CAPTURED BY PIRATES

≈≈≈≈≈

Twenty-two Firsthand Accounts
of Murder and Mayhem on the High Seas

EDITED BY

John Richard Stephens

BARNES & NOBLE
NEW YORK

THIS BOOK IS DEDICATED TO
Martha and Jim Goodwin

This 2006 edition published by Barnes & Noble Publishing, Inc.
by arrangement with Fern Canyon Press.

Design and production by Judy Gilats

2006 Barnes & Noble Publishing

ISBN-13: 978-0-7607-8537-9
ISBN-10: 0-7607-8537-6

Printed and bound in the United States of America

1 3 5 7 9 10 8 6 4 2

Contents

Acknowledgments

≋≋≋≋≋

John Richard Stephens wishes to express his appreciation to Martha and Jim Goodwin; Scott Stephens; Elaine Molina; Marty Goeller; Terity, Natasha, and Debbie Burbach; Brandon, Alisha, and Kathy Hill; Jeff and Carol Whiteaker; Doug and Michelle Whiteaker; Norene Hilden; Doug and Shirley Strong; Stan and Barbara Main; Joanne and Monte Goeller; and to his agent, Charlotte Cecil Raymond.

NOTES ON TEXTUAL CHANGES

Since the time when many of these narratives were written, the way punctuation is used has changed considerably. In order to make them more understandable and easier to read, I have modernized the punctuation. I have also standardized and corrected the spelling and tense of words and I have filled out some abbreviated words. I have not changed any words or their order, except on the accounts by the two presidents of Panama, Mendez Pinto and St. Vincent de Paul which were translated from Spanish and French. With these, I used different translations to make corrections and make them easier to read.

Because some of the terms explained in the footnotes may be difficult to remember and because some readers may read the accounts out of order, I have repeated some of the footnotes. I hope this is more helpful than it is distracting.

I Could See Death Staring Me in the Face

≋≋≋≋≋≋

Anonymous

This account was originally a letter that appeared in the February 1824 issue of the American Monthly Magazine.

In the early part of June [1822] I sailed from Philadelphia in the schooner *Mary*, on a voyage to New Orleans. My principal object in going round by sea was the restoration of my health, which had been for many months declining. Having some friends in New Orleans, whose commercial enterprises were conducted on an extensive scale, I was charged with the care of several sums of money in gold and silver, amounting altogether to nearly $18,000. This I communicated to the captain and we concluded to secure it in the best manner our circumstances would admit. A plank was accordingly taken off the ribs of the schooner in my own cabin, and the money being deposited in the vacancy, the plank was nailed down in its original place and the seams filled and tarred over. Being thus relieved from any apprehension that the money would be found upon us in case of an attack from pirates, my mind was somewhat easier. What other articles of value I could conveniently carry about with me, I did so.

I had also brought a quantity of banknotes to the amount of $15,000. Part of these I caused to be carefully sewed in the left lapel of my coat, supposing that in case of my being lost at sea, my coat, should my body be found, would still contain the most valuable of my effects. The balance was carefully quilted into my black silk cravat.[1] Our crew consisted of the captain and four men with a supply of live stock for the voyage and a Newfoundland dog, valuable for his fidelity and sagacity. He had once saved his master from a watery grave when he had been stunned and knocked overboard by a sudden shifting of the boom. I was the only passenger on board. Our voyage at first was prosperous and time went rapidly. I felt my strength increase the longer I was at sea, and when we arrived off the southern coast of Florida my feelings were like those of another man.

It was towards the evening of the fourteenth day, two hours before sunset, that we espied a sail astern of us. As twilight came, it neared us with astonishing rapidity. Night closed and all around was impenetrable darkness. Now and then a gentle wave would break against our bow and sparkle for a moment, and at a distance behind us we could see the uneven glow of light, occasioned by the foaming of the strange vessel. The breeze that filled our canvas was gentle, though it was fresh.

We coursed our way steadily through the night, though once or twice the roaring of the waves increased so suddenly as to make us believe we had passed a breaker.

At the time it was unaccountable to me, but I now believe it to be occasioned by the schooner behind us coming rather near in the darkness of the night. At midnight I went on deck. Nothing but an occasional sparkle was to be seen and the ocean was undisturbed. Still it was a fearful and appalling darkness, and in spite of my endeavors, I could not compose myself. At the windlass on the forecastle,[2] three of the sailors, like myself unable to sleep, had collected for conversation. On joining them I found our fears were mutual. They all kept their eyes steadily fixed upon the unknown vessel as if anticipating some dreadful event. They informed me that they had put their arms in order and were determined to stand or die.

At this moment a flash of light, perhaps a musket burning priming, proceeded from the vessel in pursuit and we saw distinctly that her deck was covered with men. My heart almost failed me. I had never been in battle and knew not what it was. Day at length dawned, and setting all her canvas, our pursuer gained alarmingly upon us. It was evident that she had followed us the whole night, being unwilling to attack us in the dark. In a few minutes she fired a gun and came alongside. She was a pirate. Her boat was lowered and about a dozen hideous-looking objects jumped in, with a commander at their head. The boat pushed off and was fast nearing us, as we arranged ourselves for giving her a broadside. Our whole stock of arms consisted of six muskets and an old swivel,[3] used as a signal gun, belonging to the *Mary*, and a pair of pistols of my own, which I carried in my belt. The pirate boat's crew were armed with muskets, pistols, swords, cutlasses, and knives; and when she came within her own length of us, we fired five of our muskets and the swivel into her.

Her fire was scarcely half given when she filled and went down, with all her crew. At this success we were inclined to rejoice, but looking over the pirate schooner we observed her deck still swarming with the same description of horrid-looking wretches. A second boat's crew pushed off with their muskets pointed directly at us the whole time. When they came within the same distance as the other, we fired, but with little, if any, effect. The pirate immediately returned the fire and with horrid cries jumped aboard us. Two of our brave crew were lying dead upon the deck and the rest of us expected nothing better. French, Spanish and English were spoken indiscriminately and all at once. The most horrid imprecations were uttered against us and threats that fancy cannot imagine.

A wretch whose black, shaggy whiskers covered nearly his whole face, whose eyes were only seen at intervals from beneath his bushy eyebrows, and whose whole appearance was more that of a hell-hound than of a human being, approached me with a drawn cutlass in his hand. I drew one of my pistols and snapped it in his face, but it flashed in the pan, and before I could draw the other, the pirate with a brutality that would have disgraced a cannibal, struck me over the face with his cutlass and knocked me down. I was too much wounded to resist, and the blood ran in torrents from my forehead. In this situation the wretch seized me by the scalp and thrusting his cutlass in my cravat, cut[ting] it through completely. I felt the cold iron glide along my throat, and even now the very thought makes me shudder.

The worst idea I had ever formed of human cruelty seemed now realized, and I could see death staring me in the face. Without stopping to examine the cravat, he put it in his pocket, and in a voice of thunder exclaimed, *"Levez vous."* I accordingly rose to my feet and he pinioned [i.e. bound] my hands behind my back, led me to the vessel's bulwark, and asked another of the gang in French whether he should throw me overboard. At the recollection of that scene I am still staggered. I endeavored to call the prospects of eternity before me, but could think of nothing except the cold and quiverless apathy of the tomb. His infamous companion replied, *"Il est trop bien habillé, pour l'envoyer an diable,"* and led me to the foremast, where he tied me with my face to the stern of the vessel. The cords were drawn so tight around my arms and legs that my agony was excruciating. In this situation he left me.

On looking round, I found them all employed in plundering and ransacking everything we had. Over my left shoulder one of our sailors was strung up to the yardarm and apparently in the last agonies of death, while before me our gallant captain was on his knees and begging for his life. The wretches were endeavoring to extort from him the secret of our money, but for a while he was firm and dauntless. Provoked at his obstinacy, they extended his arms and cut them off at the elbows. At this human nature gave way, and the injured man confessed the spot where we had concealed our specie.[4] In a few moments it was aboard their own vessel. To revenge themselves on our unhappy captain, when they had satisfied themselves that nothing else was hidden, they spread a bed of oakum[5] on the deck, and after soaking it through with turpentine, tied the captain on it, filled his mouth with the same combustibles, and set the whole on fire. The cries of the unfortunate man were heart-rending, and his agonies must have been unutterable, but they were soon over. All this I was compelled to witness. Heartsick with the sight, I once shut my eyes, but a musket discharged close to my ear was a warning sufficient to keep them open.

On casting my eyes towards the schooner's stern, I discovered that our boatswain had been nailed to the deck through his feet, and the body spiked through to the tiller.[6] He was writhing in the last agonies of crucifixion. Our fifth comrade was out of sight during all this tragedy; in a few minutes, however, he was brought upon the deck blindfolded. He was then conducted to the muzzle of the swivel and commanded to kneel. The swivel was then fired off and his head was dreadfully wounded by the discharge. In a moment after it was agonizing to behold his torments and convulsions—language is too feeble to describe them. I have seen men hung upon the gibbet, but their death is like sinking in slumber when compared with his.

Excited with the scene of human butchery, one of those wretches fired his pistol at the captain's dog. The ball struck his shoulder and disabled him. He finished him by shooting him again, and at last by cutting out his tongue! At this last hell-engendered act, my blood boiled with indignation at such savage brutality on a helpless, inoffensive dog! But I was unable to give utterance or action to my feelings.

Seeing that the crew had been every one dispatched, I began to think more of myself. My old enemy, who seemed to forget me, once more approached me, but shockingly besmeared with blood and brains. He had stood by the side of the unfortunate sailor who suffered before the swivel, and supported him with the point of his bayonet. He drew a stiletto from his side, placed its point upon my heart and gave it a heavy thrust. I felt its point touch my skin, but the quilting of my bank bills prevented its further entrance. This savage monster then ran it up my breast as if intending to divide my lungs, and in doing so the bank notes fell upon the deck. He snatched them up greedily and exclaimed, "*Ah! laissez mois voir ce qui reste!*" My clothes in a few moments were ripped to pieces at the peril of my life. He frequently came so near as to tear my skin and deluge me with blood, but by the mercy of Providence, I escaped from every danger. At this moment a heavy flaw[7] struck the schooner and I heard one of the pirates say, "*Voila un vaisseau!*" They all retreated precipitately, and gaining their own vessel, were soon out of sight.

Helpless as I now was, I had the satisfaction of knowing that the pirates had been frightened by the appearance of a strange sail, but it was impossible for me to see it. Still tied to the foremast, I knew not what was my prospect of release. An hour or two had elapsed after they left me and it was now noon. The sun played violently upon my head, and I felt a languor and debility that indicated approaching fever. My head gradually sank upon my breast, when I was shocked by hearing the water pouring into the cabin windows. The wretches had scuttled the schooner and left me pinioned to go down with her. I commended my spirit to my Maker and gave myself up for lost. I felt myself gradually dying away, and the last thing I remembered was the foaming noise of the waves. This was occasioned by a ship passing by me. I was taken in, restored to health, and am now a poor, ruined, helpless man.

Notes

1. Cravat: a neckcloth or scarf.

2. Windlass: a winch-like hoisting apparatus with a horizontal, rotating cylinder, around which a rope or chain is wrapped. Forecastle (pronounced "fok' sl"): the foremost part of the deck and the seaman's quarters just below.

3. Swivel: a small cannon-like gun mounted on the ship's railing and could be swung from side to side.

4. Specie: hard currency (i.e. gold, silver or coins).

5. Oakum: old ropes untwisted into loose twine that was used for caulking the seams of ships, stopping leaks, etc.

6. Tiller: the lever fitted into the head of the rudder, used for turning it.

7. Flaw: a sudden gust of wind.

The Most Villainous-Looking Rascals

≋≋≋≋≋

Captain Sabins

In 1822, Captain Sabins was sailing his brig[1] Dover for Charleston, South Carolina, and had just left the town of Matanzas[2] in Cuba when he was attacked by pirates. He recorded what happened in his log book.

Jan. 16, 1822, sea account, at 1 P.M.—Pan of Matanzas bearing s saw a boat coming to us from a small drogher,[3] which came out of Matanzas the night before us, with five Spaniards armed with long knives, pistols, cutlasses, etc. When they got within hail, they fired a musket at us, cheered and came on board. They were the most villainous-looking rascals that anyone had probably ever beheld. They immediately drew their weapons and, after beating us up severely with their cutlasses, drove us below. They then robbed us of all our clothes except what we had on, our watches and everything of value. We were afterwards called up singly. Four men with drawn knives stood over the captain and threatened him if he did not give up his money, they would kill all hands and burn the vessel. After robbing the people they commenced plundering the brig. They broke open hatches, made us get out our boat and carry their plunder to their vessel. They took from us one compass, five bags coffee, one barrel sugar, nearly all our provisions, our colors [i.e. flags], rigging, and cooking utensils. They then ordered us to stand north or they would overhaul us, murder the crew, and burn the vessel. We made sail and shortly after were brought to by another boat of the same character, which fired into us, but left us upon being informed that we had been already robbed.

Notes

1. Brig or brigantine: a two-masted merchant ship with primarily square sails.

2. Matanzas is on Cuba's northern coast about 50 miles east of Havana. Cuba still belonged to Spain at this time.

3. Drogher: a West Indian coasting vessel with long, light masts and triangular-shaped sails.

A Desperate Fight with Knives Ensued

Aaron Smith

Aaron Smith was captured by pirates and forced to join them. He finally escaped, only to be arrested as a pirate and put on trial three times—once in Cuba and twice in England. He recorded his experiences in his book, The Atrocities of the Pirates *(1824). Because of the length of his book, only excerpts are included here.*

Smith originally sailed from England to the West Indies in June 1821. After working there awhile, he found his health was impaired by the climate. He also missed his family and his fiancée, so he decided to return to England. On June 29, 1822, he sailed from Kingston, Jamaica, as the first mate on a merchant brigantine Zephyr. *The captain had two routes to choose from; they could sail up between Haiti and the eastern end of Cuba, which was a shorter distance but against the wind, or they could sail around the western end of Cuba and through the straits of Florida, which would put them at greater risk of encountering pirates. The captain chose the latter course. The* Zephyr *made it safely around Cape San Antonio, which is the western end of Cuba, and was heading eastward along Cuba's northern coast when the pirates found them.*

Smith was apparently in his late twenties at the time since a newspaper reported that he appeared to be about thirty at his trial almost two years later.

At two o'clock P.M., while walking the deck in conversation with Captain Cowper [who was one of the ship's eleven passengers], I discovered a schooner[1] standing out towards us from the land. She bore a very suspicious appearance and I immediately went up aloft with my telescope to examine her more closely. I was instantly convinced that she was a pirate and mentioned it to Cowper who coincided with me, and we deemed it proper to call Mr. Lumsden [the ship's captain] from below and inform him. When he came on deck we pointed out the schooner and stated our suspicions, recommending him to alter his course and avoid her. We were at this moment about six leagues[2] from Cape Roman,[3] which bore se by e. Never did ignorance with its concomitant obstinacy betray itself more strongly than on this occasion. He rejected our advice and refused to alter his course, and was infatuated enough to suppose that because he bore the English flag, no one would dare to molest him. To this obstinacy and infatuation I must attribute all my subsequent misfortunes—the unparalleled cruelties which I have suffered, the persecutions and prosecutions which I have undergone, the mean and wanton insults which have been heaped upon me, and the villainy and dishonesty to which I have been exposed from the author of them all; who, not satisfied with having occasioned my sufferings, would have basely taken advantage of them to defraud my friends of what little of my property had escaped the general plunder.

In about half an hour after this conversation, we began to discover that the deck of the schooner was full of men and that she was beginning to hoist out her boats. This circumstance greatly alarmed Mr. Lumsden and he ordered the course to be altered two points, but it was then too late for the stranger was within gunshot. In a short time she was within hail and in English ordered us to lower our stern boat and send the captain on board of her. Mr. Lumsden either did not understand the order or pretended not to do so, and the corsair[4]—for such she now proved to be—fired a volley of musketry. This increased his terror, which he expressed in hurried exclamations of "Aye, aye! Oh, Lord God!" and then gave orders to lay the main yard aback. A boat from the pirate now boarded the *Zephyr*, containing nine or ten men of a most ferocious aspect armed with muskets, knives, and cutlasses, who immediately took charge of the brig and ordered Captain Cowper, Mr. Lumsden, the ship's carpenter, and myself to go on board the pirate, hastening our departure by repeated blows with the flat part of their cutlasses over our backs and threatening to shoot us. The rapidity of our movements did not give us much time for consideration; and while we were rowing towards the corsair, Mr. Lumsden remarked that he had been very careless in leaving the books which contained the account of all the money on board on the cabin table. The captain of the pirate ordered us on deck immediately on our arrival. He was a man of most uncouth and savage appearance, about five feet six inches in height, stout in proportion, with aquiline nose, high cheek bones, a large mouth and very large full eyes. His complexion was sallow and his hair black and he appeared to be about two and thirty years of age. In his appearance he very much resembled an Indian, and I was afterwards informed that his father was a Spaniard and his mother a Yucatan squaw. He first addressed Mr. Lumsden and inquired in broken English what the vessels were that he saw ahead. On being informed that they were French merchantmen, he gave orders for all hands to go in chase. The *Zephyr* was observed in the meantime to make sail and stand in the direction of Cape Roman.[. . .]

[The French ships escaped and the pirates headed back to their prize.]

Supper having been prepared, the captain and his officers (six or seven in number) sat down to it and invited us to join them, which, for fear of giving offense and exciting their brutality, we did. Our supper consisted of garlic and onions chopped fine and mixed up with bread in a bowl, for which there was a general scramble, everyone helping himself as he pleased, either with his fingers or any instrument with which he happened to be supplied.

During supper Mr. Lumsden begged to be allowed to go on board the *Zephyr* to the [five or six] children [that were passengers], as he was fearful that they would be alarmed at our absence and the presence of strangers, in which request I joined; but he replied that no one would injure them and that as soon as the two vessels came to an anchor, he would accompany us on board.

The corsair was at this time fast approaching the *Zephyr*. When the captain ordered a musket to be fired and then tacked in shore, the signal was immediately answered and the brig followed our movements. One of our boat's crew was then ordered to the lead with directions to give notice the moment he found soundings and the captain then inquired if we had any Americans on board as seamen. He expressed himself very warmly against them and declared he would kill all belonging to that nation in revenge for the injuries that he had sustained at their hands—one of his vessels having been lately taken and destroyed by them—adding at the same time that if he discovered that we had concealed the fact from him, he would punish us equally. To the Americans he said that he should never give quarter,[5] but as all nations were hostile to Spain, he would attack all.[. . .]

At daylight we perceived the pirates on board beating the *Zephyr's* crew with their cutlasses and began to tremble for our own safety. After this we perceived the sailors at work hoisting out her boats and hauling a rope cable from the after-hatchway and coiling it on deck, as if preparing to take out the brig's cargo. The crew of the corsair meanwhile began to take their coffee and the officers invited us to partake of some, which we willingly did and found it very refreshing after a night spent in sleepless apprehension.

At seven o'clock the captain hailed his crew from the *Zephyr* (where he passed the night) and ordered the boat to be sent, in which he returned in a short time with some curiosities belonging to myself. On his arrival he approached me, and brandishing a cutlass over my head, told me to go on board the *Zephyr* and bring everything necessary for the purposes of navigation, as it was his determination to keep me. [The pirates needed a navigator and Capt. Lumsden, in order to prevent the pirates from keeping himself, had told them that Smith was an excellent one and that he also had some medical knowledge.] To this mandate I made no reply. So brandishing his cutlass again, he asked me with an oath if I heard him. I replied that I did. When, with a ferocious air, he said, "Mind and obey me then or I will take off your skin." At this threat I went into the boat and pulled towards the *Zephyr*, and on my arrival found Mr. Lumsden at the gangway. I told him the nature of my visit, at which he expressed his sorrow but advised me not to oppose the pirate lest it might produce bad usage, as he seemed bent upon detaining me. He then informed me that they had taken possession of everything and that he himself had narrowly escaped assassination on account of his watch.

On entering my cabin, I found my chest broken to pieces and its contents taken away, with two diamond rings and some articles of value. From a seaman I received my gold watch, sextant, and some other valuable things which I had previously given to him to conceal; and with these I returned to my own stateroom and proceeded to pack up what few clothes had been left by the plunderers. My books, parrot and various other articles, I gave in charge to Mr. Lumsden, who engaged to deliver them safely into the hands of my friends should he reach England.[. . .]

Even the playful innocence of the children could not protect them from the barbarity of these ruffians. Their ear-rings were taken out of their ears and they were left without a bed to lie upon or a blanket to cover them.

They next commenced taking out the ship's stores, with all the live-stock and some water, and Mr. Lumsden and Captain Cowper were then ordered on the quarter-deck and told that if they did not either produce the money or tell where it was concealed, the *Zephyr* should be burned and they with her. On this occasion the same answer was given as before and the inhuman wretch instantly prepared to put his threat into execution by sending the children on board the schooner and ordering those two gentlemen to be taken below decks and to be locked to the pumps. The mandate was no sooner issued than it was obeyed by his fiend-like myrmidons,[6] who even commenced piling combustibles around them. The apparent certainty of their fate extorted a confession from Lumsden, who was released and taken on deck, where he went to the round house[7] and produced a small box of doubloons,[8] which the pirate exhibited with an air of exultation to the crew. He then insisted that there was more and—notwithstanding that the other made the most solemn asseverations to the contrary, and that even what he had given was not his own—he was again lashed to the pumps.

The question was then applied to Captain Cowper and fire was ordered to be put to the combustibles piled around him. Seeing his fate inevitable, he offered to surrender all he had; and being released, he gave them about nine doubloons, declaring that what he had produced was all he had and had been entrusted to his care for a poor woman, who, for aught he knew, might at this moment be in a state of starvation.

"Do not speak to me of poor people," exclaimed the fiend, "I am poor and your countrymen and the Americans have made me so. I know there is more money, and will either have it or burn you and the vessel."

The unfortunate man was then once more ordered below and fire directed to be applied. In vain did they protest that he had got all; he persisted in his cruelty. The flames now began to approach their persons and their cries were heart-rending, while they implored him to turn them adrift in a boat at the mercy of the waves rather than torture them thus, and keep the *Zephyr*, when, if there was money, he would surely find it.

Finding that no further confession was extorted, he began to believe the truth of these protestations and ordered his men to throw water below and quench the flames. The unfortunate sufferers were then released and taken into the round house; and the seamen, children, and myself [were] allowed to go on board the brig. There we were left for a while at liberty, while the pirates caroused and exulted over their booty.

When they had finished their meal, the captain told them that it was now time to return to their own vessel and ordered me to accompany them. I hesitated at first to obey, but he was not to be thwarted, and drawing his knife, threatened with an oath to cut my head off if I did not move instanter.[. . .]

When I had reached the deck of the corsair, he asked me if I had got every instrument necessary to the purposes of navigation; and if not, to go and get them, for he would have no excuses by and by, and if I made any he would kill me. I answered that I had gotten all that was necessary. And he then gave orders to cast loose from the *Zephyr*, and told Mr. Lumsden he might proceed on his voyage, but on no account to steer for the Havana for, if he overtook him on that course, he would destroy him and his vessel together. He promised that he would not touch there and the vessels were accordingly cast loose in a short time afterwards. Mr. Lumsden, Captain Cowper, and the children, stood on the gangway and bade me *adieu*, and my heart sunk within me as the two vessels parted.

The horrors of my situation now rushed upon my mind. I looked upon myself as a wretch, upon whom the world was closed forever: exposed to the brutality of a ferocious and remorseless horde of miscreants; doomed to destruction and death, and perhaps to worse, to disgrace and ignominy; to become the partaker of their enormities; and be compelled I knew not how soon to imbrue my hands in the blood of a fellow-creature, and perhaps a fellow countryman. The distraction, grief, and painful apprehensions of my parents, and of one to whom I was under the tenderest of all engagements,[9] filled my mind with terror. I could no longer bear to look upon the scene my fancy presented to me and I would have sought a refuge from my own moveable thoughts, in self-destruc-tion, but my movements were watched and I was secured and a guard set over me. The captain then addressed me and told me that if I made a sec-ond attempt I should be lashed to a gun and there left to die through hunger. And for the sake of security, ordered me below, but at my earnest entreaty I was allowed to remain on deck till it was dark.

The *Zephyr* had got under weigh and had set her sails, but I could per-ceive that her boats had either been cut or set adrift. This did not escape the notice of the pirate, who called to me and said, "Look at that rascal, he has cut loose his old boats and when he gets home he will say that I have taken them and get new ones from the underwriters, but I will write to Lloyd's and prevent it."

He then appeared very anxious to know whether I thought they would go to the Havana; of which he seemed so apprehensive that he would have gone after the *Zephyr* and destroyed her, had I not said that they would in all probability pursue a direct course. The wind was light and the sea calm, but the weather was thick and heavy. Both vessels moved slowly through the water from one another and I kept my eyes upon the *Zephyr* as long as she was visible and then gave way to melancholy reflections on my forlorn and wretched condition.

At dusk we anchored at the edge of the reef and a boat was dispatched to the shore to inform the inhabitants of their good success. At daylight, the pirate stood to the southwest, and at nine o'clock in the morning entered a delightful harbor, where she anchored in two fathoms[10] water.

This harbor, called by the Spaniards Rio Medias, is large, commodious, and capable of containing a hundred sail. The anchorage is good, being a compound of clay and mud, and it is protected from every wind except the north. Vessels within it ride very safe and easy, as the reef breaks off the force of the sea. The distance of it is about three miles from the edge of the reef to the southward, and the entrance intricate and hazardous.

At two o'clock in the afternoon, I perceived a number of boats and canoes pulling towards the corsair and the captain told me that he expected a great deal of company from the shore; and among others, two or three magistrates and their families, and some priests, observing also that I should see several pretty Spanish girls. I remarked that I wondered he was not afraid of the magistrates. He laughed, and said I did not know the Spanish character. "Presents of coffee and other little things," said he, "will always ensure their friendship. And from them I receive intelligence of all that occurs at the Havana and know every hostile measure [with] time enough to guard against it."

Two magistrates, a priest, and several ladies and gentleman now came on board and were received in great pomp by the captain, whom they congratulated on his success. I was then introduced to them as a captive detained to navigate the vessel and underwent questioning from all of them as to my country and whether I came from London and of what religion I was. Refreshments were then introduced and the whole party drank to the captain's health. Dancing was then proposed by the females, and preparations made for it. The parties stood up for their favorite amusement, and to my great annoyance, I was selected as a partner for one of the magistrate's daughters [who was named Seraphina].[. . .]

[A few hours later they prepared to auction off their plunder.] The sale then commenced and I was placed at the steelyards[11] to weigh out the coffee to the purchaser. To this, however, they [i.e. the buyers] objected, as they suspected I would cheat them; but they had no alternative as no one else understood the use of steelyards and the captain having informed them that I was a captive and bore no share in the profits, they were content to let the sale go on.

The best coffee was sold for ten dollars per hundred weight—its supposed value in Havana—and the inferior at a similar rate. I observed that the purchasers all brought sacks and bags with them as precautionary measures to prevent detection and destroy every clue to the market in which it was purchased. Having weighed their several portions, a gun was fired. When two schooners of a small size came out from the land and when [they were] within hail, [they] were ordered to come alongside and take the coffee on board. Neither the captain nor any part of his crew understood arithmetic, so that my next task was to make out the several bills; and their amount having been paid, a large dinner was prepared from the stock taken from the *Zephyr*.

While these preparations were going on, the captain told me in English, which the rest did not understand, to make a strong mixture of spirituous liquors, that would rapidly intoxicate and bring it up after dinner as an English cordial. In the mean time, he informed the company that after dinner he should set up to auction all the wearing apparel he had taken in this prize. They had all made perfectly free with the wine taken from the *Zephyr* and the captain then told me to bring up the pretended cordial—which I made from a mixture of wine, rum, gin, brandy, and porter[12]—and recommended it to his guests, who drank it greedily and praised it. Its intoxicating effects were soon visible and the auction then commenced.

The different trunks were brought upon deck one by one and as the contents of one was disposed of, another was opened in order that the good and bad might be sold alike. My own shared the fate of the rest and I was obliged to see them pass into the hands of strangers without daring to claim them. The cordial now had its intended effect and the state of intoxication in which they were caused them to contest every article, and accordingly enormous sums were bid for the most trifling.[. . .]

What the cordial had begun, additional quantities of wine had completed. The whole party were very much intoxicated and universal disorder prevailed. A quarrel took place between two of the crew and a desperate fight with knives ensued, of which the rest were cool spectators. The battle was for a long time doubtful, as both fought with equal skill and an equal degree of caution, notwithstanding they were intoxicated, until one fell with a severe stab in the left breast, bleeding profusely.

I was instantly called to administer to the wounded man and it was in vain for me to declare that I knew nothing of the healing art. The captain swore at me and said he knew to the contrary, for the master of the *Zephyr* had informed him that I had cured and saved the life of his sailmaker, who had fallen down the hold. And therefore if I did not cure him, he would serve me in the same manner. I saw it would be useless to make any reply and therefore, having procured bandages, I stanched the blood and dressed his wounds in the best manner I was able. Having attended to one patient, I was then obliged to turn my attention to his antagonist, who had not escaped unhurt. When I had completed my task, I was carelessly complimented on my skill and asked if the wound was mortal; which question I evaded by saying I hoped not.

This brutal exhibition rendered me quite melancholy, and while I was standing lost in thought, Seraphina came up to me and asked the reason. I told her, and added that such ruffianly conduct was not suffered in England. She said it was the custom of the country, and therefore I should not mind it.[. . .]

[The party soon ended and the buyers and guests departed in their boats and canoes.]

The guests were scarcely gone when the captain went below and inquired of the least injured of the wounded men the cause of their quarrel. He [i.e. the wounded man] hesitated at first to tell and supplicated that he might be forgiven for his neglect in not having furnished him with the important intelligence before. This being granted, he told the pirate that his antagonist was one of the party formed by the chief mate to assassinate him and the whole crew and take possession of the ship and plunder. That officer, he informed him, had gone to the Havana for the express purpose of bringing some more men, and that they were to put the plan into effect when himself and the crew were either asleep or inebriated.

I saw that his brutal temper was excited by this information. His eyes flashed fire and his whole countenance was distorted. He vowed destruction against the whole party, and rushing upon deck, assembled the crew and imparted what he had heard. The air rang with the most dreadful imprecations. They simultaneously rushed below and dragged the helpless wounded wretch upon deck and—without taking into consideration that the accusation against him might be unfounded—proceeded to cut off his legs and arms with a blunt hatchet, then mangling his body with their knives, threw the yet warm corpse overboard. Not contented with having destroyed their victim, they next sated their vengeance on his clothes and every thing belonging to him, which they cut in pieces and threw into the sea.

Having glutted their vengeance in this summary manner, they went below and questioned the informer as to his accomplices, but he told them that the murdered man was the only one of the conspirators on board, that he had been persuading him to join them; and on his threatening to reveal the plot, had taunted him with cowardice, struck him, and provoked the quarrel in order to put him out of the way. The ruffians seemed satisfied with this answer and the captain told me to pay particular attention to his wounds and cure him as fast as possible.

This dreadful scene threw a damp over my spirits. All hope of escape left me and I looked upon every hour as my last, for I knew not how soon I might undergo the same fate. I determined, however, to be upon my guard and by a ready compliance in everything, prolong my existence[. . .]

When his fury had subsided, the captain asked me what I thought of the Spanish mode of fighting and added that I must learn the use of the knife, observing that it was the first thing his father had taught him. He then told me that if ever I knew or heard of anything inimical to himself or his crew going on and did not give him information, I should undergo the same fate as the man whom they had just punished for his perfidy. The watch was then set, the crew sharpened their knives as if preparing for attack, and I was ordered down below for the night.[. . .]

In the afternoon a boat full of men appeared coming towards the schooner, which upon examination was found to contain some of the chief mate's party. No sooner was this known than the captain declared he would kill them all and ordered thirty muskets to be loaded and brought on deck. When the boat was about two hundred yards from the schooner, the men ceased rowing and held up a white handkerchief for a signal, as if doubtful of their safety, which was answered by a similar one from the board, and they again advanced. When within reach of the musketry, the dreadful order of "fire" was given. Five of the men fell in the boat, the sixth leaped over and began to swim, after whom a boat was dispatched. On his being brought on board, the captain told him the accusation that was against him and his party and threatened him with a cruel and lingering death if he did not confess the whole truth. In vain did he declare his innocence and ignorance of any plot. The ruffian was resolved to glut his vengeance and ordered him to be stripped and exposed—naked, wounded, and bleeding as he was—to the scorching fervor of a July sun . . . the July sun of a tropical climate!

The feelings of humanity got the better of my caution and I entreated the captain not to torture the poor wretch in that dreadful manner, declaring that I firmly believed him innocent, for had he been guilty, torture and terror would have wrung a confession from him. In vain I pleaded. In vain I represented the inhumanity of punishing a poor wretch in all probability innocent of the crime laid to his charge. He was deaf to my entreaties and threatened me with vengeance for my interference, declaring that he had not done half that he intended to do.

Having said this, he turned to the man, told him that he should be killed, and therefore advised him to prepare for death or confess himself to any of the crew whom I chose to call aside for that purpose. The man persisted in his plea of innocence, declared that he had nothing to confess, and entreated them all to spare his life. They paid no attention to his assertions, but by the order of the captain, the man was put into the boat, pinioned, and lashed in the stern; and five of the crew were directed to arm themselves with pistols and muskets and to go in her. The captain then ordered me to go with them, savagely remarking that I should now see how he punished such rascals, and giving directions to the boat's crew to row for three hours backwards and forwards through a narrow creek formed by a desert island and the island of Cuba. "I will see," cried he, exultingly, "whether the mosquitoes and the sand-flies will not make him confess."

Prior to our leaving the schooner, the thermometer was above ninety degrees in the shade and the poor wretch was now exposed naked to the full heat of the sun. In this state we took him to the channel, one side of which was bordered by swamps full of mangrove trees and swarming with the venomous insects before mentioned.

We had scarcely been half an hour in this place when the miserable victim was distracted with pain. His body began to swell and he appeared one complete blister from head to foot. Often in the agony of his torments did he implore them to end his existence and release him from his misery, but the inhuman wretches only imitated his cries and mocked and laughed at him. In a very short time, from the effects of the solar heat and the stings of the mosquitoes and sand-flies, his face had become so swollen that not a feature was distinguishable. His voice began to fail and his articulation was no longer distinct. I had long suspected that the whole story of the conspiracy was a wicked and artful fabrication, and the constancy with which this unfortunate being underwent these tortures, served to confirm my suspicions. I resolved therefore to hazard my interference, and after much entreaty and persuasion, prevailed upon them to endeavor to mitigate his sufferings and to let the poor wretch die in peace, as the injuries which he had already sustained were sufficient of themselves to occasion death. At first they hesitated, but after consulting for some time among themselves, they consented to go to the other side of the island where they would be secured from observation and untie him and put something over him. When we had reached that place, we lay upon our oars and set him loose, but the moment he felt the fresh sea breeze, he fainted away. His appearance at this time was no longer human and my heart bled at seeing a fellow creature thus tormented. When our time was expired, we again tied him as before to prevent the fury of the captain for our leniency, and once more pulled for the passage on our way to the vessel.

On our arrival, his appearance was the source of merriment to all on board and the captain asked if he had made any confession. An answer in the negative gave him evident disappointment and he inquired of me whether I could cure him. I told him he was dying. "Then he shall have some more of it before he dies," cried the monster, and directed the boat to be moored within musket shot in the bay. This having been done, he ordered six of the crew to fire at him. The man fell and the boat was ordered alongside. The poor wretch had only fainted and when they perceived that he breathed, a pig of iron[13] was fastened around his neck and he was thrown into the sea. Thus ended a tragedy, which—for the miseries inflicted on the victim and for the wanton and barbarous depravity of his fiend-like tormentors—never perhaps had its equal.

The inhuman wretches who had been the chief participators in this horrid deed, seemed to regard it as an everyday occurrence. The guitar tinkled and the song went around as if nothing had happened, and the torments which their victim had just undergone and the cries that he had uttered, seemed to form the subject of their jests and to be echoed in their barbarous mirth.

At nine o'clock at night I was ordered below as usual, but the image of what had occurred haunted my slumbers and my sleep was broken by constant apprehensions of assassination. Morning brought around my appointed task of attending the sick, after which I was ordered to make a new gaff-topsail.[14] I went aloft and took the measure of the sail and then informed the captain that it would be necessary to take the canvas on shore to cut it out. The very mention of the shore excited his fury and he immediately accused me of intending to escape, observing that any endeavor would be fruitless, as he could have me apprehended in less than two hours after I should go. I told him I had merely said so with a view of expediting the work, and then proceeded to cut out the canvas upon deck in the best manner I could, using all diligence in making the sail. My exertions seemed to please him and he frequently addressed me in a cheerful manner.

Our attention was now excited by a cry of "a sail, a sail," from the mast-head and I was driven up aloft (with the usual threat) to reconnoiter, while the vessel got under weigh. I informed them that she was a merchant brig and orders were given to go in chase immediately. The pilot [was] undertaking to take her through the channels, while I was called down and consulted as to the best mode of fighting in case she should resist. The corsair having gained on the brig, fired a gun and hoisted Spanish colors, which the other answered by heaving to and displaying the English ensign. From the painted ports and figurehead of the brig, the pirate began to suspect that she was a man-of-war and was fearful of approaching any nearer. He therefore ordered the fore-topsail[15] to be laid aback and said that he should send the boat to board her under my directions.

This intimation greatly alarmed me and I pointed out to him the perils I should run in obeying his orders, and that should I be captured hereafter, I should assuredly suffer an ignominious death. "And what are you, sir," cried he ferociously, "that you should not suffer as well as myself? The schooner shall never be captured, for when I can no longer defend her, I shall blow her up. If you do not instantly go, I will shoot you."

I told him that he might shoot me if he pleased, but that I would not commit an act that might subject me and my family to disgrace. Seeing me resolute and inclined to dispute his authority, he ordered his crew to blindfold me and carry me forward, and told me to prepare myself for death. I was carried as he had directed, and he then came to me and asked me "if I was prepared." I answered firmly, "Yes." He then left me and immediately a volley of musketry was fired, but evidently only with a view to frighten me. The captain immediately came up to me and asked if I was not desperately wounded. I answered I was not, but begged if it was his intention to destroy me, to do it at once and not trifle with me, as I preferred death to disgrace and ignominy. He then gave directions that I should be taken and lashed to the main-mast and the bandage removed from my eyes. This order was quickly obeyed by his myrmidons. As soon as I was fastened to the mast, the captain cut up a number of cartridges and placed the powder around me on the deck with a train to it, and gave orders for the cook to light a match and send it aft. He then repeated his order and asked if I would obey him. I persisted in my refusal, and without any further hesitation he communicated the fire to the powder. The explosion deprived me of my senses and stunned me for the moment, but I soon recovered to undergo the most horrid torture. The flames had caught my clothes, which were blazing around me, and my hands were so pinioned that I could not relieve myself. I begged them for God's sake to dispatch me at once, but they only laughed at me and the captain tauntingly asked me if I would obey him now? The excruciating agony in which I was, extorted my acquiescence and I was ordered to be released, but I fainted before that could be done.[16]

When I recovered my senses, I found myself stretched on a mattress in the cabin and in the most dreadful pain. In the frenzy and delirium of the moment, I meditated self-destruction, but no weapons were near me and the shattered state of my legs did not allow me to seek any. The steward was below and I begged him to lend me his knife, but he suspected my intention and informed the captain, who descended in a fury. "You want to kill yourself, young man, I understand," cried he, "but I do not mean that you should die yet. I shall blow you up again, for I see it is the only way to make you obey me."

He then ordered them to keep a watch over me and help me to sit up and dress my wounds. I found my legs dreadfully injured, the flesh lacerated, and the bone in some parts laid bare, and by this time, large blisters had risen on various parts of my body. I asked for a sheet to cover me and a pillow for my head, and the captain, who now seemed to relent, ordered the steward to give me all that I required. I begged that the medicine chest might be placed near me, which they did and I seized that opportunity of swallowing the contents of a small vial of laudanum[17]—about a hundred and thirty drops—hoping that I should wake no more in this world. The cook, who seemed to pity and feel for my sufferings, now brought me a little arrow-root and wine, and made up my bed for me. I asked him where the corsair was and he told me in the harbor at anchor. I expressed my surprise at the circumstance; when he informed me the captain was so convinced that the brig was a man-of-war and that I had meant to decoy them to be taken, that he was afraid to attack and had returned into harbor shortly after I was brought down below.

From this poor fellow I received a great deal of kindness and he seemed possessed of much humanity. "The captain," said he, bending over me with a look of compassion, "is a very bad man and has killed more than twenty people with his own hand in cool blood, and he would kill you too, were he not in want of your services." He then cautioned me to appear cheerful and satisfied at all times, and that then they would treat me well. He also told me that he would prepare any little thing for me that I might want and attend me by day and by night, and with this kind assurance, left me to my repose.

I now began to feel the soporiferous effects of the laudanum, and laying myself down upon my mattress, commended my soul into the hands of the God who gave it, beseeching him to forgive me for the act I had committed, and resigned myself, as I thought, into the arms of death. I soon fell into a profound sleep which lasted the whole night, and in the morning they found such difficulty to arouse me that they imagined I had poisoned myself and was dead. The captain accused me of having done so and threatened me with a second torturing if I ever made another attempt. I told him I had merely taken some opiate medicine to render me insensible to the pain I suffered and that it had taken an unusually powerful effect upon me.

He then asked me if I could attend to the sick. I said that I would endeavor to do so, but upon attempting to rise, I found my strength fail and my limbs so stiff and in such a state that I began to think that I had lost their use. A mattress was however placed under me to help me to sit up and the medicine chest placed by my side, and in this manner—although it put me to excruciating agony—I began to perform my task. Having attended to the sick, I next dressed my own wounds, which had assumed a dangerous appearance.

While thus occupied below, the master of a coasting schooner brought intelligence that the *Zephyr* had arrived at the Havana and that all the circumstances of her capture and plunder had been made known. Frantic at this information, he rushed into the cabin. "See," cried he, "what dependence can be placed on your countrymen. That old rascal has gone to the Havana and broken a solemn promise. But for this I should not care, had he told the truth, [but] he has told the authorities there that I have plundered him of specie[18] to the amount of fifteen hundred pounds sterling, whereas I did not obtain half that amount. He has said also, that I maltreated the children. And he must have known that it was only on their account that I did not destroy the vessel, but allowed him to proceed on his voyage. But this will be a lesson to me not to trust the English again, for I now find them as treacherous as the Americans."

This he uttered all in a breath and then paused as if considering something. A malignant scowl passed over his face and he proceeded, "He thinks he is out of my reach, but mark me, if he remains a few days longer at the Havana, he shall never live to see England. I have three or four already on the watch to assassinate him. They must be new to the trade or it would have been done ere this. But there is one on board who will soon accomplish it, a man who has already dispatched several. I shall send him there in an hour, and to make sure of his performing it, I will give him ten doubloons for the deed. Nay, should he be fortunate enough to escape this time, I may take him again at some other, and then I will tie him to a tree in the forest and let him starve."

During this conversation, the villain [i.e. the assassin] had been preparing himself and now announced that he was ready to proceed on his sanguinary mission. The boat was then ordered to put him on shore, where he was to procure a horse and direct his course to the Havana, and the savage entered it with an air of exultation and with loud promises of his performing his task faithfully.

The hope of revenge seemed to have calmed his [i.e. the pirate captain's] turbulence and he began asking me how soon I should be able to proceed with the sail and to go up aloft, adding that my own foolish obstinacy had occasioned all my sufferings. I told him that I was very ill and could not then attempt it, to which he coolly answered that he was anxious to have the vessel completely fitted with new sails and hoped that I should be able to do so very soon. He then turned about and left the cabin.

The whole schooner's company now went to their evening meal, and as was usual, to drink, play the guitar and carouse. Their merriment was however soon interrupted by the dashing of approaching oars. They instantly flew to quarters and made every preparation for acting on the defensive, and I was dragged on deck, wounded as I was, to hail the boat in English. Immediately on my doing so, the boat stopped and I repeated the hail, but they did not answer, upon which the captain called to them in Spanish. His voice was soon recognized and they came alongside. All were eager to learn the object of their visit and rapid in their inquiries. They then informed the captain that a boat containing some more of the chief mate's party had arrived, and having heard of the fate of their associates, had vowed revenge. For this purpose they had gone in pursuit of the man who had been just set on shore—of whose arrival they were informed—and had, when they left, followed him towards the magistrate's house, where he had gone to procure a pass for his journey. They added that if he wished to preserve the man's life, he must lose no time in sending him assistance.

A general panic seemed to have seized the whole crew at this intelligence and no one seemed inclined to go upon this hazardous enterprise. The captain now upbraided, now threatened, and now abused them by turns, but with no visible effect and was on the point of abandoning his emissary to his fate, when one man—apparently bolder than the rest, but evidently with hesitation—offered his services and even declared his resolution to perish in the attempt. This example had the desired effect and nine stepped forward. They were hastily supplied with arms and ammunition and dispatched on shore, strictly charged by the captain to give the assailants no quarter.

When this expedition was dispatched, the pirate asked me whether (if I had been well) I would have volunteered to rescue Stromeda (for so the man was called). Wishing for an opportunity to lull his suspicions against me, I answered in the affirmative, adding at the same time that he ought to be on his guard for this report might have been a stratagem to withdraw part of the crew in order to attack the schooner more easily. The hint staggered him. He confessed the idea had never occurred to him and thanked me for my precautionary advice, adding, "I see now that necessity is the best teacher and I shall at last make something of you."

I was then sent below again and the captain proceeded to take measures to guard against surprise. A watch was set on deck and everyone lay down with his arms by his side. All was silence and watchful anxiety till midnight, when the boat returned with only five of the men. These informed the captain that on the beach they had met a servant dispatched by the magistrate, who informed them that Stromeda was a prisoner and that the captors had vowed to put him to death, and bade them hasten to his rescue. The party had, on hearing this, taken a circuitous route through the wood and, having eluded the scouts of the chief mate's gang, had surprised four of them playing at cards and drinking under a tree. Having secured these, they proceeded to the magistrate's residence, and firing through the doors and windows, discharged their blunderbusses[19] into the house, regardless of who might be within, whether friend or foe; and had, in so doing, unfortunately wounded the magistrate himself. Stromeda they found bound hand and foot lying on the floor, but as he had not been injured, and having loosed him, he proceeded on his journey. Two of the chief mate's party, they said, had been killed, two more were prisoners, and two who where acting as scouts, perceiving what had happened, had escaped after firing their muskets and wounding one of the corsair's crew. They concluded this long narration with an earnest request on the part of the magistrate and wounded man that I might be instantly dispatched to dress their wounds, as there was no medical man near them.

I was in consequence ordered to prepare for my new task as quick as possible. In vain did I remonstrate on the cruelty of the measure and try to move their pity by showing them the mangled and deplorable state in which I was, I was told in reply that as much care as possible should be taken not to hurt me in moving, but that go I must. Seeing them resolved, I prepared to comply. A mattress stretched on one of the hatches was placed in the boat and I was lowered down upon it, and the party who had charge of me, having received orders to be careful and gentle in their usage, shoved off the boat and rowed towards shore.

It was past two in the morning before we reached the shore and landed close to a house, where we found a horse and a man in waiting for us. I was taken into the house while they formed a sort of a litter for me with a bed fastened on the animal's back. Upon this I was placed and the party proceeded about two miles and a half through a forest to the magistrate's residence. On our arrival at the door, I was taken off the litter and the first object that met my view was Seraphina, who rushed into my arms, crying, "For God's sake, take me, for they have just killed my father," and burst into tears. The distress in which she was, made me conclude that he was dead, and when I was carried into a miserable apartment, meanly furnished, I was met by her mother, to whom Seraphina exclaimed, "Oh, my dear mother, this is the good Englishman come to cure my father." In the room, there were only two beds and a leather-bottomed chair. Upon one of the beds was stretched the magistrate covered with blood and on the other the wounded pirate. Being placed by the side of the former, I gave directions to have him stripped and then proceeded to examine his wound. One ball had slightly fractured his left arm and passed into the shoulder and another had lodged in the arm. The latter, I easily extracted and reduced the fracture in the best manner I was able and bound up the wound. The wife and daughter remained silent but anxious spectators of my operations, and when I had concluded, asked me if the old man would survive. To which I gave a favorable answer and then dressed the wounds of the other sufferer. The house, while I was attending to the wounded man, was thronged with the villagers, part of whom had come from curiosity to see me and part to inquire after their magistrate. During these operations, the pirates who had accompanied me had been absent, but on their return, they told me that they had been burying Pepe, one of their comrades, who had been killed in the *rencontre*. [20] They had with them the two prisoners they had taken, bound hand and foot, and beside them on the ground where the bleeding corpses of the other two, mangled in a dreadful manner. One of these they threw across a horse, and taking the two prisoners, they proceeded towards the beach, leaving four men to take care of me. The prisoners were fastened on each side of the horse to the dead body and in this manner they marched in triumph through the village without being interfered with.[. . .]

The horses had now returned from conveying the prisoners, and the men entering to inform me of their arrival, interrupted our conversation. I bade Seraphina *adieu* and[. . .]suffered them to carry me to the litter, which was made the same as formerly. Before we set off the magistrate sent word to beg that I might be allowed to visit him on the following day. The body of the other man was now fastened across one of the horses and the party proceeded towards the beach. When we arrived at the place where the boat was stationed, the dead body was cut from the horse and flung into the sea. A line was then fastened to the neck and attached to the boat for the purpose of towing it into deep water, where they intended to sink it and had brought a stone with them for that purpose.

It was at this time broad daylight and we had scarce rowed a hundred and fifty yards from the shore when we perceived a man closely pursued by the inhabitants rush towards the shore, plunge into the sea and swim after the boat. The crew pulled towards him and took him in. On inquiry, he proved to be one of the chief mate's party and they deliberately told him that he must die, pointing out to him at the same time, the mangled body of his late associate. The poor wretch seeing that he had only escaped from one set of barbarians to fall into the hands of a worse, burst into an agony of tears and implored them to have mercy on him. The inhabitants, in the meantime demanded with loud cries, that he should be delivered up, and the boat returned apparently for that purpose, but after some altercation, they resolved to keep and murder him themselves, and again left the shore with the determination to torture him in the swampy passage where they had already destroyed one victim. When they had arrived at the entrance of that pestiferous spot, they sunk the dead body after inflicting some indignities upon it, and thence proceeded to strip their lately acquired prisoner, whom they lashed on the boat, gagged and pinioned, and pulled into the channel. The body of the miserable being was soon covered with mosquitoes and sand-flies, and he writhed with the agony of their stings. In this state they carried him to where a tree projected into the waters, on which they placed him, blindfolded, shot him, and then made the best of their way to the corsair.

On their arrival, they exultingly told their companions of their cruelty, not only what I had witnessed, but what they had inflicted on the other two captives whom I had seen bound at the magistrate's residence. These poor wretches they had fastened to trees and fired at them as targets, and one monster boasted that he had lost a bet of a doubloon because he had not killed his man first.

Weak and fatigued as I was from want of rest, I was ordered to attend to the sick on board. The wounded man I found was now quite well and

I endeavored to impress upon his mind that he owed his life entirely to my exertions, which he verily believed, for he declared that I should never want [for] a friend while he was on board. Having performed this office, I dressed my own wounds, which I found less painful and assuming a more favorable aspect. The captain came in and examined them and expressed a hope that I should soon be able to make the sail and go up aloft, which I told him I should be able to do in three or four days. He then questioned me on the subject of the magistrate's disaster, and told me that I must pay every possible attention to him as he was a very worthy man and his best friend. In order to lull his suspicions, I pretended unwillingness to go so frequently ashore and recommended him to send for a medical man, but he overruled my objections and said that he was quite confident in my skill.

On this day he was perfectly sober, which was seldom the case, and he began to display a feeling of kindness towards me, remarked I must be fatigued and recommended me to take a few hours' sleep—a recommendation that I willingly followed, and slept till I was called up to dinner. After dinner I tried to continue making the sail, with which he was highly pleased. I worked at it till near nine in the evening, when he told me I had done enough and had better go to bed.[. . .]

At ten o'clock [the following night], the sea breeze blew rather fresh and they entered the harbor, where the corsair was brought to anchor and the Dutch ship [they had just captured] run on shore. A boat was then dispatched for me, and on my arrival, the captain, who had passed the night on board, desired me to go below and dress the wounds of one of the pirates whom he had punished for insolence during the night. When I found the man had received a very severe cut with a sword on the side of the head, the wound extending from the left temple to the ear. When I had cleaned and dressed the wound, the fellow seemed very grateful for my attention and said that when he was well, he would assist me to escape, but I was too fearful of treachery to intimate a wish to that effect to him.

After dinner I was sent ashore to the magistrate, but on our way thither became an unwilling participant in an unexpected *rencontre*. As one boat was approaching the entrance of the narrow passage (which I have had occasion to mention before), we perceived another with six men rowing rapidly towards us from the shore. Our first idea was that it was a man-of-war's boat and the pirates made immediate preparation for defense, being apparently determined to sell their lives very dearly consulting me upon what mode of fighting they should adopt and insisting on my being their leader. One of the men however recognized the chief mate as one of the party, and from their movements it appeared they were going to attack us. Knowing that indiscriminate slaughter would ensue and that I should suffer the same as the rest, I consented to direct them how to defend their boat, and while considering on the best means to do so, a musket was fired across our bows and signals made for us to go to them. No time was to be lost, so I desired two of the men to lie down in the boat with their blunderbusses and the other two to keep at their oars, having theirs ready by them to use at a preconcerted signal. Then taking the helm in my hand, guided the boat direct upon the others. When I found that the boat had sufficient way upon her, I desired the rowers to desist and take their weapons and be ready to jump into the other with their cutlasses the instant that they had discharged their pieces. My instructions were fully obeyed and the result was in our favor. The suddenness of our attack completely disconcerted them. Three of them fell by our fire, the rest made but a feeble resistance—two of whom were instantly massacred by the pirates and the other leaped into the sea, wounded as he was, and endeavored to swim off, but was followed and taken. We only lost one man, who received a ball in the head and instantly expired.

The unfortunate prisoner was interrogated as to the cause that had induced him to join the chief mate in his designs. He replied, that he had left the Havana with no other view than to join the pirate, but having heard on shore of the unprovoked slaughter of their associates, they had determined to be revenged. When they observed the corsair bring in her prize, they knew that there would be frequent communications with the shore and resolved to cut off the boats, seriatim,[21] as fast as they were sent. He then declared that he had told them the truth and hoped that as he was not the instigator of the deed, they would be satisfied with having taken the lives of his companions and spare his own. But the appeal was made in vain, for he was almost instantaneously stabbed to the heart by one of the crew. Thus did I become the unwilling actor in a scene of blood and assist by my advice in the destruction of six of my fellow creatures. I did then, and do now, often reflect upon it with horror, but I had no alternative and must have been massacred myself had I not complied with the mandates of the ferocious wretches, among whom it was the misfortune of my life to be thrown. On our arrival on shore a hole was dug and the murdered man buried. I was then placed upon a litter as before and taken to the magistrate's house.[. . .]

On the day after, the other prize-master returned from Havana with a merchant schooner, the owner of which was come to purchase the remainder of the Dutchman's cargo. The assassin who had been dispatched to murder Mr. Lumsden returned on board of her and reported that his intended victim had sailed some time before his arrival.[. . .]

The succeeding day presented another scene of atrocity and murder. In the morning while at anchor, a sail was discovered in the offing and in order to alter the sailing of the schooner, the crew were employed in removing some of the ballast more aft. In this place, the French cook of the Dutch prize was placed for security, as since his capture, the ill treatment which he had undergone and terror combined had affected his mind and he had shown evident symptoms of insanity. The inhuman wretches teased the poor maniac until they made him rave, and in his frenzy he caught hold of a hatchet and wounded one of his tormentors. The blow was no sooner given than the rest plunged their knives into his body and threw him overboard while yet breathing, accompanying their barbarity with the most horrid expressions. I was on the top during this scene, but was called down to dress the wounded man.[. . .]

On the following morning, the corsair sailed for the Morillia, where she remained idle for nearly three weeks. At the end of that time, a French vessel fell into the hands of the pirate. The usual scene of cruelty and atrocity took place, and when they had taken all the money and the valuable part of her cargo, and destroyed and damaged the remainder, they cut away her mizzen mast[22] and the starboard main rigging, and in this crippled state dismissed them to pursue their voyage, forbidding them however to go to the Havana.

The pirate returned with his plunder into the Morillia, where he anchored. Discord, however, began to rear her head among this horde of savages. Someone had insinuated that they had not been fairly dealt by and that the captain had secreted large sums for himself.[23] Discontent manifested itself, first in whispered insinuations, and at last in open accusations, and two parties were consequently formed—one who believed him innocent and the other guilty. Things were in this state, and each waiting only for a plausible pretext to attack the other, when murder and massacre would have ensued, but an unexpected event suspended the quarrel. The man at the mast head descried the gun boats steering towards the corsair and they were shortly after heard to scale their guns. These warlike preparations seemed to denote an immediate attack, and their private animosities were forgotten in the hurry of self-defense. The alarm however was without foundation, for they all passed on without noticing the pirate. A fisherman, who boarded the schooner soon after, informed us that the commanding officer of the flotilla had told him that he was well aware that the schooner was a pirate, but that he had no time to go in chase of her, as he was on his return. Thus ended this boasted expedition for the suppression of piracy without effecting one single object for which it was furnished and sent out. And no wonder; for I am convinced from personal observation, that from the governor to the mere clerk or officer, all derive some degree of benefit from the acts of those lawless ruffians, and therefore it is against their interest to injure them.

The discontent that existed previous to the late alarm, now broke out afresh and the two parties would have proceeded to extremities but for the timely arrival of two gentlemen from the Havana, who I understood were the owners of the corsair. By their interference, all differences were arranged, and the newly acquired plunder being shipped on board two coasting vessels, they returned with them.

The captain, on the following day, was attacked by a fever and felt himself so indisposed that he was apprehensive of death. He sent for me in a terrible state of alarm and promised me my liberty if I cured him. The promise I knew would be broken the moment he was well, so I resolved to take advantage of his illness to make my escape. For this, I thought the best thing would be to confine him to the cabin, and as he promised to follow my directions implicitly, I gave this injunction the first thing, and an opportunity soon after offered. Two fishermen came on board on the following afternoon and exchanged their cargo of fish for spirits. The evening being wet and stormy, they remained on board, and the crew inviting them to carouse, the whole were very shortly intoxicated. No further danger from the gun-boats being apprehended, the watch was neglected, and the moment I perceived this fancied state of security, hope dawned in my bosom. I knew that intoxication would make the rest sleep sound, and in order to secure the captain, in making him a mess of arrow root and wine, I infused a quantity of opiate.

At midnight all were asleep. The inclemency of the night had driven the usual sleepers on deck below, and therefore no one could see me. Not a sound was heard save the sullen roar of the waters around me or the wind and the rain beating against the shrouds. Not a star was to be seen and the scud[24] was flying thick and heavy. With a palpitating heart, I seized my bag that held my instruments, and in which I had secured some biscuit, and crept softly up the companion ladder and from thence to the stern of the corsair, where the fishermen's canoe was moored. Into this I gently dropped my bag, and then letting myself down, cut the painter[25] and let her drift away with the current in order not to rouse them by any noise. When I judged myself to be out of hearing, I trimmed the canoe and set the sail, steering her in the direction, as I imagined, of the Havana, and committing my future fate to the hands of that providence who had hitherto preserved me. In the morning, according to my calculation, I found myself about forty miles from the place where the pirate was at anchor, and consequently out of the reach of pursuit. The wind blew from the southwest, and what appeared to me a special Providence, continued to do so the whole day—a thing very unusual in that climate. All that day and the following night, I was upon the ocean without seeing a single vessel and at the mercy of the waves in a frail canoe in which, at any other time and under any other circumstances, I should have been afraid to trust myself. At six o'clock of the second morning of my escape, I entered the Havana, and seeing a person walking the deck of a schooner whose face appeared familiar to me, I ran my canoe along side and found him to be a Captain Williams, whom I had known some years before in America. He welcomed me on board, gave me refreshments, and seeing me weak and exhausted, begged me to lie down and sleep, promising in the afternoon to introduce me to the master of a vessel, who was in want of a mate. I willingly complied with his request, for I was completely faint and exhausted with my exertions of the day and night previous.

I now imagined my sufferings were at an end, but alas! I had yet to pass through another ordeal, as cruel and as severe as that from which I had just escaped.

Aaron Smith went into Havana the next day looking for Captain Williams but was spotted by a Spanish army captain who had been held prisoner for a few days by the pirates. This captain promptly summoned the authorities and Smith was arrested for being one of the pirates. He was held in Havana for several weeks and then put on trial. He complained that his testimony was altered by the interpreter, but the judge said he was still inclined to find him innocent . . . especially if he would pay a bribe. This judge had previously released four convicted pirates after they each gave him 100 doubloons. Smith, of course, had nothing to bribe him with.

At the request of a British admiral in Jamaica, Smith was turned over to the British Navy and returned to London to stand trial there for the piracy of two ships that were both taken on August 7, 1822. The trial was held on December 19, 1823. An outline of the trial was published in the Morning Herald *the following morning. The testimony was mixed. One of the prosecution's more damaging witnesses was a seaman named Oldham, who had been on one of the ships taken by the pirates while Smith was with them. He said the following:*

I was a seaman on board the *Victoria*.[26] I saw the prisoner on 7th August 1822 board the brig in a boat with three seamen who came from a privateer.[27] He ordered the captain, the second mate, and three seamen into a boat and sent them on board the schooner. He continued on board the *Victoria* and assumed command. He ordered the jib[28] and the foresail to be lowered, and swore at the crew if they did not do it quickly, he would shoot them, and fired a pistol amongst them. We had one seaman named Dean on board the *Victoria*. The prisoner cut him on the head with a cutlass and swore he would cut him down if Dean did not direct the ship in its due course after the brig. Dean afterwards went down the forecastle to get a chaw of tobacco. On his return the prisoner struck him with his cutlass on the neck and shoulders, which were sorely injured. Dean cried for mercy and then he was ordered to go aft by the prisoner. Another of the crew was afterwards struck by the prisoner with a cutlass, for not steering to please him, and another man was afterwards struck in the same manner by him without any cause whatever and the prisoner fired a pistol at the man's head and told him that if he fired again he would do it to some purpose. The prisoner had two pistols, which he fired twice each. While we were hoisting the fore-topmast and studding sail,[29] he fired his pistol at the crew, and afterwards ordered the steward to give us a glass of brandy each. A glass was offered to me, but I refused to drink it, and the prisoner said, "Who is it that refuses to drink a glass of brandy?" He afterwards asked me what countryman I was and if I was an American. I said no, I was an Englishman. He asked what countrymen the captain and mate were and if they were allowed private trading. I said they were allowed to trade privately and that they were Englishmen and that the captain lived in Newport Street, London. He then asked me if Dean was an Englishman. I told him he was an Irishman. He replied, "Then he is none the better for that." The prisoner ordered me to keep the ship pumped, as it leaked, and when I said the captain lived in Newport Street, London, he replied, "Don't tell me of London, I know nothing of it." He asked me of what the ship's cargo consisted and I told him. He said I must do the same as if the captain was on board, for he was the captain then. It began to rain and became so squally, and the prisoner put on a pair of the captain's shoes and the second mate's boat cloak. The prisoner ordered all the arms that were on board to be brought on deck and shown to him. They consisted of three cutlasses and two guns, and the prisoner wanted to ascertain if they were loaded. He found they were not. He saw an American schooner heave in sight and the prisoner went aloft with his telescope, and on coming down he ordered the long boat to be launched and four of the men to be ready to tow the *Victoria* ahead. The wind blew fresh and we got ahead of the American schooner. We kept a heavy press of sail and we thought at times the mast would be blown away. We were afterwards put on board the *Industry*[30] [the other ship taken by the pirates on the same day]. When I was going over the side of the *Victoria* I was told I must join the piratical schooner, but I went to the *Industry*.

[Seaman Oldham made the following testimony during the cross-examination.]

The schooner was within pistol-shot of the *Victoria* all the time, and could have fired into us and killed us had we attempted to escape. When the American schooner was in sight, the *Victoria* might, I think, then have been dropped for it to come up, if the prisoner had wished to relieve us. I am sure it was an American schooner that chased us.

Thomas Davis, the Victoria's *boatswain, was also a witness for the prosecution. He testified as follows:*

The prisoner ordered Dean, a seaman, to the wheel and other sailors were directed to hoist the jib. While Dean was steering the ship, the prisoner struck him on the head with a cutlass, which inflicted a wound three or four inches long. The prisoner ordered Hownam, the cook, to kill six fowls for dinner. Dean had done nothing to deserve the violent treatment of the prisoner. The prisoner then sent Dean aft and ordered Lewis, another sailor, to the wheel, and he not pleasing him, received a blow on the head with the prisoner's telescope. I was then ordered by the prisoner to steer after the pirate schooner and he swore if I did not steer to his liking he would fire at me, and while I was steering he fired his pistol at my head. The pistol was loaded for the ball whistled by my head. He afterwards threatened to run me through the body with his sword if I did not clear the wheel ropes, which had got foul, and he attempted to do it, but the Spaniard, Antonio, prevented him and said to him, "Don't be so cruel, he can't steer the ship while the wheel ropes are foul." Wm. Lewis, a seaman, went to the wheel after me. When the prisoner returned from aloft after spying the American schooner, he said, "I think the schooner arming towards us is a rogue" (meaning an enemy), and then he ordered the long boat out to enable them to get away if becalmed. The prisoner addressed this language to Antonio, the Spaniard. They spoke part in English and part in Spanish. I understand Spanish a little. The prisoner said that he thought the schooner that was in sight was an American which he had seen some days before. The Spaniard said that he thought so too. When the prisoner left the ship he had Mr. Sadler's [the *Victoria*'s second mate's] cloak on.

[Davis was then cross-examined.]

The prisoner was three yards from me when he fired the pistol. He had two pistols. I can't say that both were loaded. There was nothing between him and me. He could have blown out my brains if he had chosen. He was angry with me because I did not steer the ship in the due course. All the Spaniards spoke very bad English. The prisoner spoke good English. The squall had begun when the prisoner put the mate's cloak on.

[Davis was re-examined by the prosecution.]

At the time the American schooner hove in sight the pirate schooner was two miles behind the *Victoria*. I think the prisoner might have escaped from the pirate on board of the American schooner if he had pleased. It was a dark and squally night, and [i.e. but] I cannot speak positively.

Aaron Smith testified in his defense, but it was summarized by the newspaper. They reported:

The prisoner took from his pocket a written paper which he read to the jury, but was so affected with his situation that for some time he could not give utterance to a single word. The defense was well drawn up and was to the following effect: He was mate on board a merchant ship called the *Zephyr* in June 1822 and when sailing off Cape San Antonio, the *Zephyr* was boarded by a Spanish privateer and he and other persons were taken out of the ship on board the piratical schooner. He was carried forcibly away by the pirates and was obliged to work the ship. He underwent the most shocking tortures to force him to navigate the vessel and to assist them in their wicked enterprise. He had been confined to a solitary dungeon, lashed to the vessel and flogged, powder was placed at his feet and set fire to, and the flesh blown off his legs and his clothes consumed, because he merely evinced some objection to join a diabolical crew of miscreants against the property and lives of his own countrymen. All that he had done had been from fear. His spirit had been broken by the cruelties practiced upon him by the most diabolical monster that ever was in human shape—the captain of the pirates—and the circumstances which had been detailed by the witnesses as acts of cruelty, were done by him to save himself from further torture. When he fired the pistol (as it had been stated) at the ship's crew, he took care to fire in a direction that should injure no one and also when he fired by the side of the head of the man steering the *Victoria*, he could, if he had chosen, have shot him dead. This appearance of cruelty was assumed on his part to deceive the pirates and he declared to God most solemnly that he did not intend to cut the man on the head, for he struck him with the flat part of the cutlass. He called upon the jury to weigh well his case before they consigned him to an ignominious death, for though there might be appearances of guilt against him, yet God, the searcher of all hearts, knew that he was forced to do what he had done and that he had no opportunity of escaping from the pirate. He had always enjoyed a good reputation and never received a penny, or the value of it, from the pirates. And when he was taken, he had only two half-crowns[31] about his person and his dress was most wretched, which must in some degree convince the jury that he had no share in the piracy. He was on his way to England to join his friends and to marry one that he loved dearer than his life, when his hopes were blasted by his detention by the pirates and his sufferings had been almost beyond human endurance. While he had been under the lash of the monster, the captain of the pirates, he had repeatedly called upon him in mercy to put him to death and his answer had been, "No. I want your services and I will have them." Such was his situation when the captain of the pirates ordered him to board the *Victoria*, and had he [not] followed his commands, not a soul would have been left alive on board. He again appealed to his Maker that he was not a voluntary actor in the scenes described by the witnesses and trusted the jury by their verdict would acquit him.

Aaron Smith called twenty witnesses in his defense. One of them was his fiancée.

Miss Sophia Knight, a female of considerable personal attractions, was called. She was exceedingly agitated and the prisoner burst into tears as she entered the witnesses box. She said, "I have been intimately acquainted with the prisoner for more than three years. This letter (a letter put into her hands) is from him. It is the last that ever reached me. It is dated Oct., 1821. After the date of the letter, I expected on the prisoner arriving in England that I should become his wife. It was so arranged." Here she wept, and the prisoner appeared deeply affected.

In the end, the jury found Aaron Smith innocent of piracy and determined that he was a forced man. Some felt the jury was swayed by the testimony of Smith's fiancée.

Smith returned to sea and eventually commanded a merchant ship involved in trade with China. While on one journey to the Far East, he was attacked and almost taken by Borneo pirates. He quit the sea in 1834 and became an underwriter in London. Then in 1850, a Mr. Cobden and Capt. Cook (who had been captain of the Industry*) were quoted in the London* Times *calling Smith a pirate. Smith—described at this time as a burly seafaring man—sued Cook for libel. The lawsuit evolved into another trial to determine his innocence or guilt of piracy. As twenty-eight years had passed since his previous trial in London, Smith's witnesses had either died or disappeared, plus there was no official report of that trial. Still, the verdict was in his favor, though he was only awarded £10 in damages.*

Notes

1. Schooner: a small ship with two or more masts and primary sails that run from masts toward the stern. Each mast may be topped with one or more square sails. The ship has triangular sails towards the bow.

2. League: a measurement usually of about three miles.

3. Cape Roman (Cayo Romano) is actually a large island on the northeastern side of Cuba, about 275 miles east of Havana. At this time, many maps showed it as part of the mainland.

4. Corsair: a pirate, though this term is usually used to refer to pirates of the Mediterranean, the Red Sea, and the Indian Ocean.

5. Quarter: to refrain from slaying someone and often to accept them as a prisoner.

6. Myrmidons: an unquestioning follower or subordinate who blindly carries out orders.

7. Round house: a cabin in the after part of the quarter-deck having the poop (a raised deck at the stern) as its roof.

8. Doubloons: Spanish gold coins.

9. His fiancée.

10. Fathom: a measurement equal to six feet.

11. Steelyard: a type of suspended scales from which the object to be weighed is hung from the shorter arm and a weight is moved along the longer arm.

12. Porter: a dark brown beer made from charred or browned malt.

13. Pig of iron: an oblong casting of iron.

14. Gaff-topsail: a triangular or quadrilateral set above the gaff (i.e. a spar extending diagonally upward behind a mast and which supports a primary sail).

15. Fore-topsail: the sail on the fore-mast above the foresail, or the second sail in ascending order from the deck on the ship's forward mast.

16. Later he did board ships that were taken.

17. Laudanum: a solution of opium in alcohol, which was primarily used as a pain killer or sedative.

18. Specie: hard currency (i.e. gold, silver, or coins).

19. Blunderbusses: short rifles with a flared muzzles.

20. *Rencontre*: French for "rencounter," a hostile encounter or battle.

21. Seriatim: in a regular order, one by one.

22. Mizzen mast: the mast nearest the stern.

23. Which was true, as the captain had told Aaron Smith to tell the others the plunder was less than it actually was so he could pocket the rest.

24. Scud: spray carried swiftly by the wind.

25. Painter: a rope at the bow of a boat.

26. The *Victoria*, from Black River, Jamaica, sailed for England under Capt. Septimus Hern with a crew of thirteen. It had a cargo of coffee and dye wood.

Smith was charged with stealing 636 barrels of coffee valued at £5,000 and 110 barrels of coffee worth £1,000, plus other articles.

27. Privateering was a legal form of piracy, used by countries to supplement their armed forces. A privateer was a privately owned warship which operated under a commission making it legal for them to capture and plunder ships of a specific country or countries. The government granting the commission usually received a portion of the booty. In England from the fifteenth through the seventeenth centuries these commissions were issued by the King. (Capt. Kidd's commission was signed by King William the Third.) After 1702 they were issued by the Lord High Admiral, and later by colonial governors, some of whom were corrupt and granted commissions to pirates to make them "legal." Privateering was last used by Chile against Spain in 1865.

28. Jib: a triangular sail which usually extends from the foremast to the bowsprit.

29. Fore-topmast: the mast above the fore-mast and at the head of which stands the fore-topgallant mast. Studding sail: the sail extending beyond the side edge of a square sail, used to make the most of light winds.

30. The *Industry*, sailing under Capt. Cook, carried a cargo of rum. The pirates must have been well-stocked with alcohol or were unable to get a decent price for it, because they showed no interest in this cargo. Apparently little was taken, since Smith was only charged with seizing this ship.

31. Half-crowns: British silver coins, worth two shillings and sixpence, used before Britain adopted a decimal monetary system.

They Hoisted the Bloody Flag, a Signal for Death

≋≋≋

Captain Jacob Dunham

Jacob Dunham (age 42) was captain of the schooner Combine, *which had sailed from Catskill, New York, to Jérémie in
what is now Haiti. While in the West Indies, he became
deathly ill with a fever and began to think he would never see
his home again, so he ordered his ship to head back to New
York. While rounding Cape San Antonio, which is the western
tip of Cuba, he ran into pirates. He wrote about his experience
in his book* Journal of Voyages *(1850).*

About nine o'clock [October 13, 1821], while doubling [i.e. rounding]
the Cape, we discovered three small schooners, one small sloop,[1] and a
large open boat lying at anchor about two miles from the land. In about
the space of fifteen minutes the whole fleet got under weigh and bore
down for us. One of the largest schooners ran down within musket-shot
of us, fired a gun, and we hove to, while the rest of the fleet surrounded
us. The largest schooner immediately sent a boat alongside of us containing eight or nine men, who boarded us with muskets and drawn cutlasses in their hands, each of them having a long knife and a dagger
slung by his side. Immediately after getting on deck, one of them cried
out, "Forward," two or three times in broken English, pointing at the
same time toward the forecastle. The mate, sailors, and two passengers
who were on board,[2] ran forward and jumped into the forecastle. I being
very weak, dragged along slowly, when the man who gave the order
commenced beating me severely with the broad side of his cutlass. I
remonstrated with him, saying I was sick and could not walk any faster;
he answered me, "*No intende.*" I then discovered he was a Portuguese,
and not understanding that language, I excused myself as well as I could

in the French language, hoping he understood me; but I found it did not relieve my back, as he continued to beat me all the way to the fore-scuttle,[3] and there giving me a heavy blow on the head as I descended, closed it, where we remained about half an hour. They in the meantime appeared to be searching the vessel.

After letting us up from the forecastle they ordered the sailors to work the vessel in near the land and anchor her, which was soon accomplished. While beating the vessel toward the shore, they told me if I would give up my money they would let me go with my vessel. This I readily complied with, hoping to save the vessel and cargo. I then gave them all the money I had, consisting of four hundred and eighty dollars in gold and silver. After they had received it they broke open our trunks, seized all our clothes, taking the finest shirts and vests, and putting them on one over another.

As soon as they had anchored my vessel they hauled their largest schooner alongside, while the rest of the fleet were laying within a few rods[4] of us, and then all hoisted the bloody flag, a signal for death.[5] I was ordered into the cabin, where one of the pirates, having found a bottle of cordial, took it up in one hand, and drawing his cutlass with the other, struck off the neck and handed it to me, flourishing his cutlass over my head and making signs for me to taste it, which I found it difficult to do on account of the broken particles of glass. After I had tasted it he went to a case of liquor standing in the cabin, took out the bottles and compelled me to taste of them. After this ceremony was over one of the pirates drew a long knife from its sheath, and taking hold of the hair on the top of my head, drew the knife two or three times across my throat near the skin, saying, "Me want to kill you." Another pirate soon approached me with a dagger, with which he pricked me lightly in the body, two or three times, saying, "Me kill you by-and-by." I was then dismissed from the cabin and driven into the forecastle with the sailors and passengers. My cook was put on board the schooner lying alongside of us. Some of the pirates went aloft on board my vessel and cut loose her squaresail, topsail, and top-gallant-sail, and afterwards took our foresail,[6] boat, oars, loose rigging, one compass, one quadrant, all our beds and bedding, tea-kettle, all our crockery, knives and forks, buckets, etc. leaving us destitute of every kind of cooking utensil except the caboose.[7]

We remained some time in the forecastle, when suddenly the fore-scuttle was opened and the mate called on deck, and the scuttle again closed, leaving us in the dark in a state of uncertainty. We soon heard them beating the mate. After that noise had ceased, we heard the word, "Fire," given with a loud voice, then after a moment's pause another voice was heard, saying, "Heave him overboard." I had a desperate sailor, called Bill, who flew to his chest for his razor to cut his own throat, saying he would be damned before he would be murdered by them rascals. The pirates had previously robbed the sailors' chests of all the articles they contained, and among them Bill's razor. After a little while the scuttle was again opened, when they called for a sailor. There were four in the forecastle, who looked earnestly at each other, when Brown, a favorite old sailor, arose and addressed me, saying, "Captain, I suppose I might as well die first as last," then taking me by the hand gave it a hearty shake, saying, "Good-bye." I told Brown to plead with them in the French language, as I thought I had seen some Frenchmen among them, and knew that he spoke French fluently. When he had got upon deck I heard him speak a few words in that language, but soon after we heard them beating him severely. As soon as they had finished beating him we again heard the word "Fire," and soon after, "Heave him overboard." Shortly after, the scuttle was again opened and the captain was loudly called. I crawled up the scuttle, being very feeble. They then told me if I did not tell them where the money was they would serve me as they had the mate and sailor, shoot and then throw me overboard. I still persisted that there was no money on board, and entreated them to search the vessel. An old Spaniard was pointed out to me who they said was the commodore. I asked him what he wanted of me, looking him earnestly in the face. He replied he wanted my money. I told him I had no money, but if I had I would give it to him; that the property belonged to him, but he had no right to take my life, as I had a family depending on me for support. Previous to this, the man who had flogged me before had made a chalk ring on the deck, saying, "Stand there," beating me with the flat side of a heavy cutlass until the blood ran through my shirt. During my conversation with the commodore, finding all my entreaties unsuccessful, and my strength much exhausted, I took a firm stand in the ring marked out for me, hoping to receive a ball through the heart, fearing if I was wounded I should be tortured to death to make sport for the demons. Two of the pirates with loaded muskets took their stand and fired them toward me, when I cast my eyes down toward my feet looking for blood, thinking that I might have been wounded without feeling the pain.

During this time the man who had beat me before commenced beating me again, pointing aft toward the cabin door, where I proceeded, followed by him, beating me all the time. He forced me into the cabin, at the same time giving me a severe blow over the head with his cutlass. When I entered I found both the mate and sailor there who I supposed had been murdered and thrown overboard. The next person called out of the forecastle was Mr. Peck, a passenger, who was immediately asked where the money was. He told them he knew of no more money on board. One man stood before him with a musket and another with a cutlass, they knocked him down and beat him for some time, took him by the hair and said they would kill him. He was then ordered to sit upon the bit of the windlass[8] to be shot and thrown overboard, as the captain and others had been. He took his station by the windlass, when a musket was fired at him; he was then driven into the cabin.

They then called up the remainder of the men from the forecastle, one after the other, and beat and drove them into the cabin also, except a Mr. Chollet, a young man, passenger, who escaped beating. We were kept in the cabin some time, and after repeated threats that they would kill us, were all driven into the forecastle again. They took out all our cargo, consisting of coffee, cocoa, tortoise-shell, eight kedge anchors,[9] all our provisions, except part of a barrel of beef and about thirty pounds of bread. After they had taken all the cargo, spare rigging, etc. of any value, they shifted all the ballast in the hold of the vessel in search of money, and calling us on deck, we were told to be off.

After getting under weigh we proceeded but slowly, having no other sails left but the two jibs[10] and the mainsail. We looked back with a great deal of anxiety, and saw the pirates seated on the deck of the largest schooner, drinking liquor and making themselves merry, while we feared they might change their minds, pursue us and take our lives. Night beginning to approach, I thought best to go down into the cabin and see what we had left to eat or drink. As soon as I had reached the cabin, it being dark, I stumbled against something on the floor, which I found to be our cook, whom we supposed we had left behind, having seen the pirates put him on board the schooner which was lying alongside of us, but knew nothing of his return. I spoke to him, but received no answer, I hustled him about the cabin, but could not make him speak. I at last got a light and looked about for some provisions, cooking utensils, etc., and found about thirty pounds of bread, a little broken coffee, and most of a barrel of beef, but no cooking utensils except the caboose, with one or two pots set in it.

The next morning I called all hands into the cabin, showed all the bread we had left, and told them it was necessary to go on allowance of one biscuit a day per man, which was agreed to, until we could get further supplies. I then questioned the cook (knowing that he was driven into the hold of the pirate schooner) as to what kind of a cargo she had. He said there were calicoes[11] and all kinds of dry goods scattered about, and more than a hundred demijohns[12]; and "O captain, it was the best old Jamaica rum that you ever tasted." I told him if the pirates had caught him drinking their rum they would have killed him. He said it looked so tempting he thought he would try it. I suppose that after having drank a large quantity he made his escape on board of the *Combine* before he felt the effects of it, as he was not aware of our release.

The next day we were boarded by a boat from a Spanish man-of-war brig.[13] I plead hard with the officer who boarded us to go in pursuit of the pirates, which he refused to do, saying it was out of their limits to cruise. I asked him for a supply of bread, which he denied me. In our crippled state we reached Havana in nine days, where we put in for supplies.

Two days later on October 15, 1821, the ship Aristides *was taken by the same pirates and they ran vessel the shore. The next morning, while the pirates were plundering this ship, a U.S. Navy man-of-war sailed into view. The pirates abandoned their prize and tried to escape along the shore in their vessels. The commander of the* Aristides, *Captain Couthony, wrote of the arrival of the man-of-war in a letter:*

"She proved to be the United States brig *Enterprise*, L. Kearny,[14] Esq., commander. I stated to him my dreadful situation and pointed out to him the five piratical vessels in shore. He immediately made all sail in pursuit, but a reef prevented his getting within gunshot. He armed all the boats, and with the crews of the ship *Lucies* and an English brig,[15] which were likewise in the hands of the pirates, gave them chase, overhauling them fast. They rowed their vessels on shore inside the Cape, set the loaded one on fire, and took to the woods. Lieutenant McIntosh, who went on the expedition, took four of the vessels—the boat having escaped. The vessel set on fire was entirely destroyed; but few remnants of goods were saved, and these partly burnt. The pirates had a train of powder to blow up the vessel on the approach of the boats.

In a report to the Secretary of the Navy dated November 12, 1821, Lieutenant Kearny wrote, "I have the honor to report my arrival here [in Charleston, S.C.] from a cruise in the Bay of Mexico. Off Cape San Antonio on the 16th ult.[16] *we had the fortune to capture four piratical schooners and a sloop. They were manned by Spaniards about 70 or 80 strong. The pirates ran their vessels on shore when pursued by our boats and made their escape except one man now a prisoner on board this vessel."*

These pirates decided to build two forts in order to protect themselves better. In January 1822, Lieutenant Ramage in the U.S. schooner Porpoise again attacked these pirates, destroying another five vessels and taking three prisoners. By the following July, it was reported that the pirate Raphaelina was the head of a fleet of vessels which were operating around Cape San Antonio.

Notes

1. Sloop: a single-masted vessel that was a favorite of pirates because of its shallow draught and maneuverability.

2. There were nine people on this ship: the captain, mate, the cook, four crew members and two passengers.

3. Fore-scuttle: the forward hatchway or opening in the deck, large enough for a man to pass through and covered with a lid.

4. Rod: a measurement equal to 16½ feet or 5½ yards.

5. Pirates raised the black flag to show they were pirates and to demand surrender without a fight—the skull and crossbones or skeletons indicating the consequences of fighting back. The red or bloody flag was raised to say that no quarter would be given, meaning they would take no prisoners. This was sometimes just a scare tactic because occasionally the pirates would still take those who surrendered as prisoners even after they said no quarter would be given or displayed the bloody flag.

6. Topsail: the sail above the mainsail, or the second sail in ascending order from the deck. Topgallant sail: the sail above the topsail, or the third sail in ascending order from the deck. Foresail: the primary sail on the foremast.

7. Caboose: the galley, or ship's kitchen.

8. Windlass: a winch-like hoisting apparatus with a horizontal, rotating cylinder, around which a rope or chain is wrapped.

9. Kedge anchors: small anchors that are used to keep a ship from riding over its bow anchor in a change of wind or tide.

10. Jibs: triangular sails which usually extend from the foremast to the bowsprit.

11. Calico: any of several types of cotton cloth.

12. Demijohns: large bottles of earthenware or glass, with a narrow neck and a wicker casing and handle.

13. Brig or brigantine: a two-masted merchant ship with primarily square sails.

14. Lieutenant Lawrence Kearny.

15. The *Lucies* was an American ship and the English brig was the *Larch*.

16. Ult.: the abbreviation for "ultimo," meaning the previous month.

Dead Cats Don't Mew

≋≋≋≋

John Battis

On the 20th of August in 1832, the Spanish slave ship Panda *sailed from Havana on its way to buy more slaves on the west coast of Africa. The mate and owner of the* Panda *was Don Bernardo de Soto (age 25), the son of Spanish official and the son-in-law of a wealthy merchant. The captain was Don Pedro Gilbert (36), the son of a high-ranking Spanish nobleman. The crew of about forty consisted primarily of Spanish, with a few Portuguese, South Americans, and half-castes. A month later, they spotted an American brig on its way from Salem, Massachusetts, to Rio de Janeiro, Brazil. They decided to see if this ship had any money on board and, if so, to take it as a prize.*

John Battis was one of the thirteen men on the American brigantine Mexican *when it was taken by the Spaniards. He later recorded what happened in the following narrative.*

I was at Peabody's store house [in Salem] on the morning of the day of sailing and others of the crew came soon after. After waiting quite awhile, it was suggested that we go after the cook, Ridgely, who then boarded with a Mrs. Ransom, a colored woman living in Becket Street, so we set out to find him. He was at home but disinclined to go, as he wished to pass one more Sunday home. However, after some persuading he got ready and we all started out of the gate together. A black hen was in the yard and as we came out the bird flew upon the fence, and flapping her wings, gave a loud crow. The cook was wild with terror and insisted that something was going to happen; that such a sign meant harm and he ran about in search of a stone to knock out the brains of the offending biped. The poor donkey did not succeed in his design, but followed us grumbling.[1]

At about ten o'clock we mustered all present and accounted for, and commenced to carry the specie,[2] with which we were to purchase our return cargo, on board the brig. We carried aboard twenty thousand dollars in silver, in ten boxes of two thousand dollars each; we also had about one hundred bags of saltpeter and one hundred chests of tea. The silver was stored in the "run" under the cabin floor, and there was not a man aboard but knew where the money was stored. At last everything being ready we hove anchor and stood out to sea in the face of a southeast wind. As soon as we got outside and stowed anchor we cleared ship and the captain called all hands and divided the crew into watches. I was in the first mate's watch and young Thomas Fuller[3] was in the captain's watch.

On account of the several acts of piracy previously committed on Salem ships, Captain Butman undoubtedly feared, or perhaps had a premonition of a later happening to his vessel, for the next day while I was at work on the main rigging, I heard the captain and first mate talking about pirates. The captain said he would fight a long while before he'd give his money up. They had a long talk together, and he seemed to be very much worried. I think it was the next day after this conversation between Captain Butman and Mr. Reed that I was at the wheel steering when the captain came and spoke to me. He asked me how I felt about leaving home, and I replied that I felt the same as ever, "all right." I learned afterwards that he put this question to the rest of the crew.

We sailed along without anything occurring worthy of note until the night of the nineteenth of September (1832). After supper we were all sitting together during the dog-watch (this being between six and eight o'clock P.M.) when all seemed bent on telling pirate yarns, and of course got more or less excited. I went below at twelve o'clock and at four next morning my watch was called. Upon coming on deck the first mate came forward and said that we must keep a sharp look out as there was a vessel 'round, and that she had crossed our stern and gone to the leeward.[4] I took a seat between the knight-heads[5] and had been sitting there but a few minutes when a vessel crossed our bows and went to the windward of us.

We were going at a pretty good rate at the time I sang out and the mate came forward with a glass, but he could not make her out. I told him he would see her to the windward at daylight. At dawn we discovered a top-sail schooner about five miles off our weather quarter, standing on the wind on the same tack as we were. The wind was light, at south southwest, and we were standing about southeast. At seven o'clock the captain came on deck and this was the first we knew of the schooner being about us.

I was at the wheel when the captain came out of the cabin; he looked toward the schooner, and as soon as he perceived her he reached and took his glass and went onto the main top. He came down and closing the glass said, "That is the very man I have been looking for. I can count thirty men on his deck." He also said that he saw one man on her fore-topgallant yard,[6] looking out, and that he was very suspicious of her. He then ordered us to set all sail (as the schooner didn't seem to sail very fast) thinking we might get away from her.

While I was up loosing the main-royal[7] I sat on the yard, and let them hoist me up to the truck so that I could have a good look around. I saw another vessel, a brig, to the eastward of us and reported it. The schooner had in the meantime sailed very fast, for when I started to come down she was off our beam. From all appearances and her manner of sailing we concluded afterwards that she had a drag[8] out. We then went to breakfast, the schooner kept ahead of us and appeared to be after the other vessel. Then the captain altered the brig's course, tacking to the westward, keeping a little off from the wind to make good way through the water to get clear of her if possible. After breakfast when we came on deck the schooner was coming down on us under a full press of sail. I noticed two kegs of powder alongside our two short carronades,[9] the only guns we had. Our means of defense, however, proved utterly worthless as the shot was a number of sizes too large for the guns.

A few moments before this the schooner had fired a shot at us to heave to, which Captain Butman was on the point of doing as I came on deck. The schooner then hoisted patriotic colors (Colombian flag), backed her main-topsail[10] and laid to about half a mile to the windward. She was a long low straight topsail schooner of about one hundred and fifty tons burden, painted black with a narrow white streak, a large fig-ure-head with a horn of plenty painted white; masts raked aft, and a large main topsail, a regular Baltimore clipper.[11] We could not see any name. She carried thirty or more men, with a long thirty-two pound swivel[12] amidships, with four brass guns, two on each side.

A hail came in English from the schooner, asking us where we were from and where bound and what our cargo was. Captain Butman replied, "Tea and saltpeter." The same voice from the schooner then hailed us for the captain to lower a boat and come alongside and bring him his papers. The boat was got ready and Captain Butman and four men—Jack Ardissone, Thomas Fuller, Benjamin Larcomb and Fred Trask—got in and pulled to the schooner. When they parted, Captain Butman shook hands with the mate, Mr. Reed, and told him to do the best he could if he never saw him again.

The *Mexican*'s boat pulled up to the gangway of the schooner but they ordered it to go to the forechains where five of the pirates jumped into our boat, not permitting any of our men to go on board the schooner and pushed off, ordering the captain back to the brig. They were armed with pistols in their belts and long knives up their sleeves. While at the schooner's side, after getting into our boat, one of the pirates asked their captain in Spanish what they should do with us, and his answer was: "Dead cats don't mew—have her thoroughly searched and bring aboard all you can—you know what to do with them."

The orders of the captain of the schooner being in Spanish were understood by only one of the *Mexican*'s crew then in the boat, namely Ardissone, who burst into tears and in broken English declared that all was over with them.

Our boat returned to the brig and Captain Butman and the five pirates came on board. Two of them went down in the cabin with us and the other three loafed around the deck. Our first mate came up from the cabin and told us to muster aft and get the money up. Larcomb and I, being near the companion-way, started to go down into the cabin when we met the boatswain of the pirate coming up, who gave the signal for attack.

The three pirates on deck sprang on Larcomb and myself, striking at us with the long knives across our heads. A Scotch cap I happened to have on with a large cotton handkerchief inside, saved me from a severe wounding as both were cut through and through. Our mate, Mr. Reed, here interfered and attempted to stop them from assaulting us whereupon they turned on him.

We then went down into the cabin and in to the run. There were eight of us in all. Six of our men then went back into the cabin and the steward and myself were ordered to pass the money up, which we did, to the cabin floor and our crew then took it and carried it on deck.

In the meantime the pirate officer in charge (the third mate) had

hailed the schooner and told them they had found what they were looking for. The schooner then sent a launch containing sixteen men, which
came alongside and they boarded us. They made the crew pass the boxes
of money down into the boat, and it was then conveyed on board the
pirate. The launch came back with about a dozen more men, and the
search began in earnest. Nine of them rushed down into the cabin where
the captain, Jack Ardissone, and myself were standing. They beat the
captain with the long knives and battered a speaking trumpet to pieces
on his head and shoulders. Seeing we could do nothing, I made a break to
reach the deck by jumping out of the cabin window, thinking I could get
there by grasping hold of the boat's davits[13] and pulling myself on deck.
Jack Ardissone, divining my movement, caught my foot as I was jumping
and saved me, or I should probably have missed my calculation and gone
overboard. Jack and I then ran and the pirates after both of us, leaving
the captain whom they continued to beat and abuse, demanding more
money. We ran into the steerage. Jack, not calculating the break of the
deck soon went over into the hold, and I on top of him. For some reason
the pirates gave up the chase before they reached the break between the
decks, or they would have gone down with us. By the fall Jack broke two
of his ribs. Under deck we had a clean sweep, there being no cargo, so we
could go from one end of the vessel to the other.

The crew then got together in the forecastle and stayed there. We
hadn't been there long before the Mr. Reed, came rushing down, chased
by the boatswain of the pirate, demanding his money. The mate then
told Larcomb to go and get his money, which he had previously given
Larcomb to stow away for him in some safe place. There were two hundred dollars in specie and Larcomb had put it under the wood in the
hold. Larcomb went and got it, brought it up and gave it to the pirate,
who untied the bag took a handful out, retied the bag and went up on
deck and threw the handful of money overboard, so that those on the
schooner could see that they had found more money.

Then the pirates went to Captain Butman and told him that if they
found any more money which they hadn't surrendered they would cut
all our throats. I must have followed them into the cabin, for I heard
them tell the captain this. Previous to this, we of the crew found that we
had about fifty dollars, which we secured by putting into the pickle keg,
and this was secretly placed in the breast-work forward. On hearing this
threat made to the captain I ran back and informed the crew what I had

heard, and we took the money out of my keg and dropped it down the air-streak, which is the space between the inside and outside planking. It went way down into the keelson.[14] Our carpenter afterwards located its exact position and recovered every cent of it. Strange to say the first thing they searched on coming below was the pickle keg. The search of our effects by the pirates was pretty thorough, and they took all new clothes, tobacco, etc. In the cabin they searched the captain's chest, but failed to get at seven hundred dollars which he had concealed in the false bottom; they had previously taken from him several dollars which he had in his pocket, and his gold watch, and had also relieved the mate of his watch.

About noon it appeared to be very quiet on deck, we having been between decks ever since the real searching party came on board. We all agreed not to go on deck again and to make resistance with sticks of wood if they attempted to come down, determined to sell our lives as dearly as possible. Being somewhat curious, I thought I'd peep up and see what they were doing; as I did so a cocked pistol was pressed to my head and I was ordered to come on deck and went, expecting to be thrown overboard. One took me by the collar and held me out at arm's length to plunge a knife into me. I looked him right in the eye and he dropped the knife and ordered me to get the doors of the forecastle which were below. I went down and got them, but they did not seem to understand how they were to be used, and they made me come up and ship them. There were three of them and as I was letting the last one in I caught the gleam of a cutlass being drawn, so taking the top of the door on my stomach, I turned a quick somersault and went down head first into the forecastle. The cutlass came down, but did not find me; it went into the companionway quite a depth. Then they hauled the slide over and fastened it, and we were all locked below.

They fastened the after companionway leading down into the cabin, locking our officers below as well. From noises that came from overhead, we were convinced that the pirates had begun a work of destruction. All running rigging, including tiller ropes, were cut, sails slashed into ribbons, spars cut loose, ship's instruments and all movable articles on which they could lay their hands were demolished, the yards were tumbled down and we could hear the main boom swinging from side to side. They then, as appears from later developments, filled the caboose, or cook's galley, with combustibles, consisting of tar, tarred rope yarn, oakum,[15] etc., setting fire to the same, and lowered the dismantled mainsail so that it rested on top of the caboose. In this horrible suspense we waited for an hour or more when all became quiet save the wash of the sea against the brig. All this time the crew had been cooped up in the darkness of the forecastle, of course unable to speculate as to what would be the next move of the enemy, or how soon death would come to each and all of us.

Finally about three o'clock in the afternoon, Thomas Fuller came running forward and informed us that the pirates were leaving the ship. One after another of the crew made their way to the cabin and on peering out of the two small stern windows saw the pirates pulling for the schooner. Captain Butman was at this time standing on the cabin table, looking out from a small skylight, the one means of egress the pirates had neglected to fasten. We told him that from the odor of smoke, we believed they had fired the brig. He said he knew it and ordered us to remain quiet. He then stepped down from the table and for several moments knelt in prayer, after which he calmly told us to go forward and he would call us when he wanted us.

We had not been in the forecastle long before he called us back, and directed that we get all the buckets under deck and fill them with water from the casks in the hold. On our return he again opened the skylight and drew himself up on deck. We then handed him a small bucket of water, and he crept along the rail in the direction of the caboose, keeping well under the rail in order to escape observation from the schooner. The fire was just breaking through the top of the caboose when he arrived in time to throw several handfuls of water on top so as to keep it under. This he continued to do for a long while, not daring to extinguish it immediately lest the pirates should notice the absence of smoke and know that their plan for our destruction had been frustrated. When the fire had been reduced to a reasonable degree of safety he came and opened the aft companionway and let us all up. The schooner being a fast sailor was in the distance about hull down.

The fire in the caboose was allowed to burn in a smoldering condition for perhaps a half-hour or more, keeping up a dense smoke. By this time the pirate schooner was well nigh out of sight, or nearly topsails under, to the eastward. On looking about us, we found the *Mexican* in a bad plight, all sails halyards[16] and running gear were cut, headsails[17] dragging in the water, and on account of the tiller ropes being cut loose, the brig was rolling about in the trough of the sea. We at once set to work repairing damages as speedily as possible and before dark had bent new sails and repaired our running gear to a great extent.

Fortunately through the shrewdness and foresight of Captain Butman, our most valuable ship instruments, compass, quadrant, sextant, etc., had escaped destruction. It seems that immediately on discovering the true character of the stranger, he had placed them in the steerage and covered them with a quantity of oakum. This the pirates somehow overlooked in their search, although they passed and re-passed it continually during their visit. The brig was then put before the wind, steering north, and as by the intervention of Divine Providence, a strong wind came up, which before dark developed into a heavy squall with thunder and lightning, so we let the brig go before the fury of the wind, not taking in a stitch of canvas. We steered north until next morning, when the brig's course was altered, and we stood due west, tacking off and on several courses for a day or two, when finally a homeward course was taken which was kept up until we reached Salem October 12th, 1832.

Notes

1. It was once commonly believed that a crowing hen foretold death or misfortune and the only way to avoid it was by killing the hen, usually by stoning or beheading. This superstition still exists today in some rural parts of Europe.

2. Specie: hard currency (i.e. gold, silver, or coins).

3. Thomas Fuller later became a captain. He was 20 years old when this happened.

4. Leeward: the side of the ship away from the wind.

5. Knight-heads: the two pieces of timber rising on either side of the bowsprit to secure its inner end.

6. Fore-topgallant yard: the yard that holds the topgallant sail, which is the sail above the topsail, or the third sail in ascending order from the deck.

7. Main-royal: the sail on the main mast above the topgallant, or the fourth sail in ascending order from the deck.

8. Drag: a kind of floating anchor, usually of spars and sails, used to keep the ships head to the wind or diminish leeway.

9. Carronade: a light cannon of large caliber used for short range.

10. Main-topsail: the sail on the mainmast above the mainsail, or the second sail in ascending order from the deck on the ship's primary mast.

11. Clipper: a ship designed for speed, with a sleek bow and backward sweeping masts.

12. Swivel: a gun mounted on the ship's railing and could be swung from side to side.

13. Davits: uprights of timber or iron that project over the side of a vessel that are used for hoisting or lowering objects.

14. Keelson: heavy timber set above the keel and over the floor timbers to secure the latter.

15. Oakum: old ropes untwisted into loose twine that was used for caulking the seams of ships, stopping leaks, etc.

16. Halyards: vertical ropes for hoisting sails.

17. Headsails: sails that are forward of the foremast.

They Threatened Us with Instant Death

≋≋≋≋≋≋

Captain John Butman

The following is Captain John G. Butman's statement of what happened on the Mexican.

Nothing remarkable had happened on board, until half past two o'clock in the morning of September 20th [1832], in lat. 38°0' N., lon. 24°30' W. The attention of the watch on deck was forcibly arrested by the appearance of a vessel which passed across our stern about half a mile from us. At 4 A.M. saw her again passing across our bow, so near that we could perceive that it was a schooner with a fore-topsail and topgallant sail.[1] As it was somewhat dark she was soon out of sight. At daylight saw her about five miles off the weather quarter standing on the wind on the same tack we were on, the wind was light at SSW and we were standing about SE.

At 8 A.M. she was about two miles right to windward of us. [We] could perceive a large number of men upon her deck and one man on the fore-topgallant yard looking out; was very suspicious of her, but knew not how to avoid her. Soon after [I] saw a brig on our weather bow steering to the NE. By this time the schooner was about three miles from us and four points forward of the beam. Expecting that she would keep on for the brig ahead of us, we tacked[2] to the westward, keeping a little off from the wind to make good way through the water, to get clear of her if possible.

She kept on to the eastward about ten or fifteen minutes after we had tacked, then wore[3] round, set square sail, steering directly for us, came down upon us very fast, and was soon within gun shot of us, fired a gun and hoisted patriot colors and backed main-topsail.[4] She ran along to windward of us, hailed us to know where we were from, where bound, etc., then ordered me to come on board in my boat.

Seeing that she was too powerful for us to resist, I accordingly went, and soon as I got along-side of the schooner, five ruffians instantly jumped into my boat, each of them being armed with a large knife, and told me to go on board the brig again. When they got on board they insisted that we had got money, and drew their knives, threatening us with instant death and demanding to know where it was. As soon as they found out where it was, they obliged my crew to get it up out of the run upon deck, beating and threatening them at the same time because they did not do it quicker.

When they had got it all upon deck and hailed the schooner, they got out their launch and came and took it on board the schooner, viz. ten boxes containing twenty thousand dollars. [They] then returned to the brig again, drove all the crew into the forecastle, ransacked the cabin, overhauling all the chests, trunks, etc. and rifled my pockets, taking my watch, and three doubloons which I had previously put there for safety. [They] robbed the mate of his watch and two hundred dollars in specie, still insisting that there was more money in the hold. Being answered in the negative, they beat me severely over the back, said they knew that there was more, that they should search for it, and if they found any they would cut all our throats. They continued searching about in every part of the vessel for some time longer, but not finding any more specie, they took two coils of rigging, a side of leather, and some other articles, and went on board the schooner, probably to consult what to do with us; for, in eight or ten minutes they came back, apparently in great haste, shut us all below, fastened up the companion way, fore-scuttle[5] and after hatchway, stove our compasses to pieces in the binnacles, cut away tiller-ropes, halyards, braces,[6] and most of our running rigging, cut our sails to pieces badly; took a tub of tarred rope-yarn and what combustibles they could find about deck, put them in the caboose house and set them on fire; then left us, taking with them our boat and colors. When they got alongside of the schooner they scuttled our boat, took in their own, and made sail, steering to the eastward.

As soon as they left us, we got up out of the cabin scuttle, which they had neglected to secure, and extinguished the fire, which if it had been left a few minutes, would have caught the mainsail and set our masts on fire. Soon after we saw a ship to leeward of us steering to the SE the schooner being in pursuit of her did not overtake her whilst she was in sight of us.

It was doubtless their intention to burn us up altogether, but seeing the ship, and being eager for more plunder they did not stop fully to accomplish their design. She was a low strait schooner of about one hundred and fifty tons, painted black with a narrow white streak, a large head with the horn of plenty painted white, large main topmast but no yards or sail on it. Mast raked very much, mainsail very square at the head, sails made with split cloth and all new; had two long brass twelve pounders[7] and a large gun on a pivot amidships, and about seventy men, who appeared to be chiefly Spaniards and mulattos.

Soon after this, an English warship found the Panda *on the west coast of Africa. While some of the pirates got away, fifteen[8] were taken prisoner. These were clapped in irons, hauled off to England, and eventually extradited to the United States. One of the pirates agreed to turn State's evidence and two others, who had turned pirate after the taking of the* Mexican, *appeared as witnesses. The remaining twelve stood trial on November 11, 1834. During the trial, when asked to identify one of the pirates, Thomas Fuller went over and punched the pirate's shoulder. Five were found innocent because the jury wasn't convinced that they were part of the crew when the* Mexican *was taken. Seven were sentenced to death—though one was pardoned by President Andrew Jackson after his 17-year-old wife had gained an audience with Jackson where she pleaded for her husband's life and because in 1830 he had risked his life and vessel to rescue seventy-two Americans from a ship that was wrecked on the Bahama reefs and caught fire. This was Don Bernardo de Soto, the owner and mate of the* Panda. *The execution of another was postponed because he had pleaded insanity.*

Shortly before their execution, the five pirates agreed to commit suicide in order to "die with dignity." One cut his throat with a piece of tin and, even though this was discovered and the wound was patched up, he didn't regain consciousness. Captain Gibert was found to have a piece of glass, which was taken away before he could attempt suicide and another was prevented in his attempt to slash his arms. A fourth had cut his own throat, but not seriously enough. He had washed the blood out of his shirt in the morning and his suicide attempt went undiscovered until after the execution.

Protesting their innocence to the end, the five pirates were hung as scheduled. The one who was unconscious was hung while sitting in a chair. It was decided three months later that the sixth pirate was sane and he too went to the gallows. Since no murder was committed, the bodies were not sent to the local college for dissection, as would normally have been the case.

Notes

1. Fore-topsail: the sail on the fore-mast above the foresail, or the second sail in ascending order from the deck on the ship's forward mast. Topgallant sail: the sail above the topsail, or the third sail in ascending order from the deck.

2. Tack: changing direction by changing the position of the sails.

3. Wore: to veer away from wind so that it blows from astern.

4. Main-topsail: the topsail on the mainmast.

5. Fore-scuttle: the forward hatchway or opening in the deck, large enough for a man to pass through and covered with a lid.

6. Binnacles: wooden boxes at the tiller which hold the compass, log glasses, and lights for night readings. Tiller-ropes: ropes used to steer a vessel. Halyards: vertical ropes for hoisting sails. Braces: ropes that enable yards to be swung by someone on the deck.

7. Twelve pounder: a cannon that fires twelve pound balls.

8. One source says there were sixteen. If this is correct, I have not been able to discover what happened to the extra man.

Captain Morgan Sacks Panama

~~~~~~

Don Juan de Guzman
PRESIDENT OF PANAMA

Jumping back in time almost two centuries to the height of the Buccaneer[1] Period, the greatest of the buccaneers, Captain Henry Morgan, had decided to attempt a monumental feat— the taking of Panama. Panama (the city, as the country didn't exist at this time) was the repository for the gold from that area's gold mines while it was waiting to be loaded on a galleon[2] for shipment to Spain. While it is not known how much gold Spain took from the New World, records indicate that the Veraguas mine—which shipped its gold through Panama—produced over two tons of this precious metal in one year. At this time, the area around Panama was the greatest producer of gold in the world. It made a very tempting target for the pirates, but it was very heavily guarded. No one had ever attempted to take the city before.

Capt. Morgan had already achieved a great reputation among the buccaneers. He even tried to establish a refuge and sanctuary for pirates on an island off Nicaragua. Though his privateering commission allowed him to plunder Spanish ships, he decided on his own to sack the towns of El Puerto del Principe (now Camagüey) in Cuba, Portobello[3] on the Caribbean coast of what is now the country of Panama, and Maracaibo in Venezuela. With all these successes, when he announced his raid on Panama, pirates and privateers from all over the West Indies flocked to join him. This excursion was in direct violation of the 1670 peace treaty between England and Spain in which England agreed to end attacks on Spanish towns in the West Indies and the Caribbean.

It was January 1671 when the 35-year-old Morgan and 1,200 men by canoe and foot traveled about one hundred miles

*winding through the jungle to reach Panama on the Pacific
side of the Isthmus of Darien.[4] By the time they arrived, they
were starving and exhausted. Since they brought very few
supplies on their nine day trip, hoping to capture them on the
way, many of men had resorted to eating leather.*

*Preparing to face these pirates was Don Juan Perez de Guz-
man, the President of Panama and Captain-General of Tierra
Firma, with his force of 2,700 soldiers—600 of which were
cavalry. Perez was an old man, but he had many years experience as a soldier. Having distinguished himself in campaigns
in Netherlands, he was made the captain general and president
of Panama before Morgan became a buccaneer. After it was all
over, Perez wrote a letter to the Queen-Regent, María Anna
of Spain, informing her of what happened. It was intercepted
and brought to Capt. Morgan. This is that letter.*

Señora,

Having had advice from the Governor of Cartagena,[5] which he sent
me by way of Darien on the 15th day of December last year, 1670, that
the English of Jamaica, assisted by the French, intended with an army of
three thousand men to invade Cartagena or Panama, I presently
ordered two hundred men to march to Portobello and one hundred and
fifty to Chagre[6] and to the Castellan[7] Don Francisco Saludo, I sent an
order that with five hundred men he should guard the passage of the
river and fortify it.

About five months before this I had consulted Don Juan de Aras,
Capeliar [or chaplain] of *audiencia*,[8] and other intelligent persons, and
they persuaded me that the forts on the river, as well as the castle, were
all impregnable; and in reiterated letters which I had from Don Pedro
de Lisardo, he assured me the same of Chagre, and that I needed not to
take care for them, for that although six thousand men should come
against them, he should, with the fortifications and men he had, be able
to secure himself and destroy them. Similarly, those who were at the
passages of the river confidently assured me.

This being the state of affairs, with all our positions well supplied
with food and war material, on January 6th [1671], the Feast of the
Epiphany, at two o'clock the enemy attacked the castle of Chagre with
more than 600 men.[9] They came from two directions, and they fought
from the hour named until nightfall. Those of the castle defended them-

selves with great valor and resolution, killing above two hundred men and repulsing above six assaults, until the English, taking advantage of the night and by the help of their fireballs, set on fire the fortifications— the outsides of which were made of wood. The arms which they had stacked on the parapets, such as swords, spears, shields and muskets, were destroyed. They likewise burnt the castellan's (or governor's) house, being thatched with palm, and consumed the rest of the armaments that were stored within.[10] More than half the people were killed, including the lieutenant and the castellan, who all had behaved themselves with great valor and, had it not been for the fire, the enemy would have never gained it.

At the unhappy news of the loss of this considerable castle, those on the river were extremely astonished. Fearing the English would come up to them with two thousand men, Luis de Castillo, captain of the mulatto's (whom the Castellan Saludo had ordered to his post—a place called Barro Colorado[11]), having called a council of war of those officers under his command, without having any order of mine or power to do it, retired to Barbacoa, forsaking his post without so much as ever seeing the face of the enemy. The Castellan Saludo did the same, quitting the fortifications of Barbacoa[12] and retiring with his men to Cruzes.[13] Before this, at the first notice I had of the loss of the castle of Chagre, two mestizes[14] named the Sollices and a Negro named Abrego—all expert scouts and guides—offered with a hundred men to regain the castle or disorder the enemy in case they should attempt to come up the river, as to hinder them. And for fear they should gain the castle of Santos, I sent Gil de la Torre, who had been lieutenant there, to govern and defend it. But neither of these complied with their undertaking; for having sent two hundred and fifty chosen men (instead of the one hundred they had desired) with the Sollices, who meeting the enemy on the river, neither dared they stay to fight him, as they might have done, nor did they pass on to regain the castle of Chagre; but rather went round by the mountain and came out at Capira, after which they all dispersed without doing any good at all.

At this conjuncture, having had the misfortune to have been lately blooded three times for an erysipelas[15] I had in my right leg, I was forced to rise out of my bed and march to Guiabal with the rest of the people that I had raised in Panama. There I stayed until I understood the exact course of the enemies march, because I wanted to be sure not to miss them, for they might have gone by Barbacoa, Port Gilloa and Puerto de los Naos.

With me, I took eight hundred men and three hundred Negroes that were vassals and slaves of the *Assentistaes*. And from the aforesaid place, I sent to Cruzes three hundred men, amongst whom went one hundred Indians of Darien with their commanders. of these I had greater credit and opinion than of any others, yet they did not have the courage to perform anything.

Having been a day in Guiabal, and my men pretty well refreshed, I received a letter from a Negro captain called Prado in which he assured me that the enemy marched against us two thousand strong. This news discouraged my men so much that they ceased not to importune and press me to return to the town, protesting they would defend themselves in it to the last; but it being impossible then to fortify it, the town having many entrances and the houses of wood—so soon as the enemy should once make a breach, we should quickly be exposed to their fury, and forced miserably to shift for ourselves—for these reasons I consented not to them. The next morning at break of day, I found myself with less than one third of my men—the rest having deserted me—so I was constrained to return back to the city to persuade them to fight there at Panama, there being no other remedy.

I arrived on Saturday night at Panama and Sunday morning went to the great church, where having received the Holy Communion before our blessed Lady of the Immaculate Conception with great devotion, I went to the principal guard, and to all that were present I expressed myself to this effect: That all those who were true Catholics, defenders of the faith, and devotees of our Lady of the Pure and Immaculate Conception should follow my person, being that same day at four o'clock in the afternoon resolved to march out to seek the enemy, but with this caution, that he that should refuse to do it also should be held as infamous and a coward, basely slighting so precise an obligation.

All proffered me their assistance, except those who had slunk from me at Guiabal, and when I had drawn them up in order, I carried the chief of them to the great church where in the presence of our Lady of the Pure and Immaculate Conception I made an oath to die in her defense. I then gave her a diamond ring with a value of 4,000 pieces-of-eight[16] in token of compliance with my word and I heartily invoked her aid. And all those present made the same oath with much fervor.

The Images of the Pure and Immaculate Conception, ever since the day of the fight at Chagre Castle, had been carried out in general procession, attended by all the religious and by the fraternity of the Cathedral of St. Francis, that of the nuns of our Lady of the Rosario, those of San Domingo, and those of the Mercedes, together with all the saints and patrons of the religious. And always the most holy sacrament in all churches was uncovered and exposed to public view. Masses were continually said for my happy success. I parted with all my jewels and relics collected in my pilgrimage, presenting them to the aforesaid images, saints and patrons.

After this, I marched with my army about a league[17] from Panama, having with me three field pieces[18] covered with leather and charged. And from that place I ordered another party with two other guns, made up of the men which came from the river,[19] being above three hundred, to advance towards the enemy, neither of which did any good.

This body of men which I had thus brought with me, was compounded of two sorts: valiant military men and faint-hearted cowards. Many of them having all their estates or pay due to them left in the castle of Chagre and Portobello, and a great part of my men were Negroes, mulattos and Indians, to the number of about twelve hundred, besides two hundred Negroes more belonging to the *Astiento*. Our firearms were few and bad in comparison of those the enemy brought, for ours were carbines, harquebusses[20] and fowling pieces, but few muskets for they had likewise been left in Portobello and Chagre.

Now having formed the army into two double squadrons and the cavalry (which were two hundred mounted on the same tired horses which had brought them thither) and with two great herds of oxen and bulls, drove thither by fifty cow-keepers on purpose to disorder the enemy. The army all appeared brisk and courageous, desiring nothing more than to engage; nor wanted there anything of Regalo to infuse spirit into them. So that it seemed to me, by what I saw and what they told me, that they would be able to charge the enemy like lightning.

On Wednesday morning, the 28th of this month [January], the enemy appeared, seeming to direct their march towards our rear in three squadrons, wherein they had two thousand three hundred men (as I understood for certain afterwards), but by-and-by they taking a compass, advanced to the front of our army.

I had put for leader of our left wing Don Alonso Alcaudete and for leader of the right wing the Governor of Beragues, Don Juan Portando, and in the center the sergeant major; to these I gave first command that none should move without my order and that coming within shot, the three first ranks should fire on their knees, and after this charge, they should give place to allow the rear to come up and fire, and that although they should chance to see any fall dead or wounded, they should not quit their stations, but to the last extremity observe these their orders.

I was at this time in the right wing of the vanguard, watching the enemy's motion, which was hasty, by the foot of a hill and in a narrow place, about three muskets shot from the left wing of our army. When all of a sudden I heard a loud clamor, crying out, "Advance, Advance! They are fleeing!" At which Don Alonso de Alcaudete was not able to keep them in their ranks nor stop them from running forward, even though he cut them with his sword, but they all fell into disorder.[21] And I, well knowing the fatality of this, gave command that they should drive in the herds of cattle and charge with the horse.[22] So putting myself at the head of the squadron of the right wing, saying, "Come along boys, there is no other remedy now but to conquer or die; follow me." I went directly to the enemy, and hardly did our men see some fall dead and others wounded, but they turned their backs and fled; leaving me there with only one Negro and one servant that followed me. Yet I went forward to comply with my word to the Virgin, which was to die in her defense, receiving a shot in a staff which I carried in my hand upright close to my cheek. At which moment came up to me a priest of the great church called Juan de Dios (who was wont to say mass in my house) beseeching me to retire and save myself, but I twice sharply reprehended him. But the third time he persisted, telling me that it was mere desperation to die on that manner and not like a Christian. With that I retired, it being a miracle of the Virgin to bring me off safe from amidst so many thousand bullets.[23]

After this I endeavored with all my industry to persuade the soldiers to turn and face our enemies, but it was impossible; so that nothing hindering them, they entered the city, to which the slaves and owners of the houses had put fire[24]; and being all of boards and timber, was most of it quickly burnt, except the *audiencia*, the governor's house, the Convent of the Mercedes, San Joseph, the suburbs of Malambo, and Pierde Vidas, at which they say the enemy fretted very much for being disappointed of their plunder and because they had brought with them an Englishman[25] whom they called "The Prince," with intent to crown him "King of the Tierra Firma."

The English, having thus got possession of the relics of our town,[26] found a bark in the Fasca, although I had given order there should be none, yet had they not complied with my command, and when they would have set it on fire, the enemy came fast and put it out, and with it did us much damage for they took three more with it and made great havoc of all they found in the Islands of Taboga, Otoque, and las Islas del Rey,[27] taking and bringing from thence many prisoners.

After this misfortune, I gave order to all the people I met that they should stay for me at Nata,[28] for there I intended to form the body of an army to once more encounter the English. But when I came to that city I found not one soul therein, for all were fled to the mountains.

The same happened to me at the town from whence I dispatched a vessel to Peru with the sad news of our misfortune, as I had done by land to Guatemala, Mexico, and by Portobello to Sparue.

And although I afterwards attempted several times to form an army, yet I could not do any good of it because no man would be persuaded to follow me. So that I remained utterly destitute of any guard, till such time as the Englishmen marched back to the castle of Chagre to make their voyage for Jamaica.

Embarking for Peru without seeing the face of an enemy were the Castellan Saludo, (whom I did not believe to be such a one) Don Juan de Aras, Francisco Gonzales Carasco being a young lively captain, and many others.

This, Your Majesty, has been a chastisement from heaven, and the same might have happened to that great captain Gensalo Fernando de Cordova as did to me, if his men had deserted him—for one man alone can do little.

In the middle of all this torrent of affliction, it was no small good fortune to have the Fort of San Geromino in Portobello finished and to have the fortifications of those two castles made there anew, because their [i.e. the pirates'] first intent was to have attacked the said castles, which are, as report goes, well furnished with men and ammunition.

If all were lost, I hope God would give me patience to suffer so great a punishment. But so it is that all the presidents together which this kingdom has ever had, have not done the third part of what I have done

in order to prevent these mischiefs. But I know myself so unfortunate
as to not have people sent me out of Spain that are paid [i.e. paid professional soldiers]; and so long as that shall not happen in this kingdom,
and that Chagre and Panama shall not be fortified, they will be in perpetual danger of losing the Indies.

This is what has passed, omitting infinite particulars, not to enlarge
too much, and which is all I have to say to you, whose life God preserve
many years.

Penonomé,[29] February 19, 1671
Don Juan Perez de Guzman

*Morgan marched back to Chagre with 200 pack-mules laden with gold,
silver, and other valuables. Once on the coast, they divided some of the
spoils, though Morgan took off with most of the loot, leaving many
men stranded on the coast of Darien to fend for themselves. Some say
that each of his men received only £50. Morgan assessed his gains at
£30,000, though one of his surgeons on this trip, Richard Browne,
estimated it at £70,000. Whatever the amount was, it was only a frac-
tion what it could have been if the city hadn't caught fire or if the
galleon hadn't escaped.*

*Despite the treaty between England and Spain, the Council of Jamaica
passed a vote of thanks to Morgan for his successful expedition. Capt.
Morgan became Sir Henry Morgan in 1674 when he was knighted by
King Charles II and made the Lieutenant Governor of Jamaica and commander of the English armed forces there. Now he found himself in the
position of having to bring pirates to justice. Because of his intense fond-
ness for rum and his abrasive nature, he was removed from these offices
in 1683. He died in Jamaica in 1688 at the age of 53.*

*Don Juan Perez de Guzman faded into history following his defeat
and what happened to him after that is uncertain.*

*Capt. Morgan's journey to Panama was repeated in 1680 by another
pirate expedition led by a group of captains which included Capt. John
Coxon, Capt. Peter Harris, Capt. Richard Sawkins, Capt. Bartholomew
Sharp, and Capt. Edmund Cook. This time it took the 327 men eighteen days to cross through the jungles of Darien. Arriving at Panama
on April 23, they found the town abandoned. Since the city had burned
down by accident three more times since Capt. Morgan's raid, there
probably wasn't much for the Spaniards to defend. At any rate, rather*

*than fight the pirates, the Spanish soldiers and citizens all ran away to
wait for the pirates to leave, which they soon did.*

*Then on March 1, 1685, another group of French and English bucca-
neers landed on Darien and set out through the jungles. It took them
more than a month to cross the isthmus. On reaching the South Sea,
met up with more pirates, since by this time many pirates were ventur-
ing into the South Sea—either by crossing the isthmus or by sailing
around the horn—and were conducting raids up and down the Pacific
Coast of Central and South America. Like these others, instead of trying to take the city of Panama, they began sailing up and down the coast
attacking ships and smaller towns . . . and hoping to find one of the
Spanish treasure galleons.*

*After several reorganizations, the group came under the leadership of
Capt. Grogniet. There were around two hundred pirates altogether—
about 150 were French and the rest English. They were sailing in three
barks with several canoes. In August of 1686, they were sailing in the
vicinity of Panama, taking every ship or boat the came across.*

*What happened next is described in a letter written by the President
of Panama to the Governor of Costa Rica. It was one of several papers
belonging to the President that these pirates later found in a town they
captured.*

Sir,

This is to inform you of the reports I've received from Cartagena,[30] by
the way of Portobello. The King of France, supposing he had received
some affront from our nation, sent eighty sails [i.e. ships] of the all sorts
before Calix to exact retribution. Seeing so vast an inequality of force
upon this occasion, we agreed to give him half a million [pieces-of-eight]
to withdraw his ships and return to their ports.

You know that my Lord Bishop on the 22nd of August [1686] forced
me to send out three ships to fight the pirates that constantly sailed past
our port and took all the barks[31] and canoes that were coming in. Our
ships surprised them at break of day, causing the pirates to slip their
cable,[32] which was done not to escape, but to attack our commander.
From my ramparts, I watched the fight, which seemed to go in our
favor.[33] Having seen them draw near the shore, I sent a shallop[34] to
bring away the anchor of that vessel that had slipped her cable so we
could anchor her in our port [after we captured her]. As soon as I saw

the anchor was raised, I dispatched away two long barks to learn the news and to bring any of the enemy that survived before me—though my orders were that no quarter[35] should be given to any that were found upon deck so that we might rid the world of these enemies of God and His saints, who profane His churches and destroy His servants.[36]

In the evening they sent one of our men requiring me to give up five men of theirs that I had prisoners in my town, but since my prince had forbidden me to do this, I refused.[37] These new Turks[38] then sent me twenty heads and I decided that in order to prevent the slaughter of so many Christians, I ought to send them their men with ten thousand pieces-of-eight for the ransom of ninety of our people (most of whom were wounded), which they sent us out of the three hundred and thirty they'd taken. Thus you see how God is pleased to afflict us on all sides, let's attribute it to His divine mercy.

Notes

1. Buccaneer: the Spanish name for privateers and pirates. It generally refers to those operating in the West Indies and the Caribbean during the seventeenth and eighteenth centuries.

2. Galleon: the largest of the Spanish merchant ships, often used as a man-of-war or to transport the treasures of the New World and the Far East to Spain. They usually had four decks with as many batteries of cannon.

3. While celebrating on board his ship after capturing this town, the ship suddenly exploded killing over 300 men, but Capt. Morgan survived.

4. The Isthmus of Darien is now called the Isthmus of Panama and is now the eastern portion of the country of Panama and a small portion of Columbia. At that time it was part of the province of Tierra Firma, which in turn was part of the Spanish colony of New Spain.

5. Cartagena: a city on Columbia's Caribbean coast.

6. Chagre: a town on the Caribbean side of the Isthmus of Darien, about 30 miles west of Portobello. It was protected by the Lorenzo Castle (also called Fort San Lorenzo).

7. Castellan: the governor of a castle.

8. The *audiencia* was a governing body that acted to keep the president in check (similar to our congress).

9. The primary source for Capt. Morgan's exploits is John Esquemeling (a.k.a. Alexander Oliver Exquemelin or Oexmelin), who was a pirate surgeon with Morgan on this expedition. He later wrote about what happened in his book *The Buccaneers of America* (1678). He reports that in the attack on Chagre, 400 pirates went up against 314 entrenched Spaniards. Over 100 pirates were killed and

more than 70 wounded, but the Spaniards suffered more. Only 30 remained alive and only about 10 of these escaped being wounded. Morgan left 500 pirates in the fort to guard their escape route and another 150 in their ships and he headed off for Panama with 1,200 men.

10. Esquemeling writes, "One of the pirates was wounded with an arrow in his back, which pierced his body to the other side. This instantly he pulled out with great valor at the side of his breast. Then taking a little cotton that he had about him, he wound it about the said arrow, and putting it into his musket, he shot it back at into the castle. But the cotton, being kindled by the powder, occasioned two or three houses that were within the castle, as being thatched with palm-leaves, to take fire, which the Spaniards perceived not so soon as was necessary. For this fire, meeting with a parcel of powder, blew it up, and thereby caused great ruin."

11. Barro Colorado is now an island in the Panama Canal.

12. The pirates reached this place on their fifth day. They desperately wanted to fight the Spaniards by this time in the hope of winning some supplies and food, as they were close to starving. Morgan was doing his best to distribute among the most needy anything edible that they came across.

13. Cruzes (Venta de Cruces) was a town on the River Chagre about fifteen miles northwest of Panama on the Spanish road to Portobello.

14. Mestizo: a person mixed Spanish and Native American blood.

15. Erysipelas: an infectious disease characterized by spreading deep-red inflammation of the skin.

16. Pieces-of-eight: a Spanish eight real (pronounced "ree'-al") coin or portions of it. These coins were sometimes cut into two, four, or eight pieces to make smaller denominations, each of which was a piece-of-eight.

17. League: a measurement usually of about three miles.

18. Field piece: a mobile cannon.

19. Saludo's men from Cruzes.

20. Carbine: a short rifle. Harquebus: a small caliber long gun with a matchlock or wheel-lock mechanism.

21. Capt. Morgan surprised the Spaniards by not attacking them head-on as armies normally did at this time. Instead of gallantly charging into the thick of it, he sent out small parties to provoke the Spaniards into breaking their ranks. As this failed and both sides hesitated to attack, he circled his men around through a thick forest to a hill on Perez's right where he gained the advantages of height, wind and the sun. This took several hours, but they caught the Spaniards completely off guard. Perez suddenly found his cannons were facing the wrong direction.

22. Perez intended to stampeded the herd of 2,000 cattle Morgan's attacking forces in order to break them up and throw them into disarray. He didn't get the

chance to do this. Instead he tried to run the cattle at the pirates from behind, but the noise of the battle scared the cattle away.

23. In this battle, which lasted two hours, Esquemeling estimates that 600 Spaniards died and many others were wounded or taken prisoner. Morgan puts the fatalities at 400 with the loss of only five pirates and ten wounded.

24. Esquemeling says that Capt. Morgan set the Panama on fire, though it makes little sense to do this before plundering the city and trying to get a ransom for it. Morgan flatly denied doing it, saying that Perez ordered his city to be burned. Morgan said, "There we were forced to put the fire out of the enemy's houses, but it was in vain, for by 12 at night it was all consumed that might be called the City; but of the suburbs was saved two churches and about 300 houses; thus was consumed that famous and ancient City of Panama, which is the greatest mart for silver and gold in the whole world, for it receives the goods into it that comes from Old Spain in the King's great Fleet, and likewise delivers to the Fleet all the silver and gold that comes from the mines of Peru and Potosi." A month later, the fire still had not gone out. Panama was the second largest city in the New World (next to Cartagena) with some 7,000 houses. Only two churches and about 300 houses were saved.

25. Captain Morgan.

26. Esquemeling reports that most of these actually got away, saying that "one certain galleon[. . .]miraculously escaped their [i.e. the pirates'] industry, being very richly laden with all the King's plate [i.e. silver bars] and great riches of gold, pearl, jewels, and other most precious goods of all the best and richest merchants of Panama. On board of this galleon were also the religious women belonging to the nunnery of the said city, who had embarked with them all the ornaments of their church, consisting in great quantity of gold, plate, and other things of value."

27. These are all islands in the Gulf of Panama (which is on the Pacific side of the isthmus).

28. Nata: a town on the coast southwest of the city of Panama.

29. Penonomé is about 70 miles southwest of Panama. In his letter, Perez says Morgan already "marched back to the castle of Chagre" by this date, but most books on Capt. Morgan say he didn't depart from Panama until February 24th as this is the date given by Esquemeling. Esquemeling's dates are more suspect as he was writing longer after the event. He also puts the attack on Chagre on August 18, 1670, though "August" is obviously a typo for "December" since he has Morgan setting out for Chagre on December 16th. Perez places that attack on January 6, 1671.

30. Cartagena: a city on Columbia's Caribbean coast.

31. Barks: a ship with the two forward masts square-rigged and the rear mast rigged fore-and-aft.

32. Slip their cable: to throw the anchor's cable overboard, rather than taking the time and effort to haul up the anchor.

33. Actually the pirates had captured the two larger ships—a frigate and a bark. One of the pirates later wrote, "We hurled a number of grenades over on their largest vessel, one of which hit the mark and exploded some loose powder, burning several men. This ended the fight sooner than might otherwise have happened. At the same time, we neared the ship which appeared a mass of flames and climbed aboard by rope-ladders where, despite the stiff fight they put up from behind temporary barricades, we forced them to seek quarter, and made ourselves masters of their ship." The third boat was chased by the pirates' galley and two canoes until they ran it ashore, wrecking it. Only about a dozen of these Spaniards escaped. On the frigate they took eighty prisoners, the remaining forty in the crew being either dead or wounded. Only nineteen out of seventy on the bark were still alive.

34. Shallop: a large boat with one or two masts, propelled by oars or sails, and rigged like a schooner.

35. Quarter: to refrain from slaying someone and often to accept them as a prisoner.

36. To fool the two barks into thinking they'd been captured, the pirates ran up the Spanish flag on all the vessels and put the English and French flags at half-mast. The two boats pulled up alongside the first bark and were taken completely by surprise. The pirates called for their surrender, but in the sudden confusion, the Spaniards panicked and started firing wildly. The pirates promptly threw some grenades into one of the boats causing it to catch fire and sink. The other surrendered, but on boarding her the pirates found cords cut to bind them with and papers saying the Spaniards were to kill all prisoners except the surgeons. This infuriated the pirates and slaughtered everyone on this bark. The next day they spotted another ship and quickly captured her. This proved to be the shallop, returning from raising their anchor. The evening of the following day pirates sent a message requesting the return of five of their men captured in an earlier engagement and that some medical supplies be sent.

37. The pirates responded to his refusal by saying that unless their demands were complied with, they would send him the heads of all their prisoners. After receiving a reply from the bishop saying the prisoners had converted to Catholicism and wished to stay in Panama, the pirates responded by sending them twenty heads. The President then sent them the prisoners and medical supplies. The pirates then sent a message saying, "Had you acted in this wise when we demanded the five prisoners just returned, you would have saved the lives of those poor men whose heads you received and whom you caused to perish. We are sending in exchange twelve of your men and demand from you 20,000 pieces-of-eight to ransom those who remain. Failing this, we will destroy you for

having used against us poison bullets which is so manifestly a breach of law and the practices of clean warfare that if we wished to punish you in accordance to your treatment of us, we would not give quarter to a single one of your men." The President said that after scouring the city, he could only raise 6,000. They replied by telling him to send 10,000 or they'd enter the city and find it themselves. He sent them 10,000 and they released all their prisoners.

38. Turks: a citizen of the Ottoman Empire that had Constantinople (now Istanbul, Turkey) as its capital. These Turks were usually Muslim Arabs. The Christians at that time looked on them as barbarians. To the very Catholic Spaniards, the pirates seemed like a new wave of anti-Christian barbarians.

Left on a Little Spot of Sand in the Midst of the Ocean

Captain Barnabas Lincoln

While many pirates were marooned after displeasing their comrades, it doesn't seem to have been a common practice for their victims. If it was, few survived to talk about it. One who did was Capt. Barnabas Lincoln. He was captured off Cuba on December 17, 1821. After surviving numerous adversities, he wrote his account and published it as the pamphlet Narrative of the Capture, Sufferings and Escape of Capt. Barnabas Lincoln and His Crew *(1822).*

I have reluctantly yielded to the urgent solicitations of friends to give a short narrative of the capture, sufferings and escape of myself and crew, after having been taken by a piratical schooner called the *Mexican,* December, 1821. The peculiar circumstances attending our situation gave us ample opportunity for learning the character of those cruisers which have lately infested our southern coasts, destroying the lives and plundering the property of so many peaceable traders. If this narrative should effect any good or urge our government to still more vigorous measures for the protection of our commerce, my object will be attained.

I sailed from Boston, bound for Trinidad[1] in the Island of Cuba on the 13th of November, 1821, in the schooner *Exertion*, burden one hundred and seven tons, owned by Messrs. Joseph Ballister and Henry Farnam, with a crew consisting of the following persons:

Joshua Bracket,	mate,	Bristol [England]
David Warren,	cook,	Saco [Maine]
Thomas Goodall,	seaman,	Baltimore [Maryland]
Thomas Young,	"	Orangetown [?]
Francis de Suze,	"	St. John's [Newfoundland]
George Reed,	"	Greenock, Scotland

The cargo consisted of flour, beef, pork, lard, butter, fish, beans, onions, potatoes, apples, ham, furniture, sugar box shooks,[2] etc., invoiced at about eight thousand dollars. Nothing remarkable occurred during the passage, except much bad weather, until my capture, which was as follows:

Monday, December 17th, 1821, commenced with fine breezes from the eastward. At daybreak saw some of the islands northward of Cape Cruz,[3] called keys[4]—stood along northwest; everything now seemed favorable for a happy termination of our voyage. At three o'clock P.M. saw a sail coming around the keys into a channel called Boca de Clavolone[5] by the chart, nearly in latitude 20°55" north, longitude 79°55" west. She made directly for us with all sail set, sweeps [i.e. long oars] on both sides (the wind being light), and was soon near enough for us to discover about forty men on her deck armed with muskets, blunderbusses,[6] cutlasses, long knives, dirks,[7] two carronades, one a twelve, the other a six-pounder.[8] She was a schooner, wearing the patriot flag (blue, white and blue) of the Republic of Mexico.[9]

I thought it not prudent to resist them—should they be pirates—with a crew of seven men and only five muskets. [I] accordingly ordered the arms and ammunition to be immediately stowed away in as secret a place as possible, and suffer her to speak us, hoping and believing that a republican flag indicated both honor and friendship from those who wore it, and which we might expect even from Spaniards. But how great was my astonishment when the schooner, having approached very near us, hailed in English and ordered me to heave [i.e. lift] my boat out immediately and come on board of her with my papers.

Accordingly my boat was hove out, but filled before I could get into her. I was then ordered to tack[10] ship and lay by for the pirate's boat to board me; which was done by Bolidar, their first lieutenant, with six or eight Spaniards armed with as many of the before mentioned weapons as they could well sling about their bodies. They drove me into the boat and two of them rowed me to their privateer (as they called their vessel), where I shook hands with her commander, Captain Jonnia, a Spaniard, who, before looking at my papers, ordered Bolidar, his lieutenant, to follow the *Mexican* in, back of the key they had left, which was done. At 6 o'clock P.M. the *Exertion* was anchored in eleven feet of water near their vessel and an island which they called Twelve League Key (called by the chart Key Largo[11]), about thirty or thirty-five leagues from Trinidad.

After this strange conduct, they began examining my papers by a Scotchman who went by the name of Nickola, their sailing master. He spoke good English, had a countenance rather pleasing, although his beard and mustachios had a frightful appearance. His face, apparently full of anxiety, indicated something in my favor. He gave me my papers, saying, "take good care of them, for I am afraid that you have fallen into bad hands."

The pirate's boat was then sent to the *Exertion* with more men and arms; a part of them left [i.e. stayed] on board her, the rest returning with three of my crew to their vessel, viz., Thomas Young, Thomas Goodall, and George Reed. They treated them with something to drink and offered them equal shares with themselves and some money if they would enlist, but they could not prevail on them. I then requested permission to go on board my vessel, which was granted, and further requested Nickola should go with me, but was refused by the captain, who vociferated in a harsh manner, "No, No, No," accompanied with a heavy stamp upon the deck.

When I got on board I was invited below by Bolidar, where I found they had emptied the case of liquors and broken a cheese to pieces and crumbled it on the table and cabin floor. The pirates, elated with their prize (as they called it), had drank so much as to make them desperately abusive. I was permitted to lie down in my berth, but, reader, if you have ever been awakened by a gang of armed desperadoes who have taken possession of your habitation in the midnight hour, you can imagine my feelings. Sleep was a stranger to me and anxiety was my guest.

Bolidar, however, pretended friendship and flattered me with the prospect of being soon set at liberty. But I found him, as I suspected, a consummate hypocrite; indeed, his very looks indicated it. He was a stout and well-built man of a dark, swarthy complexion with keen, ferocious eyes, huge whiskers, and beard under his chin and on his lips four or five inches long. He was a Portuguese by birth, but had become a naturalized Frenchman—had a wife, if not children, (as I was told) in France and was well-known there as commander of a first-rate privateer. His appearance was truly terrific. He could talk some in English and had a most lion-like voice.

Tuesday, 18th [December 1821]. Early this morning the captain of the pirates came on board the *Exertion*, took a look at the cabin stores and cargo in the state rooms, and then ordered me back with him to his vessel, where he, with his crew, held a consultation for some time respecting the cargo. After which the interpreter, Nickola, told me that "the captain had or pretended to have a commission under General Traspelascus, commander-in-chief of the Republic of Mexico, authorizing him to take all cargoes whatever of provisions bound to any Spanish royalist port. That my cargo, being bound to an enemy's port, must be condemned, but that the vessel should be given up and put into a fair channel for Trinidad, where I was bound."

I requested him to examine the papers thoroughly and perhaps he would be convinced to the contrary, and told him my cargo was all American property taken in at Boston and consigned to an American gentleman agent at Trinidad. But the captain would not take this trouble, but ordered both vessels under way immediately and commenced beating up[12] amongst the keys through most of the day, the wind being very light.

They now sent their boats on board the *Exertion* for stores and commenced plundering her of bread, butter, lard, onions, potatoes, fish, beans, etc., took up some sugar box shooks that were on deck, and found the barrels of apples, selected the best of them and threw the rest of them overboard. They inquired for spirits, wine, cider, etc. and were told they had already taken all that was on board. But not satisfied, they proceeded to search the state rooms and forecastle, ripped up the floor of the latter and found some boxes of bottled cider, which they carried to their vessel, gave three cheers in an exulting manner to me, and then began drinking it with such freedom that a violent quarrel arose between officers and men, which came very near ending in bloodshed. I was accused of falsehood for saying they had already got all the liquors that were on board, and I thought they had. The truth was, I never had any bill of lading of the cider and consequently had no recollection of its being on board. Yet it served them as an excuse for being insolent. In the evening, peace was restored and they sang songs. I was suffered to go below for the night and they placed a guard over me, stationed at the companion way.

Wednesday, 19th [December 1821], commenced with moderate easterly winds beating towards the northeast, the pirate's boats [were] frequently going on board the *Exertion* for potatoes, fish, beans, butter, etc., which were used with great waste and extravagance. They gave me food and drink, but of bad quality—more particularly the victuals, which were wretchedly cooked. The place assigned me to eat was covered with dirt and vermin. It appeared that their great object was to hurt my feelings with threats and observations, and to make my situation as unpleasant as circumstances would admit.

We came to anchor near a key called by them Brigantine, where myself and mate were permitted to go on shore, but were guarded by several armed pirates. I soon returned to the *Mexican* and my mate to the *Exertion* with George Reed, one of my crew, the other two being kept on board the *Mexican*. In the course of this day I had considerable conversation with Nickola, who appeared well-disposed towards me. He lamented most deeply his own situation, for he was one of those men whose early good impressions were not entirely effaced, although confederated with guilt.

He told me, "those who had taken me were no better than pirates and their end would be the halter,[13] but," he added with peculiar emotion, "I will never be hung as a pirate," showing me a bottle of laudanum[14] which he had found in my medicine chest, saying, "if we are taken, that shall cheat the hangman before we are condemned."

I endeavored to get it from him, but did not succeed. I then asked him how he came to be in such company, as he appeared to be dissatisfied. He stated that he was at New Orleans last summer, out of employment, and became acquainted with one Captain August Orgamar, a Frenchman, who had brought a small schooner of about fifteen tons and was going down to the bay of Mexico to get a commission under General Traspelascus, in order to go a privateering under the patriot flag. Captain Orgamar made him liberal offers respecting shares and promised him a sailing master's berth, which he accepted and embarked on board the schooner without sufficiently reflecting on the danger of such an undertaking.

Soon after she sailed from Mexico, where they got a commission, and the vessel was called *Mexican*. They made up a complement of twenty men, and after rendering the General some little service in transporting his troops to a place called ———————, proceeded on a cruise; took some small prizes off Campeche[15]; afterwards came on the south coast of Cuba, where they took other small prizes and the one which we were now on board of. By this time the crew was increased to about forty— nearly one-half Spaniards, the others Frenchmen and Portuguese. Several of them had sailed out of ports in the United States with American protections, but, I confidently believe, none are natives, especially of the northern states.[16] I was careful in examining the men, being desirous of knowing if any of my countrymen were among the wretched crew, but am satisfied there were none and my Scotch friend concurred in the opinion.[17] They had an excellent pilot named Baltizar, belonging to Spirito Santo,[18] near Trinidad de Cuba, who was able to pilot them safely among all the small keys or islands and find their hiding places.

They soon came to a conclusion to destroy the little old *Mexican* which they first had and take the present one for a cruiser[19] and apply the old commission to her and call her by the same name. This shows their respect for the government from which they obtained that commission.

And now, with a new vessel, which was the prize of these plunderers, they sailed up Manganeil Bay; previously, however, they fell in with an American schooner from which they bought four barrels of beef and paid in tobacco.

At the bay was an English brig belonging to Jamaica, owned by Mr. John Louden of that place. On board of this vessel the Spanish part of the crew commenced their depredations as pirates, although Captain Orgamar and Nickola protested against it and refused any participation; but they persisted, and like so many ferocious bloodhounds, boarded the brig, plundered the cabin stores, furniture, captain's trunk, etc., took a hogshead[20] of rum, one twelve-pound carronade, some rigging and sails. One of them plundered the chest of a sailor who made some resistance so that the Spaniard took his cutlass and beat and wounded him without mercy. Nickola asked him [i.e. the pirate] why he did it. The fellow answered, "I will let you know," and took up the cook's ax and gave him a cut on the head which nearly deprived him of life.[21] Then they ordered Captain Orgamar to leave his vessel, allowing him his trunk, and turned him ashore to seek for himself. Nickola begged them to dismiss him with his captain, but "no, no," was the answer, for they had no complete navigator but him. After Captain Orgamar was gone, they put in his stead the present brave (or as I should call him cowardly) Captain Jonnia, who headed them in plundering the before mentioned brig and made Bolidar their first lieutenant, and then proceeded down among those keys or islands where I was captured. This is the amount of what my friend Nickola told me of their history.

Thursday, 20th [December 1821], continued beating up, wind being light. The pirate's boats were sent to the *Exertion* for more stores, such as bread, lard, etc. I this day discovered on board the *Mexican* three black girls, of whom it is well to say no more. It is impossible to give an account of the filthiness of this crew, and were it possible it would not be expedient. In their appearance they were terrific, wearing black whiskers and long beards, the receptacles of dirt and vermin. They used continually the most profane language, had frequent quarrels, and so great was their love of gambling that the captain would play cards with the meanest man on board. All these things rendered them to me objects of total disgust (with a few exceptions, as will hereafter appear). I was told they had a stabbing match but a few days before I was taken and one man came near being killed. They put him ashore at a fisherman's hut and there left him to perish. I saw the wound of another, who had his nose split open.

Friday, 21st. After laying at anchor through the night in ten fathoms water, [we] made sail and stood to the eastward. By this time I was out of my reckoning, having no quadrant, chart, or books. The pirate's boats were again sent for stores. The captain for the second time demanded of me where my wine, brandy, etc., were. I again told him they had already got the whole. They took the deep sea line and some cordage from the *Exertion*, and at night came to anchor.

Saturday, 22nd. Both vessels underway standing to the eastward, they ran the *Exertion* aground on a bar, but after throwing overboard most of her deckload of shooks, she floated off. A pilot was sent to her and she was run into a narrow creek between two keys, where they moored her head and stern alongside the mangrove trees, sent down her yards and topmasts, and covered her mastheads and shrouds with bushes to prevent her being seen by vessels which might pass that way. I was then suffered to go on board my own vessel and found her in a very filthy condition; sails torn, rigging cut to pieces, and everything in the cabin in waste and confusion. The swarms of mosquitoes and sand-flies made it impossible to get any sleep or rest. The pirate's large boat was armed and manned under Bolidar and sent off with letters to a merchant (as they called him) by the name of Dominico, residing in a town called Principe[22] on the main island of Cuba. I was told by one of them who could speak English that Principe was a very large and populous town, situated at the head of St. Maria, which was about twenty miles northeast from where we lay, and the keys lying around us were called Cotton Keys.[23] The captain pressed into his service Francis de Suze, one of my crew, saying he was one of his countrymen. Francis was very reluctant in going and said to me with tears in his eyes, "I shall do nothing only what I am obliged to do and will not aid in the least to hurt you or the vessel. I am very sorry to leave you." He was immediately put on duty and Thomas Goodall sent back to the *Exertion*.

Sunday, 23rd. Early this morning a large number of the pirates came on board of the *Exertion*, threw out the long boat, broke open the hatches and took out considerable of the cargo, in search of rum, gin, etc., still telling me "I had some and that they would find it," uttering the most awful profaneness. In the afternoon the boat returned with a pirogue,[24] having on board the captain, his first lieutenant, and seven men of a patriot or piratical vessel that was chased ashore at Cape Cruz by a Spanish armed brig. These seven men made their escape in said boat and after four days, found our pirates and joined them, the remainder of the crew being killed or taken prisoners.

Monday, 24th. Their boat was manned and sent to the before mentioned town. I was informed by a line from Nickola that the pirates had a man on board, a native of Principe, who, in the garb of a sailor, was a partner with Dominico, but I could not get sight of him. This lets us a little into the plans by which this atrocious system of piracy has been carried on. Merchants having partners on board of these pirates! thus pirates at sea and robbers on land are associated to destroy the peaceable trader.

The willingness exhibited by the seven above-mentioned men to join our gang of pirates seemed to look like a general understanding among them; and from there being merchants on shore so base as to encourage the plunder and vend the goods, I am persuaded there has been a systematic confederacy on the part of these unprincipled desperadoes under cover of the patriot flag, and those on land are no better than those on the sea. If the governments to whom they belong know of the atrocities committed (and I have but little doubt they do), they deserve the execration [i.e. abhorrence] of all mankind.

Tuesday, 25th [December 1821, Christmas]. Still on board the *Exertion*—weather very calm and warm. The pirate's boat returned from St. Maria and came for candles, cheese, potatoes, etc., they saying they must have them and forbid my keeping any light on board at night. [They] took a case of trunks for the captain's use and departed. Their irritating conduct at this time can hardly be imagined.

Wednesday, 26th. I was told by Bolidar that three Spanish cruisers were in search of them, that they could fight two of them at once (which, by the way, I believe was not true) and were disappointed in not finding them. [That] same evening they took both of my boats and their own men, towed their vessel out of the creek and anchored at its mouth to get rid of sand-flies, while they obliged us to stay on deck under an awning, exposed to all the violence of these flies. We relieved ourselves in some measure by the burning of tobacco, which lasted but for a short time.

Thursday, 27th. A gang of the pirates came and stripped our masts of the green bushes, saying, "she appeared more like a sail than trees" [and] took one barrel of bread and one of potatoes, using about one of each everyday. I understood they were waiting for boats to take the cargo, for the principal merchant had gone to Trinidad.

Friday, 28th. Nothing remarkable occurred this day. [We] were frequently called upon for tar and butter and junk to make oakum.[25] Capt. Jonnia brought on board with his new captain and officer before mentioned. Again they asked for wine and were told as before they had gotten the whole.

Saturday, 29th. Same insulting conduct continued. Took a barrel of crackers.

Sunday, 30th. The beginning of trouble! This day, which peculiarly reminds Christians of the high duties of compassion and benevolence [i.e. Sunday], was never observed by these pirates. This, of course, we might expect, as they did not often know when the day came; and if they knew it, it was spent in gambling. The old saying among seamen, "no Sunday off soundings,"[26] was not thought of, and even this poor plea was not theirs, for they were on soundings and often at anchor [sic]. Early this morning the merchant, as they called him, came with a large boat for the cargo. I was immediately ordered into the boat with my crew, not allowed any breakfast, and carried about three miles to a small island out of sight of the *Exertion* and left there by the side of a little pond of thick, muddy water, which proved to be very brackish, with nothing to eat but a few biscuit. One of the boat's men told us the merchant was afraid of being recognized and when he had gone the boat would return for us, but we had great reason to apprehend they would deceive us, and therefore passed the day in the utmost anxiety. At night, however, the boats came and took us again on board the *Exer-*

tion, when, to our surprise and astonishment, we found they had broken open the trunks and chests and taken all our wearing apparel, not even leaving a shirt or pair of pantaloons, not sparing a small miniature of my wife which was in my trunk. The little money I and my mate had, with some belonging to the owners, my mate had previously distributed about the cabin in three or four parcels while I was on board the pirate, for we dare not keep it about us. One parcel in a butter pot they did not discover.

Amidst the hurry with which I was obliged to leave my vessel to go to the before-mentioned island, I fortunately snatched my vessel's papers and hid them in my bosom, which the reader will find was a happy circumstance for me. My writing desk, with papers, accounts, etc., all Mr. Lord's letters (the gentleman to whom my cargo was consigned) and several others were taken and maliciously destroyed. My medicine chest, which I so much wanted, was kept for their own use. What their motive could be to take my papers I could not imagine, except they had hopes of finding bills of lading for some Spaniards to clear them of piracy. Mr. Bracket had some notes and papers of consequence to him, which shared the same fate. My quadrant, charts, books, and some bedding were not yet taken, but I found it impossible to hide them and they were soon gone from my sight.

Monday, 31st. We complained to them, expressing the necessity of having clothes to cover us, but as well might we have appealed to the winds, and rather better, for they would not have upbraided us in return. The captain, however, sent word he would see to it and ordered their clothes-bags to be searched, where he found some of our things, but took good care to put them into his own cabin. I urgently requested him to give me the miniature, but "no" was all I could get.

Tuesday, January 1st, 1822. A sad New Year's Day to me. Before breakfast orders came for me to cut down the *Exertion*'s railing and bulwarks on one side, for their vessel to heave out by and clean her bottom. On my hesitating a little, they observed with anger, "Very well, captain, suppose you no do it quick, we do it for you." Directly afterwards another boat, full of armed men, came alongside. They jumped on deck with swords drawn and ordered all of us into her immediately. I stepped below in hopes of getting something which would be of service to us, but the captain hallooed, "go in the boat directly or I will fire upon you."

Thus compelled to obey, we were carried together with four Spanish prisoners to a small, low island or key of sand in the shape of a half moon and partly covered with mangrove trees, which was about one mile from and in sight of my vessel. There they left nine of us with a little bread, flour, fish, lard, a little coffee and molasses two or three kegs of water (which was brackish), an old sail for a covering, and a pot and some other small articles no way fit to cook in. Leaving us these, which were much less than they appear in the enumeration, they pushed off, saying, "we will come to see you in a day or two."

Selecting the best place, we spread the old sail for an awning, but no place was free from flies, mosquitoes, snakes, the venomous santipee [centipede?]. Sometimes they were found crawling inside of our pantaloons,[27] but fortunately no injury was received. This afternoon the pirates hove[28] their vessel out by the *Exertion* and cleaned one side, using her paints, oils, etc. for that purpose. To see my vessel in that situation and to think of our prospects was a source of the deepest distress. At night we retired to our tent, but having nothing but the cold damp ground for a bed and the heavy dew of the night penetrating the old canvass; the situation of the island being 50 miles from the usual track of friendly vessels and 135 from Trinidad; seeing my owner's property so unjustly and wantonly destroyed; considering my condition, the hands at whose mercy I was, and deprived of all hopes, rendered sleep or rest a stranger to me.

Wednesday, 2nd. The pirates hove out and cleaned the other side. She then commenced loading with the *Exertion*'s cargo, which appeared to be flour and lard. In the afternoon their boat came and took two of the Spaniards with them to another island for water and soon after returned with four kegs of poor, unwholesome water, and left us, saying they should not bring us provisions again for some time, as they were going away with goods from the prize, to be gone two or three days. Accordingly they brought a present supply of beef, pork, and a few potatoes, with some bedding for myself and mate. The mangrove wood afforded us a good fire, as one of the Spanish prisoners happened to have fireworks, and others had tobacco and paper with which we made cigars. About this time one of my men began to be unwell. His legs and body swelled considerably, but having no medicine I could not do much to relieve him.

Thursday, 3rd. The pirates had dropped off from the *Exertion*, but kept their boats employed in bringing the cargo from her; I supposed it to be kegs of lard to make stowage. They then got underway with a pirogue in tow, both deeply laden, run out of the harbor, hauled on the wind to the eastward till out of sight behind the keys, leaving a guard on board the *Exertion*.[. . .]

[Lincoln then gives a detailed description of the pirate's vessel "in hopes that some American cruiser may fall in with her and that they may not be deceived by her wearing the patriot flag."]

Friday, 4th, commenced with light wind and hot sun. [We] saw a boat coming from the *Exertion*, apparently loaded. She passed between two small keys to the northward, supposed to be bound for Cuba. At sunset a boat came and inquired if we wanted anything, but instead of adding to our provisions, [they] took away our molasses and pushed off. We found one of the *Exertion*'s water casks and several pieces of plank, which we carefully laid up in hopes of getting enough to make a raft.

Saturday, 5th. Pirates again in sight coming from the eastward. They beat up alongside their prize and commenced loading. In the afternoon Nickola came to us, bringing with him two more prisoners, which they had taken in a small sailboat coming from Trinidad to Manganeil—one a Frenchman, the other a Scotchman, with two Spaniards who remained on board the pirate and who afterwards joined them. The back of one of these poor fellows was extremely sore, having just suffered a cruel beating from Bolidar with the broad side of a cutlass. It appeared that when the officer asked him where their money was and how much [they had], he answered, he was not certain, but believed they had only two ounces of gold. Bolidar furiously swore he said "ten," and not finding any more, gave him the beating.

Nickola now related to me a singular fact, which was, that the Spanish part of the crew were determined to shoot him [i.e. Nickola]; that they tied him to the mast and the man was appointed for the purpose, but Lyon—a Frenchman, his particular friend—stepped up and told them if they shot him, they must shoot several more. Some of the Spaniards sided with him and he was released. Nickola told me the reason for such treatment was that he continually objected to their conduct towards me, and their opinion was if he should escape, they would be discovered, as he declared he would take no prize money.

While with us he gave me a letter written in great haste, which contains some particulars respecting the cargo, as follows:

January 4th, 1822.

Sir,

We arrived here this morning and before we came to anchor had five canoes alongside ready to take your cargo, part of which we had in; and as I heard you express a wish to know what they took out of her to this moment, you may depend on this account of Jamieson[29] for quality and quantity. If I have the same opportunity, you will have an account of the whole. The villain who bought your cargo is from the town of Principe, his name is Dominico, as to that, it is all I can learn. They have taken your charts on board the *Mexican* and I suppose mean to keep them, as the other captain has agreed to act the same infamous part in the tragedy of his life. Your clothes are here on board, but do not let me flatter you that you will get them back; it may be so, and it may not. Perhaps in your old age, when you recline with ease in a corner of your cottage, you will have the goodness to drop a tear of pleasure to the memory of him whose highest ambition should have been to subscribe himself—though devoted to the gallows—your friend.

Nickola Monacre.

Excuse haste.

P.S. Your answer in writing when I come again.

Sunday, 6th. The pirates were underway at sunrise with a full load of the *Exertion*'s cargo going to Principe again to sell a second freight, which was done readily for cash. I afterwards heard that the flour brought only five dollars per barrel, when it was worth at Trinidad thirteen, so that the villain who bought my cargo at Principe made very large profits by it.

Monday, 7th. The pirates brought more water, but being very brackish, it was unfit for use. We were now greatly alarmed at Thomas's ill health, being suddenly attacked with a pain in the head and swelling of the right eye, attended with derangement. He, however, soon became better, but his eye remained swollen several days without much pain. In the evening we had some heavy showers of rain and having no secure cabin, no sheltered retreat, our exposure made us pass a very uncomfortable night.

Tuesday, 8th. Early this morning the pirates [are] in sight again with fore-topsail and topgallant sail[30] set. [They] beat up alongside of the

Exertion and commenced loading, having, as I supposed, sold and discharged her last freight among the inhabitants of Cuba. They appeared to load in great haste and the song "O He Ho," which echoed from one vessel to the other, was distinctly heard by us. How wounding was this to me! How different was this sound from what it would have been had I been permitted to pass unmolested by these lawless plunderers, had been favored with a safe arrival at the port of my destination, where my cargo would have found an excellent sale. Then would the "O He Ho" on its discharging have been a delightful sound to me. In the afternoon she sailed with the pirogue in tow, both with a full load, having chairs, which was a part of the cargo, slung at her quarters.

Wednesday, 9th. Very calm and warm. The swarms of mosquitoes and flies made us pass a very uncomfortable day. We dug in the sand for water, but were disappointed in finding none so good as they left us. In walking around among the bushes, I accidentally discovered a hole in the sand and saw something run into it. Curiosity led me to dig about it. With the help of Mr. Bracket, I found at the distance of seven feet from its mouth and one from the surface, a large solitary rat apparently several years old. He had collected a large nest of grass and leaves, but there was not the least appearance of any other being on the island.

Thursday, 10th. No pirates in sight. The day was passed in anxious suspense, David Warren being quite sick.

Friday, 11th. They came and hauled alongside of the *Exertion*, but I think took out none of her cargo, but had, as I supposed, a vendue [i.e. an auction] on board, wherein was sold among themselves all our books, clothing, quadrants, charts, spyglasses, and everything belonging to us and our fellow-prisoners. I was afterwards told they brought a good price, but what they could want of the Bible, prayer book, and many other books in English was matter of astonishment to me.

Saturday, 12th. They remained alongside the *Exertion*; took the paints, oil, brushes, etc. and gave their vessel a new coat of paint all around and a white boot top. [They] took the pirogue to another key and caulked her. There was no appearance of their taking any cargo out. The *Exertion*, however, appeared considerably high out of water. About sunset the pirates went out of the harbor on a cruise. Here we had been staying day after day, and exposed night after night. Apprehensions for our safety were much increased. What was to become of us seemed now to rush into everyone's mind.

Sunday, 13th. Deprived of our good books, deprived in fact of everything save life, and our ideas respecting our fate so gloomy, all tended to render time—especially the Lord's day—burdensome to all. In the afternoon a boat came for cargo, from, as I supposed, that villain Dominico.

Monday, 14th. They again hove in sight, as usual, alongside their prize. While passing our solitary island they laughed at our misery, which was almost insupportable—looking upon us as though we had committed some heinous crime, and they had not sufficiently punished us. They hallooed to us, crying out, "Captain! Captain!" accompanied with obscene motions and words (with which I shall not blacken these pages), yet I heard no check upon such conduct, nor could I expect it among such a gang who have no idea of subordination on board, except when in chase of vessels, and even then but very little. My resentment was excited at such a malicious outrage and I felt a disposition to revenge myself, should fortune ever favor me with an opportunity. It was beyond human nature not to feel and express some indignation at such treatment. Soon after, Bolidar with five men, well-armed, came to us, he having a blunderbuss, cutlass, a long knife and pair of pistols. But for what purpose did he come? He took me by the hand, saying, "Captain, me speak with you. Walk this way." I obeyed and when we were at some distance from my fellow-prisoners (his men following), he said, "the captain send me for your wash." I pretended not to understand what he meant and replied, "I have no clothes nor any soap to wash with. You have taken them all"—for I had kept my watch about me, hoping they would not discover it. He demanded it again as before and was answered, "I have nothing to wash." This raised his anger, and lifting his blunderbuss, he roared out, "What the devil you call him that make clock, give it me." I considered it imprudent to contend any longer and submitted to his unlawful demand. As he was going off he gave me a small bundle, in which was a pair of linen drawers sent to me by Nickola and also the Rev. Mr. Brooks's *Family Prayer Book*. This gave me great satisfaction. Soon after he returned with his captain, who had one arm slung up, yet with as many implements of war as his diminutive wicked self could conveniently carry. He told me (through an interpreter who was a prisoner) "that on his cruise he had fallen in with two Spanish privateers and beat them off, but had three of his men killed and himself wounded in the arm." Bolidar turned to me and said, "It is a damn lie," which words proved to be correct for his arm was not wounded, and when I saw him again, which was soon afterwards, he forgot to sling it up. He further told me, "after tomorrow you shall go with your vessel and we will accompany you towards Trinidad." This gave me some new hopes, and why I could not tell. They then left us without rendering any assistance. This night we got some rest.

Tuesday, 15th [January 1822]. The words "go after tomorrow" were used among our Spanish fellow-prisoners as though that happy tomorrow would never come. In what manner it came will soon be noticed.

Wednesday, 16th. One of their boats came to inquire if we had seen a boat pass by last night, for their small sloop sailboat was gone and two men deserted. I told them "no." At heart I could not but rejoice at the escape and approve the deserters. I said nothing however to the pirates. On their return they manned three of their boats and sent them in different directions to search, but at night came back without finding boat or men. They now took our old sail—which hitherto had somewhat sheltered us—to make, as I supposed, some small sail for their vessel. This rendered our night more uncomfortable than before, for in those islands the night dews are very heavy.

Thursday, 17th, was passed with great impatience. The *Exertion* having been unmoored and swung to her anchor, gave some hopes of being restored to her, but was disappointed.

Friday, 18th, commenced with brighter prospects of liberty than ever. The pirates were employed in setting up our devoted schooner's shrouds, stays, etc. My condition now reminded me of the hungry man chained in one corner of the room, while at another part was a table loaded with delicious foods and fruits, the smell and sight of which he was continually to experience, but, alas! his chains were never to be loosed that he might go and partake. At almost the same moment they were thus employed, the ax was applied with the greatest dexterity to both her masts and I saw them fall over the side! Here fell my hopes. I looked at my condition and then thought of home. Our Spanish fellow-prisoners were so disappointed and alarmed that they recommended hiding ourselves if possible among the mangrove trees, believing, as they said, we should now certainly be put to death or, what was worse, compelled to serve on board the *Mexican* as pirates. Little else, it is true, seemed left for us. However, we kept a bright lookout for them during the day, and at night "an anchor watch," as we called it; determined, if we discovered their boats coming towards us, to adopt the plan of hiding. Although starvation stared us in the face, yet [we] preferred that to instant death. This night was passed with sufficient anxiety. I took the first watch.

Saturday, 19th. The pirate's large boat came for us. It being daylight and supposing they could see us, [we] determined to stand our ground and wait the result. They ordered us all into the boat, but left everything else. They rowed towards the *Exertion*. I noticed a dejection of spirits in one of the pirates and inquired of him where they were going to carry us. He shook his head and replied, "I do not know." I now had some hopes of visiting my vessel again, but the pirates made sail, ran down, took us in tow and stood out of the harbor. Bolidar afterwards took me, my mate, and two of my men on board and gave us some coffee. On examination I found they had several additional light sails, made of the *Exertion*'s. Almost every man [had] a pair of canvass trousers and my colors [i.e. flags] [were] cut up and made into belts to carry their money. My jolly boat was on deck and I was informed all my rigging was disposed of. Several of the pirates had on some of my clothes and the captain one of my best shirts, a cleaner one than I had ever seen him have on before.

He kept at good distance from me and forbid my friend Nickola's speaking to me. I saw from the companion way in the captain's cabin my quadrant, spyglass, and other things which belonged to us, and observed by the compass that the course steered was about west by south, distance nearly twenty miles, which brought them up with a cluster of islands called by some "Cayman Keys."[31] Here they anchored and caught some fish (one of which was named guard fish), of which we had a taste.

I observed that my friend Mr. Bracket was somewhat dejected and asked him in a low tone of voice what his opinion was in respect to our fate. He answered, "I cannot tell, but it appears to me the worst is to come." I told him that I hoped not, but thought they would give us our small boat and liberate the prisoners. But mercy even in this shape was not left for us. Soon after, [I] saw the captain and officers whispering for some time in private conference. When [this was] over, their boat was manned under the command of Bolidar and went to one of those islands or keys before mentioned.[32] On their return another conference took place. Whether it was a jury upon our lives, we could not tell. I did not think conscience could be entirely extinguished in the human breast, or that men could become fiends.

In the afternoon, while we knew not the doom which had been fixed for us, the captain was engaged with several of his men in gambling, in hopes to get back some of the five hundred dollars they said he lost but a few nights before, which had made him unusually fractious.

A little before sunset he ordered us all into the large boat with a supply of provisions and water and to be put on shore. While we were getting into her, one of my fellow-prisoners, a Spaniard, attempted, with tears in his eyes, to speak to the captain, but was refused with the answer, "I'll have nothing to say to any prisoner, go into the boat." In the meantime Nickola said to me, "My friend, I will give you your book" (being Mr. Colman's *Sermons*). "It is the only thing of yours that is in my possession. I dare not attempt anything more." But the captain forbid his giving it to me and I stepped into the boat. At that moment Nickola said in a low voice, "never mind, I may see you again before I die."

The small boat was well-armed and manned, and both set off together for the island where they had agreed to leave us to perish! The scene to us was a funeral scene. There were no arms in the prisoners' boat and, of course, all attempts to relieve ourselves would have been throwing our lives away as Bolidar was near us, well-armed. We were rowed about two miles northeasterly from the pirates to a small, low island, lonely and desolate. We arrived about sunset and for the support of us eleven prisoners they only left a ten-gallon keg of water and perhaps a few quarts in another small vessel (which was very poor), part of a barrel of flour, a small keg of lard, one ham and some salt fish, a small kettle and an old broken pot, an old sail for a covering, and a small blanket—which was thrown out as the boat hastened away. One of the prisoners happened to have a little coffee in his pocket and these comprehended all our means of sustaining life, and for what length of time we knew not. We now felt the need of water and our supply was comparatively nothing. A man may live twice as long without food as without water.

Look at us now, my friends, left benighted on a little spot of sand in the midst of the ocean, far from the usual track of vessels, and every appearance of a violent thunder tempest and a boisterous night. Judge of my feelings and the circumstances which our band of sufferers now witnessed. Perhaps you can and have pitied us. I assure you we were very wretched, and to paint the scene is not within my power.

When the boats were moving from the shore, on recovering myself a little, I asked Bolidar if he was going to leave us so. He answered, "No, only two days. We go for water and wood, then come back, take you." I requested him to give us bread and other stores, for they had plenty in the boat and at least one hundred barrels of flour in the *Mexican*. "No, no, suppose tomorrow morning me come, me give you bread," and [they] hurried off to their vessel. This was the last time I saw him.

They then set about the work of building a shelter, creating fire, and deal-ing with the "thousands of creeping insects, scorpions, lizards, crickets, etc." The damp gave most of them severe colds. Their island was one acre of sand rising about three feet above sea level with a few bushes and small mangroves. Finding food and water was definitely a problem. Sharks made attempts to swim to other keys difficult, but not impossible, and by doing this they were able to gather up enough debris tossed by the pirates from the Exertion *to build a boat—though they were afraid that if the pirates returned and caught them doing this, they would all be murdered.*

On the 28th of January, their tenth day on the key, David Warren suddenly died at the age of 26. They buried him at the highest spot in the sand they could find. By the 31st they had a crude boat built, which leaked badly and could only hold six, meaning four would have to remain behind. Lincoln decided to stay, with George Reed, Thomas Goodall, and Manuel, to await a rescue boat sent by the others. Joshua Bracket went with the Spaniards.

Their situation was gradually getting worse. Lincoln wrote, "Our provisions nearly expended, no appearance of rain since the night we first landed, our thirst increasing, our strength wasting, our few clothes hanging in rags, our beards of great length and almost turned white, nothing like relief before us, no boat in sight. . . . We had marked out for each one the place for his grave. I looked at mine and thought of my wife and family."

By the 5th of February, they had assembled a small raft that could carry two people. Then at 10 A.M. they spotted a boat about a mile off and George and Thomas set off after her in the raft. It took them five hours to reach her, only to discover it was the boat they'd built, but no one was on board and it was full of water. It took them another eight hours to get back ashore.

Suddenly on February 6, 1822 a rescue ship arrived, but it was not from their six fellow captives who set out in the crude boat—it was Nickola, Thomas Young and three Frenchmen. After recovering a bit

with some food and water, Lincoln left a note in a bottle for the other six men and set off to search for them.
Nickola then explained how they had gotten away from the pirates.

As nearly as I can recollect his own words, he said, "A few days since, the pirates took four small vessels, [who] I believe [were] Spaniards. They, having but two officers for the first two, the third fell to me as prize-master, and having an understanding with the three Frenchmen and Thomas, [I] selected them for my crew and went on board with orders to follow the *Mexican*, which I obeyed. The fourth, the pirates took out all but one man, and bade him [to] also follow their vessel. Now, our schooner leaked so bad that we left her, and in her stead agreed to take this little sloop (which we are now in), together with the one man. The night being very dark, we all agreed to desert the pirates, altered our course, and touched at St. Maria, where we landed the one man. [We] saw no boats there, could hear nothing from you, and agreed one and all—at the risk of our lives—to come and liberate you if you were alive; knowing as we did that you were put on this key to perish.

"On our way, we boarded the *Exertion*, thinking possibly you might have been there. On board her we found a sail and paddle.[33] We took one of the pirate's boats, which they had left alongside of her, which proves how we came by two boats.

"My friend, the circumstance I am now about to relate will astonish you. When the pirate's boat with Bolidar was sent to the before-mentioned key [i.e. the key they were marooned on] on the 19th of January [1822], it was their intention to leave you prisoners where there was nothing but salt and mangroves and no possibility of escape. This was the plan of Baltizar, their abandoned pilot, but Bolidar's heart failed him and he objected to it. Then after a conference, Captain Jonnia ordered you to be put on the little island from whence we have taken you. But after this was done that night, the French and Portuguese part of the *Mexican*'s crew protested against it, so that Captain Jonnia, to satisfy them, sent his large boat to take you and your fellow-prisoners back again; taking care to select his confidential Spaniards for this errand. And will you believe me, they set off from the *Mexican*, and after spending about as much time as would really have taken them to come to you, they returned and reported they had been to your island and landed and that none of you were there, somebody having taken you off!

"This all my companions here know to be true. I knew it was impossible you could have been liberated and therefore we determined among ourselves that should an opportunity occur, we would come and save your lives, as we now have."

He then expressed—as he hitherto had done (and I believe with sincerity)—his disgust with the bad company which he had been in and looked forward with anxiety to the day when he might return to his native country.

I advised him to get on board an American vessel whenever an opportunity offered and come to the United States, and on his arrival direct a letter to me, repeating my earnest desire to make some return for the disinterested friendship which he had shown towards me. With the Frenchman I had but little conversation, being unacquainted with the language. Here ended Nickola's account. "And now," said the Frenchman, "our hearts be easy."

Nickola observed he had left all and found us. I gave them my warmest tribute of gratitude, saying I looked upon them, under God, as the preservers of our lives, and promised them all the assistance my situation might ever enable me to afford. This brings me to—

Thursday evening, 7th, when, at 11 o'clock, we anchored at the creek's mouth, near the *Exertion*. I was anxious to board her [and] accordingly took with me Nickola, Thomas, George, and two others, well-armed, each with a musket and cutlass. I jumped on her deck [and] saw a fire in the caboose, but no person there. I called aloud Mr. Bracket's name several times, saying, "It is Captain Lincoln. Don't be afraid, but show yourself," but no answer was given. She had no masts, spars, rigging, furniture, provisions, or anything left, except her bowsprit and a few barrels of salt provisions of her cargo. Her sealing had holes cut in it, no doubt in their foolish search for money. I left her with peculiar emotions, such as I hope never again to experience, and returned to the little sloop, where we remained till—

Friday, 8th. When I had a disposition to visit the island on which we were first imprisoned. [We] found nothing there, [but] saw a boat among the mangroves near the *Exertion*. Returned and got underway immediately for Trinidad. In the night, while under full sail, [we] run aground on a sunken key, having rocks above the water resembling old stumps of trees. We, however, soon got off and anchored. Most of these keys have similar rocks about them, which navigators must carefully guard against.

Saturday, 9th. Got under way again, and stood along close in for the main island of Cuba, in order that if we should see the pirates, to take our boats and go on shore.

Sunday, 10th. [We] saw the highlands of Trinidad. At night [we] came to anchor in sight of the town, near a small key. Next morning—

Monday, 11th. [We] underway and saw a brig at anchor about five miles below the mouth of the harbor. We hoped to avoid her speaking [to] us, but when we opened in sight of her, [we] discovered a boat making towards us with a number of armed men in her. This alarmed my friends and as we did not see the brig's ensign hoisted, they declared the boat was a pirate and looking through the spy-glass, thought they knew some of them to be the *Mexican's* men!

This state of things was quite alarming. They said, "we will not be taken alive by them." Immediately the boat fired a musket. The ball passed through our mainsail. My friends insisted on beating them off. I endeavored to dissuade them, believing as I did that the brig was a Spanish man-of-war who had sent her boat to ascertain who we were. I thought we had better heave to. Immediately another shot came. Then they insisted on fighting and said, if I would not help them I was no friend. I reluctantly acquiesced and handed up the guns. [We] commenced firing upon them, and they upon us. We received several shots through the sails, but no one was hurt on either side. Our two boats had been cast adrift to make us go the faster and we gained upon them, continuing firing until they turned from us and went for our boats, which they took in tow for the brig. Soon after this it became calm. Then I saw that she had us in her power. She armed and manned two more boats for us. We now concluded—since we had scarcely ammunition—to surrender and were towed down alongside the brig, taken on board, and were asked by the captain, who could speak English, "what for you fire on the boat?" I told him we thought her a pirate and did not like to be taken by them again, having already suffered too much, showing my papers.

Nickola and the three Frenchmen were immediately arrested as pirates. Capt. Lincoln, George Reed, Thomas Goodall, Thomas Young, and Manuel were arrested as pirates on reaching the port of Casilda, just a few miles from Trinidad, Cuba. While Lincoln and his men were released after he presented his papers to the governor, he was less successful in securing the others' release as they were still held on the Spanish man-of-war, which had put to sea again. The three Frenchmen enlisted into the Spanish Navy to improve their situation. Lincoln sailed from Trinidad on February 20th and arrived in Boston on March 25th.

Lincoln later learned that Joshua Bracket and the marooned Spaniards reached the Exertion and took one of her boats, letting the one they made float away. They then made their way to Principe, where the authorities provided Bracket with several soldiers as a search party, but after traveling only a short distance, the soldiers refused to go any further and force him to turn back. Unable to do anything further, being a lone foreigner unable to speak Spanish, he set off over land to Havana, where took passage on a ship to Boston. He and Capt. Lincoln were at last reunited.

Nickola made it to Boston to see Capt. Lincoln in August 1824. While on the Spanish man-of-war, Nickola had received a musket ball through his arm in a battle with a Colombian privateer. He and a number of other wounded men were taken to a hospital on shore, from which he escaped and made his way to Jamaica. Nickola stayed with Lincoln until his death five years later.

Lincoln says that he later met a commercial agent named Stewart who was in Trinidad about the time of his captivity, writing, "He informed me that the piratical schooner Mexican was afterwards chased by an English government vessel from Jamaica, which was cruising in search of it. Being hotly pursued, the pirates deserted their vessel and fled to the mangrove bushes on an island similar to that on which they had placed me and my crew to die. The English surrounded them, and thus they were cut off from all hope of escape. They remained there, I think, fourteen days, when, being almost entirely subdued by famine, eleven surrendered themselves and were taken. The others probably perished among the mangroves. The few who were taken were carried by the government vessel into Trinidad. Mr. Stewart said that he saw them himself, and such miserable objects that had life he never before beheld. They were in a state of starvation, their beards had grown to a frightful length, their bodies were covered with filth and vermin, and their countenances were hideous. From Trinidad they were taken to Kingston, Jamaica, and there hung. Thus there is every reason to believe that this horde of monsters was at last broken up and dispersed."

Capt. Lincoln also mentions that before coming to Boston, Nickola *"saw the villainous pilot of the Mexican—the infamous Baltizar—with several other pirates, brought into Montego Bay, from whence they were to be conveyed to Kingston to be executed. . . . Baltizar was an old man and, as Jamieson [i.e. Nickola] said, it was a melancholy and heart-rending sight to see him borne to execution with those gray hairs which might have been venerable in virtuous old age, [but were] now a shame and reproach to this hoary villain, for he was full of years and old in iniquity."*

Notes

1. Trinidad is midway along the southern coast of Cuba and about 175 miles from Havana. It should not be confused with island of Trinidad.

2. Shooks: boards to the boxes that are disassembled and bound together to make them easier to transport.

3. Cape Cruz (Cabo Cruz) is the tip of a peninsula that points westward at the southeastern end of Cuba and is about 170 miles west of what is now the U.S. Naval Station at Guantanamo Bay.

4. Keys: reefs or low islands.

5. Boca de Clavolone (Canal de Caballones) is between two groups of islands—the Cayos de las Doce Leguas and the Laberinto de las Doce Leguas—just south of the Cuban mainland, about 100 miles northwest of Cape Cruz.

6. Blunderbusses: short rifles with a flared muzzles.

7. Dirks: short daggers.

8. Carronades: light cannons of large caliber used for short range. The twelve and six-pounds referring to the weight of the cannonballs they fire.

9. Mexico became independent of Spain on September 27, 1821. Cuba remained a Spanish posssession until 1898 when the United States took the island away from Spain.

10. Tack: changing direction by changing the position of the sails.

11. This is the Cuban Cayo Largo, not the Key Largo in Florida. Cayo Largo is just south of the Cuban mainland at the eastern end of a string of keys that trail westward to a large island—Isla de la Juventud. It is about 260 miles northwest of Cape Cruz; just over halfway from Cape Cruz to Cape San Antonio, which forms the western tip of Cuba

12. Beating up: sailing against the wind, especially on alternate tacks.

13. Halter: a hangman's noose.

14. Laudanum: a solution of opium in alcohol, which was primarily used as a pain killer or sedative.

15. Campeche is in southeastern Mexico on the western coast of the Yucatán Peninsula.

16. In 1821 there were twenty-four states.

17. [Lincoln's note:] The Spaniards at Havana have been in the habit of saying to those who arrive there, after suffering the horrid abuse of cutting, beating, hanging, robbing, etc., "it is your countrymen [i.e. Americans] that do this."

18. Spirito Santo (Sancti Spiritus) is about 35 miles east of Trinidad.

19. Cruiser: an armed patrol ship.

20. Hogshead: a barrel or cask containing from 100 to 140 gallons.

21. [Lincoln's note:] He showed me the wound, which was quite large and not then healed.

22. Principe (Camagüey) is about two-thirds of the way along Cuba's length toward the east and is centered about 35 miles inland from both the northern and the southern coasts. It's one of the towns sacked by Capt. Morgan.

23. It appears they were back in the general area of Boca de Clavolone, where they first encountered the pirates.

24. [Lincoln's note:] A boat built of two halves of a large tree, hollowed out and so put together as to carry about thirty barrels.

25. Junk: old or inferior rope. Oakum: old ropes untwisted into loose twine that was used for caulking the seams of ships, stopping leaks, etc.

26. Off soundings: any place where the water is too deep for the depth to be measured with a weighted line.

27. Pantaloons: originally these were tight trousers fastened below the calf, though later it came to mean any trousers.

28. Hove: turned the vessel on its side for cleaning.

29. [Lincoln's note:] This is the real name of Nickola.

30. Fore-topsail: the sail on the fore-mast above the foresail, or the second sail in ascending order from the deck on the ship's forward mast. Topgallant sail: the sail above the topsail, or the third sail in ascending order from the deck.

31. These were probably not Cayman Islands, which are about 150 miles south of Cuba and about 100 miles southwest of where they were first taken. While Capt. Lincoln may have misjudged the distance, they were still close enough to the *Exertion* for its debris to float ashore, as he later mentions.

32. [Lincoln's note:] This key was full of mangrove trees, whose tops turn down and take root, forming a kind of umbrella. The tide at high water flows two feet deep under them. It is therefore impossible for human beings to live long among them, even with food and water.

33. [Lincoln's note:] This proved to me that Mr. Bracket had been there, these being the ones which he took from the island.

The Bloody-Minded Villain
Came on to Kill Me

≋≋≋≋

Captain William Snelgrave

During the period when pirates haunted the waves searching for their victims, slave ships were busy dragging African natives away from the families and off to a life of severe hardships in the New World. Humans had become a more valuable commodity in Africa than spices, ivory, and gold, making the slave trade a very lucrative business venture, yielding profits up to $120,000 on an investment of only $10,000. This frightful profession brought ships with valuable cargoes right into the pirates' West Indian hunting grounds and attracted the pirates to the slavers' hunting grounds along the coasts of Africa.

Slave ships would pick up merchandise in Europe and transport it to Africa where it would be traded for slaves. Sometimes these ships would sit on the coast for weeks while their holds slowly filled with human cargo. They would then set off for the West Indies, where the ships would exchange their cargo for money, rum, sugar, and other West Indian commodities that could be sold for a good price in Europe.

In November of 1719, William Snelgrave was made captain of the slave ship Bird Galley[1] *and sailed from London to Holland, where he took on a cargo of goods to trade in Africa for slaves. Changing winds and several storms brought the ship to Ireland. After some repairs, they set off for Guinea— which at that time covered a much larger area than the current country by that name. In Snelgrave's day, most of western-central Africa was called Guinea. The coast of Guinea stretched 3,000 miles from present-day Senegal to Gabon. Snelgrave arrived at the mouth of the River Sierra Leone (now called Rokel, in the country of Sierra Leone), which was a new home for pirates that had been chased out of Nassau by the ex-privateer, now governor of the Bahamas, Woodes Rogers. In about 1719, thirty ex-privateers and ex-pirates set up a secret trading settlement at the River Sierra Leone delta, where they operated in defiance of the Royal African Company's monopoly on trade in this region. This was a natural place for active pirates to spend part of the winter. What happened to Capt. Snelgrave when he arrived there is recorded in his book,* A New Account of Some Parts of Guinea and the Slave Trade *(1734).*

[. . .]we sailed from that place [Kinsale, Ireland] with a northerly wind the 10th day of March 1718–19 [*sic*] and had a short and fine passage to the River Sierra Leone on the north coast of Guinea, in the latitude of 8 deg. 30 min., where we arrived the first day of April 1719. We met with nothing remarkable in our passage, except that near the Canary Islands we were chased by a ship whom we judged to be a Sallec rover,[2] but our ship outsailing her, they soon gave over the chase.

There were, at the time of our unfortunate arrival in the above mentioned river, three pirate ships, who had then taken ten English ships in that place. As it is necessary for illustrating this story, to give an account how these three ships came to meet there, I must observe that the first of them which arrived in the river was called the *Rising Sun*, one Cocklyn[3] commander, who had not with him above twenty-five men. These having been with one Captain Moody,[4] a famous pirate, some months before in a brigantine which sailed very well and took the *Rising Sun*, they were marooned by him, (as they call it) that is forced on board that ship and deprived of their share of the plunder taken formerly by the brigantine. These people being obliged to go away in her with little provision and ammunition, chose Cocklyn for their commander and made for the River Sierra Leone, where arriving they surprised in his sloop, one Segnor[5] Joseph, a black gentleman, who had been formerly in England and was a person of good account in this country. This man's ransom procured the pirates a sufficient supply of provision and ammunition. Moreover, several Bristol[6] and other ships arriving soon after were likewise taken, and many of their people entering with the pirates, they had when I fell into their hands near eighty men in all.

The crew of the brigantine, who with their Captain Moody, had thus forced their companions away in the *Rising Sun*, soon after repenting of that action, it bred great discontents among them so that they quarreled with their captain and some others whom they thought the chief promoters of it, and at last forced him with twelve others into an open boat, which they had taken a few days before from the Spaniards of the Canary Islands, and as they never were heard of afterwards, doubtless they perished in the ocean.[7] After this, they chose one Le Bouse,[8] a Frenchman for their commander, who carried them to the River Sierra Leone where they arrived about a month after their parting with the *Rising Sun*.

At the first appearance of this brigantine, Cocklyn and his crew were under a great surprise, but when they understood how Moody and some others had been served by them, they cheerfully joined their brethren in iniquity.

On the same day also arrived one Captain Davis,[9] who had been pirating in a sloop and had taken a large ship at the Cape Verde Islands.[10] He, coming into Sierra Leone with her, it put the other two pirates into some fear, believing at first it was a man-of-war, but upon discovering her black flag at the main-topmast-head, which pirate ships usually hoist to terrify merchantmen, they were easy in their minds and a little time after, saluted one another with their cannon.[11]

This Davis was a generous man and kept his crew, which consisted of near 150 men, in good order. Neither had he consorted or agreed to join with the others when I was taken by Cocklyn, which proved a great misfortune to me (as will appear afterwards), for I found Cocklyn and his crew to be a set of the basest and most cruel villains that ever were; and indeed they told me after I was taken that they chose him for their commander on account of his brutality and ignorance, having resolved never to have again a gentleman-like commander as, they said, Moody was.

Upon mentioning this, I think it necessary to observe in this place that the captain of a pirate ship is chiefly chosen to fight the vessels they may meet with. Besides him, they chose another principal officer whom they call quartermaster, who has the general inspection of all affairs and often controls the captain's orders. This person is also to be the first man in boarding any ship they shall attack or go in the boat on any desperate enterprise. Besides the captain and quartermaster, the pirates had all other officers as is usual on board men-of-war.

I come now to give an account how I was taken by them. The day that I made the land, which I was with in three leagues[12] of the river's mouth, it became calm in the afternoon. Seeing a smoke on shore, I sent for my first mate Mr. Simon Jones—who had been formerly at Sierra Leone, where I had not—bidding him take the pinnace[13] and go where the smoke was to inquire of the natives how affairs stood up the river. But he replied it would be to little purpose, for no people lived there. As to the smoke we saw, he believed it might be made by some travelers who were roasting of oysters on the shore and would be gone before he could get a mile from the ship. Moreover, as night drew on, it would be difficult for him to find the ship again.

Thinking this answer reasonable, I did not press him further, though I understood afterwards there was a town where the smoke appeared. But I did not then in the least suspect Mr. Jones would have proved such a villain as he did afterwards.

About five o'clock in the afternoon, a small breeze arising from the sea and the tide of flood setting strong,[14] we stood for the river's mouth. At sun-setting we perceived a ship at anchor a great way up the river, which was the pirate that took us soon after. The other two pirate ships, with their prizes, were hid from our sight by a point of land.

It becoming calm about seven o'clock and growing dark, we anchored in the river's mouth. Soon after which I went to supper with the officers that usually ate with me. About eight o'clock, the officer of the watch upon deck sent me word he heard the rowing of a boat. Whereupon we all immediately went upon deck, and the night being very dark, I ordered lanterns and candles to be got ready, supposing the boat might come from the shore with some white gentlemen that lived there as free merchants, or else from the ship we had seen up the river a little while before we came to an anchor. I ordered also, by way of precaution, the first mate to go into the steerage[15] to put all things in order and to send me forthwith twenty men on the quarter-deck with fire arms and cutlasses, which I thought he went about.

As it was dark, I could not yet see the boat, but heard the noise of the rowing very plain; whereupon I ordered the second mate to hail the boat, to which the people in it answered they belonged to the *Two Friends*, Captain Elliot of Barbados. At this, one of the officers who stood by me said he knew the captain very well and that he commanded a vessel of that name. I replied, "It might be so, but I would not trust any boat in such a place," and ordered him to hasten the first mate with the people and arms upon deck, as I had just before ordered. By this time our lanterns and candles were brought up and I ordered the boat to be hailed again; to which the people in it answered they were from America." And at the same time fired a volley of small shot at the ship, though they were then above pistol shot from us; which showed the boldness of there villains, for there was in the boat only twelve of them, as I understood afterwards, who knew nothing of the strength of our ship; which was indeed considerable, we having sixteen guns and forty-five men on board. But as they told me after we were taken, they judged we were a small vessel of little force. Moreover, they depended on the same good fortune as in the other ships they had taken, having met with no resistance for the people were generally glad of an opportunity of entering with them. Which last was but too true.

When they first began to fire, I called aloud to the first mate to fire at the boat out of the steerage portholes, which not being done and the people I had ordered upon deck with small arms not appearing, I was extremely surprised; and the more, when an officer came and told me the people would not take up arms. I went thereupon down into the steerage, where I saw a great many of them looking at one another. Little thinking that my first mate had prevented them from taking arms, I asked them with some roughness why they had not obeyed my orders. Calling upon some brisk fellows by name, that had gone a former voyage with me, to defend the ship, saying it would be the greatest reproach in the world to us all if we could be taken by a boat. Some of them replied they would have taken arms, but the chest they were kept in could not be found. The reason of which will be related hereafter.

By this time the boat was along the ship's side, and there being nobody to oppose them, the pirates immediately boarded us; and coming on the quarter-deck, fired their pieces several times down into the steerage and shot a sailor in the reins,[16] of which wound he died afterwards. They likewise threw several granado-shells,[17] which burst amongst us so that it is a great wonder several of us were not killed by them or by their shot.

At last some of our people bethought themselves to call out for quarter,[18] which the pirates granting, the quartermaster came down into the steerage inquiring where the captain was. I told him I had been so till now. Upon that he asked me how I dared order my people to fire at their boat out of the steerage, saying, that they had heard me repeat it several times. I answered, I thought it my duty to defend the ship if my people would have fought. Upon that he presented a pistol to my breast, which

I had but just time to parry before it went off so that the bullet passed between my side and arm. The rogue finding he had not shot me, he turned the butt-end of the pistol and gave me such a blow on the head as stunned me, so that I fell upon my knees, but immediately recovering myself, I forthwith jumped out of the steerage upon the quarter-deck where the pirate boatswain was.

He was a bloody villain, having a few days before killed a poor sailor because he did not do something so soon as he had ordered him. This cruel monster was asking some of my people where their captain was. So at my coming upon deck, one of them, pointing to me, said, "There he is." Though the night was very dark, yet there being four lanterns with candles, he had a full sight of me; whereupon lifting up his broadsword, he swore no quarter would be given to any captain that offered to defend his ship, aiming at the same time a full stroke at my head. To avoid it I stooped so low that the quarter-deck rail received the blow and was cut in at least an inch deep, which happily saved my head from being cleft asunder, and the sword breaking at the same time with the force of the blow on the rail, it prevented his cutting me to pieces.

By good fortune his pistols that hung at his girdle were all discharged. Otherwise he would doubtless have shot me. But he took one of them, and with the butt-end endeavored to beat out my brains, which some of my people that were then on the quarter-deck observing, cried out aloud, "For God's sake don't kill our captain, for we never were with a better man." This turned the rage of him and two other pirates on my people and saved my life. But they cruelly used my poor men, cutting and beating them unmercifully. One of them had his chin almost cut off and another received such a wound on his head that he fell on the deck as dead; but afterwards, by the care of our surgeon, he recovered.

All this happened in a few minutes, and the quartermaster then coming up, ordered the pirates to tie our people's hands, and told me that when they boarded us, they let their boat go adrift and that I must send an officer with some of my people in our boat to look for theirs. Whereupon my first mate, Mr. Simon Jones, who stood by, offered to go; and the quartermaster telling him he must return quickly, otherwise he should judge that they were run away with the boat in order to go on shore, and if they did so he would cut me to pieces. Mr. Jones replied he would not stay above a quarter of an hour, but return whether he found the boat or not. Happily for me he soon found her and returned (though it was very dark) in less time than he had promised.

Then the quartermaster took me by the hand and told me my life was safe provided none of my people complained against me. I replied, "I was sure none of them could."

The pirates next loaded all their small arms and fired several volleys for joy they had taken us, which their comrades on board their ship hearing, it being then very near us, though we could not see it for the darkness of the night, they concluded we had made resistance and destroyed their people.

It will be proper to observe here that soon after we had anchored in the mouth of the River Sierra Leone, it became calm and the tide of ebb beginning to come down, the pirates cut their cable and let their ship drive down with the tide towards us from the place where we had seen her at anchor; having sometime before sent their boat against the tide of flood to discover us. The ship being by that means come near us and see-ing our lights, without asking any questions, gave us a broadside with their great guns, verily believing we had destroyed their boat and people. This put the pirates on board us into confusion, which I observing, asked the quartermaster why he did not call with the speaking trumpet and tell their ship they had taken us. Upon that he asked me angrily whether I was afraid of going to the Devil by a great shot. For, as to his part, he hoped he should be sent to Hell one of these days by a cannon ball. I answered, "I hoped that would not be my road." However, he followed my advice and informed their ship they had taken a brave prize with all manner of good liquors and fresh provisions on board.

Just after this, Cocklyn, the pirate captain, ordered them to dress a quantity of these victuals; so they took many geese, turkeys, fowls and ducks, making our people cut their heads off and pull the great feath-ers out of their wings, but they would not stay till the other feathers were picked off. All these they put into our great furnace, which would boil victuals for five hundred Negroes, together with several West-phalia[19] hams and a large sow with pig, which they only boweled, leav-ing the hair on. This strange medley filled the furnace, and the cook was ordered to boil them out of hand.

As soon as the pirate ship had done firing, I asked the quartermaster's leave, for our surgeon to dress my poor people that had been wounded, and I likewise went into the steerage to have my arm dressed, it being very much bruised by the blow given me by the pirate boatswain. Just after that, a person came to me from the quartermaster desiring to know what o'clock it was by my watch. Which judging to be a civil way of demanding it, I sent it him immediately, desiring the messenger to tell him it was a very good going gold watch. When it was delivered to the quartermaster, he held it up by the chain and presently laid it down on the deck, giving it a kick with his foot, saying it was a pretty foot-ball. On which, one of the pirates caught it up, saying he would put it in the common chest to be sold at the mast.

I would not mention such trifling circumstances, but that I judge they serve to show the humors and temper of these sort of people.

By this time I was loudly called upon to go on board the pirate ship. As soon as I came upon deck, they hurried me over our ship's side into the boat, but when we arrived along the side of the pirate vessel, I told them I was disabled in my arm and so desired their help to get me into their ship, which was readily done. Then I was ordered to go on the quarter-deck to their commander, who saluted me in this manner:

"I am sorry you have met with bad usage after quarter given, but it is the fortune of war sometimes. I expect you will answer truly to all such questions as I shall ask you, otherwise you shall be cut to pieces. But if you tell the truth and your men make no complaints against you, you shall be kindly used, and this shall be the best voyage you ever made in your life, as you shall find by what shall be given you."

I thanked him for his good intentions, telling him I was content to stand on the footing he had proposed to me.

Having answered all his questions, one of which was how our ship sailed, both large and on a wind. I replying, "Very well." He then threw up his hat, saying she would make a fine pirate man-of-war. When I heard that, I must own I could not but be concerned for having answered so truly in that particular, but then considering that some of my people would no doubt have told them the same, and moreover my journal, when they looked into it, would have made it plainly appear, which might have proved my destruction, I satisfied my mind with these reflections.

As in this whole affair, I greatly experienced the providence of Almighty God, in his goodness delivering me from the hands of these villains and from many dangers; so the same good providence gave me such a presence of mind that when I believed I was upon the point of being killed, such terrors did not arise, as I had formerly experienced, when in danger of shipwreck. And though I faired very hard and endured great fatigues during the time I was their prisoner; yet praised be God, I enjoyed my health, submitting with that resignation to the will of the Almighty, as a man ought to do in such severe misfortunes.

But to return to my narrative, which the remembrance of my past dangers had interrupted.

As soon as I had done answering the captain's questions, a tall man with four pistols in his girdle and a broad sword in his hand, came to me on the quarter-deck, telling me his name was James Griffin and that we had been school-fellows. Though I remembered him very well, yet having formerly heard it had proved fatal to some who had been taken by pirates to own any knowledge of them, I replied I could not remember any such person by name. Upon that he mentioned some boyish pranks that had formerly passed between us. But I still denying any knowledge of him, he told me he supposed I took him to be one of the pirate's crew because I saw him armed in that manner, but that he was a forced man[20] and had been lately chief mate to Captain James Creichton of Bristol, who was then with his ship in the possession of the pirates in the river and had not been destroyed by them, at his earnest entreaty. That since his being forced, they had obliged him to act as master of the pirate ship; and the reason of his being so armed was to prevent their imposing on him, for there was hardly any among the crew of pirates belonging to Captain Cocklyn but what were cruel villains, misusing much better men than themselves, only for having the misfortune to fall into their hands, as I had already experienced and might find hereafter, but he would himself take care of me that night, in which would be my greatest danger because many of their people would soon get drunk with the good liquors found in my ship.

This generous declaration was very acceptable to me and I then readily owned my former acquaintance with him. Then he turned to Captain Cocklyn and desired a bowl of punch might be made. Which being done, the captain desired Mr. Griffin my school-fellow to show me the way to the great cabin, and he followed himself.

There was not in the cabin either chair or anything else to sit upon, for they always kept a clear ship ready for an engagement, so a carpet was spread on the deck upon which we sat down cross-legged. Captain Cocklyn drank my health, desiring I would not be cast down at my misfortune, for one of the boat's crew who had taken us had told him my ship's company in general spoke well of me and they had goods enough left in the ships they had taken to make a man of me. Then he drank several other healths, amongst which was that of the pretender, by the name of King James the Third,[21] and thereby I found they were doubly on the side of the gallows, both as traitors and pirates.

It being by this time midnight, my school-fellow desired the captain to have a hammock hung up for me to sleep in, for it seems every one lay rough, as they called it, that is, on the deck—[even] the captain himself not being allowed a bed. This being granted and soon after done, I took leave of the captain and got into the hammock, though I could not sleep in my melancholy circumstances. Moreover, the execrable oaths and blasphemies I heard among the ship's company shocked me to such a degree that in Hell itself I thought there could not be worse; for though many seafaring men are given to swearing and taking God's name in vain, yet I could not have imagined human nature could ever so far degenerate as to talk in the manner those abandoned wretches did.

After I was got into the hammock, Mr. Griffin, according to his promise, walked by me with his broad sword in his hand to protect me from insults. Some time after, it being about two o'clock in the morning, the pirate boatswain (that attempted to kill me when taken) came on board very drunk, and being told I was in a hammock he came with his cutlass near me. My generous school-fellow asked him what he wanted. He answered, to slice my liver, for I was a vile dog for ordering my people to fire on their boat, neither would I deliver my watch when the quartermaster first demanded it. Upon hearing that, I told Mr. Griffin the last was false for I had immediately sent it by a messenger, who only asked what o'clock it was, supposing the quartermaster expected it. Then Griffin bid the boatswain keep his distance or else he would cleave his head asunder with his broad sword. Nevertheless, that bloody-minded villain came on to kill me, but Mr. Griffin struck at him with his sword, from which he had a narrow escape and then ran away, so I lay unmolested till daylight. By that time the fumes of the liquor being gone off by sleep among most of the pirates, Mr. Griffin complained to the quartermaster and company of the cruel intention of the boatswain towards me, representing they ought to observe strictly that maxim established among them, not to permit any ill usage to their prisoners after quarter given.

At the hearing of this, many of them voted for his being whipped, though he was a great favorite of several others. But though I wished him hanged in my mind, yet I thought it prudent to plead for him, saying I believed it was his being in liquor that was the cause of his using me in that manner. So he received a general order not to give me the least offense afterwards; yet did that vile wretch attempt once more to kill me, as shall be related in its due place.

I come now to relate how Mr. Simon Jones, my first mate and ten of my men entered with the pirates. The morning after we were taken he came to me and said his circumstances were bad at home. Moreover, he had a wife whom he could not love, and for these reasons he had entered with the pirates and signed their articles.[22] I was greatly surprised at this declaration and told him I was very sorry to hear it, for I believed he would repent to it when too late, and as he had taken this resolution rashly, without communicating it to me, all I could say now would be to no purpose; neither would it be proper for me for the future to have any discourse with him in private. I saw this poor man afterwards despised by his brethren in iniquity, and have since been informed he died a few months after they left the River Sierra Leone. However, I must do him the justice to own he never showed any disrespect to me; and the ten people he persuaded to enter with him remained very civil to me and of their own accord always manned the side for me whenever I went on board the ship they belonged to.

Several of these unhappy people soon after repented and desired me to intercede for them that they might be cleared again, for they dared not themselves mention it to the quartermaster—it being death by their articles—but it was too nice a matter for me to deal in, and therefore I refused them.

Some days after this, one of these poor men, whose name was Thomas Wilder, discovered [i.e. revealed] things to me of which I only had a suspicion before. After cursing Mr. Jones for persuading him to enter with the pirates, he said to me that several times in the night watch before we came to Sierra Leone, he had heard a him say that he hoped we should meet with pirates when we came to that river, which he then thought to be spoken only in jest, but now he found it too true. As I seemed not to believe this, he called another of our people, who confirmed what he had told me. Then I asked them the reason why the chest of arms was put out of the place where it usually stood at the steerage, and where it was hid in the time we were taken. They answered, I might remember that the morning we made land I ordered the steerage to be cleaned, to do which all the chests there were carried between decks, and after the steerage was cleaned all the chests were brought back again in their places, except the chest of arms, which was left behind by the mate's order, [so] that when I called to the people in the steerage to fire on the pirate boat, supposing Mr. Jones had delivered them arms according to my order, many of the men would have broken the chest open, but he prevented them by declaring this was the opportunity he had wished for and that if they fired a musket, they would all be cut to pieces. And they further assured me that to induce them to enter with the pirates, he had declared to them that I had promised him to enter myself. Putting all this together with what several of the pirates told me afterwards—namely, that he had been the chief occasion of their keeping my ship—it was a wonder that I escaped so well, having such a base wretch for my principal officer.

But to resume the thread of my story. As soon as the fumes of the liquor were gone out of the pirates' heads, they all went on board the prize (as they called my ship) about eight o'clock in the morning, it being the second day of April [1719]. Mr. Jones, who had been my first mate, went with them; and he having confirmed them in their intention of keeping the ship for their own use, all hands went to work to clear the ship by throwing overboard bales of woolen goods, cases of India goods, with many other things of great value, so that before night they had destroyed between three and four thousand pounds[23] worth of the cargo, for they had little regard to these things—money and necessaries being what they chiefly wanted. The sight of this, much grieved me, but I was obliged in prudence to be silent, for my school-fellow told me I was still under the displeasure of many of them on account of my ordering my people to fire on their boat when they took me.

There were then residing at Sierra Leone several Englishmen who traded on their own accounts; and among the rest, one Captain Henry Glynn, who was since governor for the Royal African Company at Gambia, and died there. This gentleman was an honest, generous person, and of so much integrity that though he had suffered by the pirates when they first landed, yet he would never accept of any goods from them, which they had often pressed him to receive for his own use. This conduct, with an engaging deportment, so gained him the goodwill of the pirates that they were ready to oblige him in whatever he requested.

Captain Glynn and myself having formerly been acquainted, as soon as he heard of my being taken, he engaged Captain Davis and Le Bouse, the commanders of the two other pirate ships, who were then on shore at his house, to come on board with him to see me. I was very agreeably surprised with his coming that afternoon, and both the pirate captains that came with him saluted me civilly.

Captain Davis told me he knew me, though I never could recollect where I had seen him, and I found he did not care to tell where he had seen me.

Soon after this, Captain Cocklyn with his quartermaster and others, came from the prize on board their old ship to compliment Captain Davis and the rest that came with him. After the compliments were over, Captain Davis generously said he was ashamed to hear how I had been used by them. That they should remember their reasons for going a pirating were to revenge themselves on base merchants and cruel commanders of ships. That as for the owner of the prize,[24] he had not his fellow [i.e. that there was not his equal] in London for generosity and goodness to poor sailors, as he had formerly heard from others, and now from Captain Glynn, that as for my part, no one of my people— even those that had entered with them—gave me the least ill character, but by their respect since shown me, it was plain they loved me. That he indeed had heard the occasion of my ill usage and of the ill-will some still bore me was because I had ordered my people to defend the ship, which he blamed them exceedingly for, saying if he had had the good fortune to have taken me and I had defended my ship against him, he should have doubly valued me for it. That as he was not in partnership with them, he would say no more at present, but that he hoped they would now use me kindly and give me some necessaries with what remained undestroyed of my private adventure.[25] This was by no means relished by this pack of miscreants, for in their hearts they hated Captain Davis because he kept his ship's company in good order, though they were almost double their number, and being a brave, generous man, they dreaded his resentment. However Cocklyn, and the chief of his people putting a good face on the matter, invited him and Captain Glynn on board the prize, and they two desiring I might accompany them, it was readily granted.

Soon after we were on board, we all went into the great cabin, where we found nothing but destruction. Two scrutoires[26] I had there were broke to pieces, and all the fine goods and necessaries in them were all gone. Moreover, two large chests that had books in them were empty and I was afterwards informed they had been all thrown overboard, for one of the pirates, upon opening them, swore there was jaw-work enough (as he called it) to serve a nation and proposed they might be cast into the sea for he feared there might be some books amongst them that might breed mischief enough and prevent some of their comrades from going on in their voyage to Hell, whither they were all bound; upon which the books were all flung out of the cabin windows into the river.

After the company were all sat down in the cabin, they were treated with all sorts of liquors and other things that had once been mine. By this means, the chief pirates being put into a good humor, my friend Captain Glynn took the opportunity of begging of the quartermaster several necessaries for me, which being readily granted, they were tied up in bundles and Captain Glynn designed to take them on shore with him to his house for me, but an unlucky accident happened which made me lose them all again. For some of Captain Davis's people coming on board at that time, one of them—a pert young fellow of eighteen—broke a chest open to plunder it. The quartermaster hearing of it, went out of the cabin and asked the reason of his so doing. The young man replied, as they were all pirates, he thought he did what was right. On that the quartermaster struck at him with his broad sword, but the young man [by] running away escaped the blow and fled for protection into the great cabin to his master Captain Davis. The quartermaster pursued him in a great passion, and there not being room amongst so many of us to make a stroke at him, he made a thrust with sword and slit the ball of one of the young man's thumbs and slightly wounded at the same time Captain Davis on the back of one of his hands. Davis upon that was all on fire and vowed revenge, saying that though his man had offended, he ought to have been first acquainted with it, for no other person had a right to punish him in his presence; and immediately [he] went on board his own ship, where, telling the story to his ship's company, they all resolved forthwith to revenge this great injury done to one of their comrades and the indignity shown their captain. Upon that they slipped one of their cables and began to heave on the other in order to come and board Cocklyn's ship and destroy such a set of vile fellows as they called him and his crew.

When Captain Davis went from the prize, Cocklyn soon followed and went on board his own ship to get all things in a readiness to defend himself. Captain Glynn and myself only remained behind and hoped quickly to have seen hot work between them, but Cocklyn, having consulted his people and judging they should be no ways able to cope with Captain Davis, hastily came on board the prize again and desired Captain Glynn to go on board Davis with him in order to make up matters. My friend would have refused this unpleasant office if he dared, but on his not readily complying, Cocklyn grew enraged. I, fearing the consequences, persuaded him to go, which Cocklyn was so well pleased with that he often spoke of it afterwards to my advantage. By the time they came on board Davis, his ship was just heaving up their anchor; and though Captain Glynn was a well-spoken, ingenious man, he found it very difficult to compromise the matter; which at last was done on these terms: that Captain Davis and his ship's company should have their share of liquors and necessaries on board the prize and that the quartermaster who had wounded the young man belonging to Davis, should before all his crew acknowledge his fault and ask pardon for the same.

Night now approaching, Captain Glynn was obliged to go on shore without calling upon me for the things he had begged, intending to come next day for them. Being thus left on board the prize with only three or four of the pirates—amongst whom the bloody-minded boatswain (formerly mentioned) was one—and there being no boat along the side at that time, I resolved to stay where I was all night and not hail their pirate ship to send their boat for me.

The pirate carpenter was then lying on my bed in the stateroom, so I sat some time by myself in the cabin, having a candle by me on a table. When he awoke, he civilly desired me to go and take some rest, saying he feared I had not had any since I was taken. I returned him thanks, saying I would sit up till eight o'clock. Whereupon he came and sat down by me on the locker, abaft[27] in the cabin. The boatswain came down soon after this, and being a little in liquor, began to abuse me. On that the carpenter told him he was a base villain, and turned him out of the cabin. Soon after, a puff of wind coming in at one of the cabin windows, put our candle out, and the carpenter and I rising up together to blow the candle again, but not being able to do it. We accidentally shifted places in the dark, he seating himself just over against the cabin door, where I sat before. And having no tinder-box, we were at a great loss how to light the candle again.

While we were considering how to do it, the boatswain came into the steerage and finding the candle out, began to swear and rant, saying I had put it out purposely with design to go into the powder-room undiscovered and blow the ship up, but the carpenter called to him and told him it was done by accident and that I still sat by him on the locker. So he came to the cabin door, and by the starlight that came in at the windows, perceived us sitting, but could not distinguish our faces. Thinking I still sat in the place where he had seen me before, he presented a pistol and drew the trigger, swearing at that instant he would blow my brains out.

By good fortune the pistol did not go off, but only flashed in the pan. By the light of which, the carpenter observing that he should have been shot instead of me, it so provoked him that he ran in the dark to the boatswain, and having wrenched the pistol out of his hand, he beat him, with that and his fist to such a degree that he almost killed him.

The noise that was made in this fray being heard on board the pirate ship that lay close to us, a boat was sent from her; and they being informed of the truth of the matter, the officer that was in her thought fit to carry away this wicked villain, who had three times attempted to murder me.

After this I slept soundly, having been much fatigued; but I was awakened early in the morning by a great number of Captain Davis's crew, who came on board to take part of the liquors and necessaries, according to [the] agreement. It was very surprising to see the actions of these people. They and Cocklyn's crew (for Le Bouse's were not yet admitted) made such waste and destruction that I am sure a numerous set of such villains would in a short time have ruined a great city. They hoisted upon deck a great many half hogsheads[28] of claret and French brandy, knocked their heads out, and dipped cans and bowls into them to drink out of. And in their wantonness threw full buckets of each sort upon one another. As soon as they had emptied what was on the deck, they hoisted up more. And in the evening washed the decks with what remained in the casks.

As to bottled liquor of many sorts, they made such havoc of it that in a few days they had not one bottle left, for they would not give themselves the trouble of drawing the cork out, but nicked the bottles (as they called it)—that is, struck their necks off with a cutlass—by which means one in three was generally broke. Neither was there any cask-liquor left in a short time, but a little French brandy.

As to eatables, such as cheese, butter, sugar and many other things, they were as soon gone, for the pirates being all in a drunken fit—which held as long as the liquor lasted—no care was taken by anyone to prevent this destruction, which they repented of when too late. As for my things which the quartermaster had given me at Captain Glynn's request and which were accordingly bundled up, a company of drunken pirates came into the cabin and stumbled over some goods that lay on the floor. They took them, with three of my bundles, and threw them overboard, swearing they had like to have broken their necks by those things lying in their way.

I had then but one bundle left, in which was a black suit of cloths and other things which this gang had spared. They being gone out of the cabin, a pirate who was tolerably sober came in soon after, and seeing my bundle, said he would see what was in it, which in prudence I did not oppose. He then took out my black cloth clothes, a good hat and wig, and some other things, whereupon I told him Captain Cocklyn's quartermaster had given them to me and I hoped he would not deprive me of them, for they were of no service to him in so hot a country, but would be of great use to me, as I should soon return to England.

I had hardly done speaking, when he lifted up his broad sword and gave me a blow on the shoulder with the flat side of it, whispering at the same time these words in my ear:

"I give you this caution: never to dispute the will of a pirate. For, supposing I had cleft your skull asunder for your impudence? What would you have got by it but destruction? Indeed, you may flatter yourself I should have been put to death for killing a prisoner in cold blood, but assure yourself, my friends would have brought me off on such an occasion."

I gave him thanks for his admonition and soon after he put on the clothes, which, in less than half an hour after, I saw him take off and throw overboard, for some of the pirates, seeing him dressed in that manner, had thrown several buckets of claret upon him. This person's true name was Francis Kennedy. He was afterwards hanged at Execution Dock.[29] But he told me at the time he put my clothes on that his name was Sun, asking me if I did not know his father—who was then commander of a ship that used the Barbados trade—and that if ever the old dog fell in his way, he would kill him." To which I answered, "I knew no such person."

When night came on, I had nothing left of what had been bundled up, but a hat and wig. I must own that whenever they plundered me, no affront was offered to my person, but several brought me liquor and slices of ham broiled, a biscuit being my plate, saying they pitied my condition. The hat and wig I had left, being hung on pins in the cabin, a person half drunk came in about eight o'clock at night, and put them on, telling me he was a great merchant on shore and that his name was Hogbin. But supposing him to be a pirate, I said little to him. By this time there was a great quietness in the ship, most of the pirates being dead drunk. After a little conversation, as Mr. Hogbin was going out of the cabin with my hat and wig on, he met Cocklyn's quartermaster, who knowing him not to be one of the crew, asked him how he came by the things he had on, To which the fellow not returning a direct answer, the quartermaster beat him very severely for taking things he had no right to. Then coming to me, he asked in a kind manner how I had fared in the hurly burly of that day. When I told him I had lost all the necessaries he had given me the day before, he expressed much concern and said he would take care the next day to recover what he could for me. But he did not prove so good as his word.

The next day, which was the third since my being taken, Le Bouse's crew were permitted to come on board the prize, where they finished what was left of liquors and necessaries, acting in the same destructive manner as their vile brethren in iniquity had done before. Being quite weary of such company, and understanding the three pirate captains were on shore at my friend Captain Glynn's house, I asked leave of the quartermaster to go to them, which he readily granted. On this I got into a canoe, and as we rowed towards the shore, we had like to have been overset through the drunkenness of one of the pirates that was with us. If providence had not prevented this accident, we should undoubtedly have all been lost, for the tide ran very strong and several voracious sharks were then near us. When I came to Captain Glynn's, he and the pirate captains received me in a very civil manner, and upon my telling them how I had lost all my necessaries that had been given me, the captains promised that the next day they would do what they could to recover some of them again for me. Then I begged a shirt of my friend Captain Glynn, for I had been three days without shifting, which is very uneasy in so hot a country where people sweat so much.

Being greatly refreshed with that clean shirt and having stayed all night with him, where I had more rest than I before had for a good while, [the] next day I went on board in company with the pirate captains. Captain Davis desired Cocklyn to order all his people on the quarter-deck and made a speech to them in my behalf, which they relishing better than that he had formerly made, it was resolved to give me the ship they designed to leave, in order to go into the prize with the remains of my cargo that was undestroyed. And there being a large quantity of goods likewise remaining in several prizes, they concluded to give me them also, which, with my own, were worth several thousand pounds. One of the leading pirates proposed to the rest that they should take me along with them down the coast of Guinea, where I might exchange the goods for gold. And if, in order to make a quick sale, I sold them at prime cost, I should get money enough by them. That, no doubt, as they went down the coast, they should take some French and Portuguese vessels, and then they might give me as many of their best slaves as would fill the ship. That then he would advise me to go for the island of St. Thomas[30] in the West Indies—a free port belonging to the Danes—and sell them there with the vessel. And after rewarding my people in a handsome manner, I might return with a large sum of money to London and bid the merchants defiance. This proposal was unanimously approved of by them, but it struck me with a sudden damp, apprehending it would be fatal to me, so I began to insinuate it would not be proper for me to accept of such a quantity of other peoples goods, as they had so generously voted for me and going on to give my reasons, I was immediately interrupted by several of the pirates, who began to be very angry that I did not readily accept of what had been proposed, so much for my advantage, as they thought; for many of them were so ignorant, as to think their gift would have been legal.

On this, Captain Davis said, "I know this man and can easily guess his thoughts concerning this matter, for he thinks if he should act in the manner you have proposed, he shall ever after lose his reputation. Now, I am for allowing everybody to go to the Devil in their own way, so desire you will give him the remains of his own cargo, with what is left of his private adventure, and let him do with it what he thinks fitting." This was readily granted and they advised me to take Le Bouse's brigantine—which he had then just quitted, having fitted one of the prizes for a pirate ship for him and his crew—and carry her along the side of my ship in order to save the goods then left undestroyed in her, allowing me some of my own people to do it. By this means we saved a considerable part of the cargo, but of my private adventure not above thirty pounds sterling; for that chiefly consisting in necessaries and liquors, with fine goods, was soon destroyed by them. One instance of which out of many I shall give. The pirates took several pieces of fine holland,[31] and opening them, spread them on the deck, and being almost drunk, lay down on them. Then others came and threw buckets of claret upon them which roused them up, and the hollands being thereby rained, they flung the pieces overboard.

Captain Davis likewise further obtained for me that I might lie on board the *Two Friends*, Captain Elliot of Barbados—whom they had taken and forced to be their store ship—and that I might go on shore when I pleased to my friend Captain Glynn's house, on condition I should return whenever they sent for me.

And now, the tide being turned, they were as kind to me as they had been at first severe. So we got the brigantine along the side of the prize and as bale goods and cases came to hand, we got them into her. Only now and then we lost some by the ill-nature of two or three leading pirates, for if we could not receive the goods so fast as they expected with the few people I had of my own then with me, they would let them drop overboard.

The same they did by a quantity of Irish beef, the first day after I was taken, for they despised it, having found so much English in the several prizes they had met with in the River. This sight moved me to entreat Captain Cocklyn to give me the Irish beef they were going to throw overboard for the use of my poor people that had not entered with them. But I being then under the high displeasure of him and his crew, he brutishly replied there is horse-beans enough in the prize to serve you and your people six months. To which I answered, it was [a] coarse diet. But finding this put him into a passion, I held my tongue and the beef was all cast into the sea.

In this place I think it proper to acquaint the reader [about] what danger all the prisoners [i.e. the captains and crews of the prizes who hadn't joined the pirates] were in, by [i.e. because of] a false report brought on board the prize ships that afternoon. For it was confidently averred by some Negroes that one of their [i.e. the pirate's] crew was murdered by two captains, whose names were Bennet and Thompson, who had been obliged to fly into the woods from the rage of the pirates. And they added that these two gentlemen coming to the house of one Mr. Jones (who lived a great way up the river) to seek for provisions, they there met with the person whom they had killed [i.e. there they met the pirate and killed him].

Upon this report the pirates resolved to revenge themselves on us who were their prisoners, which obliged me to argue with them, and observe how great a cruelty it would be to punish us who were wholly innocent, for the faults of others. Moreover, I said the report might be false, it coming from the shore Negroes, and I hoped at least they would defer their resentment against us till they had a more certain account of the matter.

This calmed their rage a little, when, to our great joy, the person that was reported to be killed came on board soon after and told his comrades that he had met with Captain Bennet and Thompson at Mr. Jones's house, who threatened him—from which the report arose that they had killed him—but that they had not otherwise misused him. So on this, their passion was entirely calmed.

As I have mentioned these two captains, Bennet and Thompson, I shall give an account of their misfortunes, which I had afterwards from their own mouths. Captain John Bennet, being bound from Antigua[32] to the coast of Guinea, was taken at Cape Verde Islands[33] by Davis. Who, after plundering him, restored him his ship and he went into the River Sierra Leone, where Captain Thompson was arrived before him. Upon Cocklyn the Pirate's coming into the river, they carried their ships a good way up to a place called Brent's Island—being the settlement of the Royal African Company, where one Mr. Plunket was governor. Having got their ships very near the shore, they made a battery thereon, and having landed ammunition, resolved with their people to defend themselves to the utmost, thinking at that time they would remain faithful.

Le Bouse being arrived in his brigantine and hearing that several ships were up the river, he resolved to have one of them for his use, so he went up to attack them, and they bravely defended themselves against him. But, soon after, Cocklyn coming with his ship to the assistance of Le Bouse, their people began to falter. And these gallant captains were, for saving [i.e. in order to save] their lives, [were] obliged, with Mr. Plunket and several of their officers, to fly into the woods, where for many weeks they remained, having nothing to subsist on but rice, with now and then some oysters which they got by night from the riverside. Neither dared they appear near the place where the pirates were (as long as they remained there) for they had vowed to cut them to pieces if ever they fell into their hands. Moreover, their ships were burnt, and Le Bouse took for his own use one Captain Lamb's ship, which at that time lay farther up the river.

I thought proper to relate this, in order to set the story in a better light, though it happened some weeks before I was taken. But now, to return to my subject. I was relating how we were employed in saving what goods we could. This took us up four days; and I slept every night on board their tender[34] commanded by Captain Elliot, who was very kind to me and had a great ascendant over the leading pirates, so that he had seldom the company of the common sort, having orders to drive them away whenever they came on board him. And I have often been amazed to hear and see what he has done to some of them when they were impudent—beating them and saying he was sure he should see them hanged in due time at Execution Dock. However, by this means we were generally very easy on board him, which was no little satisfaction to me in my circumstances.

About this time the quartermaster who took me, fell sick of a fever, which increasing, he sent to speak with me. And having desired all present, except my self to withdraw, he told me that at the time I was taken, he designed to have killed me when he presented the pistol to my breast; begging I would forgive him for his cruel intention. Which I readily doing, he further said that he had been a most wicked wretch, having been guilty of all manner of abominable crimes, and that now believing he should die, his conscience sadly tormented him, fearing he should be punished as he deserved in Hell-fire, which so often in their vile discourse he had made light of.

Upon hearing that, I exhorted him to sincere repentance, telling him the Christian religion assured us of God's mercies if we are truly penitent; and I instanced the goodness of God to myself, in that he was graciously pleased to preserve me the night I was taken from being murdered by him and others, which great mercies I believed were shown me because I put my hope and trust in Almighty God, and exhorted him to do the same.[35]

But he replied, with a sad countenance, "Oh, sir, my heart is hardened. However, I will endeavor to follow your good counsel." As he was going on, expressing his sorrow for his former course of life, some of the pirates broke in upon us to ask him how he did, so he called his boy and, as a mark of his goodwill towards me, ordered him to take the key of his chest and let me take out what necessaries I would. Accordingly I took that opportunity of providing myself with shirts, stockings and several other things.

As I was taking them out, a pirate coming from the deck and knowing nothing of the quartermaster's order, called out aloud, "See how that dog is thieving there. He does it as cleverly as any rogue of us all." But being told it was with the quartermaster's leave, he came and helped me to bundle the things up and I sent them on board the tender. These were the first necessaries which I could call my own, since my misfortune. The quartermaster that evening falling into a delirium, died before morning in terrible agonies cursing his maker in so shocking a manner, that it made a great impression on several new entered men; and they afterwards came privately to me, begging that I would advise them how to get off from so vile a course of life, which led them into destruction both of body and soul. Some of them proposed to fly into the woods and remain there till their ships were gone if I would promised to protect them afterwards, but this being too nice a matter for me to meddle with at that juncture, I declined it; exhorting them in general, not to be guilty of murder or any other cruelty to those they should take. For if ever they should by a general consent resolve to embrace the King's Pardon, it would be a great advantage to them to have the unfortunate people they had taken give them a good character in that respect.

Having mentioned the King's Pardon, I shall here relate what I before omitted with relation to his late Majesty's proclamation for a pardon to pirates that should surrender themselves at any of the British plantations by the first of July 1719.[36] This proclamation I had on board, with a declaration of war against Spain. The quartermaster, finding them amongst my papers and not being able to read, he brought them to me the next day after I was taken and bid me read them aloud to all then present, which I did, but there being rewards offered in the proclamation to those that should take or destroy pirates, so much for a captain and in proportion for the other officers and common pirates, this put them into such a rage that I began to apprehend myself in some danger. But Captain Cocklyn ordering silence to be made, bid me read the other paper, which was the declaration of war against Spain.

When I had read it, some of them said they wished they had known it before they left the West Indies. From thence I took occasion to observe to them that if they thought fit to embrace his Majesty's most gracious pardon, there was not only time enough for them to return to the West Indies, (there being still three months to come of the time limited in the proclamation) but now that war was declared against Spain, they would have an opportunity of enriching themselves in a legal way by going a privateering, which many of them had privately done. This seemed to be relished by many, but several old buccaneers who had been guilty of murder and other barbarous crimes, being no ways inclined to it, they used the King's proclamation with great contempt and tore it in pieces. I thought myself well off that no resentment or ill-usage was shown me on this occasion. Amongst the several pirates that came to consult me how they should get off. There was one Ambrose Curtis, who was in a bad state of health and generally walked the deck in a silk night-gown. This person finding me shy in answering his questions, he told me, although I had forgot him, yet he had not me; for he was eleven years ago at sea with my father, who had used him severely for being an unlucky boy. That I might remember, my father died in Virginia and I commanded the ship afterwards and brought her home to England; having been very kind to him, except in one thing, which was that he—having confessed to me he was a servant[37] and run away from his master—I refused to pay him his wages till he brought a person who gave me security that I should not pay them twice, and then he had his wages to a farthing.[38] Adding, he had told this to several leading pirates, who had persuaded him to revenge himself on me, but as I had been kind to him, and in his conscience he believed I was in the right to demand security when I paid him his wages, so he bore no ill-will to me on that account; and when my necessaries came to be sold at the mast, he would buy some of them for me; in which he proved as good as his word.

But as to his questions about getting off, I replied as I had done to others, assuring him if ever it came to be in my power to save him, I would not spare for money nor pains to do it. But this poor fellow died before the pirates left Sierra Leone.

I hope the reader will pardon me for mentioning several things, which are not so coherent as I could wish, as also several little incidents.

The reason why I mention them is because I think they display the true humors and ways of these miscreants. Amongst my adventure of goods, I had in a box three secondhand embroidered coats. One day the three pirate captains coming on board the prize together, inquired for them, saying they understood by my book such clothes were in my ship. I told them they were in a box under the bed place in the stateroom. So they ordered them to be taken out and immediately put them on. But the longest coat falling to Cocklyn's share, who was a very short man, it almost reached as low as his ankles. This very much displeased him and he would fain [i.e. gladly] have changed with Le Bouse or Davis, but they refused, telling him they were going on shore amongst the Negro ladies, who did not know the white men's fashions, [so] it was [of] no matter. Moreover, as his coat was scarlet embroidered with silver, they believed he would have the preference of them (whose coats were not so showy) in the opinion of their mistresses. This making him easy, they all went on shore together.

It is a rule amongst the pirates, not to allow women to be on board their ships when in the harbor. And if they should take a prize at sea that has any women on board, no one dares, on pain of death, to force them against their inclinations. This being a good political rule to prevent disturbances amongst them, it is strictly observed. So now being in a harbor, they went on shore to the Negro women, who were very fond of their company, for the sake of the great presents they gave them. Nay, some white men that lived there did not scruple to lend their black wives to the pirates purely on account of the great rewards they gave.

The pirate captains having taken their clothes without leave from the quartermaster, it gave great offense to all the crew, who alleged if they suffered such things, the captains would for the future assume a power to take whatever they liked for themselves. So upon their returning on board next morning, the coats were taken from them and put into the common chest to be sold at the mast. And it having been reported that I had a hand in advising the captains to put on these coats, it gained me the ill-will in particular of one Williams, who was quartermaster of Le Bouse's ship. He seeing me in the tender's boat going on board a French Ship lately taken, where he then was, he swore that if I came there, he would cut me to pieces for the advice I had given the captains. But Captain Elliot, who was then in the boat, whispered [to] me, saying, "Don't be afraid of him, for it is his usual way of talking. But be sure call him captain as soon as you get on board." It seems this villain had been commander of a pirate sloop, who, with a brigantine two years before, took Captain Lawrence Prince in the *Whidaw Galley* near Jamaica; and being now quartermaster, which he did not like, he loved to have the title of captain given him.

So when I came into the French ship, I addressed myself to him, saying, "Captain Williams, pray hear me upon the point you are so offended at." Upon that he gave me a slight blow on the shoulder with the flat of his cutlass, swearing at the same time he had not the heart to hurt me. When I had told him how the affair had really happened, which he had been so angry about, he gave me a keg of wine and was my friend ever after.

The French ship just now mentioned, fell into their hands about a fortnight after I was taken by them in this manner. It was not bound to Sierra Leone, but having not had an observation in several days because the sun was near their zenith, they made land unexpectedly; and not knowing certainly whereabouts they were, but seeing several ships in the river at an anchor, they came boldly towards them.

I was then on board Captain Cocklyn's old ship—for they had not quite fitted mine for their use, not having at that time any guns mounted—so I saw the great fear and confusion that was amongst them. My mate, who had entered with them, said he believed, by the ship's coming in so boldly, it was the *Launceston* man-of-war of forty guns, whom we had left in Holland. For he had heard me say, she was to follow us to the coast of Guinea.

Happy would it have been for us and many more, if it had been so. For had that or even a smaller ship of twenty guns with the King's Commission come in at that time or any other while I was in their hands, I am persuaded they would have easily destroyed them, for the new-entered-men had little courage and the far greater part both of old and new pirates were so much in drink that there could have been no order or conduct amongst them in an engagement. So that it would have been very easy to have subdued them and prevented that terrible destruction which happened to above one hundred sail of ships that fell afterwards into their hands in their going down the coast of Guinea, together with those damages that happened a good while after in the East Indies by some of this gang; and the great ravage made by Roberts[39] (who rose out of Davis's ashes) the second time on the coast of Guinea, till he was happily destroyed by Sir Chaloner Ogle in the *Swallow* man-of-war.[40] But the reason why no timely care was taken to prevent so great a destruction is not proper for me to mention in this place.

As I had no business to be on board the pirate ship in time of action, I asked Captain Cocklyn's leave to go on board their tender, which he readily granted. Just as I was going, several of my people who had entered with him said they would go along with me, for they had never seen a gun fired in anger. Cocklyn hearing that, told them that now they should learn to smell gunpowder, and caned them heartily.

So I went on board Captain Elliot, where I soon saw the French ship taken. For coming so unexpectedly into the pirates hands, they made no resistance. And because the captain did not strike [his flag] on their first firing, they put a rope about his neck and hoisted him up and down several times to the main-yard-arm till he was almost dead. Captain Le Bouse coming at that instant, luckily saved his life; and highly resenting this their cruel usage to his countryman, he protested he would remain no longer in partnership with such barbarous villains. So to pacify him, they left the Frenchmen with the ship in his care; and after the cargo was destroyed, they cut the ship's masts by the board and ran her on shore, for she was very old and not fit for their purpose. After the affair of the French ship was over, I was employed for several days in landing out of the brigantine the goods that had been given me out of my own ship's cargo, and carrying them to my friend Captain Glynn's house, in which both he and I worked very hard—for my own people that did not enter with the pirates were mostly obliged to work on board the prize in fitting her for them, and the natives who served Captain Glynn at his house were grown so insolent by the large quantity of goods given them by the pirates, that they would do nothing but what they pleased. However, at last, with much trouble we got them housed.

By this time, which was about the 20th of April [1719], the ship they had taken from me was completely fitted, and the next day was appointed to name her, to which ceremony I was invited. When I came on board, the pirate captains told me it was not out of disrespect they had sent for me, but to partake of the good cheer provided on this occasion, so they desired I would be cheerful and go with them into the great cabin. When I came there, bumpers[41] of punch were put into our hands, and on Captain Cocklyn's saying aloud, "God bless the *Windham Galley*," we drank our liquor, broke the glasses, and the guns fired.

The ship being galley-built[42] with only two flush decks, the cover of the scuttle[43] of the powder-room was in the great cabin and happened at that time to be open. One of the aftermost guns blowing at the touch hole,[44] set fire to some cartouch boxes[45] that had cartridges in them for small arms, the shot and fire of which flew about us and made a great smother. When it was over, Captain Davis observed there had been great danger to us from the scuttle's being open; there being under in a room above [i.e. there being in a room underneath more than] twenty thousand weight of gunpowder. Cocklyn replied he wished it had taken fire, for it would have been a noble blast to have gone to Hell with.

Then all going upon deck, three prizes that remained undestroyed were ordered to be burned. Upon hearing that, I privately represented to Captain Davis how hard it would be upon us who were prisoners to remain in that country without necessaries and without food to subsist on. Besides, there was no manner of prospect of our getting away quickly. That to the many obligations I owed him, I hoped he would add one more, and, by his interest, at least save one of the vessels for us to return to England in. That as he had several times hinted to me how much he disliked that course of life, hoping he should have an opportunity of leaving it in a short time; so I wished he would put it in my power to report to his advantage, the good deed I then requested of him, for, in my opinion, next to murder and cruelty too often practiced by pirates, nothing could make them more odious to the world than their destroying, out of mere wantonness, so many ships and cargoes, as had been done by Cocklyn and Le Bouse's crews (in which I knew he had no hand). And if he would be pleased to procure my entire liberty at the same time that he pleaded for one of the vessels for us, it would be a double obligation on me to gratitude in case it ever fell in my power to serve him.

This he readily promised, and by his management, the ships were saved from being burned, and they made a bonfire only of the old *Rising Sun*, being the ship they had quitted for mine. And now obtaining through Captain Davis's means, my entire liberty, I went on shore to my friend Captain Glynn's house again.

Two days after this Captain Elliot sent his boat for me, desiring I would forthwith come on board his ship, because he wanted very much to speak with me. I had too many obligations to this gentleman to refuse going (though I had a sort of an aversion.) Upon coming on board, he privately represented to me that I knew he had been obliged against his will by the pirates to receive into his ship a great quantity of other people's goods, for which he might hereafter be called to an account; therefore he desired I would give him a certificate testifying the truth of it. Knowing this to be true, I readily complied, for he was a very honest man, as appeared soon after. For the pirates compelling him to go out of the river with them as their tender, he took the first opportunity of getting from them, which he did in a tornado or sudden gust of wind that arose in the night. And having the good fortune to succeed in his attempt, he made a good voyage for his owners with slaves to Barbados, where he fell sick and died.

While I was in his ship, the three pirate captains called along the side. Not expecting to see me there, they seemed very glad of it and invited me to go and sup with them on board Captain Davis. This I declined, being desirous of going on shore to Captain Glynn's. But Captain Davis insisting on it, I thought it prudent to comply, that I might not lose that gentleman's good-will, who had been so kind to me.

After we had been some time on board his ship, supper was brought up about eight o'clock in the evening and the music was ordered to play, amongst which was a trumpeter that had been forced to enter out of one of the prizes. About the middle of supper, we heard upon deck an outcry of fire, and instantly a person came to us and said the main hatchway was all in a flame, so we all went upon deck.

At that time, besides the pirate ship's crew—who were mostly drunk—there was on board at least fifty prisoners and several boats along the side, into which many people jumped and put off. I being then on the quarter-deck with the captains, observed this to them, but they all in confusion said, "We know not what to do in the matter." Upon that I told them if the sober people were allowed to go away with the boats, no one would endeavor to save the ship; and we that were left should be lost—for the other ships were above a mile from us and the tide of flood then running strong, that their boats could not row against it to save us. So I proposed to them to fire the quarter-deck guns at the boats that had just put off, to oblige them to come on board again; which being instantly done, it so frightened the people in them that they forthwith came back and all that were able, and not drunk, lent their helping hand to put out the fire, which by this time was come to a great head in the ship's hold.

After this I went down into the steerage, where I saw one Golding—

who was gunner's mate and a brisk active fellow—put his head up the after-hatchway, calling for blankets and water, which if not brought immediately, he said, the bulkhead of the powder room would be fired and the ship soon blown up. Observing the stupidity of the people about me, who stood looking on one another, I caught up several blankets and rugs which lay scattered about and flung them to him, and so did others by my example. Then I ran out of the steerage upon deck, where meeting with some people that were sober, I got them to go over the side and draw up buckets of water; and others handing them to Golding, who had by this time placed the blankets and rugs against the bulkhead of the powder room, he slung this water on them and thereby prevented the flames from catching the powder, and consequently from blowing up the ship, which must otherwise have happened for there was then on board at least thirty thousand pounds of gunpowder which had been taken out of several prizes—it being a commodity much in request amongst the Negroes.

There was still great confusion amongst us, occasioned by the darkness of the night and the many drunken people who were not sensible of the great danger we were in. Moreover, the people in the hold gave us as yet no hopes of their getting the mastery of the fire. So I went again on the quarter-deck and considered with myself [that] if fire could not be conquered, as I could not swim, I should have no chance of being saved; and even those that could [swim], would, I knew, be exposed to be torn to pieces by voracious sharks, which abound in that river. So I took one of the quarter-deck gratings and lowered it by a rope over the ship's side, designing to get on that if I should be forced to quit the ship. For though the boats had been once obliged to come back, yet it being a dark night, some people unperceived had slipped again away with them and were quite gone away.

Whilst I stood musing with myself on the quarter-deck, I heard a loud shout upon the main-deck with a huzza,[46] "For a brave blast to go to Hell with," which was repeated several times. This not only much surprised me, but also many of the new entered pirates, who were struck with a panic fright, believing the ship was just blowing up, so that several of them came running on the quarter-deck and accidentally threw me down, it being very dark. As soon as I got upon my legs again, I heard these poor wretches say in a lamentable voice one to another, "Oh! that we could be so foolish as to enter into this vile course of life!

The ship will be immediately blown up and we shall suffer for our villainies in hellfire." So that when the old hardened rogues on the maindeck wished for a blast to go to Hell with, the other poor wretches were at the same time under the greatest consternation at the thoughts of it.

The apprehension of the ship's being just ready to blow up was so universal that above fifty people got on the boltsprit and spritsail-yard,[47] thinking they should have there a better chance for their lives, but they much deceived themselves for had so great a quantity of powder as was at that time on board been fired, it would have blown them up to atoms.

There was one Taylor, master of this pirate ship, as brisk and courageous a man as ever I saw (who afterwards commanded the *Cassandra*, an English East India Ship, and carried her to New Spain where he and his crew separated). This person, with fifteen more, spared no pains to extinguish the fire in the hold, and though they were scalded in a sad manner by the flames, yet they never shrunk till it was conquered; which was not till near ten o'clock at night when they came upon deck, declaring the danger was over. So the surgeons were called to dress their burns. This was joyful news to us all on deck, for we little expected to escape.

I shall now relate how this fire happened, from which our deliverance was almost miraculous. About half an hour after eight o'clock in the evening, a Negro man went into the hold to pump some rum out of a cask, and imprudently holding his candle too near the bunghole,[48] a spark fell into the hogshead and set the rum on fire. This immediately fired another cask of the same liquor, whose bung had been through carelessness left open. And both the heads of the hogsheads immediately flying out with a report equal to that of a small cannon, the fire run about the hold. There were twenty casks of rum, with as many barrels of pitch and tar, very near the place where the rum lay that was fired, yet it pleased God none of these took fire, otherwise it would have been impossible for us to escape.

After this was over, I was obliged to stay on board till morning, all the boats being run away with. In that time Golding, the gunner's mate, told the pirate's crew several things to my advantage: How I had handed the blankets to him and ordered water to be thrown on them, which saved the bulkhead where the powder lay from being fired and consequently the ship from being blown up. So now I was more than ever in their favor, for several of them desired me to come on board the *Windham Galley* the day things were sold there at the mast and then they would be kind to me. Likewise Captain Davis pressed me to come, asking me whether the gold watch that was taken from me was a good one. To which I answering it was very good at that time. He then said he would buy it for his own use at any rate.

While he and I were talking thus, one of the mates came half drunk on the quarter-deck, saying to him, "I propose in behalf of the ship's company, that this man shall be obliged to go down the coast of Guinea with us, for I am told we cannot have a better pilot. This was a great surprise to me, but my generous friend Davis soon put me out of pain, for he told him they wanted no pilot. And the fellow still insisting on my going, Captain Davis caned him off the quarter-deck and I heard no more of it; for soon after I went on shore to my friend Captain Glynn's house.

Two days after this, a small vessel came into the river and was taken by them. It was called the *Dispatch*, Captain Wilson, belonging to the Royal African Company. Mr. Simon Jones, formerly my first mate, who had entered with the pirates, (as I have before related) told them on this occasion that he had once commanded a ship which was hired and freighted by the African Company and that he had been very unjustly used by them, so he desired the *Dispatch* might be burned, that he might be revenged of them. This being immediately consented to, and forthwith ordered to be executed, one John Stubbs, a witty, brisk fellow, stood up and desired to be heard first saying, "Pray, gentlemen, hold a little and I will prove to you, if this ship is burnt, you will thereby greatly serve the company's interest. This drawing everyone's attention, they bid him go on. Then he said, "The vessel has been out these two years on her voyage, being old and crazy, and almost eaten to pieces by the worms; besides, her stores are worth little; and as to her cargo, it consists only of a little redwood and Melegette-pepper; so if she should be burned, the company will lose little; but the poor people that now belong to her and have been [on] so long a voyage will lose all their wages, which I am sure is three times the value of the vessel and of her trifling cargo, so that the company will be highly obliged to you for destroying her. The rest of the crew being convinced by there reasons, the vessel was spared and delivered again to Captain Wilson and his people, who afterwards came safe to England in it.

The 29th of April [1719], such of the pirates as were my friends sent me word on shore that the sale of necessaries was to begin that day in the afternoon in the *Windham Galley*, Captain Cocklyn. So I went on board in a large canoe belonging to two men that lived ashore, who went at the same time with me. At the sale, several of the pirates bought many necessaries that had been mine and gave them to me. Likewise, Mr. James Griffin, my school-fellow, was so civil as to beg from those that were not so kind to me as he hoped they would have been. The two white men that went with me in the canoe, minded their own business so well that they got several great bundles of clothes and goods, which they put into the canoe with mine.

By this time several pirates being half drunk with brandy, looked over the side and seeing so many bundles in the canoe, which they supposed to be all mine, they swore I was insatiable and that it would be a good deed to throw them overboard. This my kind school-fellow hearing, he came and told me of it, advising me to go immediately on shore; which I accordingly did, and it proved very happy for me, for soon after my watch was put up to sale, and many bidding for it, some of them out of spite to Captain Davis, it was run up to one hundred pounds, which he paid down. One of the pirates being greatly vexed at it, said he believed the cases of the watch were not good gold, and calling for a touch-stone, he tried them on it. The touch looking of a copperish color (as indeed all gold cases of watches do on the touch by reason of the quantity of alloy put in to harden them), this pretense served the turn of this villain, who thereupon exclaimed against me, saying I was a greater rogue than any of them who openly professed piracy, since I was so sly as to bring a base metal watch and endeavor to put it off for a gold one.

This speech procured me the anger of many who knew no better; they believing every word of what he said to be true. And though Captain Davis laughed at it, yet several swore if I had not been gone on shore, they would have whipped me. And as their drunkenness increased, they talked of sending for me to be punished for so great a villainy, as they called it. But my school-fellow apprehending they would really offer me some violence, was so kind as to send me word of what had passed by a white man living on shore, who was then on board, advising me to go into the woods, for they should sail quickly out of the river.

The next morning early, which was the last day of April [1719], as I was just going to follow his advice, I was agreeably surprised with the arrival of one Mr. James Bleau, my surgeon, whom they designed to take by force with them. This honest man had been very much cast down at it, and had often desired me to intercede for his liberty. Accordingly I had done it, representing that he grieved himself so much that if he did not die quickly, yet he would be of no use to them. But this had no effect. However, at last a fortunate accident cleared him when he least expected it, for that very evening after I was come on shore, the surgeon of the French ship entered with them; whereupon they gave Mr. Bleau his liberty the next morning.

Mr. Bleau brought us the agreeable news that the three pirate ships with their tender were under sail going out of the river. This gave us all on shore the highest satisfaction, for I had been then in their hands a month, and many others much longer. Mr. Bleau, whom I have here mentioned, lives now at Woodford-Row on Epping-Forest [just to the northeast of London], where he follows his business.

I shall now inform the reader what became of my kind school-fellow Griffin and my generous friend Davis. The first took an opportunity of getting out of the hands of the pirates by taking away a boat from the stern of the ship he was in when off the road of Anamabu[49] on the coast of Guinea. He was driven on shore there unperceived in the night-time and from thence went to Cape Coast Castle,[50] belonging to the Royal African Company; from which place he went passenger to Barbados in an English ship, where he was taken with a violent fever and died.

As to Davis, having discovered a few days after they left the River Sierra Leone a conspiracy to deprive him of his command, which was carried on by one Taylor—that was master of the ship under him—he timely prevented it, but he and some others left their ship and went on board the *Windham Galley*, Captain Cocklyn, by whom he found Taylor had been set on to displace him. This causing him to leave their partnership, he took a few days after one Captain Plumb in the *Princess*[51] of London, whose second mate Roberts[52]—so famous afterwards for his villainies—entered with him; and Davis's crew, after plundering the ship, restored her to Captain Plumb again. After this, Captain Davis went for the island Princess,[53] belonging to the Portuguese, which lies in the Bay of Guinea. Here the pirates gave out [that] they were a King's ship, but the people soon discovered what they were by their lavishness in purchasing fresh provisions with goods, but the governor winked at it on account of the great gains he and others of the chief of his people made by them. But at last, some putting him in mind that if this affair should come to the King of Portugal's ear it might prove his ruin, he plotted how to destroy Davis and his crew in order to color over what he had so basely permitted in allowing them a free trade after discovering they were pirates.

Captain Davis being one day on shore with the governor, he told him they designed to sail from the island in three days and that he would come and take his leave of him the day before. Accordingly he went on a Sunday morning, taking with him his first surgeon, the trumpeter, and some others, besides the boat's crew. At their coming into the governor's house, they saw nobody to receive them, so they went on till they came into a long gallery fronting the street. Here the governor's major-domo[54] presently came to them, saying his master was at his country house, but he had sent a messenger to him when they saw Captain Davis coming on shore and no doubt he would soon be in town. But the surgeon observing that many people had got together in the street with arms in their hands, he said to his captain, "I am sure we shall see no governor today," and advised him immediately to go away. So Davis and the surgeon went out of the house, whereupon the major domo called to the people in the street to fire at them. The surgeon and two more were killed on the spot and the trumpeter was wounded in the arm, who seeing two Capuchin friars[55] (from whom I had this account at the island Princess) fled to them. One of them took him in his arms to save him, but a Portuguese came and shot him dead without any regard to the friar's protection. Captain Davis, though he had four shots in diverse parts of his body, yet continued running towards the boat, but being closely pursued, a fifth shot made him fall, and the Portuguese being amazed at his great strength and courage, cut his throat that they might be sure of him.[56]

The boat's crew hearing the firing, put off in good time at some distance from the shore; and seeing the Portuguese advancing to fire at them, they rowed on board their ship, where relating what had happened, as they supposed, to their captain and to the rest left on shore, it set the pirates all in a flame, and they directly chose Roberts for their commander, vowing a severe revenge on the Portuguese.

The water was so shallow that they could not get their ship near the town, so they prepared a raft, on which they mounted several pieces of cannon with which they fired at the place, but the inhabitants having quitted it, and all the houses being of timber, they did little damage to the town. Neither dared they land to burn the place for fear of the great number of people, whom they perceived in the bushes with small arms, so they returned to their ship and the next day sailed out of the harbor.[57]

Thus fell Captain Davis, who (allowing for the course of life he had been unhappily engaged in) was a most generous humane person. And thus Roberts arose, who proved the reverse of him and did afterwards a great deal of mischief in the West Indies and on the coast of Guinea till he and his crew were happily suppressed by Sir Chaloner Ogle in the *Swallow* man-of-war, and in the engagement, Roberts and several of his people were killed.

After stocking up two vessels as well as they could, the pirates' victims sailed for England. Capt. Snelgrave and sixty others left the River Sierra Leone on May 10th in the Bristol Snow, which was commanded by Captain John Morris. They arrived safely in Bristol on August 1, 1719. This was four months after Snelgrave's slave ship was captured. He was given command of another ship soon after his return.

Notes

1. Galley: a low flat-built vessel, all or partly propelled by oars.

2. Rover: pirate.

3. Capt. Thomas Cocklyn was at the Bahama Islands in 1717 when the new governor Woodes Rogers arrived with the King's offer of pardon for all pirates who came in and surrendered themselves (see note on page 136). Only a year after recieving the pardon, Capt. Cocklyn was again plundering ships in the twenty-four gun *Rising Sun*. His career ended on the gallows.

4. Capt. Christopher Moody, with two ships under his command, was very active on the Carolina coast in 1717. (Carolina at this time included North Carolina, South Carolina, Georgia and about half of Florida.)

5. Probably a misspelling of *signor, seignior,* or *señor,* all of which mean "sir."

6. Bristol: either ships from the town of Bristol, England, or a type of ship manufactured in Bristol.

7. Capt. Moody came to light again in 1722 when he was taken prisoner by a British man-of-war on Capt. Bartholomew Roberts's *Royal Fortune.* He had been serving Roberts as one of his chief men. Moody was tried at Cape Coast Castle in what is now Ghana and hung at the age of 28.

8. Capt. Oliver la Bouche was a French pirate who roamed the east and west coast of Africa in 1718 and1719. Oliver la Bouche means "Oliver the Mouth." For some reason Snelgrave calls him "*Le Bouse,*" which means "the Cow Pie."

9. Welsh seaman Howell Davis was captured by Captain Edward England while sailing from Nassau to Madagascar in 1718. Though he refused to join the pirates, he got along well with them, charming them with his light-hearted manner. When the ship was released, its crew clapped Davis in irons and on

arriving at their destination, Davis was jailed for three months. Since he couldn't be charged with being a pirate, he was released. Despite his never being charged, he soon found he was unable to get work, since his reputation as a pirate preceeded him. Going to the Bahamas, he joined a trading ship that had a crew of ex-pirates who had accepted the King's pardon. In Martinique, he assisted in the crew's mutiny and was elected as their captain. They then set off for the western coast of Africa where they began taking prizes and soon came across the ships of Cocklyn and La Bouche.

10. The Cape Verde Islands are a group of ten larger islands and several smaller ones that lie about 320 miles off the coast of Africa.

11. They then proceeded to spend the next two days in celebration, with considerable drinking and singing.

12. League: a measurement usually of about three miles.

13. Pinnace: a boat usually rowed with eight oars, usually thinner, shallower and longer than a yawl. It is generally used as a tender (i.e. a boat that is carried or towed by a ship). It can also be a larger, two-masted vessel.

14. Flood tide: an rising or incoming tide; as opposed to an ebb tide.

15. Steerage: the forward part of the stern cabin, under the quarter-deck.

16. Reins: the kidneys or the lower part of the back.

17. Granado-shells: probably an type of early grenade. At this time grenades were usually square-faced case bottles containing gunpowder, small shot and bits of old iron.

18. Quarter: to refrain from slaying someone and often to accept them as a prisoner.

19. Westphalia is now part of northwestern Germany.

20. Forced men usually had some special skill or knowledge that the pirates needed. They included surgeons, navigators, carpenters, blacksmiths and musicians.

21. Many believed James III was the rightful heir to the throne because of heredity, but the act of settlement of 1701 prohibited any Roman Catholic from taking the throne, so when Queen Anne died in 1714, her closest Protestant heir was George I—a German who knew nothing of English customs and society and could not even speak English. He assumed the throne and created the office of prime minister, who he installed to run the country for him. Support of James III was considered treason, which was punished by being hanged by the neck until not quite dead, drawn (i.e. disemboweled), and then killed by beheading, with the body being quartered (cut into four parts) and the parts hung on display in different places in London.

22. Articles: the rules or laws that the pirates sail under and each pirate must sign upon joining a pirate crew. They were drawn up and agreed upon by the entire company on setting out on a voyage.

23. Pound: the British unit of monetary measurement, currently equal to about one and a half dollars.

24. Humphrey Morrice, a merchant in London.

25. "My private adventure" refers to the merchandise on the ship that was owned by Capt. Snelgrave, as opposed to most of the merchandise which was owned by the ship's owner or other London merchants.

26. Scrutoires: writing desks.

27. Abaft: towards the stern.

28. Hogsheads: barrels or casks containing from 100 to 140 gallons.

29. Execution Dock: the usual place for pirate hangings in London. It is at Wapping Old Stairs on the Thames.

30. St. Thomas: one of the Virgin Islands.

31. Holland: a certain kind of fine linen originally manufactured in Holland.

32. Antigua: one of the islands of the Lesser Antilles at the eastern end of the Caribbean Sea.

33. The Cape Verde Islands are a group of ten larger islands and several smaller ones that lie about 320 miles off the coast of Africa.

34. Tender: a boat that is carried or towed by a ship.

35. Such self-righteous statements sound strange coming from a slave trader, who would today be considered morally as bad or worse than the pirate he was preaching to, but in his day slavery was not only legal, it was also sanctioned by many religious authorities. Some priests even owned slaves (see page 163).

36. This pardon, also known as an Act of Grace, brought about the surrender of many pirates, though some later returned to their former profession. The proclamation read:

By the King
A PROCLAMATION FOR SUPPRESSING OF PIRATES

Whereas we have received information that several persons, subjects of Great Britain, have, since the 24th day of June in the year of our Lord, 1715, committed diverse piracies and robberies upon the high seas in the West Indies or adjoining to our plantations, which hath and may occasion great damage to the merchants of Great Britain and others trading into those parts; and though we have appointed such a force as we judge sufficient for suppressing the said pirates, yet the more effectually to put an end to the same, we have thought fit, by and with the advice of our Privy Council, to issue this our Royal Proclamation; and we do hereby promise and declare that in case any of the said pirates shall on or before the 5th of September in the year of our Lord 1718, surrender him or themselves to one of our principal secretaries of state in Great Britain or Ireland, or to any governor or deputy governor of any of our plantations beyond the seas; every such pirate and pirates so surrendering him or themselves, as aforesaid, shall have our gracious pardon, of, and for such, his or their piracy or piracies by him or them committed before the fifth of January next ensuing. And we do hereby strictly charge and command all our admirals, captains, and other officers at sea, and all our governors and commanders of any forts, castles, or other places in our plantations, and all other our officers civil and military, to seize and take such of the pirates, who shall refuse or neglect to surrender themselves accordingly. And we do hereby further declare that in case any person or persons, on or after the 6th day of September, 1718, shall discover or seize, or cause or procure to be discovered or seized, any one or more of the said pirates, so refusing or neglecting to surrender themselves as aforesaid, so as they may be brought to justice, and convicted of the said offense, such person or persons so making such discovery or seizure, or causing or procuring such discovery or seizure to be made, shall have and receive as a reward for the same, viz. for every commander of any private ship or vessel, the sum of £100 for every lieutenant, master, boatswain, carpenter and gunner, the sum of £40 for every inferior officer, the sum of £30 and for every private man, the sum of £20. And if any person or persons belonging to and being part of the crew of any pirate ship and vessel, shall on or after the said sixth day of September, 1718, seize and deliver, or cause to be seized or delivered, any commander or commanders of such pirate ship or vessel, so as that he or they be brought to justice and convicted of the said offense such person or persons, as a reward for the same shall receive for every such commander the sum of £200 which said sums the Lord Treasurer or the commissioners of our treasury for the time being, are hereby required and desired to pay accordingly.

Given at our court at Hampton-Court, the fifth day of September, 1717, in the fourth year of our reign.

GEORGE R.
God save the King.

37. An indentured servant was someone who sold themselves into service for two to seven years in return for their sea passage to the New World colonies. On arrival at their destination, the captain would auction them off to the highest bidder. Some historians estimate that up to three-fourths of all immigrants to America prior to 1775 came over in this manner.

38. Farthing: a small British coin equal to one fourth of their penny.

39. Capt. Bartholomew Roberts set the record for the most prizes known to be taken by any pirate with over 400 vessels plundered in three years.

40. At Parrot Island off the coast of Gabon on February 10, 1722, the British 60-gun man-of-war came upon Roberts's two ships early in the morning as Roberts was eating his breakfast of Salmagundi (a mixture of chopped meat, eggs and anchovies, flavored with oil, vinegar, pepper and onions). Most of his crew were still drunk from the night before or suffering from severe hangovers and were unable to put up strong resistance. Roberts tried to rally his men, but was killed early in the engagement when he was hit in the throat by grapeshot, which are a cluster of iron balls shot from a cannon. Unable to escape, his crew

soon surrendered and 254 pirates (70 of which were Africans) were taken prisoner. Capt. Chaloner Ogle, the captain of the *Swallow*, was later knighted for killing Roberts and capturing his crew.

41. Bumpers: cups or glasses filled to the brim or so that they run over.

42. Galley-built: a merchant ship that has a continuous deck along her entire length; as opposed to frigate-built ships which have a split-level deck with a descent of four or five steps from the quarter-deck and forecastle into the waist.

43. Scuttle: a hatchway or opening in the deck, large enough for a man to pass through and covered with a lid.

44. When the cannon went off, some ignited debris blew out through the small hole in the top where the flame is applied to fire the cannon.

45. Cartouch boxes: ammunition boxes for holding cartridges or cannon balls.

46. Huzza: to shout "huzza," a cheer of approval.

47. Boltsprit: a bowsprit (i.e. spar projecting from the bow of the ship) which pivots on a bolt so it can be raised or lowered. Spritsail-yard: a yard set on the underside of the bowsprit to carry the spritsail.

48. Bunghole: the hole in the side or end of a barrel or cask from which it is filled or emptied.

49. Anamabu is in what is now Ghana.

50. Cape Coast (or Corso) Castle: a castle with underground slave dungeons at Cape Coast in what is now Ghana.

51. The *Princess* was a slave ship that sailed from London for Guinea in November 1719.

52. Bartholomew Roberts was 36 years old when he was captured by fellow-Welshman Capt. Davis on June 5, 1719. He was a forced on board the pirate ship at pistol-point and would have little to do with the pirates. As a religious man who read the Bible, kept the Sabbath with prayer and by abstaining from work, and who didn't drink, swear or dance, he obviously felt out of place among these brutish, riotous drunks. Still, he was more knowledgable and skillful seaman than many captains, having already had more than twenty years experience. The pirates recognized and appreciated his talents and bravery. Six weeks later, when Capt. Davis was killed, the crew elected Roberts to take his place. He accepted, probably because he was prevented him from realizing his dream of becoming a captain otherwise because his lower-class background. He also knew that if the pirates were captured by a man-of-war, he would probably be tried as a pirate even though he was a forced man. Later he explained his decision, saying, "It is better to be a commander than a common man, since I have dipped my hands in muddy water and must be a pirate." He knew he it was impossible to stop his crew from drinking, but he did insist that the crew swear to abide by certain rules: no gambling for money; no fighting on board, with all

quarrels settled on shore by a duel; no women or boys allowed among the crew and anyone who seduced any woman would be put to death; and lights had to be put out at 8 P.M., while those who wished to continue drinking and carousing after this hour had to move up on the deck. The crew accepted these restrictions and Roberts suddenly found himself the commander of "a floating anarchy of outlaws" (as one writer vividly described it). He quickly rose to the head of his profession as one of the most successful and bloody of the pirate captains. His crew called him "Black Bart" and as time went on he became increasingly less religious and more bloody.

53. This was actually Prince's Island (now called Príncipe), which lies about 175 miles southwest of Cameroon.

54. Major-domo: the chief steward, or person in charge of running another's estate.

55. Capuchin friars: monks of a certain Franciscan order that wear a long pointed hood.

56. When Davis arrived at Prince's Island, he told the Portuguese authorities that he commanded a Royal Navy man-of-war that was hunting pirates and they treated him with all honors due the Royal Navy. When a French merchant arrived in the harbor, he quickly plundered it, telling the island's authorities that the French ship had been trading with pirates and he had confiscated its cargo "for the King's use." Davis then invited the island's chief men and some friars to a party on board the pirate ship. He intended to clap them in irons and hold them for a £40,000 ransom. Before he could carry out this plan, the Portuguese discovered what he was up to. When the pirates landed the next morning to escort the guests back to their ship, the town ambushed them.

57. Other reports say that Roberts and a force of armed men went ashore and marched right up the steep hill to the fort. The Portuguese fired a volley, but the determined pirates kept on coming, so they fled the fort, abandoning their guns and supplies. Roberts took everything of value, spiked the cannons, and fired a few cannon shots at the town from his ship as he departed.

They Hoisted a Red Flag with a Death's Head

≈≈≈

Captain Z. G. Lamson

Z. G. Lamson was captian the brigantine Belvidere *out of Beverly, Massachusetts. While he was sailing from Port-au-Prince, Jamaica, to New Orleans, he was attacked by pirates off Cay Sal, an island that is about ninety miles south of Florida and about forty miles north of Cuba. Here is an excerpt from his log.*

May 2[, 1822], fell in with a schooner and three launches, which gave chase; blowing heavy and being to windward, succeeded in getting from them the next day. At 10 A.M. made a schooner on our larboard[1] bow, lying under mainsail and jib[2]; at 11, she was on our lee quarter,[3] fired a shot, and coming up very fast; at 20 minutes past 11, gave us a second shot and hoisted a red flag with death's head and cross under it.

Finding I had a hard character to deal with, I prepared for him as well as we were able and immediately brailed up[4] my topsails,[5] hauled up my courses, clewed[6] down topgallant sails,[7] hauled down jib, braced to the main-topsail, and kept off two points, fired a musket and hoisted colors. At 12, she came alongside within ten yards distance—hailed with "God damn you, send your boat on board, or I will murder all hands of you."

He had not discovered our gun at that time. I told him I would send her directly. He immediately gave me a whole volley of musketry and blunderbusses.[8] Before I had answered him, our gun was pointed and cloth removed and we commenced as smart a fire as possible with our 24 pound carronade,[9] four muskets and seven pistols; and on our first fire six of them were seen to fall, the captain among them, or leader, being the one that hailed me. He only discharged his long gun three times alongside, as our third shot broke his carriage and his gun fell into the lee scupper.[10] He then kept up as smart a fire as he was able with muskets and blunderbusses, and dropped near the stern expecting to find more comfortable quarters, but there he got a most terrible cutting up from a brass three pounder,[11] by which he was raked within twenty yards distance with a round and two bags of forty musket balls each, which completely fixed him. I did not receive any fire from, nor even hear a word spoken on board of him, and in fact did not see anyone on deck. His vessel holding such a wind and sailing so fast she was soon clear of grapeshot range and wore[12] ship, when we counted six or seven of them, which appeared to be all that was left; the captain I saw distinctly laid on deck. Our loss was one man killed, shot through the head; about forty musket balls through the rudder case, tiller, skylight, companion way, our fore-topsail halyards[13] shot away and our try-sail halyards cut in three pieces. The pirate was 36 to 40 tons; we counted twenty-two men when he came alongside; he had a brass six or nine pounder amidships, and muskets and blunderbusses.

Z. G. Lamson

Captain Lamson had previously been taken by pirates. After being robbed and badly abused, he determined not to be taken again. To this end he had prepared his ship and crew beforehand in case they encountered pirates.

To show their gratitude for fighting off the pirates, the Louisiana State Insurance Company gave Captain Lamson $300 worth of silver and another $200 for his crew.

Notes

1. Larboard: to the left (or port) side when facing the bow.

2. Jib: a triangular sail which usually extends from the foremast to the bowsprit.

3. Lee quarter: the corner of the ship that is away from the wind.

4. Brailed up: furled the sails by tying them to the yard or mast.

5. Topsail: the sail above the mainsail, or the second sail in ascending order from the deck.

6. Clewed: wound up into a ball.

7. Topgallant sail: the sail above the topsail, or the third sail in ascending order from the deck.

8. Blunderbus: a short rifle with a flaired muzzle.

9. Carronade: a light cannon of large caliber used for short range. The "24 pound" mentioned here is the weight of the ball it fires.

10. Lee: on the side away from the wind. Scupper: the channel cut through the ship's side at the deck line to allow water to drain off the deck.

11. A very small cannon that fires three pound balls and was probably mounted on the ship's railing.

12. Wore: to reach the opposite tack by coming about in a three-quarter circle, instead of by swinging across the wind.

13. Fore-topsail halyards: vertical ropes for hoisting the sail above the foresail on the foremast.

Cocked Pistols were Clapped to Our Chests

Captain J. Evans

In 1724, Captain Charles Johnson published a classic book on pirates called A General History of the Robberies and Murders of the Most Notorious Pyrates.[1] *The book was so popular that Capt. Johnson set about expanding the book into a two-volume version. These volumes were published in 1726 and 1728 respectively. While the book contains some errors and exaggerations, overall it is quite authoritative and much of what we know today of the pirates of that period comes directly from this work.*

One error in the 1724 edition, prompted one pirate victim to write a letter to Capt. Johnson explaining the error and providing additional details of his capture. Johnson published this letter as an appendix to the second volume.

Sir,

Though I can contribute nothing to your second volume of pirates you have (as I hear) in hand, yet by your character of veracity, I persuade myself I shall oblige you in rectifying a mistake you made in your first. In [the chapter] "The Life of Captain Martel," you say the *Greyhound* galley of London, which I then commanded, fell into the hands of that pirate, who plundered her of some gold-dust, elephants' teeth, and forty slaves. The latter part of this is just, except the elephants' teeth [i.e. tusks], of which I lost, I think, none. But you are misled in the former, for Martel's company had deposed him on account (as they themselves told me) of his cruelty [and] had given him—and those who were willing to follow his fortunes—a sloop. And sending him away, [they] chose a more righteous in his place, whose name was Kennedy—by descent an Irishman, by birth a Spaniard of Cuba, and a hunter.

On my coming on board the pirate, Captain Saunders of the *Weymouth*—who was taken the day before—was the first man who spoke to me, telling me he was sorry for my misfortune. I took him for the commander of the pirate, but I soon found my mistake by his carrying me aft to the captain, who bid me welcome and drank to me in a can of wine. And some of the crew told me that it was happy for me I did not fall into the hands of their late captain, for a ship with madeira[2] wine thought fit to give them the trouble to lose some time and fire a couple of chase guns[3] before she shortened sail, which Captain Martel took for so great an affront that all the company was cut off.

But I shall now give you the particulars of my being taken. As I have said, I commanded the *Greyhound* galley on board of which I had 250 slaves bound from the coast of Guinea to Jamaica, and consigned to Messieurs Peak and Aldcroft on account of Mr. Bignell and others. On the 16th of October, 1716, about ten leagues[4] ssw from the Island of Mona,[5] in the gray of the morning, my second mate came down and acquainted me that a ship was almost on board us. We then steered about w half South and the pirate stood to the SE. His coming very near us made us edge away from him and call out to desire he would keep his luff[6] or he would be on board us. No answer was given and not a soul appeared on his decks but the man at the helm and about two more; however, the *Greyhound* got clear and crowded as usual for a market.[7] As soon as the pirate got into our wake, she wore[8] and made all the sail she could, by which means she soon came up with us (for she was clean and we foul)[9] and clewing[10] up her spritsail,[11] fired a gun with shot and at the same time let fly her jack, ensign and pennant,[12] in which was the figure of a man with a sword in his hand and an hourglass before him [and] with a death's head and bones.[13] In the jack and pendant were only the head and cross bones. I did not think fit to shorten sail, which occasioned a second shot from the pirate, which went through our main topsail.[14] Upon this I consulted my officers, and they advised the shortening sail, as we were no way in a capacity to make any defense. I followed their advice and was ordered on board the pirate, who asked me pretty civilly the usual questions: "Whence I came?" "Whither bound?" etc. My second mate and some of my men were soon shifted into the pirate, [along] with forty of the best men slaves. The women slaves they diverted themselves with and took off the irons from all the Negroes I had on board. The captain asked me if I had no gold. I assured him I had not; and, indeed, I had no more than 100 ounces—which, before I went on board the pirates, my carpenter had let into the ceiling of the great cabin. He answered only, it was very strange that I should take no gold on the coast. I answered, I had taken a considerable quantity, but as I took it in one place, I parted with it in another; which, if he would inspect my books, he would find exactly as I said. We had no more discourse then on the subject, but a while after, I and my mate were sent for into the great cabin, where the council sat. Immediately cocked pistols were clapped to our breasts and we were threatened with death in case we did not confess what gold we had on board and where it was hid. I denied that we had any and desired he would satisfy himself of the truth by examining my books. The mate answered he knew nothing of my dealings on the coasts and therefore could give no answer. He knew, indeed, I had received gold on the coast, as he had seen it brought on board, but he had seen a considerable quantity carried out of the ship. Upon this, we were ordered to withdrawal and nothing more was said. But I hearing [sic] their design was to torture me with lighted matches betwixt my fingers, I thought the loss of the use of my hands would be but poorly compensated with the saving 100 ounces of gold and therefore desired to speak to the captain himself; to him I discovered what I had and where it was concealed. He immediately sent his boat on board the *Greyhound* with my carpenter and half a dozen of his own crew, who were so impatient to be at the gold, they made a mere pincushion of the fellow's breech,[15] continually pricking his backside with their swords to hasten him. My lodging was in the hold, where one Taffier, the gunner, came down to me and snapped a pistol at my breast, which he fired afterwards upon deck. And the same man, one day as I was on the quarter-deck, struck me in the presence of his captain with his cutlass, after having reproached me with my private confession and asking if every man there had not as good and just pretension to the gold as the captain. Whether it was by accident or design that he struck with the flat of his cutlass, I know not, but the blow knocked me down and deprived me of my senses for some time.

Captain Kennedy, who seemed to have more humanity than is commonly found in men of his profession, resented this treatment of me so far that he got into his yawl[16] and put off from the ship, swearing he would not sail with men who so barbarously abused their prisoners. He, however, returned on board at their persuasions and on their promise that nothing like it should happen for the future. The night of the day in which we were taken, the pirate came to an anchor under the Island of Savona,[17] where he kept us till the 20th and then let us go in company with Captain Saunders of the ship *Weymouth*, from Boston, laden with fish and lumber for Jamaica, at which island we arrived and anchored at Port Royal the 25th in the morning.

The pirate, a little before I was taken, had met with two interloping Dutch men supposed to be bound for the Main,[18] who gave him a rough entertainment and made him glad to sheer off.

The *Weymouth* had two women passengers on board. How they passed their time I need not say; though I fancy, as they had formerly made a trip or two to the bay,[19] there was no rape committed.[20]

Notwithstanding the melancholy situation I was in, I could not refrain laughing when I saw the fellows who went on board the *Greyhound* return to their own ship, for they had, in rummaging my cabin, met with a leather powder bag and puff with which they had powdered themselves from head to foot[. They] walked the decks with their hats under their arms, minced their oaths, and affected all the airs of a beau with an awkwardness [that] would have forced a smile from a cynic.

When I was permitted to return on board the *Greyhound* and prosecute my voyage, I found all my papers torn and everything turned topsy-turvy. But this was nothing to their leaving all my Negroes out of irons, of whom I was more in fear than I had been of the pirates—for among them, the captain's humanity protected us—but we could expect no quarter[21] from the Negroes should they rebel; and in such case, we had no prospect of quelling them, for the pirates had taken away all our arms. And by opening a cask of knives, which they had scattered about the ship, they had armed the Negroes—one of whom had the insolence to collar and shake one of my men.

I therefore called my people aft and told them our security depended altogether on our resolution; wherefore, arming [our]selves with hand-spikes,[22] we drove the Negroes into the hold and afterwards, calling them up one by one, we put on their irons (which the pirates had not taken with them), took away their knives, and by these means arrived safely at our port.

If this detail is of any service to you, I have my ends. I hope, if you intend a third volume, it may induce others who have had the same misfortune of falling into the hands of pirates to assist you with their minutes.

I am, sir, your very humble servant,

J. Evans

Feb. 2, 1728

P.S. Four of my men took on with the pirates, though I remember the names of two only: Bryant Ryley, John Hammond.

Notes

1. In the past some scholars attributed this book to Daniel Defoe, though it is generally accepted today that this was wrong. In 1932, Defoe scholar J. R. Moore decided this book and several others were actually written by Defoe. Though his opinion was widely accepted for many years, it was based on very shaky internal evidence. Several modern scholars have presented stronger evidence that this and the other books were not written by Defoe afterall.

2. Madeira: a strong white wine made on the Island of Madeira.

3. Chase guns: cannons at the bow used when chasing a ship.

4. League: a measurement usually of about three miles.

5. Island of Mona is an island in the Mona Passage between what is today the Dominican Republic and Puerto Rico.

6. Luff: to keep the ship's head windward.

7. Market: two or more ships coming together to buy, sell, or trade merchandise.

8. Wore: to veer away from wind so that it blows from astern.

9. This refers to the barnacles, etc. that grow on the hull of a ship and slow her down. Pirate ships were careened often because they wanted their vessels to sail as fast as possible so they could catch prizes or escape from a man-of-war.

10. Clewing: taking in a sail.

11. Spritsail: a sail hanging from the spritsail-yard on the bowsprit.

12. Jack: the flag that shows the ship's nationality, usually flown at the bow. Ensign: a military flag or banner. Pennant: a long, narrow, usually triangular flag, usually used for signaling or decoration.

13. This sounds like the following flag which belonged to the French Captain Dulaïen, who became a pirate in 1726:

14. Main topsail: the sail on the mainmast above the mainsail, or the second sail in ascending order from the deck on the ship's primary mast.

15. Breech: the buttocks or rump.

16. Yawl: a small boat usually with four to six oars and/or a sail, usually broader, deeper and shorter than a pinnace. It is generally used as a tender.

17. The Island of Savona (Saona) is on the southeast tip of what is today the Dominican Republic.

18. The Spanish Main was the mainland of the Americas adjacent to the Caribbean, primarily from the Isthmus of Panama to the mouth of the Orinoco River in Venezuela.

19. Bay: (? possibly the Bay of Honduras).

20. Capt. Evans seems to have believed that these must have been loose women or prostitutes, and therefore their rape could not be considered rape or that they charged the pirates for their services.

21. Quarter: to refrain from slaying someone and often to accept them as a prisoner.

22. Handspike: a sort of crowbar or lever, usually made of wood.

I Waited to Have My Doom Determined

Captain George Roberts

Captain George Roberts sailed from London in September 1721 as the chief mate of the twenty-two gun ship King Sagamore, *under Capt. Andrew Scott. They were headed for Virginia, by way of Barbados. When he reached Virginia, Capt. Roberts was to take possession of sloop called* Dolphin *and fit her out with cargo to trade for slaves in Guinea. On arriving in Virginia, Capt. Scott—who was apparently deeply in dept—could neither pay Capt. Roberts his wages nor some money he had borrowed before the voyage. Instead Capt. Scott offered to buy a ship on credit, using the unsold goods as collateral, and make Capt. Roberts part owner of the ship equal to the amount he was owed. Capt. Roberts had no choice but to accept this. The sloop* Margaret *was bought and placed in their names, plus that of merchant in Barbados to whom presumably Capt. Scott also owed money. Later, when Capt. Scott told the pirate captains Low and Russel that they should capture this ship, he may have hoped to wipe out several depts at once.*

At any rate, Capt. Roberts fitted the ship out as best he could and the two ships—the King Sagamore *and the* Margaret*—headed out together for the Cape Verde Islands (which are a group of ten larger islands and several smaller ones that lie about 320 miles off the coast of Africa), but they lost each other in a storm. Capt. Scott reached these islands about two weeks before Roberts. Shortly after Roberts arrived, he was captured by the pirates.*

This incident took place in the fall of 1722. Capt. Roberts wrote about it in his book, The Four Voyages of Capt. George Roberts . . . written by Himself *(1726).*[1]

Next morning about dawn, as it was my usual custom, I turned out. It continuing still calm and as the day broke out, looking about I espied three sail of ships off the bay, one ship to the eastward, another ship to the westward, and the third right of the middle of the bay. The first of them that I made plain with my glass was the eastwardmost ship, which seemed to be a full-built and laden ship, and I took the rest to be the same, and of her company, and imagined that perhaps they might want water, etc. They had but very little wind in the offing and it continued still calm in the bay. I saw them bring to, then edge away, but could not perceive any signals made by them; and seeing them act thus, I still continued in my first opinion, that they wanted to touch at the island for wood, water, etc., but that perhaps they might be unacquainted with the roads² or harbors of the islands; insomuch that I was almost of the mind to send my mate off with the boat to conduct them in.

As soon as the day broke up clear, that they made me, the middlemost of the three stood right in for me, and as the sun rose the wind freshened and backed more to the eastward, as is usual there after calm nights. As she drew nigher, I made her with my glass to be a schooner and full of hands all in their white shirts, and likewise I saw a whole tier of great guns; and then, indeed, I began to suspect what they were: but I had no remedy but patiently to wait the event, for I could do nothing except I put the vessel ashore, which would have been mere madness to have done although I had been sure they were pirates; and I was so surrounded by them that there was no possibility of escaping from them, and especially, it holding calm within the bay; and they coming in with the day-breeze, came in as fast as the wind.

He came in under an English ensign, jack and pennant and as soon as I perceived his colors I hoisted my ensign. He had eight guns, and six pattereroes,³ and seventy men. He stretched ahead of us and haled us. I answered him. He asked where the sloop belonged to. I answered, "To London." He asked from whence we came? I told him, "From Barbados." He said it was very well; he knew that; and so brought to ahead of us and bid me send my boat on board of him; which accordingly I did with two hands in her and I myself kept walking on the deck.

The captain of the schooner, whose name was John Lopez, a Portuguese (as I was told afterwards; but then went by the name of John Russel, pretending, though falsely, that he was born in the northern parts of England) asked the people who came on board of him with the boat where the master of the sloop was, who answered that he was on board, and sent them with the boat to know what they wanted. He asked them which was the master of the sloop? So they showed me to him as I was walking the sloop's deck and then he immediately called to me saying, "You dog! You son of a bitch! You speckled-shirt dog!" (for I had a speckled holland shirt[4] on and was slip-shoed and without stockings, being just as I turned out of my cabin). So he still continued calling in that manner and I, considering what hands I was fallen into and that it would be easy for them to send a ball through me for my silence, which, perhaps, they might deem contempt of them, as indeed it was, I thought it was the safest and wisest course to answer according to the proverb, "when your hand is in the lion's mouth, get it out as easy as you can," and not in the least to seem to resent anything that they said or did to me, but endeavor to submit, if not with a willing mind, yet with a seeming patience, as in truth I could do no otherwise, except I would with a foolish rashness provoke them to be my executioners; and God knows a small provocation, nay, if they do but conceit it so, will occasion the taking any honest man's life away. So I answered him, "Ho lo." He said, "You dog, you, why did not you come on board with the boat, you son of a bitch? I will drub[5] you, you dog, within an inch of your life, and that inch too." I made him answer, "That he only commanding the boat on board, I did not think he required me, but if he pleased to send the boat, I would come and wait upon him on board." He answered, "Aye, you dog, and I will teach you better manners."

Upon this, he ordered some of the pirates into my boat to fetch me, as also eight or ten more of them to take possession of the sloop meanwhile, which accordingly was done and I came along side of the schooner. The captain of her still continued to threaten me with drubbing to teach me better manners than so to affront him. I answered, "I did not design to affront him or any of the company. "Damn you, you dog," said he, "Do not stand there to chatter. Come on board." So up the side I came, this glib-tongued captain standing at the entering-place with his cutlass ready drawn in his hand to receive me.

The least I expected was a sound drubbing bout and I had abundance of reason to apprehend even worse than that (he still continuing to threaten what he would do to me when I came in), but a man in a gold-laced hat, whom afterwards I understood to be the gunner, looked over the side as I was coming up and said, "Come up, master, you shall not be abused." After I got in, the captain came up with his cutlass as though he was going to cleave me down and said, "Dog, you, what was the reason you did not come on board when the boat first came? What do you think you deserve?" I answered, "If I had done amiss, it was through ignorance and for want of knowing better, and hoped that he would excuse this my fault, I not knowing who or what they were. Then he rapped out an oath with a "Damn you, you dog, what or who do you think we are?"

I paused a while, not well knowing what answer to make for fear of offending them again; for one displeasing word is as much as the best man in the world's life is worth while in their clutches. However, after a little pause I told him I believed they were gentlemen of fortune belonging to the sea. At which he answered and said, "You lie by God, we are pirates, by God." Then I answered again and said, "Well, gentlemen, now I know who you are, but not before, and am sorry I have not carried myself as I should; but, as I had told them before, I said it was my ignorance, never having been taken by such gentlemen as they before and therefore did not know the way of behaving myself to them as they might have expected had I been acquainted with their ways or customs (though I had been once taken by pirates before coming from Newfoundland when I was a youth, but I did not then think it proper to take notice of it to them, but the reverse, and thought it the safer course at present to pretend ignorance as the only way to appease his unmerited, though dangerous and threatening wrath.)

So after he had hectored and bounced thus a while, he asked me in a gaming way why I had not put on my best clothes when I came a visiting such gentlemen as they were. I told him that that was the common dress which I wore on board my own vessel in a morning and did not know that I should have paid a visit to such gentlemen as they were when I dressed myself. Besides, when he called me to come on board of him, he threatened me so that I came from on board my own vessel as it were in a fright that made me have but very little thought, or stomach either, to change my present dress; but if he pleased to let me go on board the sloop and grant me the liberty, it would not be too late yet to dress myself in better clothes. "No, damn you," said he, "Now it is too late. What clothes we took you in, you shall keep. But your sloop and what is in her is ours." I told him I perceived it was, but still hoped, as I wholly lay at his mercy, he would be so generous as to take only what they had occasion for and leave me the rest. He answered, as to that he could say nothing as yet, that being a company business to decide; and withal demanded of me an account of everything that was on board of the sloop, particularly of the cargo and what money I had or knew to be on board, and if I did not give a true and exact account and discover [i.e. reveal] to him everything, and if upon their rummaging they found the least thing on board which I did not discover, they would set the sloop on fire and me in her. He added that he had a full account of what cargo I brought out from Barbados and therefore if I had touched anywhere and disposed of any of it, I must not conceal the money, for if I did, I should fare the worse.

All the rest of the Johns[6] that were standing by in a seeming friendly manner, told me that it would be much better for me to make a full and true discovery of everything, especially of money, arms and ammunition, which, as they said, were the principal things they sought after; for it was their manner to punish liars and concealers, especially of those things they had now mentioned, in a very severe manner. I told them I would give them an account of everything on board as exact as my memory would suffer me; which accordingly I then did and withal told them that if I failed in giving them an exact account of everything, that it was not with a design to conceal anything from them, but merely the fault of my memory, for which, if any happened, I hoped they would excuse me and not punish me as culpable for that which was not a willful or designed omission. "But," said I, "if you please, gentlemen, to give me liberty to go on board of the sloop for my papers and to peruse them, I shall then be able to give you a very exact inventory, I think, I may say of everything on board, except what properly belonged to my men." But Captain Russel told me, no, and as for my papers, he would take care of them and if anything was found on board, more than I had given an account of, I must stand clear.

All this while the pirates were rummaging on board the sloop, which, when they had done, I suppose, as much as they thought fit, some of them came on board with an account of what they had found or seen there, which was nothing more than what I had told them of before, saving a ring and my silver buckles, which really I had forgotten, otherwise I should have mentioned them. However, they were so generous as to keep them.

By this time the priest and the blacks [i.e. some people Capt. Roberts was transporting from one island to another where they would meet the priest's ship and who had camped on shore for the night], mistrusting how the game went, were got a pretty way up the rocks in order to escape into the mountains, which the pirates observing, Captain Russel asked me if I knew who those people were. I, not knowing but the same question might have been asked of some of my people and that perhaps they might have told them, and not being willing, and indeed I may say not daring to be caught in a lie, ingenuously told them the truth and said they were the priest and some blacks with him who were to have gone with me to the Isle of Sal,[7] if I had not thus met with them. He then asked what we were to have done at the Isle of Sal. So I told him the occasion and also of the bargain which I had made with him on that head. He said the priest would never see his sloop more. I asked him if he heard anything of her. He said yes, they had taken her, and their own gang that they had put on board of her ran away with her, with a booty of eight hundred pounds in money, besides other goods; and also he said he had an account of me and what cargo I brought out of Barbados, and that in all probability, I was then arrived on St. Nicholas; which information, and also that the priest and governor of St. Nicholas had a pretty large bag of dollars,[8] which each of them had boarded up was the only occasion of their coming here, otherwise, if they had not received this information, they were designed to have gone directly from the Island of Bona Vista, after they had cleaned and fitted their vessels on their intended enterprise.

I told him I could not imagine who could give him that information of me for that I had hardly communicated my design of touching at these islands to any that I thought was or could be liable to fall into their hands, except one person. He told me it was one that came out in company with me from Barbados; and to be short, said, it was Captain Scott told them, and how that all the sloop was his, and he had filled my hold full of sugar, rum, etc. and that he was sure I was by this time arrived at the Island of St. Nicholas, St. Antonia, or some of the westward islands, unless I run away with his sloop and cargo; and likewise that he had seen, when he was last trading at St. Nicholas, both the priest's and governor's money, which, as he reported to them, he was certain, neither of them could have less than 1,600 or 2,000 dollars apiece. So I asked them how it was with Captain Scott. They told me he was but indifferent yet, they thought he was better than he deserved and told me how they had burnt his ship and that he had been put ashore by them at Bona Vista, where they believed he at present was.[9]

Russel, still eyeing the priest and blacks, asked me if I thought it was possible to go ashore and catch them. I told him I thought not. He asked me why. For he had men on board [who] could out-walk or out-run them, he was sure. I told him I believed not; for before his boat could put ashore, they would be got two or three miles up into the country, and that the way there was so steep and rocky, that I was sure his men could not climb up, much less pretend to catch them. He answered it did not signify much, for he would have him, meaning the priest, and some more of them before this time tomorrow; and asked me which was the nighest anchoring-place to the town. And also from which anchoring-place was the smoothest path or road up to it. I told him I did not know for certain, neither was I anyways acquainted on the island, having never been half a quarter of mile up from the sea-side on any part of it. He said I might have heard from the inhabitants. I told him I did hear some of the inhabitants say that the road of Paragheesi[10] was the nighest anchoring-place to the town of all the roads about the island; but what sort of pathway it was up to town, I had not so exactly inquired as to be able to satisfy him in that. "Well," says Russel, "we will go to Paragheesi, and," says he to me, "you shall pilot us thither." I told him I never had been there and did not know but there might be sunken rocks in the way; and, therefore, thought myself very unqualified to take charge of the vessel thither; but, I told him, there were two blacks on board the sloop, both natives and fishermen of that island, and that both of them was my pilot and might be, as far as I knew, very capable to pilot their vessel into the road; or perhaps might discover to them some more convenient place to anchor or land at. Upon this, he swore and damned, saying, "What! Do you think I will let a Negro pilot me? No, no"; but swore I would pilot the vessel into an anchoring-place, and stand clear if the least accident happened to her. I told him I would do as well as I could and that I acquainted him already of my little knowledge of the island. "Well," says he, "do as well as you can. Do as you would do was it your own vessel." I told him I would. "Well," said he, "we desire you to do no more"; and immediately he gave orders to make the best of our way down to Paragheesi, which accordingly was done; and the pirates on board my sloop slipped the cable because they would not take the pains to weigh the anchor, and so, through sloth and laziness, left a good cable and anchor behind.

All this time, the other two ships lay too in the offing, but as soon as they saw us make sail down to leeward,[11] the *Rose Pink*, having thirty-six guns mounted, commanded by Edward [or Ned] Low, who was then commodore of them, edged in towards us, upon which we edged off towards him and spoke with him and Russel gave him an account of what had passed, and of his design of landing that evening upon the island of St. Nicholas in order to take the priest and governor, if he approved of their resolution. Which the commodore said he did and immediately ordered his great launch to be manned, and sent some more of his ship's company to join and reinforce the schooner's crew and to go ashore with them in the expedition; which was accordingly done.

Then we haled in for the shore again and when we were got the length of Porto Lappa—which is a road or bay lying about midway or a little more between Currisal[12] and Paragheesi—one of the schooner's company raps out a great oath that that was the best place to land at and the nighest to the town; upon which Captain Russel, whom I understood then to be not only captain of the schooner, but also quartermaster general of all the companies, asked me if it was as the fellow said. I told him I could not tell; it might be so as far as I knew, for all the knowledge I had as to that was only by the relation of the inhabitants, and therefore could not be certain myself, not knowing but they might deceive me in the relations they made me. The fellow swore that he knew the place perfectly well and that he had landed there before and was acquainted with the way up to the town. Upon which, Captain Russel ordered to stand in for the Bay of Porto Lappa and likewise directed the gang that was to go ashore to have their arms ready and every man to prepare so many rounds of cartridges, both for pistols and pieces, and to be in a readiness to embark in the boats as soon as we should be got nigh enough to the land. When we came within about half a league[13] of the shore, the pirates were manned by Russel's order, who also went ashore and headed them, to the number of thirty-five, besides those which went in the boats to bring them off again. We were ordered by Russel, as soon as the boats were put off, to make the best of our way down to Paragheesi and come to an anchor and stay there till further orders, and the boats were to follow us down to the bay after they had landed the men at Porto Lappa.

All this was accordingly performed and we cast anchor in the Old Road, where I had anchored before in the sloop; and the boats, after they had landed the men, also came down and got on board of us about 6 o'clock that evening; the two ships keeping plying off and on, open with where we lay.

Here we rode all night, during which the commodore kept out a light, as we also did to answer him; and next day Captain Russel with all his company came down to Paragheesi and brought with them as prisoners, the priest and the old governor's son with five or six men blacks; and upon their haling the schooner, the boats were manned and sent ashore for them and they were all brought off together. It was about one o'clock in the afternoon when they came on board, and immediately we weighed and stood off to the ships, which were then lying to in the offing; and when we were come within call of the commodore, he haled us and asked how all fared and what luck. And was answered by Russel that he would wait on him on board and give him a full and particular account. Accordingly the launch was forthwith manned and the men sent from the commodore to join the schooner's men, for the shore expedition were ordered to embark in her to go on board their own ship; which being done, I was ordered also to get into her to present myself and pay my respects to the great Captain Low, their commodore. Accordingly I went into the launch and Russel followed us in his own boat with the priest and the other prisoners, which they had brought off the Island of St. Nicholas.

When I came on board the *Rose Pink*, the company welcomed me on board and said they were sorry for my loss; but told me I must go to pay my respects to the captain, who was in the cabin and waited for me. I was ushered in by an officer, who I think was their gunner, and who, by his deportment, acted as though he had been master of the ceremonies; though I do not remember to have heard of such an officer or office mentioned among them, neither do I know whether they are always so formal on board their commodore at the first reception of their captivated masters of vessels. When I came into the cabin, the officer who conducted me thither, after paying his respects to the commodore, told him that I was the master of the sloop which they had taken the day before and then withdrew out of the cabin, leaving us two alone.

Captain Low, with the usual compliment, welcomed me on board and told me he was very sorry for my loss and that it was not his desire to meet with any of his countrymen, but rather with foreigners, excepting some few that he wanted to chastise for their roguishness, as he called it. "But however," says he, "since fortune has ordered it so, that you have fallen into our hands, I would have you to be of good cheer and not to be cast down." I told him that I also was very sorry that it was my chance to fall into their way; but still encouraged myself in the hopes that I was in the hands of gentlemen of honor and generosity; it being still in their power whether to make this, their capture of me, a misfortune or not. He said it did not lie in his particular power; for he was but one man, and all business of this nature must be done in public and by a majority of votes by the whole company; and though neither he, nor, he believed, any of the company, desired to meet with any of their own nation (except some few persons for the reasons before mentioned) yet when they did, it could not well be avoided, but that they must take as their own what providence sent them and as they were gentlemen who entirely depended upon fortune, they dared not be so ungrateful to her as to refuse anything which she put into their way; for if they should despise any of her favors, though never so mean, they might offend her and thereby cause her to withdraw her hand from them; and so, perhaps, they might perish for want of those things which in their rash folly they slighted. He then, in a very obliging tone, desired me to sit down, he himself all this time not once moving from his seat, which was one of the great guns, though there were chairs enough in the cabin; but I suppose he thought he should not appear so martial or hero-like if he sat on a chair, as he did on a great gun.

After I had sat down he asked me what I would drink. I thanked him and told him I did not much care for drinking; but out of a sense of the honor he did me in asking, I would drink anything with him which he pleased to drink. He told me it would not avail me anything to be cast down. It was fortune of war and grieving or vexing myself might be of no good consequence in respect to my health; besides, it would be more taking, he said, with the company, to appear brisk, lively, and with as little concern as I could. "And come," says he, "you may, and I hope you will, have better fortune hereafter." So ringing the cabin-bell, and one of his *valet de chambres*, or rather *valet de cabins*, appearing, he commanded him to make a bowl of punch in the great bowl—which was a rich silver one, and held, I believe, about two gallons—which being done, he ordered likewise some wine to be set on the table and accordingly two bottles of claret were brought; and then he took the bowl and drank to me in punch; but bid me pledge him in which[ever] I liked best; which I did in wine. He told me that what he could favor me in, he would, and wished that it had been my fortune to have been taken by them ten days or a fortnight sooner; for then, he said, they had abundance of good commodities, which they took in two Portuguese outward-bound Brazil-men, viz. cloth, as well linens as woolens, both fine and coarse, hats of all sorts, silk, iron and other rich goods in abundance, and believed he could have prevailed with the company even to have loaded my sloop. But now they had no goods at all, he believed, having disposed of them all either by giving them to other prizes, etc. or heaving the rest into David Jones's Locker (i.e. the sea); but did not know, but it might be his lot, perhaps, to meet with me again when it might lie in his way to make me a retaliation for my present loss; and he did assure me that when such an occasion, as he was but now a speaking of, offered, I might depend he would not be wanting to serve me in anything that might turn to my advantage as far as his power or interest could reach. I could do no less, in common civility, and the truth is I dared do no less, than thank him.

By this time, word was brought into the cabin that the Quartermaster-General Russel was come on board with the priest and the other prisoners, which they had brought off from the Island of St. Nicholas. Captain Low ordered Captain Russel, the priest, and the governor's son of St. Nicholas to be called into the great cabin, and accordingly they came and the cabin was immediately filled with officers and some others of the principal pirates, who I suppose by their long standing or their activity in villainy had signalized [i.e. distinguished] themselves for principals of the crew; out of whom, as occasion served, they also chose their officers, etc.

The cabin having been thus filled, Low, after compliments passed, bid Russel and the prisoners sit down and then asked Russel, what news and how the game went. Upon which, Russel began his relation in these words, as near as I can remember:

"According to our last agreement in consultation," says he, "we landed with thirty-five men on the Island of St. Nicholas yesterday in the afternoon as soon as possibly we could after the taking the sloop and putting things in such order as was proper; and immediately after our landing, we apprehended two blacks of the natives who were come down to know who we were and what account we were upon, that they might go and acquaint the governor of us, as they said. But we retarded their journey by making them our guides to direct and show us the way to the town; and it was well we happened to meet them, for night coming on, we should never have found the way; and besides, if we had, we should not have been able in the dark to know whether we were going right or wrong, the way being moreover very rocky, stony and there being some very steep, as well as high ascents and descents; so that if we had not had a guide, we should have been so discouraged as to defer our journey till the succeeding day, which would have balked us; for if we had not got up to town last night before we were discovered, the rumor of our coming would, I believe, have frightened all the inhabitants out of the town and caused them to fly to the mountains, and then we should have thought that there was a booty, but that our being discovered gave them an opportunity of conveying it away. But by our taking those men, we prevented any rumor or notice of our coming and so were assured there was no booty there but what we found.

"We got to town about nine o'clock at night and by estimation from the place of our landing to the town was about twelve miles. We went directly to the governor's house, and having set a guard there to prevent anybody's going out or in that there might be no opportunity of conveying anything out of the house, I took some hands with me and went to the priest's house, whom we found not to have been long come home from Currisal and had not the least thought of our so sudden arrival here, believing it was impossible that we could reach the town till the day following, if we were designed to come up; neither had he any notice of our arrival before, till his own eyes confirmed it. But, however, he did not seem to be much surprised.

"I set a guard to prevent anything being conveyed out and the priest ordered such victuals as he had to be set on the table and wine enough and told me that he could not entertain us at such an unseasonable time of night as he would, and hoped we would excuse him for not being better provided and take the will for the deed, adding that to such as we found, we were very welcome, wishing it had been better; but if we tarried till next day, he said, we should be supplied plentifully with whatever the island afforded. Upon which I thanked him and told him I came of an errand and must perform it, which was that we had a positive information from very good hands who had been eyewitnesses that he, as also the governor, had good store of dollars, as well of gold, boarded up and that we were come to share it with them, it being one great branch of our trade not to let money lie rusting and cankering in old bags or chests, but to make it move and circulate whenever we could come at it. At which the priest, without any apparent concern, replied that whoever gave us that information, gave a false one, as anyone might easily conceive if they but gave themselves leave to consider how unlikely, nay, he might very well say, impossible it was to get money in those barren, uncultivated and commerce-less islands. I told him I was master of but two senses that could give me satisfaction whether the information was false or what he now said was true, which were seeing and feeling. He said I was welcome to make sure of those senses to my satisfaction, 'which I am sure,' says he, 'will then fully confirm the truth of what I have said'; and immediately ordered wax-candles, (they having no other there, and them only for the use of the church, being all consecrated, and sent thither by the Bishop of St. Jago,[14] whose business it is to send consecrated candles, oil, etc. for the use of the church to all the adjacent islands to be lighted; and we searched all the house, chests, trunks, and everywhere throughout and about the house and found nothing worth taking, and only about twenty dollars in money which I did not think it worth our while to take from him.

"From thence I went to the governor's house and searched here as narrowly as we could and found less there; after which I disposed of my men as I thought most convenient for the reposing and refreshing them after their fatiguing journey, but yet with a due regard withal to our own security by setting a guard and ordering the rest to repose as well as they could and not one of them to offer to stir out of the governor's house; and withal giving them a strict charge to be ready with their arms at all calls and at a moment's warning, and not one of them to unarm or unsling his pistols; which was accordingly very regularly and orderly performed; and next morning we concluded that not having lighted on the booty according to information given, or rather the information being false, no such booty being there, we had therefore agreed to seize and bring on board the governor, priest, and four or five besides of the principal inhabitants for your more ample satisfaction."

Captain Low, sitting as demure and attentive all the while, as a judge upon the bench, of a sudden started, as it were, out of a deep study and interrupting Russel in his story, said, "Zounds, what satisfaction is this to me or the company? We did not want these fellows, damn them. No, we wanted their money, if they had any; and if not, they might have stayed ashore or gone to the Devil where they belong to, so we had had the money."

To this Russel replied in a something more stern tone and said, "Captain Low, we had as much reason for and interest in getting the money, if there had been any, as you had or any of the company could have, and we did as much as could be done to find it; neither do I believe they have any more than what we saw, and which, had I taken it, could not have amounted to sixpence apiece when shared among the company and it was not worth having our name called in question for such an insignificant trifle. For my part, I am for something that is worth taking and if I cannot light with such, I will never give the world occasion to say I am a poor, pitiful, or mean-spirited fellow. No, I will rob for something of value or else will not rob at all, especially from the people among whom we may reckon one of our places of refuge in case any of us should be separated from the company, or the company break, etc. and therefore I boldly affirm that by drawing on us an odium from these people for a trifle might be of pernicious consequence to us, and more especially if any of us should be put to such extremities as might happen. For this," said he, "would by all men be accounted a narrow-souled, mean-spirited folly and we should, to all futurity, be cursed by our own fraternity as often as any of them were pinched with the effects, which would be very likely to follow such an oversight."

Hereupon Captain Low interrupting him replied that what he said was very true and carried abundance of sense and reason with it, and desired that he would proceed no farther on that head, adding that he was satisfied in what he did and believed that there was neither want of judgment or courage in the management of it; but withal desired that he would proceed to finish the history of his expedition. "But come," says he, "let us do nothing rashly"; and so fills a bumper[15] and gave his service to Captain Russel and willing me better success for the future. I thanked him, and so the cup was ordered to pass round with a full bumper to everyone, except me, who alone was permitted to drink wine.

After everyone had drank round, Captain Russel resumed his tale and proceeded thus :

"Captain Low, as I told you before, how that we had resolved to bring the priest, the governor, and four or five blacks on board to satisfy you and the company that it was not fear nor cowardice that deterred us from obtaining the booty, which we and you expected to find; so, pursuant to our resolution, I sent for the priest to come to me at the governor's house; but the person I sent found that he was fled away in the night with all his slaves, saving an old, lame woman who told them this. Hereupon I told the governor, who was a very ancient Negro, if he did not cause the priest to be brought to me in two hours time, it should be the worse for the inhabitants of the island. The governor answered that he much feared it was impossible to bring him in, by reason he heard that he was fled with some of his slaves to the mountains and that it was very easy for him to remain there several months, notwithstanding all the means which he could possibly use to discover him. He gave an instance of this in one of the priest's slaves, who formerly had run away from his master, and notwithstanding the priest used all manner of diligence to apprehend him, (and that he could do more that way than anyone) yet that slave was undiscovered for near twelve months and by most people thought to be dead. The governor added that the same slave being with him now, he had no doubt thoroughly acquainted his master with all the caverns, caves and other places of secrecy. Upon which I told him if he did not bring him or cause him to be brought and delivered to me in three hours time at farthest, I would, as soon as that time was expired, burn the town down to ashes. He answered he lay at my mercy and would use all diligence to find and cause him if possible to be delivered to me within the time limited, but hoped that after he had used his utmost endeavor, if it should prove fruitless, that I would be more considerate than to make the innocent suffer for the fault of the guilty. I told him the time was set and I would not defer burning the town down to the ground one minute after that time was expired if the priest was not delivered into my hands. Then he told me he hoped we would not kill him nor abuse him in his person. As for our goods, says he, them we leave wholly to your mercy. I told him the priest should not be hurt in his body if he came and surrendered himself within the time limited and behaved himself like a man. The governor sent immediately several parties of his blacks in quest of the priest and, in the mean time, I ordered him to kill an ox and dress it as soon as he could for my men, and also to get a pipe of wine and set it abroach,[16] which he accordingly did. In about two hours, some of the blacks who had been sent out by the governor in quest of the priest, returned and brought word that they had found the priest and secured him from escaping, but he had sent them to desire the governor to pray me not to be angry and heartily to beg my pardon, being very sorry that he had given me so much trouble, and in affiance on my goodness, he would wait upon me and cast himself entirely upon my mercy. I told the governor he might come without fear, for he should not be abused. Upon which he came and very submissively asked my pardon and hoped I would not be angry for his being so rude after I and our company had behaved ourselves so civilly; repenting that he should be so foolish as to sneak away so and abscond, having no reason, as he believed to do so, but his own groundless apprehensions; adding that he was persuaded to it, or else he should not have done it of himself neither. I bid him not be afraid, we would not hurt him, but told him he had like to have hurt the whole if and by his unadvised rashness; for if he had not come as he did, I was resolved, as soon as my men had got their victuals, to have burned the town down to ashes, church and all. He said he thanked God that he was, he hoped, come time enough to save it, and thanked me for my clemency in deferring it so long. I told him, it was very well and had him sit down, which he did, and sent to his house for wine, fowls, and an anchor of rum, which were brought and we made ourselves very merry, eat and drank heartily, kept open house and treated all the natives that came to us; the greatest part having taken example by the priest, I suppose, and fled out to the mountains for fear of us, though my design was not to hurt any of them while they continued civil.

"After we had eaten and drank and sufficiently refreshed ourselves, I told the priest and governor that they and six more whom I should choose must go on board the commodore. The priest seemed to be much surprised at this news and told me that he hoped we would not carry them quite away from the island, nor make slaves of them. Upon which I told him I was a Roman Catholic as well as he. Neither should there be any harm done to him and that they should only go on board the commodore and satisfy him that the information which he had of their having no money was false. At which he seemed to be very well contented and accordingly we came down and got on board. And now here they are, do you with them as you please."

Captain Russel having thus ended his relation, Captain Low said he had done very well and asked the priest several questions, after which he directed them to be put on board the schooner and from her to be put ashore. But I was ordered to remain on board the commodore till by a general vote of the company it should be determined how I and the sloop were to be disposed of; and Captain Low ordered a hammock and bedding to be fixed for me and told me that he would not oblige me to sit up later than I thought fit nor drink more than suited my own inclination; and that he liked my company no longer than his was agreeable to me; adding that there should be no confinement or obligation as to drinking or sitting up, but I might drink and go to sleep when I pleased without any exceptions being taken, ordering me to want for nothing that was on board; for I was very welcome to anything that was there as to eatables and drinkables. I thanked him and told him I would, with all due gratefulness, make use of that freedom which he was so generous to offer me, etc. About eight o'clock at night I took my leave of him and went to my hammock, where I continued all night with thoughts roving and perplexed enough, not being able as yet, to guess what they designed to do with me, whether they intended to give me the sloop again or to burn her—as I heard it tossed about by some—or to keep me as a prisoner on board or put me ashore.

My two boys and mate remained still on board the sloop, but all the rest they took on board of them, not once so much as asking them whether they would enter with them, only demanding their names, which the steward wrote down in their roll-book.

About eight o'clock in the morning I turned out and went upon deck, and as I was walking backwards and forwards—as is usual amongst us sailors—there came up one of the company to me and bid me good-morrow and told me he was very sorry for my misfortune. I answered, so was I. He looked at me and said he believed I did not know him. I replied it was true I did not know him; neither at present could I call to mind that ever I had seen him before in the whole course of my life. He smiled and said he once belonged to me and sailed with me when I was commander of the *Susannah* in the year 1718. (At that time I was master of a ship called the *Susannah*, about the burden of 300 tons, whereof was sole owner Mr. Richard Stephens, merchant, living at this present writing in Shad-Shames, Southwark Side, near London ————). In the interim came up two more who told me they all belonged to me in the *Susannah* at one time. By this time I had recollected my memory so far as just to call them to mind and that was all; and then I told them I did remember them. They said they were truly very sorry for my misfortune and would do all that lay in their power to serve me, and told me they had among them the quantity of about forty or fifty pieces of white linen cloth and six or eight pieces of silk, besides some other things; and they would also, they said, make what interest they could for me with their consorts and intimates, and with them would make a gathering for me of what things they could and would put it on board for me as soon as the company had determined that I should have my sloop again. They then looked about them as though they had something to say that they were not willing anybody should hear; but as it happened there was nobody nigh us, which was an opportunity very rare in these sort of ships of speaking without interruption: But we lying too all night, nobody had anything to do, but the lookers-out at the topmast-head; the mate of the watch, quartermaster of the watch, helmsman, etc. being gone down to drink a dram, I suppose, or to smoke a pipe of tobacco or the like. However it was, we had the quarterdeck entirely to ourselves and they, seeing the coast clear, told me with much seeming concern that if I did not take abundance of care, they would force me to stay with them for my mate had informed them that I was very well acquainted on the coast of Brazil and they were bound down along the coast of Guinea and afterwards designed to stretch over to the coast of Brazil: That there was not one man of all the company that had ever been upon any part of that coast; and that there was but one way for me to escape being forced; but I must be very close and not discover [i.e. reveal] what they were going to tell me; for if it was known that they had divulged it, notwithstanding they were entered men, and as much of the company as any of them, yet they were sure it would cost them no smaller a price for it than their lives. I told them I was very much obliged to them for their goodwill and did not wish them to have any occasion for my service; but if ever it should be so, they might depend it should be to the utmost of my power; and as for my betraying anything that they should tell me of, they could not fear that, because my own interest would be a sufficient tie upon me to the contrary; and were it not so, and that I was sure to get mountains of gold by divulging it to their prejudice, I would sooner suffer my tongue to be plucked out.

They said they did not much fear my revealing it, because the disclosing it would rather be a prejudice to me than an advantage, and therefore out of pure respect to me they would tell me; which was thus: "You must know," said they, "that we have an article which we are sworn to, which is not to force any married man against his will to serve us. Now we have been at a close consultation whether we should oblige you to go with us, not as one of the company, but as a forced prisoner in order to be our pilot on the coast of Brazil, where we are designed to cruise and hope to make our voyage; and your mate," continued they, "has offered to enter with us, but desires to defer it till we have determined your case. Now your mate, as yet, is ignorant of our articles,[17] we never exposing them to any till they are going to sign them. He was asked whether you were married or not and he said he could not tell for certain, but believed you were not. Upon which we spoke and said we had known you several years and had sailed with you in a frigate-built ship[18] of 300 tons or more; that you were an extraordinary good man to your men, both for usage and payment; and that to our knowledge, you were married and had four children then. However, there is one man who would fain [i.e. gladly] have the company break through their oath on that article, and tells them, they may and ought to do it because it is a case of necessity, they having no possibility of getting a pilot at present for that coast, except they take you. And in their run along the coast of Guinea, if they should light of anybody that was acquainted with the coast of Brazil, and no way exempted from serving them by the articles, then they might take him and turn you ashore, but until such is offered, he did not see but the oath might be dispensed with. But," continued they, "Captain Low is very much against it, and told them that it would be an ill precedent, and of bad consequence; for if we once take the liberty of breaking our articles and oath, then there is none of us can be sure of anything. If," said Captain Low, "you can persuade the man upon any terms to stay with us, as a prisoner or otherwise, well and good; if not, do not let us break the laws that we have made ourselves and sworn to." They went on and told me that most of the company seemed to agree with Captain Low's opinion, but Russel, said they, "seemed to be sadly nettled at it that his advice was not to be taken; and," continued they, "you will be asked the question, we reckon, by and by, when Russel comes on board and all the heads meet again; but you must be sure to say you are married and have five or six children; for it is only that that will prevent your being forced; though, you may depend upon it, Russel will do what he can to persuade the company to break the article, which we hope they will not, nor shall they ever have our consent; and indeed, there are very few of the company but what are against it, but Russel bears a great sway in the company and can almost draw them any way. However, we have put you in the best method that we can and hope it will do. But, for fear notice should be taken of our being so long together, we have told you as much as we can and leave you to manage it; and so God bless you."

Upon this, away they went, and by-and-by Captain Low turns out, and comes upon deck, and bidding me good-morrow, asked me how I did and how I liked my bed. I thanked him and told him I was very well at his service and liked my bed very well and was very much obliged to him for the care he had taken of me. After which he ordered a consultation signal to be made, which was their green trumpeter, as they called him, hoisted at the mizzen-peek. It was a green silk flag with a yellow figure of a man blowing a trumpet on it. The signal being made, away came the boats flocking on board the commodore, and when they were all come on board Captain Low told them he only wanted them to breakfast with him; so down they went into the cabin, as many as it would well hold, and the rest in the steerage[19] and where they could.

After breakfast Captain Low asked me if I was married and how many children I had. I told him I had been married about ten years and had five children when I came from home, and did not know but I might have six now, one being on the stocks when I came from home. He asked me whether I had left my wife well provided for when I came from home. I told him I had left her in but very indifferent circumstances. That having met with former misfortunes, I was so low reduced that the greatest part of my substance was in this sloop and cargo; and that, if I was put by this trip, I did not know but my family might want bread before I could supply them.

Low, then turning to Russel, said, "It will not do, Russel." "What will not do?" said Russel. Low answered, "You know who I mean; we must not, and it shall not be, by God." "It must and shall, by God," replied Russel, "self-preservation is the first law of nature, and necessity according to the old proverb has no law." "Well," says Low, "it shall never be with my consent." Hereupon most of the company said it was a pity and ought to be taken into consideration and seriously weighed amongst them and then put to the vote. At which Low said, "So it ought, and there is nothing like the time present to decide the controversy and to determine the matter." They all answered, "Aye, it was best to end it now."

Then Low ordered them all to go upon deck and bid me stay in the cabin; so up they went all hands and I sat still and smoked a pipe of tobacco, wine and punch being left on the table. And though I was very impatient to know the determination, sometimes hoping it would be in my favor, and sometimes fearing the contrary; yet I dared not go out of the cabin to hear what they said, nor make any inquiry about it.

After they had been upon deck about two hours, they came down again and Low asked me how I did and how I liked my company since they went upon deck. I thanked him and said I was very well at his service; and as for my company, I liked it very well, and it was company that few would dislike. "Why," said he, "I thought you had been all alone ever since we went upon deck." I answered, "How could you think, sir, that I was alone, when you left me three such boon, jolly companions to keep me company?"

"Zounds," says Low, and seemed a little angry. "I left nobody and ordered nobody but the boy Jack, and him I bid stay at the cabin-door with-out-side, and not go in, nor stir from the door, until I bid him." "But," I said, "sir, my three companions were not human bodies, but those which you left on the table, to wit, a pipe of tobacco, a bottle of French claret and a bowl of punch." At which they all laughed and Low said I was right. So after some discourses had passed by way of diversion, Russel said to me, "Master, your sloop is very leaky." I said, "Yes, she made water." "Water!" says he, "I do not know what you could do with her, suppose we were to give her to you. Besides, you have no hands, for all your hands now belong to us." I said, "Sirs, if you please to give her to me, I do not fear, with God's blessing, but to manage her well enough, if you let me have only those which are on board, which I hope you will: namely, my mate and the two boys." "Well," says he, "and suppose we did, you have no cargo, for we have taken to replenish our stores all the rum, sugar, tobacco, rice, flour, and, in short, all your cargo and provisions." I told him I would do as well as I could, and if the worst came to the worst, I could load the sloop with salt and carry it to the Canaries,[20] where I knew they were in great want of salt at present, and therefore was sure it would come to a good market there. "Aye, but," says he, "how will you do to make your cargo of salt, having no hands and having nothing wherewith to hire the natives to help you to make it, or to pay for their bringing it down on their asses; for you must believe," said he, "I understand trade." I told him if it did come to that extremity, I had so good interest both at the island of Bona Vista, as likewise at the Isle of May,[21] that I was sure the inhabitants would assist me all that they could and trust me for their pay till I returned again, especially when they came to know the occasion that obliged me to it; and that upon the whole, I did not fear, with God's blessing, to get a cargo of salt on board, if they would be so generous as to give me the sloop again. "Well but," says Russel, "suppose we should let you have the sloop and that you could do as you say, what would you do for provisions? For we shall leave you none; and I suppose I need not tell you, for without doubt you know it already, that all these islands to windward are in great scarcity of victuals, and especially the two islands that produce the salt which have been oppressed for many years with a sore famine." I told him I was very sensible that all he said last was true, but hoped if they gave me the sloop, they would also be so generous as to give me some provisions, a small quantity of which would serve my little company; but if not, I could go down to the Leeward Islands,[22] where, likewise, I had some small interest, and I did not doubt but I could have a small matter of such provisions as the islands afforded, namely maize, pompions, feshunes,[23] etc. with which, by God's assistance, we would endeavor to make shift, until it pleased God we could get better. "Aye but," says he, "perhaps your mate and boys will not be willing to run that hazard with you, nor care to endure such hardship." I told him as for my boys, I did not fear their compliance and hoped my mate would also do the same, seeing I required him to undergo no other hardship but what I partook of myself. "Aye, but," says Russel, "your mate has not the same reasons as you have to induce him to bear with all those hardships which you must certainly be exposed to in doing what you propose; and therefore you cannot expect him to be very forward in accepting such hard terms with you; (though I cannot conceive it to be so easy to go through with, in the manner you propose, as you seem to make it)." I answered as for the mate's inclinations, I was not able positively to judge in this affair, but I believed him to be an honest, as well as a conscientious man, and as I had been very civil to him in several respects in my prosperity, so I did not doubt if I had the liberty to talk with him a little on this affair but he would be very willing to undergo as much hardship to extricate me out of this my adversity as he could well bear, or I in reason require of him, which would be no more than I should bear myself; and when it pleased God to turn the scales, I would endeavor to make him satisfaction to the full of what, in reason, he could expect, or at least as far as I was able.

"Come, come," says Captain Low, "let us drink about. Boy! how does the dinner go forward?" The boy answered, "Very well, sir." Says Low, "Gentlemen, you must all dine with me to day." They unanimously answered, "Aye." "Come then," says Low, "toss the bowl about and let us have a fresh one, and call a fresh cause."

They all agreed to this and then began to talk of their past transactions at Newfoundland, the Western Islands, Canary Islands, etc. What ships they had taken and how they served them when in their possession; and how they obliged the governor of the island of St. Michael to send them off two boatloads of fresh meat, greens, wine, fowls, etc. or otherwise threatened to damnify the island by burning some of the small villages. Of their landing on the island of Tenerife[24] to the northward of Oratavo in hopes of meeting with a booty, but got nothing but their skins full of wine; and how they had like to have been surprised by the country, which was raised upon that occasion, but got all off safe and without any harm, except one man who received a shot in his thigh after they were got into their boats; but, they said, they caused several of the Spaniards to drop; and that they should have been certainly lost, if they had tarried but half a quarter of an hour longer in the house where they were drinking and where they expected to get the booty, which they landed in quest of, according to the information given them by one of the inhabitants of the island who was taken by them in a fishing-boat, and told them, that, that gentleman had an incredible quantity of money, as well as plate, in his house. And on this occasion they threatened the poor fisherman how severely they would punish him for giving them a false information if ever they should light of him again; but I suppose the fellow kept close ashore after they let him go, all the time they lay lurking about the island. They also boasted how many French ships they had taken upon the banks of Newfoundland and what a vast quantity of wine, especially French claret, they took from them; with abundance of such like stuff; which, as it did not immediately concern me, so I shall not trouble myself with particularizing. And, indeed, my attention was so wholly taken up with the uncertainty of my own affairs, that I gave no great heed to those subjects that were foreign to me; and which, for that reason, made but a slight impression on my memory.

In this manner they passed the time away drinking and carousing merrily, both before and after dinner, which they eat in a very disorderly manner, more like a kennel of hounds than like men, snatching and catching the victuals from one another; which, though it was very odious to me, it seemed one of their chief diversions and, they said, looked martial like.

Before it was quite dark, every one repaired on board their respective vessels, and about eight o'clock at night I went to my hammock, without observing, as I remember, anything worth remarking, save that Captain Low and I, and three or four more, drank a couple of bottles of wine after the company were gone before we went to sleep, in which time we had abundance of discourse concerning church and state, as also about trade, which would be tedious to relate in that confused manner we talked of these subjects, besides the reason I just now mentioned.

Low stayed up after me and when I was in my hammock, I heard him give the necessary orders for the night, which were that they were to lie too with their head to the north westward, as indeed we had ever since I had been on board of him; to mind the top-light, and for the watch to be sure above all things to keep a good look-out; and to call him if they saw any thing or if the other ships made any signals.

I passed this night as the former, ruminating on my present unhappy condition, not yet being able to dive into or fathom their designs, or what they intended to do with me, and often thinking on what the three men told me, as also on what the company said, but in a more particular manner, of what Russel told me concerning my mate, until sleep overpowered my senses and gave me a short recess from my troubles.

In the morning, about five o'clock, I turned out, and a little after, one of the three men who spoke to me the morning before came to me, and bid me good-morrow, and asked me very courteously how I did, and told me that they would all three, as before, have come and spoken to me but were afraid the company, especially Russel's friends, would think they held a secret correspondence with me, which was against one of their articles, it being punishable by death to hold any secret correspondence with a prisoner; but they hoped all would be well and that they believed I should have my sloop again; Russel being the only man who endeavored to hinder it, and he only on the account of having me to go with them on the coast of Brazil; but that most of the company was against it, except the mere creatures of Russel. He said I might thank my mate for it all, who, he much feared, would prove a rogue to me and enter with them; and then if they should give me my sloop, I should be sadly put to it to manage her myself with one boy and the little child. He also said that he and the other two heartily wished they could go with me in her, but that it was impossible to expect it, it being death even to motion it, by another of their articles, which says that if any of the company shall advise or speak anything tending to the separating or breaking of the company, or shall by any means offer or endeavor to desert or quit the company, that person shall be shot to death by the quartermaster's order without the sentence of a court-martial. He added that until my mate had given Russel an account of my being acquainted on the coast of Brazil, he seemed to be my best friend and would certainly have proved so, and would have prevailed with the company to have made a gathering for me, which perhaps might not have come much short in value of what they had taken from me; for there was but few in the company but had several pieces of linen cloth, pieces of silk, spare hats, shoes, stockings, gold lace, and abundance of other goods, besides the public store, which, if Russel had continued my friend, for one word speaking, there was not one of them but would have contributed to make up my loss; it being usual for them to reserve such things for no other use but to give to any whom they should take, or that formerly was of their acquaintance, or that they took a present liking to. He said further that he believed Captain Low would be my friend and do what he could for me; but that, in opposition to Russel, he could do but little. Russel bearing twice the sway with the company that Captain Low did; and that Russel was always more considerate to those they took, than Low; but now I must expect no favor from him, he was so exasperated by the opposition that the company, and especially Captain Low, made to my being forced to go with them on the coast of Brazil. He, however, bid me have a good heart and wished it lay in his power to serve me more than it did, and bid me not to take very much notice, or show much freedom with them, but rather a seeming indifference. Adding that he and his two consorts wished me as well as heart could wish, and whatever service they could do me while among them, I might assure myself it should not be wanting; desiring me to excuse him and not take amiss his withdrawing from me; concluding, with tears in his eyes, that he did not know whether he should have another opportunity of private discourse with me; neither would it be for the advantage of either of us, except some new matter offered them occasion to forewarn or precaution me, which, if it did, one of them would not fail to acquaint me with it. And so he left me.

Sometime after, Captain Low turned out and after the usual compliments passed, we took a dram of rum and entered into discourse with one or another on different subjects; for as a tavern or alehouse-keeper endeavors to promote his trade by conforming to the humors of every customer, so was I forced to be pleasant with everyone and bear a bob with them in almost all their sorts of discourse, though never so contrary and disagreeable to my own inclinations; otherwise I should have fallen under an odium with them, and when once that happens to be the case with any poor man, the Lord have mercy upon him; for then every rascally fellow will let loose his brutal fancy upon him and either abuse him with his tongue (which is the least hurtful) or kick or cuff him, or otherwise abuse him, as they are more or less cruel, or artificially raised by drinking, passion, etc.

Captain Russel, with some more, came on board about ten or eleven o'clock in the forenoon and seemed to be very pleasant to me, asking me how I did, telling me that he had been considering of what I said yesterday and could not see how I should be able to go through with it. That it would be very difficult, if not wholly impossible, and I should run a very great hazard in what I proposed. He believed, he said, that I was a man, and a man of understanding, but in this case I rather seemed to be directed by an obstinate desperation, than by reason; and for his part, since I was so careless of myself as to determine to throw myself away, he did not think it would stand with the credit or reputation of the company to put it into my power. He wished me well, he said, and did assure me that the thoughts of me had taken him up the greatest part of the night; and he had hit on a way which he was sure would be much more to my advantage and not expose me to so much hazard and danger, and yet would be more profitable than I could expect by having the sloop, though everything was to fall out to exceed my expectation; and did not doubt of the company's agreeing to it. "And this," says he, "is to take and sink or burn your sloop and keep you with us no otherwise than as you are now, viz. a prisoner; and I promise you, and will engage to get the company to sign and agree to it, the first prize we take, if you like her; and if not, you shall stay with us till we take a prize that you like, and you shall have her with all her cargo to dispose of how and where you please for your own proper use." He added that this perhaps might be the making of me and put me in a capacity of leaving off the sea and living ashore, if I was so inclined; protesting that he did all this purely out of respect to me because he saw I was a man of sense, as he said, and was willing to take care and pains to get a living for myself and family.

I thanked him and told him I was sorry I could not accept of his kind offer; and hoped he would excuse me, and not impute it to an obstinate temper because, I said, I did not perceive it would be of any advantage to me, but rather the reverse; for I could not see how I should be able to dispose of the ship or any part of her cargo, because nobody would buy, except I had a lawful power to sell; and they all certainly knew they had no farther right to any ship or goods that they took, than so long as such ship or goods was within the verge of their power; which, they were sensible, could not extend so far as to reach any place where such sale could be made. Besides, I said, if the owners of any such ship or goods should ever come to hear of it, then should I be liable to make them restitution to the full value of such ship and cargo, or be obliged to lie in a prison the remaining part of my days; or perhaps by a more rigid prosecution of the law against my person, run a hazard of my life.

Russel said these were but needless and groundless scruples, and might easily be evaded. As for my having a right to make sale of the ship and cargo which they would give me, they could easily make me a bill of sale of the ship and such other necessary powers in writing as were sufficient to justify my title to it beyond all possibility of suspicion; so that I should not have any reason to fear my being detected in the sale. And as for my apprehension of being discovered to the owners, that might as easily be prevented; for they should always know, by examination of the master, etc. and also by the writings taken on board such ship (which they always took care to seize upon) who were the owners and merchants concerned in both ship and cargo, as also their places of abode; by which I might be able to shun a possibility of their discovering me. Adding that I might have the powers and writings made in another name, which I might go by until I had finished the business, and then could assume my own; which method would certainly secure me from all possibility of discovery.

I told him, I must confess there was not only a probability but a seeming certainty in what he said and that it argued abundance of wit in the contrivance; but I assured him that were I positively certain, which I could not be, that until the hour of my death it would not be discovered, yet there was still a strong motive to deter me from accepting it; which, though it might seem perhaps to them to be of no weight and but a mere

chimera, yet it had greater force with me than all the reasons I had hitherto mentioned; and that was my conscience, which would be a continual witness against me and a constant sting, even when perhaps nobody
would accuse me. And as there could be no hearty and unfeigned repentance without making a full restitution as far as I was able to the inj red
person; I asked them what benefit would it be to me if I got thousands
of pounds and could not be at peace with my conscience until I had
restored everything to the proper owners and, after all, remain as I was
before. A great deal more I told them I could say upon this head, but
doubted that discourses of this nature were not very taking with some
of them and might seem of very little account; yet I hope, said I, and God
forbid that there should not be some of you who have a thought of a
great and powerful God and a consciousness of his impartial justice to
punish, as well as of his unfathomable mercy to pardon offenders upon
their unfeigned repentance, which would not so far extend as to encourage us to run on in sinning, thereby presuming to impose on his mercy.

Some of them said I should do well to preach a sermon and would
make them a good chaplain. Others said, no, they wanted no Godliness
to be preached there: That pirates had no God but their money, nor sav-
ior but their arms. Others said that I had said nothing but what was very
good, true, and rational, and they wished that Godliness, or at least
some humanity, were in more practice among them; which they
believed would be more to their reputation and cause a greater esteem
to be had for them, both from God and man.

After this, a silence followed which Capt. Russel broke, saying to me
again, "Master, as to your fear that you wrong your neighbor in taking
a ship from us, which we first took from him; in my judgment it is
groundless and without cause; nor is it a breach of the laws of God or
man, as far as I am able to apprehend; for you do not take their goods
from them nor usurp their property. That we have done without your
advice, concurrence, or assistance; and therefore whatever sin or guilt
follows that action, it is entirely ours, and in my opinion cannot extend to
make any unconcerned person guilty with us. It is plain, beyond disput-
ing," continued he, "that you can be no way partaker with us in any capture while you are only a constrained prisoner, neither giving your advice
or consent or any ways assisting; and therefore it may be most certainly
concluded that it is we only that have invaded the right and usurped the
property of another; and that you must be innocent, and cannot be par-

taker of the crime unless concerned in that action that made it a crime. But you seem to allow that we have a property, while we are in possession; but," added he, "I suppose you think that all the claim we have to the ships and goods that we take is by an act of violence, and therefore unjust and of no longer force than while we are capable to maintain them by the same superior strength by which we obtained them.

I told him I could not express my conceptions of it better or fuller, I thought, than he had done; but hoped neither he nor Capt. Low nor any of the gentlemen present would be offended at my taking so much liberty; which was rather to acquaint them with my reasons for not being able to accept of their kind offer, than to give any gentleman offense; adding that I had so much confidence in their favors, that if I could have accepted them, I verily believed they would all have concurred with Capt. Russel in what he so kindly and friendly designed me.

At which words they all cried, "Aye, Aye, by God," and that I was deserving of that and more.

I told them I heartily thanked them all in general and did not wish any of them so unfortunate as to stand in need of my service; yet if ever they did, they should find that the uttermost of my ability should not be wanting in retaliation of all the civilities they had shown me ever since it was my lot to fall into their hands; but, in a more special manner for this, their now offered kindness, though I could not accept it with a safe and clear conscience, which I valued above any thing to be enjoyed in this world. I said I could add further reasons to those I had already urged; but I would not trouble them longer, fearing I had already been too tedious or offensive to some of them; which, if I had, I heartily begged their pardon; assuring them once more that if it was so, it was neither my design nor intent, but the reverse.

Hereupon they all said they liked to hear us talk and thought we were very well matched. Adding that Capt. Russel could seldom meet with a man that could stand him. But, as for their parts, they were pleased with our discourse and were very sure Low and Russel were so too.

Capt. Low then said he liked it very well, but told me I had not returned Capt. Russel an answer to what he last said, which he thought deserved one.

I answered that since the gentlemen were so good-natured as not only to take in good part what I had hitherto said, but also to give me free liberty to pursue my discourse, I should make use of their indulgence and answer what Capt. Russel had said last to me in as brief and inoffensive a manner as I was capable of.

Then turning to Russel, I said, "Sir, your opinion of my notion of the right you have to any ship or goods you may take is exactly true; and I think your right cannot extend farther than your power to maintain that right; and therefore it must follow, you can transfer no other right to anyone than what you have yourselves, which will render any person who received them as guilty for detaining them from the proper owners as you for the taking them.

He said, "Be it so; we will suppose" (and seemed a little angry) "for argument sake, we have taken a ship and are resolved to sink or burn her, unless you will accept of her. Now, pray, where is the owner's property when the ship is sunk or burned? I think the impossibility of his having her again cuts off his property to all intents and purposes, and our power was the same, notwithstanding our giving her to you, if we had thought fit to make use of it."

I was loath to argue any farther, seeing him begin to be peevish; and knowing, by the information afore given me by the three men that all his pretended kindness and arguments were only in order to detain me without the imputation of having broken their articles; which he found the major part of the company very averse to; wherefore, to cut all short I told him I was very sensible of the favors designed me and should always retain a grateful sense of them. That I knew I was absolutely in their power and they might dispose of me as they pleased, but that having been hitherto treated so generously by them, I could not doubt of their future goodness to me. And that if they would be pleased to give me my sloop again, it was all I requested at their hands; and I doubted not, but that by the blessing of God on my honest endeavors, I should soon be able to retrieve my present loss; at least, I said, I should have nothing to reproach myself with, whatever should befall me, as I should have if I were to comply with the favor they had so kindly intended for me.

Upon which, Capt. Low said, "Gentlemen, the master, I must needs say, has spoke nothing but what is very reasonable, and I think he ought to have his sloop. What do you say Gentlemen?" The greatest part of them answered aloud, "Aye, Aye, by God, let the poor man have his sloop again and go in God's name and seek a living in her for his family." "Aye," said some of them, "and we ought to make something of a gathering for the poor man, since we have taken everything that he had on board his vessel. This put an end to the dispute and everybody talked according to their inclinations, the punch, wine, and tobacco being moving commodities all this time. And everyone who had an opportunity of speaking to me, wished me much joy with, and success in, my newly obtained sloop.

Towards night, Russel told Capt. Low, that as the company had agreed to give me the sloop again, it was to be hoped they would discharge me and let me go about my business in a short time; and therefore, with his leave, he would take me on board the schooner with him to treat me with a sneaker of punch before parting. Accordingly, I accompanied him on board his vessel, though I had rather stayed with Low, and he welcomed me there and made abundance of protestations of his kindness and respect to me, but still argued that he thought I was very much overseen in not accepting what he had so kindly, and out of pure respect, offered to me, and which, he said, would really have been the making of me. I told him I thanked him for his favor and goodwill; but was very well satisfied with the company's generosity in agreeing to give me the sloop again, which, I said, was more satisfactory to me than the richest prize that they could take.

"Well," says he, "I wish it may prove according to your expectation." I thanked him; so down we went into the cabin and, with the officers only, diverted ourselves in talking until supper was laid on the table.

After supper, a bowl of punch and half a dozen of claret being set on the table, Capt. Russel took a bumper and drank success to their undertaking; which went round, I not daring to refuse it. Next health was prosperity to trade, meaning their own trade. The third health was the King of France. After which, Russel began the King of England's health; so they all drank round, some saying, "The King of England's health," others only, "The aforesaid health," until it came round to me; and Capt. Russel having emptied two bottles of claret into the bowl as a recruit, and there being no liquor that I have a greater aversion to than red wine in punch, I heartily begged the captain and the company would excuse my drinking anymore of that bowl and give me leave to pledge the health in a bumper of claret.

Hereupon Russel said, "Damn you, you shall drink in your turn a full bumper of that sort of liquor that the company does." "Well, gentlemen," said I, "rather than have any words about it, I will drink it, though it is in a manner poison to me; because I never drank any of this liquor, to the best of my remembrance, but it made me sick two or three days at least after it." "And damn you," says Russel, "if it be in a manner or out of a manner, or really rank poison, you shall drink as much, and as often, as any one here, unless you fall down dead, dead!"

So I took the glass, which was one of your Holland's glasses, made in the form of a beaker without a foot, holding about three quarters of a pint, and filling it to the brim, said, "Gentlemen, here is the aforesaid health." "What health is that?" said Russel. "Why," says I, "the same health you all have drank. The King of England's health." "Why," says Russel, "who is King of England?" I answered, "In my opinion, he that wears the crown is certainly king while he keeps it." "Well," says he, "and pray who is that?" "Why," says I, "King George at present wears it." Hereupon he broke out in the most outrageous fury, damning me and calling me rascally son of a bitch; and abusing His Majesty in such a virulent manner, as is not fit to be repeated, asserting with bitter curses that we had no king.

I said I admired that he would begin and drink a health to a person who was not in being. Upon which, he whipped one of his pistols from his sash and I really believe would have shot me dead if the gunner of the schooner had not snatched it out of his hand.

This rather more exasperated Russel, who continued swearing and cursing His Majesty in the most outrageous terms, and asserting the pretender to be the lawful King of England, etc.[25] He added that it was a sin to suffer such a false traitorous dog as I was to live, and with that whipped out another pistol from his sash and cocked it and swore he would shoot me through the head, and was sure he should do God and his country good service, by ridding the world of such a traitorous villain. But the master of the schooner prevented him by striking the pistol out of his hand.

Whether it was with the fall or his finger being on the trigger, I cannot tell, but the pistol went off without doing any damage. At which the master and all present blamed Russel for being so rash and hasty; and the Gunner said, I was not to blame; for that I drank the health as it was first proposed, and there being no names mentioned, and King George being possessed of the crown and established by authority of Parliament, he did not see but his title was the best. "But what have we to do," continued he, "with the rights of kings or princes? Our business here is to choose a king for our own commonwealth, to make such laws as we think most conducive to the ends we design, and to keep ourselves from being overcome and subjected to the penalty of those laws which are made against us." He then intimated to Russel that he must speak his sentiments freely and imputed his quarrel with me to his being hindered from breaking through their articles; urging that he would appear no better than an infringer of their laws, if the matter were narrowly looked into; and that it was impossible ever to have any order or rule observed if their statutes were once broken through. He put him in mind of the penalty, which was death to anyone who should infringe their laws; and urged that if it were once admitted that a man, through passion or the like, should be excused breaking in upon them, there would be an end to their society; and concluded with telling him that it was an extraordinary indulgence in the company, not to remind him of the penalty he had incurred.

Russel, still continuing his passion, answered that if he had transgressed, it was not for the sake of his own private interest, but for the general good of the company; and therefore did not fear, neither in justice could he expect, any severity from the company for what he had done; and for that reason, whatever he (the gunner) or those of his sentiments thought of it, he was resolved, whatever came of it, to pursue his present humor.

Then says the gunner to the rest, "Well, gentlemen, if you have a mind to maintain those laws made, established, and sworn to by you all, as I think we are all obligated by the strongest ties of reason and self-interest to do, I assure you, my opinion is that we ought to secure John Russel, so as to prevent his breaking our laws and constitutions, and thereby do ourselves, and him too, good service: Ourselves, by not suffering such an action of cruelty in cold blood, as he more than once attempted to commit, as you are eyewitnesses of and, I believe, most on board have been ear-witnesses to the pistol's going of; and all this for no other reason in the world, but through a proud and ambitious humor, conceiving he is the man that is not to be contradicted and that his words, though tending to our ruin, must yet be received as an oracle, without any opposition.

At which they all said it was a pity the master should suffer, neither would they permit it; and speaking to Russel they said they would not allow him to be so barbarous; that they had always valued themselves upon this very thing of being civil to their prisoners and not abusing their persons; that, till now, he himself had been always the greatest persuader to clemency, and even to the forgiving provocations, and permitting them to go from them with as little loss as could be, after they had taken what they had occasion for. "But now," said they, "you are quite the reverse to this poor man; and for no other reason, that we know of, but as the Gunner said just now, because we would not yield a greater power to you alone then you with the whole company have when conjoined; that is, that you at any time, to gratify your own humor, shall have liberty, not only to dispense with our laws, but to act against the sentiments of the whole company."

Russel answered that he never did oppose the company before; neither could he believe any present could charge him with any cruelty in cold blood ever since he belonged to the company, but that he had a reason for what he did, or would have done, if he had not been prevented. Hereupon the master interrupting him said, "Capt. Russel, we know of no reason for your passionate design, but what we have told you; and, as you have been told before, it reflects a revenge against the company; but not being able to effect that, you turn it on that poor man, the master of the sloop, and, as it were, in despite of the company, because they have decreed him his sloop again that he may provide a living for his family, you would barbarously, nay brutishly, as well as to the company contemptuously, murder that poor man, who has given you no occasion to induce you to such an action that we know of; and if he has given you any sufficient cause to be so offended at him, we promise you this instant to deliver him up to you to suffer death, or what other punishment you think fit to inflict on him."

Russel told them that he had been in the company almost from the first and he challenged anyone to charge him with singularity or opposition to the company, or of cruelty to anyone prisoner before that rascal, as he called me, and that therefore they might be assured, he should not have taken up such resentments against me if he had not a sufficient reason to provoke him to it, which he did not think proper at that time to divulge.

"Then," says the gunner, "neither do we think proper that you shall take any man's life away in cold blood until you think fit to acquaint the company with the reasons for it, and I think it was your place to satisfy the company before you took the liberty to attempt the life of any man under the company's protection as I think all prisoners are. And, to say the truth, I do verily believe you have no other reasons to give than those hinted by the master and me; and therefore, I think it but reason to use such methods as may prevent your passionate design and secure the prisoner until morning, and then send him on board the commodore, who, with the advice of the majority, may order the matter as he thinks best.

This was consented to by all, and so Russel, having his arms taken from him, was ordered not to offer the least disturbance again, nor concern himself with or about me until after I was on board the commodore, on pain of the crew's displeasure and also of being prosecuted as a mutineer; and the gunner, master, boatswain, etc. bid me not be discouraged, assuring me that there should no harm come to me while I was on board of them, and that they would send me away now, but that there is, said they, "an express order among us, to receive no boats on board after eight at night, or nine o'clock at farthest; but they would put me on board Capt. Low in the morning, where they were sure I should be protected and secured from the revengeful hand of Capt. Russel; for they said, they were sure that Capt. Low had a great respect for me and would be a means to counter-balance Russel; and they said they would sit up with me all night for my greater security. Which they did, smoking and drinking and talking, everyone according to his inclination and so we passed the time away until day.

Russel went to sleep about two o'clock in the morning in his cabin; however, the master [i.e. navigator], the gunner, and five or six more, did not go to bed all that night, but would have had me gone to sleep, telling me I need not fear for they would take care that Russel should not hurt me.

About eight o'clock in the morning, I was carried on board Capt. Low, the gunner and steward going with me, who told him all that had passed; and acquainted him that they still believed Russel to be so implacable against me that he would murder me in cold blood before I got clear of them if he did not interpose to protect me from his violence. Capt. Low said he very well knew, and he believed so did they all, what was the reason that made Russel so inveterate and implacable to me. He added that Russel did not do well, and that I had behaved myself so inoffensively that there could be no reason to induce the most savage monster to be such an irreconcilable enemy to me; but that it was an easy matter to dive into the cause of it, to wit, his being thwarted by the company in his humor; and because they would not break through the articles which cemented them together and which were signed and swore to by them all, as the standing rule of their duty, by which only they could decide and settle controversies and differences among themselves; the least breach of which would be a precedent for the like infractions, whenever Russel or any other thought fit to give way either to revenge or ambition, and that then all their counsels would be fluctuating; and fancy, and not reason, would be the rule of their conduct; and their resolutions would be rendered more inconstant than the weathercock. He added that he hoped the company would inviolably adhere to their established laws, which, he said, were very good; and were they not, yet, as they were made by the unanimous consent of the whole company, so they ought not to be altered without the same unanimous consent; concluding, that for his part, he would rather choose to be out of the company than in it, if they did not resolve to be determined by their articles. Hereupon they answered that what he had said was very good and they were resolved to adhere to his advice.

After this they drank a dram and then returned with their boat on board the schooner, and Capt. Low told me he was sorry for Capt. Russel's disgust against me because he believed it would be a disadvantage to me; but, however, there was no remedy but patience, assuring me that Russel should neither kill me nor abuse my person, and I should have my sloop again and be discharged in as short a while as possible, that I might be clear of Russel, who, he was afraid, would always continue my foe.

All the officers and men likewise spoke very friendly to me and bid me not be daunted; so we passed the time away in several kinds of discourse until dinner, after which, Low ordered a bowl of punch to be made and said he wished I was well clear of them.

About four o'clock in the afternoon Capt. Russel came on board, as did also Francis Spriggs, who commanded the other ship, and after a little while, says Russel to Capt. Low, "The mate of the sloop is willing to enter with us as a volunteer."

Low made answer and said, "How must we do in that case? For then the master of the sloop will have nobody to help him, but one boy; for," says he, "the little child is no help at all."

Russel said he could not help that. "But," said Low, "we must not take all the hands from the poor man if we design to give him his sloop again," adding that he thought in reason there could not be less than two boys and the mate.

"Zounds," says Russel, "his mate is a lusty young brisk man and has been upon the account[26] before and told me but even now, for," said he, "I was on board the sloop but just before I came here, and Frank Spriggs was along with me and heard him say that he was fully resolved to go with us and would not go any more in the sloop unless forced; and when he came out of Barbados, he said, his design was to enter himself on board the first pirate that he met with; and will you refuse such a man, contrary to your articles which you all so much profess to follow; and which enjoin you by all means, not repugnant to them, to increase and fill your company? Besides," continued he, "he spoke to me the first day that he was resolved to enter with us."

Low replied that to give the man his sloop and no hands with him to assist him, was but putting him to a lingering death, and they had as good almost knock him on the head, as do it.

Russel answered, as to that, they might do as they pleased; what he spoke now was for the good of the whole company and agreeable to the articles, and he would fain [i.e. gladly] see or hear that man that should oppose him in it. He said he was quartermaster of the whole company, and by the authority of his place, he would enter the mate directly, and had a pistol ready for the man that should oppose him in it.

Low said, as for what was the law and custom among them (as what he now pleaded, was) he would neither oppose, nor argue against; but if they thought fit to take the man's mate from him, then they might let him have one of his own men with him.

Russel said no, for all the sloop's men were already enrolled in their books, and therefore none of them should go in her again. "Gentlemen," continued he, "you must consider I am now arguing, as well for the good of the company, as for the due maintenance and execution of the laws and articles; and as I am the proper officer substituted and entrusted by this company with authority to execute the same, so (as I told you before) I have a pistol and a brace of balls ready for anyone who dare oppose me herein," and turning to me said, "Master, the company has decreed you your sloop, and you shall have her; you shall have your two boys and that is all. You shall have neither provisions, nor anything else more than as she now is. And I hear there are some of the company design to make a gathering for you, but that also I forbid by the authority of my place because we are not certain but we may have occasion ourselves for those very things before we get more, and for that reason I prohibit a gathering; and I swear by all that is great and good that if I know anything whatsoever carried or left on board the sloop against my order or without my knowledge, that very instant I will set her on fire, and you in her.

Upon which I said that since it was their pleasure to order it thus, I begged that they would not put me on board the sloop in such a condition; but rather begged, if they so pleased, to do what they would with the sloop, and put me and my two boys ashore on one of the islands.

Russel said no, for they were to leeward of all the islands and should hardly come near any of them this season again.

I said I should rather be put ashore anywhere else, either on the coast of Guinea or on whatever coast they came at first, than be put as a victim on board the sloop, where I should have no possibility of anything but perishing, except by an extraordinary miracle.

He told me my fate was already decreed by the company and he, by his place, was to see all their orders put in execution; and he would accordingly see me safely put on board the sloop in the exact condition as he had but now mentioned.

I was going to make him a reply, but casting my eye on Capt. Low, he winked at me to be silent; and taking a bumper, drank success to their proceedings. The health went round, and Low ordered the great bowl to be filled with punch and bottles of wine to be set on the table in the cabin, to which we all resorted and spent the remaining part of the evening in discourses on different subjects. Only Frank Spriggs offered to persuade me to accept of what was first offered me, which Russel swore I should not now have, I having not once but several times already refused it. Capt. Low not being then willing to have anymore of that kind of discourse, broke it off by singing a song and enjoining everyone present to do the same, except me, whom he said he would excuse until times grew better with me. And thus they diverted themselves and passed the evening away until towards eight o'clock, and then everyone repaired on board their respective ships; and after they were gone, Low and I and two or three of his confidants smoked a pipe and drank a bottle or two of wine, in which time he told me he was very sorry that Jack Russel was so set against me. I said so was I and wondered what should be the reason of it, having given him no cause, unless by drinking that health the preceding night. I said I had imputed to liquor the fury he was then in and was in hopes that after that had worked off, his resentments also would have cooled and was not a little concerned to find it otherwise. Low said the health was not the cause, but rather the effect of his anger and a mere pretense to cloak his resentment for other disappointments. Adding that I did right to take his hint given me by winking, to answer no more. "For," says he, "I knew that everything which you could speak to him would be taken edgeways and the more you said to excuse yourself, the more it would add fuel to his anger, which he turned against you who could not resist him because he could not have his will of us, but we will endeavor to draw him off by degrees and for that reason will not discharge you, but I will keep you on board with me, where he shall not hurt nor abuse you except with his tongue, which you must bear, until we see if we can alter his temper, so as to deal with you a little more favorable than at present he designs.

I thanked him and all of them present for their favors and goodwill, and it being near midnight, we parted, and everyone retired to his rest and I to my hammock; and being pretty much fatigued the night before, as well as the preceding day, soon fell asleep; and about day-dawning, I got up and came upon deck, and walking upon the quarter deck very solitary, one of the three men mentioned before passed by me and asked me how I did and said he was very sorry for the unkindness already showed me, and like to be showed, but it was what they expected, as they had before hinted to me, and that still there was like to be a tough struggle about me. That Russel did design to be very barbarous to me and that Low and a great part of the company intended to oppose him in it; that there were a great many who were Russel's gang or clan and designed to stand by him in it, and had threatened that if there were much disturbance about it, they would shoot me and so put an end to the controversy. That there were some, on the other hand, that threatened hard if they did, to revenge my death by some of theirs; so that it was likely to be an untoward touch and he wished it might not prove to my disadvantage in the end, but would have me still to keep a good heart and trust in God and hope for the best, and by no means to speak one word or concern myself either way, but patiently wait the issue, which he hoped would be better for me than some of them intended; and so heartily wishing me well, walked his way.

Now you must believe these accounts were not a little shocking to me; but I had no friend that I could really rely on, but God, to whom I made my petitions and whose assistance I humbly besought to extricate me, in his own good time, out of these difficulties and snares which were laid for me on every side, and in the mean time, patiently so to bear them, as not to murmur and repine at his fatherly chastisements, nor by their extremity, through desperation, wound my conscience; but that in all things I might, through the guidance of the Holy Spirit, be directed so as to submit myself entirely to his will, who infinitely knew what was better for me than I knew myself.

After some time passed, Capt. Low came upon deck, who asked me how I had rested the preceding night. I told him very well, considering my present case; but, next under God, had grounded my hopes upon him to rid me of my present fears, by dispatching me away as soon as possible he could with conveniency. He told me he would do everything in his power to further my desires and hoped that what he had already done on my account would sufficiently convince me of his desire to serve me; but that things hitherto had fallen out very unluckily and cross, as I myself was able to judge by what was already passed.

I told him I had very good reasons to return him my hearty thanks and owned myself bound to him in the strictest ties of gratitude, and that if it ever should be in my power to serve him, I would not content myself with bare acknowledgments of his favor.

He said his will was at present more extensive than his power, but that he still hoped to prevail with Russel and those who were of his side to be more compassionate to me before I parted with them than at present they seemed to intend and as soon as he had brought them to a better temper, he then would procure my discharge; but if Russel still continued inexorable, which he should be very sorry for, "then you must endeavor," says he, "to keep up a good heart and patiently wait until providence brings you out of your present calamities, which I hope he will."

I thanked him and told him I would endeavor to follow his advice, though, I said, it was with some impatience that I waited to have my doom determined in a discharge from them. He bid me be easy, it should be shortly.

By this time there were several joined with us, so we broke that discourse, and fell into other talk.

About two or three o'clock in the afternoon, Capt. Russel, Capt. Spriggs, and some of their officers came on board and held a consultation, which I was not allowed to be a hearer of, but understood afterwards it was chiefly about their own affairs, in relation to the further prosecution of their intended voyage, and by the little mention that was made of me, it appeared that Russel continued still inflexible, bitterly swearing, that he would, if he had a thousand lives, lose them all, rather than miscarry in this his fixed resolution.

In this difficult situation I stood, not daring to speak freely for fear of offending, nor be silent, lest I should be thought contemptuous; not knowing how to avoid their resentments, and every resentment menacing and often bringing death. And thus I tediously, as well as dangerously, passed my time among them, until it pleased God to put it into their hearts to discharge me. Though, if seriously weighed, this my discharge seemed like sentencing me to a lingering and miserable death; yet I must needs confess, considering the whole matter, that I was in a manner miraculously befriended and supported, even in spite of malice, rage, and revenge, for which I shall always pay my humble acknowledgments to the Divine Providence.

After several efforts made by Capt. Low and others, and abundance of arguments used to bring Russel to better temper relating to me; and finding it all to no purpose, and that some of his clan had bound themselves by oath to stand by him even to my destruction if the dispute continued much longer; Capt. Low and Capt. Spriggs and others, who were my friends, resolved on sending me away as soon as possible; and for that purpose Low, the tenth day after I was taken, made a signal for a general consultation on board of him; and as soon as the officers and leading men of the other two ships were assembled, he made a speech to them to let them know the reason of his calling them to a consultation, telling them that he thought it was time to discharge me, as they had before agreed, as also to prosecute their intended voyage, they having lain a long time driving; and that, altogether out of their way, by reason they could not expect, either here or in this drift, to meet with any ships.

To this they all agreeing, Capt. Low told them he thought it would be best to discharge me first for several reasons, among which my being cumbersome to them as well as unserviceable, they being forced to sail the sloop themselves; besides, he said, it was not proper that I should be made acquainted with the design of their voyage.

They asked why he did not turn me away. Saying they did not know for what reason I had been kept so long, the company having settled that matter so long since.

Capt. Low said, "Gentlemen, you all know what arguments we have had already about this matter, and how Capt. Russel and some more were angry with the master of the sloop and, I verily believe, without any cause by him given to any of you designedly; and therefore I hope you have considered better of it since and laid aside your resentments against the poor man; neither," said he, "let us do any thing now in passion, for I do not design (nor would I, if I could) to enforce any of you to comply to anything against your will, nor would I have you think, gentlemen, that I shall ever show so much respect to any prisoner as, on his account, to cause a difference or wrangling among ourselves; but yet, gentlemen, give me leave to say that though we are pirates, yet we are men, and though we are deemed by some people dishonest, yet let us not wholly divest ourselves of humanity and make ourselves more savage than brutes. If we send this poor man away from us without provisions or hands to assist him, pray what greater cruelty can there be? I think the more lingering any death is made, the more barbarous 'tis accounted by all men; and therefore, gentlemen, I leave it to your own consideration."

To this Russel made answer that he, in the company's name, had made the master of the sloop very good and generous offers in the hearing of all the company, but that I had, in his opinion, after a very slighting manner, refused them. That it was my choice to be sent thus on board the sloop, rather than the compulsion of the company; and that notwithstanding he told me what I must trust to by insisting on the sloop and, how favorable they were designed to be to me, if I would have but a little patience until they could provide for me, yet that I had refused their favors, notwithstanding the pains he took to persuade me; adding an egregious falsehood, (but I dared not tell him so) that I had petitioned and begged of the company, rather to be put in the sloop in the condition he now proposed for me and that therefore, according to my desire, it should be so; and he hoped it could never be reckoned cruelty in them to give a person his free choice. "And, Gentlemen," says he, "we have had a great many more words about this matter already than ever we had in the like case before, but I hope you all have so much value and respect for one another and for the general peace, as that we shall have no more debate on this head, but determine at once the time when he is to be discharged, the manner of it being already settled by the major part, and I as your quartermaster, as my office requires, will see it executed and, perhaps, in a more favorable manner than at first I designed or he really deserves at mine or your hands either, but let that rest there."

Then Capt. Low said, "Mr. Russel has spoke to you, gentlemen, his sentiments, which, in the main, are reasonable and true, and I am glad he is reconciled to the master of the sloop before their parting; and I cannot say but I always believed Jack Russel to be a man of so much sense, as well as good-nature, that he would scorn to take revenge on one whose condition rendered him incapable of helping himself. And I think, gentlemen, we may discharge him as soon as you please, and this afternoon, if you are all agreed to it." They all said "Aye." Upon which Russel told them, it should be done that afternoon; telling Low that after dinner he would take me on board the schooner with him, and from thence, send me on board the sloop and see what could be done for me.

Some of Low's company said they would look out some things and give me along with me when I was going away, but Russel told them they should not, for he would toss them all into Davy Jones's Locker if they did, for I was the schooner's prize, and she had all my cargo and plunder on board of her, and therefore what was given to me should be given to me out of her. And turning to me said, "Well, master, I will this evening put you on board your own sloop and will be a better friend to you, perhaps, than them that pretended a great deal more, but I am above being led by passion, etc. They all dined on board of Low, who after dinner ordered a bowl of punch to be made in the great silver bowl and set a dozen of claret on the table, and that they said was for me to take my leave of them and part sailor-like. I thanked them; so they drank round to my good success and then to their own fortunate proceedings and good success; and Low told me he wished me very well, and hoped to meet with me again at some time when they had a good prize of rich goods and he would not fail to make me a retaliation with good advantage for my present loss. And they all present said I need not fear meeting with a friend whenever I met with them again.

About duskish they began to prepare to go on board their ships and I took my leave of Capt. Low and all his ship's company, and in particular of the three men, who I believe were my hearty friends, and returned them all thanks for their kindness, as well as good humor, showed to me since my first coming on board of them. I also took my leave of Capt. Spriggs and those of his company who were present wished me well, but not one of them, I believe, dared to give me any lumber with me, nor dared I have accepted of it had they offered it for fear of angering my but newly and seemingly reconciled enemy, who in all likelihood would have taken from me whatever they would have given me. And for that reason I believe it was that none of them offered to give me a farthing, notwithstanding all their professions of kindness to me, though this generosity is very usual with them to people that they profess much less favor for than they did to me.

Russel being ready, I was ordered to go in his boat, which I did; and as soon as we were come on board the schooner, he ordered a supper to be got ready and, in the mean time, there was a bowl of punch made and some wine set on the table. Russel invited me down into the cabin, as also all his officers, and we drank and smoked until supper was brought and then he told me I was very welcome and bid me eat and drink heartily, "for," he said, "I had as tedious a voyage to go through, as Elijah's forty days journey was to Mount Horeb, and as far as he knew, without a miracle, it must only be by the strength of what I eat now; for I should have neither eatables nor drinkables with me in the sloop.

I told him I hoped not so. He rapt out a great oath that I should find it certainly true. I told him that rather than be put on board the sloop in that manner, where there was no possibility to escape perishing without a miracle, I would submit to tarry on board until an opportunity offered to put me ashore where they pleased, or would yield to anything else they should think fit to do with me, excepting to enter into their service.

He said it was once in my power to have been my own friend, but my slighting their proffered favors and my own choosing what I now must certainly accept, had rendered me incapable of any other choice, and that therefore all apologies were but in vain; and he thought he showed himself more my friend than I could well expect or than I had deserved at his hands, having caused him to have a great deal of difference with the company more than ever he had in his life before, or ever should have again he hoped.

I told him I was very sorry that I was so unfortunate as to be the unhappy occasion of it, but could from my heart aver that it was not only undesigned, but also sorely against my inclinations; and begged of him and all the gentlemen then present to consider me as an object rather of their pity, than of their revenge.

He told me all my arguments and persuasions now were in vain, it being too late. I had not only refused their commiseration when I was offered it, but ungratefully despised it. "Therefore," says he, "as I told you before, it's in vain for you to plead anymore. Your lot is cast and you have nothing now to do, but to go through with your chance as well as you can, and fill your belly with good victuals and good drink to strengthen you to hold it as long as you can. It may be, and is very probable to be, the last meal that ever you may eat in this world. However, perhaps, such a conscientious man as you would fain [i.e. gladly] seem, or it may be are, may have a supernatural, or at least a natural means wrought by a supernatural power in a miraculous manner to deliver you. However, I cannot say but I pity the two boys and have a great mind to take them on board and let the miraculous deliverance be wrought on you alone."

The master and gunner said they heard the boys say they were willing to take their chance with their master, let it be what it would. "Nay, then," says Russel, "it's fit they should. I suppose their master has made them as religious and as conscientious as himself. However, master," says Russel speaking to me, "I would have you eat and drink heartily and talk no more about changing your allotted chance, because, as I told you before, it is all in vain; besides, it may be a means of provocation to serve you worse."

"Gentlemen," says I, "I have done. I will say no more. You can do no more than God is pleased to permit you; and I own, for that reason, I ought to take it patiently."

"Well, well," says Russel, "if it be done by God's permission, you need not fear that he will permit anything hurt to befall so good a man as you are."

About ten o'clock at night, he ordered to call the sloop's boat, which was brought by some of the pirates of his own clan who were stationed on board of her and asked them if they had done as he had ordered them, viz. to clear the sloop of everything. And they said yes, raping out a great oath or two, adding she had nothing on board except ballast and water. "Zounds," said Russel, "did not I bid you have all the casks that had water in them on board?" "So we did," said they; "but the water that we spoke of was saltwater leaked in by the vessel, and is now above the ballast; for we have not pumped her we do not know when."

Said Russel, "Have you brought away the sails I told you of?" They said all but the mainsail that was bent, for the other old mainsail that he had ordered to be left was good for nothing but to cut up for parceling, and hardly for that, it was so rotten; besides, it was so torn that it could not be brought too and was past mending, and for that reason they let it lie and would not unbend the other mainsail.

"Zounds," says Russel, "we must have it, for I want it to make us a mainsail." "Damn it," said the men, "then you must turn the man adrift in the sloop without a mainsail."

"Pish," said Russel, "the same miraculous power that is to bring him provisions, can also bring him a sail."

"What a devil, is he a conjurer?" said one of them.

"No, no," says Russel, "but he expects miracles to be wrought for him, or he never would have chosen what he had."

"Nay, nay," said they, "if he be such a one, he will do well enough." "But I doubt," says one of them, "he will fall short of his expectation; for if he be such a mighty conjurer, how the devil was it that he did not conjure himself clear of us?"

"Pish," said another, "it may be his conjuring books were shut up." "Aye, but," said another, "now we have hove all his conjuration books over board, I doubt he will be hard put to it to find them again."

"Come, come," says the gunner, "Gentlemen, the poor man is like to go through hardship enough, and very probably may perish; yet it is not impossible but he may meet with some ship or other timely succor to prevent his perishing, and I heartily wish he may; but however, you ought not to add affliction to the afflicted. You have sentenced him to a very dangerous chance, which I think is sufficient to stop your mouths from making a droll and game of him. I would have you consider," added he, "if any of you were at Tyburn or any other place to be executed, as many better and stouter men than some of you have been and the spectators, or Jack Catch should make a droll and May-game of you, you would think them a very hard-hearted, as well as an inconsiderate sort of people. And pray, gentlemen, consider the sentence which you are now going to execute on this poor man will be as bad or rather worse than one of our cases would be there, because unless providence stand his friend in an extraordinary manner, his death must as certainly ensue or be the consequence of this your sentence, as it would there be to any of us by the sentence of a judge and so much the more miserable by how much it is more lingering."

"Damn it," said Russel, "we have had enough, and too much of this already."

"Aye," said the gunner, "and take care, Russel, you have not this to answer for one day, when perhaps you will then, but too late, wish you had never done it. But you have got the company's assent in this, I cannot tell how, and therefore I shall say no more, only that I, as I believe most of the company, came here to get money, but not to kill, except in fight and not in cold blood or for private revenge. And I tell you, John Russel, if ever such cases as these be any more practiced, my endeavor shall be to leave this company as soon as I possibly can."

To which Russel said nothing in answer, but bid the men that came on board in the boat to leave the sloop's boat on board the schooner and take the schooner's boat with them on board the sloop; and, as soon as they saw the lights upon deck on board the schooner, to come away from the sloop with the schooner's boat, and bring the master of the sloop's biggest boy with them; and to take their hands out of the sloop's boat, and put the master's boy on board of the sloop's boat with his master, and let them go on board themselves with their boat and to be sure to bring the sloop's mainsail with them, and also the mate of the sloop. All of which they said they would do, so away they went; and then Russel told me he would give me something with me to remember him, which was an old musket and a cartridge of powder, but for what reason he made me that present, I cannot tell[27]; and then ordered the candles to be lighted in the lanterns and carried upon deck, and ordered two hands to step into the sloop's boat to carry me away, and to execute his former orders; and then shaking hands with me, he wished me a good voyage. I told him I hoped I should. The gunner, master, and several of the crew shook hands with me also and heartily wished me success, and hoped I should meet with a speedy and safe deliverance. I thanked them for their good wishes and told them I was now forced into a necessity of going through it, whether I would or not; but thanked God I was very easy at present, not doubting in God's mercy to me, though I was not deserving of it; and that if I was permitted to perish, I knew the worst and doubted not but he would graciously pardon my sins and receive me to his everlasting rest, and in this respect, what they had intended for my misfortune would be the beginning of my happiness; and that in the mean time, I had nothing to do but to resign myself to his blessed will and protection, and bear my lot with patience. And so bidding them farewell, I went over the side into the boat, which was directly put off; and about half way between the schooner and sloop, we met the schooner's boat and, according to their orders from Russel, they put my boy on board of me and so put away again to get on board their own vessel.

After their boat put away from us, I thought I heard the voice of my mate, but was not certain because he spoke so low, his conscience checking him I suppose for his leaving me so basely. I called to him and said "Arthur, what are you going to leave me?" He answered, "Aye." "What," said I, "do you do it voluntary or are you forced?" He answered faintly, "I am forced, I think." I said, "It was very well." He called to me again and said he would desire me to write to his brother and give him an account where he was, if ever I should have an opportunity. I told him I did not know where his brother lived. He called and said he lived in Carlingford. I told him I did not know where that was. He said it was in Ireland. "Why," said I, "you told me in Barbados that you was a Scotch-man and that all your friends lived in Scotland." But he made me no further answer, but away they rowed towards their vessel and I towards the sloop, and it being a very dark, as well as a close night, it was as much as ever I could do to see her; this being the last time that I spoke to or saw any of them, nor do I ever more desire to see them except at some place of execution.

From here, Capt. Robert's goes through many trying adventures. The elder boy was lost along with the ship's boat and the sloop ran aground on one of Cape Verde Islands at the base of a sheer cliff. He was helped by the natives, but nearly died of fever before reaching their village. After overcoming many other obstacles, he and the younger boy finally made it to England in June, 1725—about three years after he was taken.

Notes

1. This is another book that J. R. Moore attributed to Daniel Defoe in the 1930s based on some similarities in writing style. Modern scholars have cast serious doubt on this attribution.

2. Roads: a protected area near shore where a ship can anchor that is not as enclosed as a harbor.

3. Patareroes: muzzle-loading mortars which fired scattering shot, stones, spikes, nails, glass, or other debris.

4. Holland shirt: a shirt made of a certain kind of fine linen originally manufactured in Holland.

5. Drub: to beat or thrash with a stick.

6. A general name used to refer to persons whose names are unknown or unimportant.

7. Sal, St. Nicholas (São Nicolau), Bona Vista (Boa Vista) and St. Antonia (Santa Antão) are four of the Cape Verde Islands.

8. Probably pieces-of-eight.

9. The May 9, 1723 issue of the *American Weekly Mercury* reported, "Our merchants have advice that the *Sagamore*, Capt. Scot, in her voyage from Barbados to the Cape Verdes was taken and burnt by the pirates. Several of the seamen turned pirates also, and the captain was wounded and set ashore naked; and that five vessels had fallen into the hands of the pirates about the same time."

10. Paragheesi is a town on St. Nicholas.

11. Leeward: the side of the ship away from the wind.

12. Currisal is another town on St. Nicholas.

13. League: a measurement usually of about three miles.

14. St. Jago (São Tiago) is another of the Cape Verde Islands.

15. Bumper: a cup or glass filled to the brim or so that it runs over.

16. Abroach: opened so that the wine would come out.

17. The articles were the rules or laws that the pirates sail under and each pirate must sign upon joining a pirate crew. They were drawn up and agreed upon by the entire company on setting out on a voyage. These are Capt. Low's articles as printed in the *Boston News-Letter*, Aug. 8, 1723:

1. The captain is to have two full shares; the master is to have one share and one half; the doctor, mate, gunner and boatswain, one share and one quarter.

2. He that shall be found guilty of taking up any unlawful weapon on board the privateer or any other prize by us taken, so as to strike or abuse one another in any regard, shall suffer what punishment the captain and majority of the company shall see fit.

3. He that shall be found guilty of cowardice in the time of engagements, shall suffer what punishment the captain and majority of the company shall think fit.

4. If any gold, jewels, silver, etc. be found on board of any prize or prizes to the value of a piece-of-eight, and the finder do not deliver it to the quartermaster in the space of 24 hours he shall suffer what punishment the captain and majority of the company shall think fit.

5. He that is found guilty of gaming, or defrauding one another to the value of a real of plate, shall suffer what punishment the captain and majority of the company shall think fit.

6. He that shall have the misfortune to loose a limb in time of engagement, shall have the sum of six hundred pieces-of-eight, and remain aboard as long as he shall think fit.

7. Good quarter to be given when craved [meaning prisoners will not be abused].

8. He that sees a sail first, shall have the best pistol or small arm aboard of her.

9. He that shall be guilty of drunkenness in time of engagement shall suffer what punishment the captain and majority of the company shall think fit.

10. No snapping of guns in the hold.

This list of Low's articles is obviously incomplete, since several articles mentioned in this narrative are missing, such as the one concerning not allowing married men to sign, the one saying secret communication with a prisoner is punishable by death, and the one that says "if any of the company shall advise or speak anything tending to the separating or breaking of the company, or shall by any means offer or endeavor to desert or quit the company, that person shall be shot to death by the quartermaster's order without the sentence of a court-martial." Pirates usually destroyed their articles when attacked by a man-of-war because it contained their signatures (sometimes in a circle to conceal who had signed first) and could be used as evidence against them in court to prove that they weren't forced men. It's also possible it contained something too gruesome or disagreeable that they wouldn't want made public. Apparently many of the pirate articles that survive today were reconstructed from interviews with the pirates in prison, from trial testimony, or from the forced men who refused to sign.

18. Frigate-built: a merchant ship that has a split-level deck with a descent of four or five steps from the quarter-deck and forecastle into the waist; as opposed to ships which have continuous decks along the entire length, which are called galley-built.

19. Steerage: the forward part of the stern cabin, under the quarter-deck.

20. The Canary Islands are off the coast of Africa to the north of the Cape Verde Islands.

21. The Isle of May (Maio) is another of the Cape Verde Islands.

22. The Leeward Islands are a group of islands at the northern end of the Lesser Antilles, stretching from the Virgin Islands to Dominica. They are on the eastern boundary of the Caribbean Sea.

23. Maize: a type of native corn. Pompions: pumpkins. Feshunes: (?).

24. Tenerife is one of the Canary Islands.

25. Many believed James III was the rightful heir to the throne because of heredity, but the act of settlement of 1701 prohibited any Roman Catholic from taking the throne, so when Queen Anne died in 1714, her closest Protestant heir was George I—a German who knew nothing of English customs and sociey and

could not even speak English. He assumed the throne and created the office of prime minister, who he installed to run the country for him. Support of James III was considered treason, which was punished by being hanged by the neck until not quite dead, drawn (i.e. disemboweled), and then killed by beheading, with the body being quartered (cut into four parts) and the parts hung on display in different places in London.

26. "Going on account" meant "to become a pirate."

27. These were usually provided to anyone who was marooned so they could commit suicide rather than suffer a slow death from thirst or starvation.

The Monster in Human Shape

≋≋≋≋≋

Lucretia Parker

On March 11, 1825 the Eliza Ann, *sailing from St. John's[1] to
Antigua (one of the islands of the Lesser Antilles at the eastern end of the Caribbean Sea), was taken by pirates off Cuba.
The entire crew of ten was brutally murdered, except for the
ship's female passenger, Lucretia Parker. Twelve days after
her release she wrote a letter to her brother, George G. Parker,
detailing what happened and how she came to be the lone survivor. This letter was published later that same year in a pamphlet titled* Piratical Barbarity *or* The Female Captive,
*which appears to be the only time it has appeared in print
until now.*

St. John's, April 3, 1825.

Dear Brother,

You have undoubtedly heard of my adverse fortune and the shocking
incident that has attended me since I had the pleasure of seeing you in
November last. Anticipating your impatience to be made acquainted
with a more circumstantial detail of my extraordinary adventures, I
shall not on account of the interest which I know you must feel in my
welfare, hesitate to oblige you. Yet, I must declare to you that it is that
consideration alone that prompts me to do it, as even the recollection of
the scenes which I have witnessed, you must be sensible must ever be
attended with pain and that I cannot reflect on that I have endured and
the scenes of horror that I have been witness to without the severest
shock. I shall now, brother, proceed to furnish you with a detail of my
misfortunes as they occurred without exaggeration, and if it should be
your wish to communicate them to the public through the medium of
a public print or in any other way, you are at liberty to do it and shall
consider myself amply rewarded if in a single instance it proves benefi-

cial in removing a doubt in the minds of such, who, although they dare not deny the existence off a Supreme Being, yet disbelieve that be ever in any way revealed Himself to his creatures. Let philosophy (as it is termed) smile with pity or contempt on my weakness or credulity, yet the superintendence of a particular Providence interfering by second causes is so apparent to me and was so conspicuously displayed in the course of my afflictions that I shall not banish it from my mind from the beginning to the end of my narration.

On the 28th February I took passage on board the sloop *Eliza Ann*, Captain Charles Smith, for Antigua, in compliance with the earnest request of brother Thomas and family, who had advised me that they had concluded to make that island the place of their permanent residence, having a few months previous purchased there a valuable plantation. We set sail with a favorable wind and with every appearance of a short and pleasant voyage and met with no incident to destroy or diminish those flattering prospects until about noon of the 11th day from that of our departure [March 11, 1825], when a small schooner was discovered standing toward us with her deck full of men. And as she approached us, from her suspicious appearance, there was not a doubt in the minds of any on board but that she was a pirate!

When within a few yards of us, they gave us a shout and our decks were instantly crowded with the motley crew of desperadoes, armed with weapons of almost every description that can be mentioned, and with which they commenced their barbarous work by unmercifully beating and maiming all on board except myself. As a retreat was impossible and finding myself surrounded by wretches whose yells, oaths, and imprecations made them more resemble demons than human beings, I fell on my knees and from one who appeared to have the command I begged for mercy and for permission to retire to the cabin that I might not be either the subject or a witness of the murderous scene that I had but little doubt was about to ensue! The privilege was not refused me. The monster in human shape (for such was then his appearance) conducted me by the hand himself to the companion way and pointing to the cabin, said to me "descend and remain there and you will be perfectly safe, for although pirates, we are not barbarians to destroy the lives of innocent females!" Saying this he closed the companion doors and left me alone to reflect on my helpless and deplorable situation. It is indeed impossible for me, brother, to paint to your imagination what were my feelings at this moment. Being the only female on board, my terror it cannot be expected was much less than that of the poor devoted mariners! I resigned my life to the Being who had lent it and did not fail to improve the opportunity (which I thought it not improbable might be my last) to call on Him for that protection, which my situation so much at this moment required—and never shall I be persuaded but that my prayers were heard.

While I remained in this situation, by the sound of the clashing of swords, attended by shrieks and dismal groans, [I] could easily imagine what was going on on deck and anticipated nothing better than the total destruction by the pirates of the lives of all on board.

After I had remained about one hour and an half alone in the cabin and all had become silent on deck, the cabin doors were suddenly thrown open and eight or ten of the piratical crew entered, preceded by him whom I had suspected to be their leader and from whom I had received assurances that I should not be injured. By him I was again addressed and requested to banish all fears of personal injury, that they sought only for the money which they suspected to be secreted somewhere on board the vessel and which they were determined to have, although unable to extort a disclosure of the place of its concealment by threats and violence from the crew.

The pirates now commenced a thorough search throughout the cabin. The trunks and chests belonging to the captain and mate were broken open and rifled of their most valuable contents—nor did my baggage and stores meet with any better fate. Indeed this was a loss which at this moment caused me but little uneasiness; I felt that my life was in too much jeopardy to lament in any degree the loss of my worldly goods, surrounded as I was by a gang of the most ferocious-looking villains that my eyes ever before beheld of different complexions and each with a drawn weapon in his hand, some of them fresh crimsoned with the blood (as I then supposed) of my murdered countrymen and whose horrid imprecations and oaths were enough to appall the bravest heart!

The search for money proving unsuccessful (with the exception of a few dollars which they found in the captain's chest), they returned to the deck and setting sail on the sloop, steered her for the place of their rendezvous—a small island or key not far distant I imagine from the island of Cuba. There we arrived the day after our capture [March 12,

1825]. The island was nearly barren, producing nothing but a few scattered mangroves and scrubs interspersed with the miserable huts of these outlaws of civilization, among whom power formed the only law and every species of iniquity was here carried to an extent of which no person who had not witnessed a similar degree of pollution could form the most distant idea.

As soon as the sloop was brought to an anchor the hatches were thrown off and the unfortunate crew ordered on deck—a command which to my surprise was instantly obeyed, as I had harbored strong suspicions that they had been all murdered by the pirates the day previous. The poor devoted victims, although alive, exhibited shocking proofs of the barbarity with which they had been treated by the unmerciful pirates; their bodies exhibiting deep wounds and bruises too horrible for me to attempt to describe! Yet, however great had been their sufferings, their lives had been spared only to endure still greater torments. Being strongly pinioned [i.e. bound], they were forced into a small leaky boat and rowed on shore, which we having reached and a division of the plunder having been made by the pirates.

A scene of the most bloody and wanton barbarity ensued, the bare recollection of which still chills my blood! Having first divested them of every article of clothing but the shirts and trousers, with swords, knives, axes, etc. they fell on the unfortunate crew of the *Eliza Ann* with the ferocity of cannibals! In vain did they beg for mercy and entreat of their murders to spare their lives! In vain did poor Capt. S. attempt to touch their feelings and to move them to touch their feelings and to move them to pity by representing to them the situation of his innocent family— that he had a wife and three small children at home wholly dependent on him for support! But, alas, the poor man entreated in vain! His appeal was to monsters possessing hearts callous to the feelings of humanity! Having received a heavy blow from one with an ax, he snapped the cords with which he was bound, and attempted an escape by flight, but was met by another of the ruffians, who plunged a knife or dirk[2] to his heart! I stood near him at this moment and was covered with his blood. On receiving the fatal wound, he gave a single groan and fell lifeless at my feet!

Nor were the remainder of the crew more fortunate. The mate, while on his knees imploring mercy and promising to accede to anything that the vile assassins should require of him on condition of his life being spared, received a blow from a club, which instantaneously put a period to his existence!

Dear brother, need I attempt to paint to your imagination my feelings at this awful moment? Will it not suffice for me to say that I have described to you a scene of horror which I was compelled to witness! And with the expectation too of being the next victim selected by these ferocious monsters, whose thirst for blood appeared to be insatiable! There appeared now but one alternative left me, which was to offer up a prayer to Heaven for the protection of that Being who has power to stay the assassin's hands and "who is able to do exceeding abundantly above what we can ask or think." Sincerely in the language of scripture I can say, "I found trouble and sorrow, then called I upon the name of the Lord."[3]

I remained on my knees until the inhuman wretches had completed their murderous work and left none but myself to lament the fate of those who but twenty-four hours before, were animated with the pleasing prospects of a quick passage and a speedy return to the bosoms of their families! The wretch by whom I had been thrice promised protection and who seemed to reign chief among them, again approached me with hands crimsoned with the blood of my murdered countrymen and with a savage smile once more repeated his assurances that if I would but become reconciled to any situation, I had nothing to fear!

There was indeed something truly terrific in the appearance of this man, or rather monster, as he ought to be termed. He was of a swarthy complexion, near six feet in height, his eyes were large black and penetrating, his expression was remarkable, and when silent, his looks were sufficient to declare his meaning. He wore around his waist a leather belt to which was suspended a sword, a brace of pistols and a dirk. He was, as I was afterward informed, the acknowledged chief among the pirates. All appeared to stand in awe of him and no one dared to disobey his commands. Such, dear brother, was the character who had promised me protection if I would become reconciled to my situation, in other words subservient to his will! But whatever might have been his intentions, although now in his power, without a visible friend to protect me, yet such full reliance did I place in the Supreme Being who sees and knows all things and who has promised his protection to the faithful in the hour of tribulation that I felt myself in a less degree of danger than you or anyone would probably imagine.

As the day drew near to a close, I was conducted to a small temporary hut or cabin where I was informed I might repose peaceably for the night, which I did without being disturbed by anyone. This was another opportunity that I did not suffer to pass unimproved to pour out my soul to that Being who had already given me reasons to believe that he did not say to the house of Jacob "seek you me" in vain. Oh! that all sincere Christians would in every difficulty make him their refuge. He is a hopeful stay.

Early in the morning ensuing [March 13, 1825], I was visited by the wretch alone whom I had viewed as chief of the murderous band. As he entered and cast his eyes upon me, his countenance relaxed from its usual ferocity to the feigned smile. Without speaking a word, he seated himself on a bench that the cabin contained and drawing a table toward him, leaned upon it resting his cheek upon his hand. His eyes for some moments were fixed in steadfast gaze upon the ground, while his whole soul appeared to be devoured by the most diabolical thoughts! In a few moments he arose from his seat and hastily traversed the hut, apparently in extreme agitation and not infrequently fixing his eyes steadfastly upon me. But that Providence—which while it protects the innocent, never suffers the wicked to go unpunished—interposed to save me and to deliver me from the hands of this remorseless villain at the very instant when in all probability he intended to have destroyed my happiness forever! On a sudden the pirates' bugle was sounded, which, as I was afterward informed, was the usual signal of a sail in sight. The ruffian monster thereupon without uttering a word left my apartment and hastened with all speed to the place of their general rendezvous on such occasions. Flattered by the pleasing hope that Providence might be about to complete her work of mercy and was conducting to the dreary island some friendly aid to rescue me from my perilous situation, I mustered courage to ascend to the roof of my hovel to discover if possible the cause of the alarm and what might be the issue.

A short distance from the island I espied a sail which appeared to be lying to, and a few miles there from to the windward, another, which appeared to be bearing down under a press of sail for the former. In a moment this whole gang of pirates, with the exception of four, were in their boats and with their oars, etc. were making every possible exertion to reach the vessel nearest to their island. But by the time they had effected their object, the more distant vessel (which proved to be a British sloop of war disguised) had approached them within fair gunshot and probably knowing or suspecting their characters, opened their ports and commenced a destructive fire upon them.

The pirates were now—as nearly as I could judge with the naked eye—thrown into great confusion. Every possible exertion appeared to have been made by them to reach the island and escape from their pursuers. Some jumped from their boats and attempted to gain the shore by swimming, but these were shot in the water, and the remainder who remained in their boats were very soon after overtaken and captured by two well-manned boats dispatched from the sloop of war for that purpose. And soon had I the satisfaction to see them all on board of the sloop and in the power of those from whom I was fully satisfied that they would meet with the punishment due to their crimes.

In describing the characters of this piratical band of robbers, I have, dear brother, represented them as wretches of the most frightful and ferocious appearance—blood-thirsty monsters, who, in acts of barbarity ought only to be ranked with cannibals who delight to feast on human flesh—rendered desperate by their crimes and aware that they should find no mercy if [they were] so unfortunate as to fall into the hands of those to whom they show no mercy. To prevent a possibility of detection and the just execution of the laws, [they] wantonly destroy the lives of everyone, however innocent, who may be so unfortunate as to fall into their power. Such, indeed brother, is the true character of the band of pirates (to the number of thirty or forty) by whom it was my misfortune to be captured—with the exception of a single one who possessed a countenance less savage and had the appearance of possessing a heart less callous to the feelings of humanity. Fortunately for me, as Divine Providence ordered, this person was one of the four who remained on the island and on whom the command involved [i.e. fell] after the unexpected disaster which had deprived them forever of so great a portion of their comrades. From this man (after the capture of the murderous tyrant to whose commands he had been compelled to yield) I received the kindest treatment and assurances that I should be restored to liberty and to my friends when an opportunity should present or when it could be consistently done with the safety of their lives and liberty.

This unhappy man (for such he declared himself to be) took an opportunity to indulge me with a partial relation of a few of the most extraordinary incidents of his life. He declared himself an Englishman by birth, but his real name and place of nativity was, he said, a secret he would never disclose. "Although I must," said he, "acknowledge myself by profession a pirate, yet I can boast of respectable parentage and the time once was when I myself sustained an unimpeachable character. Loss of property through the treachery of those whom I considered friends and in whom I had placed implicit confidence, was what first led me to and induced me to prefer this mode of life to any of a less criminal nature. But, although I voluntarily became the associate of a band of wretches, the most wicked and unprincipled perhaps on earth, yet I solemnly declare that I have not in any one instance personally deprived an innocent fellow creature of life. It was an act of barbarity at which my heart ever recoiled and against which I always protested. With the property I always insisted we ought to be satisfied, without the destruction of the lives of such who were probably the fathers of families and who had never offended us. But our gang was as you may suppose chiefly composed of and governed by men without principle who appeared to delight in the shedding of blood and whose only excuse has been that by acting with too much humanity in sparing life, they might thereby be exposed and themselves arraigned to answer for their crimes at an earthly tribunal!

"You can have no conception, madam," continued he, "of the immense property that has been piratically captured and of the number of lives that have been destroyed by this gang alone, and all without the loss of a single one on our part until yesterday, when by an unexpected circumstance our number has been reduced as you see from thirty-five, to four! This island has not been our constant abiding place, but the bodies of such as have suffered here have always been conveyed a considerable distance from the shore and thrown into the sea, where they were probably devoured by the sharks, as not a single one has ever been known afterward to drift on our shores. The property captured has not been long retained on this island, but shipped to a neighboring port where we have an agent to dispose of it.

"Of the great number of vessels captured by us," continued he, "you are the first and only female that has been so unfortunate as to fall into our hands. And from the moment that I first saw you in our power— well knowing the brutal disposition of him whom we acknowledged our chief—I trembled for your safety and viewed you as one deprived perhaps of the protection of a husband or brother to become the victim of an unpitying wretch whose pretended regard for your sex and his repeated promises of protection were hypocritical—a mere mask to lull your fears until he could effect your ruin! His hellish designs, agreeable to his own declarations, would have been carried into effect the very morning that he last visited you, had not an all-wise Providence interfered to save you. And so sensible am I that the unexpected circumstance of his capture—as well as that of most of our gang, as desperate and unprincipled as himself—must have been by order of Him, from whose all-seeing eye no evil transaction can be hidden, that (were I so disposed) I should be deterred from doing you any injury through fear of meeting with a similar fate. Nor do my three remaining companions differ with me in opinion and we all now most solemnly pledge ourselves that so long as you remain in our powers you shall have nothing to complain of, but the deprivation of the society of those whose company no doubt would be more agreeable to you. And as soon as it can be done consistently with our own safety, you shall be conveyed to a place from which you may obtain a passage to your friends. We have now become too few in number to hazard a repetition of our piratical robberies; and not only this, but some of our captured companions to save their own lives may prove treacherous enough to betray us. We are therefore making preparation to leave this island for a place of more safety, when you, madam, shall be conveyed and set at liberty as I have promised you."

Dear brother, if you before doubted, is not the declaration of this man (which I have recorded as correctly as my recollection will admit of) sufficient to satisfy you that I owe my life and safety to the interposition of a Divine Providence! Oh yes! surely it is—and I feel my insufficiency to thank and praise my Heavenly Protector as I ought, for his loving kindness in preserving me from the evil designs of wicked men, and for finally restoring me to liberty and to my friends!

> "I cannot praise Him as I would,
> But He is merciful and good."

From this moment every preparation was made by the pirates to remove from the island. The small quantity of stores and goods which remained on hand (principally of the *Eliza Ann*'s cargo) was either buried on the island or conveyed away in their boats in the night to some place unknown to me. The last thing done was to demolish their temporary dwellings, which was done so effectually as not to suffer a vestige of anything to remain that could have led to a discovery that the island had ever been inhabited by such a set of beings. Eleven days from that of the capture of the *Eliza Ann* [March 22, 1825] (the pirates having previously put on board several bags of dollars, which from the appearance of the former, I judged had been concealed in the earth) I was ordered to embark with them, but for what price I then knew not.

About midnight I was landed on the rocky shores of an island which they informed me was Cuba. They furnished me with a few hard biscuits[4] and a bottle of water and directed me to proceed early in the morning in a northeast direction to a house about a mile distant, where I was told I would be well-treated and be furnished with a guide that would conduct me to Mantansies.

With these directions they left me and I never saw them more. Although many of my sex would doubtless in my place have considered their situations extremely perilous, yet I felt not alone—that I was yet in the presence of that sublime being who sits upon the circle of the earth and views all its inhabitants with one comprehensive glance and who has promised all those who will trust in Him that when difficulties beset them, when disappointment blasts their fond expectations, when sorrow or afflictions assail them, they can repose all their concerns and griefs on the wisdom, power and goodness of their Almighty Friend.

Having with some difficulty reached the summit of a chain of high rocks before me, my first emotion was upon my bended knees to offer up my thanksgivings to Heaven, to raise up my suppliant hands in petition to Providence to continue its mercy in affording me the means of reaching some hospitable dwelling.

At daybreak I set out in search of the house to which I had been directed by the pirates and which I had the good fortune to reach in safety in about an hour an half. It was a humble tenement thatched with canes, without any flooring but the ground, and was tenanted by a man and his wife only from whom I met with a welcome reception and by whom I was treated with much hospitality. Although Spaniards, the man could speak and understand enough English to converse with me and to learn by what means I had been brought so unexpectedly alone and unprotected to his house. Although it was the same to which I had been directed by the pirates, yet he declared that so far from being in any way connected with them in their piratical robberies or enjoying any portion of their ill-gotten gain, no one could hold them in greater abhorrence. Whether he was sincere in these declarations or not, is well known to Him whom the lying tongue cannot deceive. It is but justice to them to say that by both the man and his wife I was treated with kindness, and it was with apparent emotions of pity that they listened to the tale of my sufferings. By their earnest request I remained with them until the morning ensuing, when I set out on foot for Mantansies accompanied by the Spaniard who had kindly offered to conduct me to that place, which we reached about seven in the evening of the same day [March 23, 1825].

At Mantansies I found many Americans and Europeans by whom I was kindly treated and who proffered their services to restore me to my friends, but as there were no vessels bound direct from thence to Antigua or St. John's, I was persuaded to take passage for Jamaica, where it was the opinion of my friends I might obtain a passage more speedily for one or the other place, and where I safely arrived after a pleasant passage of four days.

The most remarkable and unexpected circumstance of my extraordinary adventures, I have yet, dear brother, to relate. Soon after my arrival at Jamaica, the Authority having been made acquainted with the circumstance of my recent capture by the pirates and the extraordinary circumstance which produced my liberation, requested that I might be conducted to the prison to see if I could, among a number of pirates recently committed, recognize any of those by whom I had been captured. I was accordingly attended by two or three gentlemen and two young ladies (who had politely offered to accompany me) to the prison apartment, on entering which I not only instantly recognized among a number therein confined the identical savage monster of whom I have had so much occasion to speak (the pirates' chief), but the most of those who had composed his gang and who were captured with him!

The sudden and unexpected introduction into their apartment of one whom they had probably in their minds numbered with the victims of their wanton barbarity, produced unquestionably on their minds not an inconsiderable degree of horror as well as surprise! And considering their condemnation now certain, they no doubt heaped curses upon their more fortunate companions for sparing the life and setting at liberty one whom an all wise Providence had conducted to and placed in a situation to bear witness to their unprecedented barbarity.

Government having though me obtained the necessary proof of the guilt of these merciless wretches, after a fair and impartial trial they were all condemned to suffer the punishment due to their crimes and seven ordered for immediate execution—one of them was the barbarian, their chief. After the conviction and condemnation of this wretch, in hopes of eluding the course of justice, he made (as I was informed) an attempt upon his own life by inflicting upon himself deep wounds with a knife which he had concealed for that purpose. But in this he was disappointed, the wounds not proving so fatal as he probably anticipated.

I never saw this hardened villain or any of his equally criminal companions after their condemnations—although strongly urged to witness their execution—and am therefore indebted to one who daily visited them for the information of their behavior from that period until that of their execution; which, as regarded the former, I was informed was extremely impenitent. That while proceeding to the place of ignominy and death, he talked with shocking unconcern, hinting that by being instrumental in the destruction of so many lives, he had become too hardened and familiar with death to feel much intimidated at its approach! He was attended to the place of execution by a Roman Catholic priest, who it was said labored to convince him of the atrociousness of his crimes, but he seemed deaf to all admonition or exhortation and appeared insensible to the hope of happiness or fear of torment in a future state. And so far from exhibiting a single symptom of penitence, declaring that he knew of but one thing for which he had cause to reproach himself, which was in sparing life and not ordering me to be butchered as the others had been! How awful was the end of life of this miserable criminal! He looked not with harmony, regard or a single penitent feeling towards one human being in the last agonies of an ignominious death. But we must shudder to reflect upon the countenance he was immediately to present before the throne of the Almighty! His fate should be a solemn admonition to the hopeless pirate that no plan of concealment or escape can enable him to elude the detection of his bloody crimes or the ignominious and fatal punishment which the laws of all countries award against them.

After remaining nine days at Jamaica, I was fortunate as to obtain a passage with Captain Ellsmore direct for St. John's. The thoughts of once

212 ≈ Captured by Pirates

more returning home and of so soon joining my anxious friends, when I could have an opportunity to communicate to my aged parents, to a beloved sister and a large circle of acquaintances the sad tale of the misfortunes which had attended me since I bid them *adieu* would have been productive of the most pleasing sensations, had they not been interrupted by the melancholy reflection that I was the bearer of tidings of the most heartrending nature to the bereaved families of those unfortunate husbands and parents who had in my presence fallen victims to piratical barbarity! Thankful should I have been had the distressing duty fell to the lot of someone of less sensibility, but unerring Providence had ordered otherwise.

We arrived safe at our port of destination after a somewhat boisterous passage of eighteen days. I found my friends all well, but the effects produced on their minds by the relation of the distressing incidents and adverse fortune that had attended me since my departure, I shall not attempt to describe. And much less can you expect, brother, that I should attempt a description of the feelings of the afflicted widow and fatherless child, who first received from me the melancholy tidings that they were so!

Thus, brother, have I furnished you with as minute a detail of the sad misfortunes that have attended me in my intended passage to Antigua in February and March last, as circumstances will admit of. And here permit me once more to repeat the inquiry, is it not sufficient to satisfy you and every reasonable person that I owe my life and liberty to the interposition of a Divine Providence? So fully persuaded am I of this, dear brother, and of my great obligations to that Supreme Being who turned not away my prayer nor his mercy from me, that I am determined to engage with my whole heart to serve Him the residue of my days on earth, by the aid of his heavenly grace, and invite all who profess to fear Him (should a single doubt remain on their minds) to come and hear what he hath done for me![. . .]

[She then goes on to preach a sermon for six more pages, concluding with:]

> I am, dear brother, affectionately yours,
> Lucretia Parker

Notes

1. Apparently this was St. John's in Newfoundland, Canada. The pamphlet prints it both as "St. John's" and "St. Johns," but gives no further information. There is a St. Johns in Antigua, a St. John in the Virgin Islands and a Saint John in New Brunswick, Canada, though these are unlikely.

2. Dirk: a short dagger.

3. Psalms 116:3-4.

4. Probably hardtack, which was a large unleavened, saltless cracker that resembled a saltine in appearance. It was approximately four inches square and a quarter-inch thick and was much denser than a saltine. Hardtack apparently tasted about as bad as it sounds, but considering the alternative was usually weevil-ridden bread, seamen couldn't afford to be particular.

He Repeated the Snapping
of His Pistol at My Head

≈≈≈≈≈

Philip Ashton, Jr.

*Pirate Captain Edward (or Ned) Low[1] was born in Westmin-
ster, England. Something of a thief and a juvenile delinquent,
he apparently never learned to read or write. He went to sea
with one of his brothers and eventually ended up in Boston
where he married Eliza Marble, who was from a good family,
in 1714. Shortly after his daughter was born, his wife died and
he lost his job, so he set to sea once more. After accidently
killing a man when he was trying to shoot the ship's captain,
he ran away with twelve of the crew and set himself up as a
pirate. He was said to be one of the bloodiest of pirates and that
his cruelty towards his crews often caused them to desert him.*

*Eventually he joined forces with Captian George Lowther,
another pirate who at that time was also short of men. Within
a few months Lowther had about a hundred pirates under his
command, but he found Captain Low to be an unruly officer
and they parted company on May 28, 1722; Low taking a
brigantine and 44 men with him.[2]*

*Low eventually gathered several ships under his command
and took 140 prizes over the next twenty months. He was
known for boldly charging into harbors and plundering ships
at anchor. Usually, he was able to take ships without a battle
by running up his black flag and telling his victims that he
would kill them all unless they surrendered immediately
without any sign of resistance.*

*Low had a reputation for murdering those who didn't join
him and scuttling the vessels. While he did let many of his
prizes go free after plundering them, his cruelty increased as
time went on. He had a particular dislike for Portuguese. On
one occasion, a Portuguese captain dropped a sack of 11,000*

gold coins overboard, rather than have it fall into the pirates'
hands. This man was tied to his ship's mast and Low sliced off
his lips with his cutlass. The pirates then cooked the lips in a
fire and forced the mate of the Portuguese vessel to eat them.
Then they murdered the entire 32-man crew of this ship. For
Portuguese prisoners, decapitation and disemboweling were
common. After the U.S. Navy captured one of his ships on June
10, 1723, Low began treating New Englanders with the same
ferocity. Sometimes he would make the captain of a New Eng-
land vessel strip naked and whip him around the deck. On tiring
of this he would shoot the victim in the head. Other times he
would cut off their ears and slit open their noses.

Fisherman Philip Ashton, Jr. was with Low through most
of this period, though he refrains from describing the more
horrendous attrocities committed by these pirates. Ashton
was captured in the harbor of Port Roseway, near what is
now Shelburne in Nova Scotia, Canada about two weeks after
Low parted ways with Lowther. His account was published in
a pamphlet titled A History of the Strange Adventures and
Signal Deliverances of Mr. Philip Ashton, Jun. of Marblehead[3] *(1725). It was transcribed by a Boston minister, which*
may account for the religious references and the missing
descriptions of the pirates' more barbarous acts.

Upon Friday, June 15th, 1722, after I had been out for some time in the
schooner *Milton* upon the fishing grounds off Cape Sable Shore, among
others, I came to sail in company with Nicholas Merritt in a shallop[4] and
stood in for Port Roseway, designing to harbor there till the Sabbath was
over; where we arrived about four of the clock in the afternoon. When
we came into the harbor, where several of our fishing vessels had arrived
before us, we spied among them a brigantine, which we supposed to
have been an inward bound vessel from the West Indies, and had no
apprehensions of any danger from her; but by that time we had been at
anchor two or three hours, a boat from the brigantine with four hands,
came alongside of us and the men jumped in upon our deck, without
our suspecting anything but that they were friends come on board to
visit or inquire what news, till they drew their cutlasses and pistols from
under their clothes and cocked the one and brandished the other and
began to curse and swear at us, and demanded a surrender of ourselves
and vessel to them. It was too late for us to rectify our mistake and think

of freeing ourselves from their power; for however we might have been able (being five of us and a boy) to have kept them at a distance, had we known who they were, before they had boarded us, yet now we had our arms to seek; and being in no capacity to make any resistance, were necessitated to submit ourselves to their will and pleasure. In this manner they surprised Nicholas Merritt, and twelve or thirteen other fishing vessels this evening.

When the boat went off from our vessel, they carried me on board the brigantine, and who should it prove [to be] but the infamous Ned Low, the pirate, with about forty-two hands, two great guns, and four swivel guns.[5] You may easily imagine how I looked and felt when, too late to prevent it, I found myself fallen into the hands of such a mad, roaring, mischievous crew; yet I hoped that they would not force me away with them, and I purposed to endure any hardship among them patiently, rather than turn pirate with them.

Low presently sent for me aft, and according to the pirates usual custom and in their proper dialect, asked me if I would sign their articles, and go along with them. I told him no, I could by no means consent to go with them. I should be glad if he would give me my liberty and put me on board any vessel, or set me on shore there. For indeed my dislike of their company and actions, my concern for my parents, and my fears of being found in such bad company, made me dread the thoughts of being carried away by them; so that I had not the least inclination to continue with them.

Upon my utter refusal to join and go with them, I was thrust down into the hold, which I found to be a safe retreat for me several times afterwards. By that time, I had been in the hold a few hours, they had completed the taking the several vessels that were in the harbor and the examining of the men; and the next day I was fetched up with some others that were there and about thirty or forty of us were put on board a schooner belonging to Mr. Orn of Marblehead [Massachusetts], which the pirates made use of for a sort of a prison upon the present occasion; where we were all confined unarmed, with an armed guard over us, till the Sultan's pleasure should be further known.

The next Lord's Day about noon, one of the quartermasters, John Russel by name, came on board the schooner and took six of us, (Nicholas Merritt, Joseph Libbie, Lawrence Fabens, and myself—all of Marblehead, the eldest of, if I mistake not, under 21 years of age[6]—with two others) and carried us on board the brigantine, where we were called upon the quarter-deck, and Low came up to us with pistol in hand and with a full mouth demanded, "Are any of you married men?" This short and unexpected question, and the sight of the pistol, struck us all dumb, and not a man of us dared to speak a word for fear there should have been a design in it, which we were not able to see through. Our silence kindled our new master into a flame, who could not bear it, that so many beardless boys should deny him an answer to so plain a question; and therefore in a rage, he cocked his pistol and clapped it to my head and cried out, "You dog! Why don't you answer me?" and swore vehemently he would shoot me through the head if I did not tell him immediately whether I was married or no.

I was sufficiently frightened at the fierceness of the man and the boldness of his threatening, but rather than lose my life for so trifling a matter, I even ventured at length to tell him I was not married as loud as I dared to speak it; and so said the rest of my companions. Upon this he seemed something pacified, and turned away from us.

It seems his design was to take no married man away with him, how young so ever he might be, which I often wondered at; till after I had been with him some considerable time, and could observe in him an uneasiness in the sentiments of his mind and the workings of his passions towards a young child he had at Boston (his wife being dead, as I learned, some small time before he turned pirate) which upon every lucid interval from reveling and drink he would express a great tenderness for, inasmuch that I have seen him sit down and weep plentifully upon the mentioning of it; and then I concluded that probably the reason of his taking none but single men was that he might have none with him under the influence of such powerful attractives as a wife and children, lest they should grow uneasy in his service and have an inclination to desert him and return home for the sake of their families.

Low presently came up to us again, and asked the old question, whether we would sign their articles and go along with them. We all told him no, we could not; so we were dismissed. But within a little while we were called to him singly, and then it was demanded of me with sternness and threats whether I would join with them. I still persisted in the denial; which through the assistance of heaven, I was resolved to do, though he shot me. And as I understood, all my six companions, who were called in their turns, still refused to go with him.

Then I was led down into the steerage[7] by one of the quartermasters, and there I was assaulted with temptations of another kind in hopes to win me over to become one of them; a number of them got about me, and instead of hissing, shook their rattles and treated me with abundance of respect and kindness in their way. They did all they could to soothe my sorrows and set before me the strong allurement of the vast riches they should gain and what mighty men they designed to be, and would fain [i.e. gladly] have me to join with them and share in their spoils. And to make all go down the more glib, they greatly importuned me to drink with them, not doubting but this wile would sufficiently entangle me and so they should prevail with me to do that in my cups, which they perceived they could not bring me to while I was sober. But all their fair and plausible carriage, their proffered kindness and airy notions of riches had not the effect upon me which they desired; and I had no inclination to drown my sorrows with my senses in their inebriating bowls and so refused their drink, as well as their proposals.

After this I was brought upon deck again and Low came up to me with his pistol cocked and clapped it to my head and said to me, "You dog you! If you will not sign our articles and go along with me, I'll shoot you through the head," and uttered his threats with his utmost fierceness and with the usual flashes of swearing and cursing. I told him that I was in his hands and he might do with me what he pleased, but I could not be willing to go with him. And then I earnestly begged of him with many tears and used all the arguments I could think of to persuade him not to carry me away, but he was deaf to my cries and unmoved by all I could say to him and told me I was an impudent dog and swore I should go with him whether I would or no. So I found all my cries and entreaties were in vain and there was no help for it, go with them I must, and as I understood they set mine and my townsmen's names down in their book, though against our consent. And I desire to mention it with due acknowledgments to God, who withheld me that neither their promises nor their threatenings nor blows could move me to a willingness to join with them in their pernicious ways.

Upon Tuesday, June 19th [1722], they changed their vessel and took for their privateer, as they called it, a schooner[8] belonging to Mr. Joseph Dolliber of Marblehead—being new, clean, and a good sailor—and shipped all their hands on board her and put the prisoners, such as they designed to send home, on board the brigantine with one who was her master and ordered them for Boston.

When I saw the captives were likely to be sent home, I thought I would make one attempt more to obtain my freedom and accordingly Nicholas Merritt, my townsman and kinsman, went along with me to Low and we fell upon our knees and with utmost importunity besought him to let us go home in the brigantine among the rest of the captives, but he immediately called for his pistols and told us we should not go, and swore bitterly if either of us offered to stir he would shoot us down.

Thus all attempts to be delivered out of the hands of unreasonable men (if they may be called men) were hitherto unsuccessful and I had the melancholy prospect of seeing the brigantine sail away with the most of us that were taken at Port Roseway, but myself and three townsmen mentioned and four of shoal-men detained on board the schooner in the worst of captivity without any present likelihood of escaping.

And yet before the brigantine sailed, an opportunity presented that gave me some hopes that I might get away from them; for some of Low's people, who had been on shore at Port Rossaway to get water, had left a dog belonging to him behind them and Low observing the dog a shore howling to come off ordered some hands to take the boat and fetch him. Two young men, John Holman, and Benjamin Ashton, both of Marblehead, readily jumped into the boat, and I (who pretty well know their inclination to be rid of such company and was exceedingly desirous myself to be freed from my present station and thought if I could but once set foot on shore, they should have good luck to get me on board again) was getting over the side into the boat, but Quartermaster Russel spied me and caught hold on my shoulder and drew me in board, and with a curse told me two was enough, I should not go. The two young men had more sense and virtue than to come off to them again, so that after some time of waiting, they found they were deprived of their men, their boat, and their dog; and they could not go after them.

When they saw what a trick was played them, the quartermaster came up to me cursing and swearing that I knew of their design to run away and intended to have been one of them, but though it would have been an unspeakable pleasure to me to have been with them, yet I was forced to tell him I knew not of their design; and indeed I did not, though I had good reason to suspect what would be the event of their going. This did not pacify the quartermaster, who with outrageous cursing and swearing clapped his pistol to my head and snapped it; but it missed fire. This enraged him the more and he repeated the snapping of his pistol at my head three times, and it as often missed fire; upon which he held it overboard and snapped it the fourth time, and then it went off very readily. (Thus did God mercifully quench the violence of the fire that was meant to destroy me!) The quartermaster upon this, in the utmost fury, drew his cutlass and fell upon me with it, but I leaped down into the hold and got among a crowd that was there, and so escaped the further effects of his madness and rage. Thus, though God suffered me not to gain my wished for freedom, yet he wonderfully preserved me from death.

All hopes of obtaining deliverance were now past and gone. The brigantine and fishing vessels were upon their way homeward, the boat was ashore and not likely to come off again. I could see no possible way of escape; and who can express the concern and agony I was in to see myself, a young lad not 20 years old carried forcibly from my parents, whom I had so much reason to value for the tenderness I knew they had for me, and to whom my being among pirates would be as a sword in their bowels and the anguishes of death to them; confined to such company as I could not but have an exceeding great abhorrence of; in danger of being poisoned in my morals by living among them; and of falling a sacrifice to justice if ever I should be taken with them. I had no way left for my comfort, but earnestly to commit myself and my cause to God and wait upon him for deliverance in his own time and way; and in the meanwhile firmly to resolve, through Divine Assistance, that nothing should ever bring me to a willingness to join with them or share in their spoils.

I soon found that any death was preferable to being linked with such a vile crew of miscreants, to whom it was a sport to do mischief; where prodigious drinking, monstrous cursing and swearing, hideous blasphemies, and open defiance of heaven, and contempt of Hell itself was the constant employment, unless when sleep something abated the noise and revelings.

Thus confined, the best course I could take was to keep out of the way, down in the hold or wherever I could be most free from their perpetual din; and fixed purpose with myself, that the first time I had an opportunity to set my foot on shore, let it be in what part of the world it would, it should prove (if possible) my taking a final leave of Low and company.

I would remark it now also (that I might not interrupt the story with it afterwards) that while I was on board Low, they used once a week, or fortnight as the evil spirit moved them, to bring me under examination and anew demand my signing their articles and joining with them; but blessed be God I was enabled to persist in a constant refusal to become one of them, though I was thrashed with sword or cane as often as I denied them; the fury of which I had no way to avoid but by jumping down into the hold where for a while I was safe. I looked upon myself for a long while but as a dead man among them and expected every day of examination would prove the last of my life, till I learned from some of them that it was one of their articles not to draw blood or take away the life of any man after they had given him quarter,[9] unless he was to be punished as a criminal; and this emboldened me afterwards so that I was not so much afraid to deny them, seeing my life was given me for a prey.

This Tuesday [June 19, 1722], towards evening, Low and company came to sail in the schooner, formerly called the *Mary*, now the *Fancy*, and made off for Newfoundland; and here they met with such an adventure as had like to have proved fatal to them. They fell in with the mouth of St. John's Harbor[10] [on July 2nd] in a fog before they knew where they were; when the fog clearing up a little, they spied a large ship riding at anchor in the harbor, but could not discern what she was by reason of the thickness of the air and concluded she was a fish trader. This they looked upon as a boon prize for them and thought they should be wonderfully well accommodated with a good ship under foot, and if she proved but a good sailer, would greatly further their roving designs and render them a match for almost anything they could meet with, so that they need not fear being taken.

Accordingly they came to a resolution to go in and take her; and imagining it was best doing it by stratagem, they concluded to put all their hands, but six or seven, down in the hold and make a show as if they were a fishing vessel and so run up along side of her, and surprise her and bring her off; and great was their joy at the distant prospect how cleverly they should catch her. They began to put their designs in execution, stowed away their hands, leaving but a few upon deck, and made sail in order to seize the prey; when there comes along a small fisherboat, from out the harbor, and hailed them, and asked them from whence they were? They told them from Barbados, and were laden with rum and sugar; then they asked the fisherman what large ship that was in the harbor, who told them it was a large man-of-war.[11]

The very name of a man-of-war struck them all up in a heap, spoiled their mirth, their fair hopes, and promising design of having a good ship at command; and lest they should catch a tartar, they thought it their wisest and safest way, instead of going into the harbor, to be gone as fast as they could; and accordingly they stretched away farther eastward and put into a small harbor, called Carbonear,[12] about fifteen leagues[13] distance; where they went on shore; took the place and destroyed the houses, but hurt none of the people (as they told me, for I was not suffered to go a shore with them).

The next day they made off for the grand bank where they took seven or eight vessels, and among them a French banker,[14] a ship of about 350 tons, and two guns. This they carried off with them and stood away for St. Michaels.[15]

Off of St. Michaels they took a large Portuguese pink[16] laden with wheat, coming out of the road, which I was told was formerly called the *Rose Frigate.*[17] She struck to the schooner, fearing the large ship that was coming down to them—though all Low's force had been no match for her, if the Portuguese had made a good resistance. This pink they soon observed to be a much better sailer than their French banker, which went heavily, and therefore they threw the greatest part of the wheat overboard, reserving only enough to ballast the vessel for the present, and took what they wanted out of the banker and then burnt her, and sent the most of the Portuguese away in a large launch they had taken.[18]

Now they made the pink, which mounted fourteen guns, their commodore, and with this and the schooner sailed from St. Michaels to the Canaries, where off of Tenerife[19] they gave chase to a sloop, which got under the command of the fortress and so escaped sailing into their hands. But stretching along to the western end of the island, they came up with a fishing boat, and being in want of water, made them pilot them into a small harbor, where they went a shore and got a supply.

After they had watered, they sailed away for Cape Verde Islands, and upon making the Isle of May,[20] they descried a sloop, which they took, and it proved to be a Bristol man,[21] one [Captain] Pare or Pier,[22] master; this sloop they designed for a tender,[23] and put on board her my kinsman Nicholas Merritt with eight or nine hands more and sailed away for Bonavista with a design to careen[24] their vessels.

In their passage to Bonavista, the sloop wronged both the pink and the schooner; which the hands on board observing, being mostly forced men or such as were weary of their employment, upon the 5th of September ran away with her and made their escape.[25]

When they came to Bonavista, they hove down the schooner and careened her, and then the pink; and here they gave the wheat—which they had kept to ballast the pink with—to the Portuguese and took other ballast.

After they had cleaned and fitted their vessels, they steered away for St. Nicholas[26] to get better water; and here as I was told, seven or eight hands out of the pink went a shore a fowling, but never came off more, among which I suppose Lawrence Fabens was one, and what became of them I never could hear to this day.[27] Then they put out to sea and stood away for the coast of Brazil, hoping to meet with richer prizes than they had yet taken. In the passage thither, they made a ship which they gave chase to, but could not come up with. And when they came upon the coast, it had like to have proved a sad coast to them for the trade-winds blowing exceeding hard at southeast, they fell in upon the northern part of the coast, near two hundred leagues to the leeward[28] of where they designed; and here we were all in exceeding great danger and for five days and nights together hourly feared when we should be swallowed up by the violence of the wind and sea, or stranded upon some of the shoals that lay many leagues off from land.[29] In this time of extremity, the poor wretches had no where to go for help! For they were at open defiance with their maker, and they could have but little comfort in the thoughts of their agreement with Hell; such mighty hectors[30] as they were in a clear sky and a fair gale, yet a fierce wing and a boisterous sea sunk their spirits to a cowardly dejection, and they evidently feared the Almighty—whom before they defied—lest He was come to torment them before their expected time; and though they were so habituated to cursing and swearing, that the dismal prospect of death, and this of so long continuance, could not correct the language of most of them, yet you might plainly see the inward horror and anguish of their minds visible in their countenances, and like men amazed or starting out of sleep in a fright, I could hear them every now and then cry out, "Oh! I wish I were at home."

When the fierceness of the weather was over and they had recovered their spirits, by the help of a little Nantes,[31] they bore away to the West Indies, and made the three islands called the Triangles, lying off the

Main[32] about forty leagues to the eastward of Surinam. Here they went in and careened their vessels again; and it had like to have proved a fatal scouring to them, for as they hove down the pink, Low had ordered so many hands upon the shrouds, and yards to throw her bottom out of water that it threw her ports, which were open, under water and the water flowed in with such freedom that it presently overset her. Low and the doctor were in the cabin together, and as soon as he perceived the water to gush in upon him, he bolted out at one of the stern-ports, which the doctor also attempted, but the sea rushed so violently into the port by that time as to force him back into the cabin, upon which Low nimbly run his arm into the port and caught hold of his shoulder and drew him out, and so saved him. The vessel pitched her masts to the ground in about six fathom[33] water and turned her keel out of water; but as her hull filled, it sunk, and by the help of her yard-arms, which I suppose bore upon the ground, her masts were raised something out of water. The men that were upon her shrouds and yards, got upon her hull when that was uppermost and then upon her top-masts and shrouds when they were raised again. I (who with other light lads were sent up to the main-top-gallant yard) was very difficultly put to it to save my life, being but a poor swimmer; for the boat which picked the men up refused to take me in and I was put upon making the best of my way to the buoy, which with much ado I recovered, and it being large I stayed myself by it till the boat came along close by it and then I called to them to take me in, but they being full of men still refused me; and I did not know but they meant to leave me to perish there. But the boat making way ahead very slowly because of her deep load and Joseph Libbie calling to me to put off from the buoy and swim to them, I even ventured it and he took me by the hand and drew me in board. They lost two men by this accident, viz. John Bell, and one they called Zana Gourdon. The men that were on board the schooner were busy a mending the sails under an awning, so they knew nothing of what had happened to the pink till the boat full of men came along side of them—though they were but about gun shot off and we made a great out-cry—and therefore they sent not their boat to help take up the men.

And now Low and his gang, having lost their frigate as their only privateer and with her the greatest part of their provision and water, were again reduced to their schooner [i.e. the *Fancy*] and in her they put to sea and were brought to very great straits for want of water; for they could not get a supply at the Triangles, and when they hoped to furnish themselves at Tobago,[34] the current set so strong and the season was so calm that they could not recover the harbor, so they were forced to stand away for Grand Grenada, a French island about eighteen leagues to the westward of Tobago, which they gained, after they had been at the hardship of half a pint of water a man for sixteen days together.

Here the French came on board and Low, having put all his men down but a sufficient number to sail the vessel, told them upon their inquiry whence he was, that he was come from Barbados and had lost his water and was obliged to put in for a recruit; the poor people not suspecting him for a pirate, readily suffered him to send his men ashore and fetch off a supply. But the Frenchmen afterwards suspecting he was a smuggling trader, thought to have made a boon prize of him and the next day fitted out a large Rhode Island-built sloop of 70 tons, with four guns mounted and about thirty hands, with design to have taken him. Low was apprehensive of no danger from them till they came close along side of him and plainly discovered their design by their number and actions and then he called up his hands upon deck, and having about ninety hands on board and eight guns mounted, the sloop and Frenchmen fell an easy prey to him and he made a privateer of her.[35]

After this they cruised for some time through the West Indies, in which excursion they took seven or eight sail of vessels, chiefly sloops.[36] At length they came to Santa Cruz,[37] where they took two sloops more and then came to anchor off the island.

While they lay an anchor here, it came into Low's head that he wanted a doctor's chest, and in order to procure one he put four of the Frenchmen on board one of the sloops, which he had just now taken, and sent them away to St. Thomas's,[38] about twelve leagues off where the sloops belonged, with the promise, that if they would presently send him off a good doctor's chest for what he sent to purchase it with, they should have their men and vessels again, but if not, he would kill all the men and burn the vessels. The poor people in compassion to their neighbors and to preserve their interest, readily complied with his demands; so that in little more than twenty-four hours the four Frenchmen returned with what they went for, and then according to promise, they and their sloops were dismissed.

From Santa Cruz they sailed till they made Curacao,[39] in which passage they gave chase to two sloops that out sailed them and got clear;

then they ranged the coast of New Spain, and made Cartagena,[40] and about mid way between Cartagena and Portobello,[41] they descried two tall ships which proved to be the [H.M.S.] *Mermaid* man-of-war and a large Guineaman.[42] Low was now in the Rhode Island sloop and one Farrington Spriggs, a quartermaster, was commander of the schooner, where I still was. For some time they made sail after the two ships, till they came so near that they could plainly see the man-of-war's large range of teeth, and then they turned tail to and made the best of their way from them; upon which the man-of-war gave them chase and over-haled them apace. And now I confess I was in as great terror as ever I had been yet, for I concluded we should be taken, and I could expect no other but to die for [the] company's sake; so true is what Solomon tells us, a companion of fools shall be destroyed. But the pirates finding the man-of-war to overhale them, separated, and Low stood out to sea, and Spriggs stood in for the shore.[43] The man-of-war observing the sloop to be the larger vessel much and fullest of men, threw out all the sail she could and stood after her, and was in a fair way of coming up with her presently. But it happened there was one man on board the sloop that knew of a shoal ground thereabouts, who directed Low to run over it. He did so and the man-of-war, who had now so forereached him as to sling a shot over him, in the close pursuit ran aground upon the shoal. And so Low and company escaped hanging for this time.

Spriggs, who was in the schooner, when he saw the danger they were in of being taken, upon the man-of-war's outsailing them, was afraid of falling into the hands of justice; to prevent which, he and one of his chief companions took their pistols and laid them down by them, and solemnly swore to each other and pledged the oath in a bumper of liquor that if they saw there was at last no possibility of escaping, but that they should be taken they would set foot to foot and shoot one another to escape justice and the halter [i.e. noose]. As if Divine Justice were not as inexorable as humane!

But, as I said, he stood in for the shore and made into Pickeroon Bay, about eighteen leagues from Cartagena, and so got out of reach of danger. By this means the sloop and schooner were parted, and Spriggs made sail towards the Bay of Honduras and came to anchor in a small island called Utila, about seven or eight leagues to leeward of Roatán,[44] where by the help of a small sloop he had taken the day before, he haled down and cleaned the schooner.

While Spriggs lay at Utila, there was an opportunity presented which gave occasion to several of us to form a design of making our escape out of the pirates company; for having lost Low and being but weak handed, Spriggs had determined to go through the Gulf and come upon the coast of New England to increase his company and supply himself with provision; whereupon a number of us had entered into a combination to take the first fair advantage to subdue our masters and free ourselves. There were in all about twenty-two men on board the schooner and eight of us were in the plot, which was that when we should come upon the coast of New England, we would take the opportunity when the crew had sufficiently dozed themselves with drink and had got sound asleep, to secure them under the hatches and bring the vessel and company in and throw ourselves upon the mercy of the government.

But it pleased God to disappoint our design. The day that they came to sail out of Utila, after they had been parted from Low about five weeks, they discovered a large sloop which bore down upon them. Spriggs, who knew not the sloop, but imagined it might be a Spanish privateer full of men, being but weak-handed himself, made the best of his way from her. The sloop greatly overhaled the schooner. Low, who knew the schooner and thought that since they had been separated she might have fallen into the hands of honest men, fired upon her and struck her the first shot. Spriggs, seeing the sloop fuller of men than ordinary (for Low had been to Honduras and had taken a sloop and brought off several bay-men, and was now become an hundred strong) and remaining still ignorant of his old mate, refused to bring to, but continued to make off and resolved if they came up with him, to fight them the best he could. Thus the harpies had like to have fallen fowl of one another. But Low hoisting his pirate colors, discovered who he was; and then, hideous was the noisy joy among the piratical crew on all sides, accompanied with firing and carousing at the finding their old master and companions and their narrow escape; and so the design of cruising upon the coast of New England came to nothing. A good providence it was to my dear country, that it did so; unless we could have timely succeeded in our design to surprise them.

Yet it had like to have proved a fatal providence to those of us that had a hand in the plot; for though our design of surprising Spriggs and company when we should come upon the coast of New England was carried with as much secrecy as was possible (we hardly daring to trust one another and mentioning it always with utmost privacy, and not plainly, but in distant hints), yet now that Low appeared, Spriggs had got an account of it some way or other, and full of resentment and rage he goes aboard Low and acquaints him with what he called our treacherous design, and says all he can to provoke him to revenge the mischief upon us and earnestly urged that we might be shot. But God who has the hearts of all men in His own hands and turns them as He pleases, so overruled, that Low turned it off with a laugh and said he did not know but if it had been his own case, as it was ours, he should have done so himself; and all that Spriggs could say was not able to stir up his resentments and procure any heavy sentence upon us.

Thus Low's merry air saved us at that time; for had he lisped a word in compliance with what Spriggs urged, we had surely some of us, if not all, have been lost. Upon this, he came on board the schooner again, heated with drink, but more chased in his own mind that he could not have his will of us, and swore and tore like a madman, crying out that four of us ought to go forward and be shot; and to me in particular he said, "You dog, Ashton, deserve to be hanged up at the yardarm for designing to cut us off." I told him I had no design of hurting any man on board, but if they would let me go away quietly I should be glad. This matter made a very great noise on board for several hours, but at length the fire was quenched and through the goodness of God, I escaped being consumed by the violence of the flame.

The next day, Low ordered all into Roatán Harbor to clean, and here it was that through the favor of God to me, I first gained deliverance out of the pirates hands; though it was a long while before my deliverance was perfected in a return to my country and friends, as you will see in the sequel.

Roatán Harbor, as all about the Bay of Honduras, is full of small islands, which go by the general name of the keys. When we had got in here, Low and some of his chief men had got ashore upon one of these small islands, which they called Port Royal Key, where they made them booths and were carousing, drinking, and firing, while the two sloops—the Rhode Island and that which Low brought with him from the bay—were cleaning. As for the schooner, he loaded her with the logwood[45] which the sloop brought from the bay and gave her, according to promise, to one John Blaze and put four men along with him in her, and when they came to sail from this place, sent them away upon their own account, and what became of them I know not.

Upon Saturday the 9th of March, 1723, the cooper with six hands in the long-boat were going ashore at the watering place to fill their casks; as he came along by the schooner I called to him and asked him if he were going a shore? He told me yes. Then I asked him if he would take me along with him. He seemed to hesitate at the first, but I urged that I had never been on shore yet since I first came on board and I thought it very hard that I should be so closely confined when everyone else had the liberty of going ashore at several times, as there was occasion. At length he took me in, imagining, I suppose, that there would be no danger of my running away in so desolate uninhabited a place as that was.

I went into the boat with only an Ozenbrigs frock and trousers on and a milled cap upon my head, having neither shirt, shoes, nor stockings, nor anything else about me; whereas, had I been aware of such an opportunity, but one quarter of an hour before, I could have provided myself something better. However, thought I, if I can but once get footing on *terra firma*, though in never so bad circumstances, I shall count it a happy deliverance; for I was resolved, come what would, never to come on board again.

Low had often told me (upon my asking him to send me away in some of the vessels, which he dismissed after he had taken them) that I should go home when he did and not before, and swore that I should never set foot on shore till he did. But the time for deliverance was now come. God had ordered it that Low and Spriggs and almost all the commanding officers were ashore upon an island distinct from Roatán, where the watering place was. He presented me in sight, when the long boat came by, the only opportunity I could have had. He had moved the cooper to take me into the boat, and under such circumstances as rendered me least liable to suspicion; and so I got ashore.

When we came first to land, I was very active in helping to get the casks out of the boat and rolling them up to the watering place. Then I lay down at the fountain and took a hearty draught of the cool water; and anon, I gradually strolled along the beach picking up stones and shells and looking about me. When I had got about musket shot off from them (though they had taken no arms along with them in the boat) I began to make up to the edge of the woods. When the cooper spying me, called after me and asked me where I was going, I told him I was going to get some coconuts, for there were some coconut trees just before me. So soon as I had recovered the woods and lost sight of them, I betook myself to my heels and ran as fast as the thickness of the bushes and my naked feet would let me. I bent my course, not directly from them, but rather up behind them, which I continued till I had got a considerable way into the woods, and yet not so far from them but that I could hear their talk when they spoke anything loud; and here I lay close in a very great thicket, being well assured if they should take the pains to hunt after me never so carefully, they would not be able to find me.

After they had filled their casks and were about to go off, the cooper called after me to come away, but I lay snug in my thicket and would give him no answer, though I plainly enough heard him. At length they set a hallooing for me, but I was still silent. I could hear them say to one another, "The dog is lost in the woods and can't find the way out again." Then they hallooed again and cried, "He is run-away and won't come again." The cooper said if he had thought I would have served him so, he would not have brought me ashore. They plainly saw it would be in vain to seek me in such hideous woods and thick brushes. When they were weary with hallooing, the cooper at last, to show his good will to me (I can't but love and thank him for his kindness) called out, "If you don't come away presently, I'll go off and leave you alone." But all they could say was no temptation to me to discover [i.e. reveal] myself and least of all that of their going away and leaving me, for this was the very thing I desired, that I might be rid of them and all that belonged to them. So finding it in vain for them to wait any longer, they put off with their water [and] without me; and thus was I left upon a desolate island destitute of all help and much out of the way of all travelers; however this wilderness I looked upon as hospitable and this loneliness as good company, compared with the state and society I was now happily delivered from.

When I supposed they were gone off, I came out of my thicket and drew down to the waterside, about a mile below the watering place where there was a small run of water, and here I sat down to observe their motions and know when the coast was clear; for I could not but have some remaining fears lest they should send a company of armed men after me. Yet I thought if they should, the woods and bushes were so thick that it would be impossible they should find me. As yet I had nothing to eat, nor indeed were my thoughts much concerned about living in this desolate place, but they were chiefly taken up about my getting clear. And to my joy, after the vessels had stayed five days in this harbor, they came to sail and put out to sea, and I plainly saw the schooner part from the two sloops and shape a different course from them.

When they were gone and the coast clear, I began to reflect upon myself and my present condition. I was upon an island from whence I could not get off. I knew of no humane creature within many scores of miles of me. I had but a scanty clothing and no possibility of getting more. I was destitute of all provision for my support and knew not how I should come at any. Everything looked with a dismal face. The sad prospect drew tears from me in abundance. Yet since God had graciously granted my desires in freeing me out of the hands of the sons of violence, whose business it is to devise mischief against their neighbor, and from whom everything that had the least face of religion and virtue was entirely banished—unless that Low would never suffer his men to work upon the Sabbath (it was more devoted to play) and I have seen some of them sit down to read in a good book—therefore I purposed to account all the hardship I might now meet with as light and easy, compared with being associated with them.

> Ashton goes on to describe the severe hardships he had to endure while he was self-marooned on Roatán Island[46] in the Bay of Honduras. He had no knife or any metal objects to fashion tools with or to catch prey with. If he could have caught an animal, he had no way to cut it up. Neither could he cook it, since he had no way of making a fire. Initially he was forced to live off wild fruit and raw turtle's eggs. The island was "greatly infested with vexatious insects." There were also snakes "as big round as a man's waist, though not above 12 or 14 feet long." On his first encounter with one of these boa constrictors, he said, "it opened its mouth wide enough to have thrown a hat into it, and blew out its breath at me." While these aren't venomous, there were several others that were—though he says he saw no rattlesnakes, except for the pirates.
>
> He found he could escape the insects by swimming over to a nearby barren island, but he had to contend with sharks and alligators while swimming back and forth. One time a shark struck his thigh, but it was in a place where the water was too shallow for the shark to maneuver to bite him. Another time he was attacked by a wild boar.
>
> Having no shoes, the sticks and rocks in the jungle and the broken shells on the beach soon tore his feet to shreds. He also became so weak that he would often suddenly pass out.

He spent the next nine months completely alone, with no one to talk to but himself. Then in November 1723, an old fisherman showed up in a canoe. After three days, the old man set out on a hunting expedition to another island and apparently drowned in a storm.

Though he was once again alone, he now had a knife and a flint which the old man had not taken with him. Having a fire was now essential as he was entering the cold, rainy winter months.

Eventually he spotted a sloop at the eastern end of the island. It took him two days and most of two nights to travel there. At one point he fell asleep at the base of a tree and awoke to the sounds of gunshots, only to discover the men from the ship were shooting at him. He quickly ran away into the jungle, but not before discerning they were Spaniards. He estimated they fired at least 150 shots at him. Though all missed, he went back the next day and found that six or seven shots had hit the tree within a foot of his head.

In June 1724, after sixteen months on the island, he was discovered barely alive by some Englishmen in two canoes. Eighteen of them and a Native American woman who was their servant were living on the nearby island of Barbarat, having fled the mainland because the Spaniards and Native Americans were about to attack them. While not much better than the pirates, they at least weren't involved in any illegal activities.[47]

Although his situation had greatly improved, he still was not out of danger. His narrative continues:

It happened, about six or seven months after these bay-men came to me [late December 1724 or early January 1725], that three men and I took a canoe with four oars to go over to Bonacca,[48] a hunting and to kill tortoise. While we were gone the rest of the bay-men haled up their canoes, and dried and tarred them, in order to go to the bay [i.e. the Bay of Honduras] and see how matters stood there, and to fetch off their effects which they had left behind them, in case they should find there was no safety for them in tarrying. But before they were gone, we, who had met with good success in our voyage, were upon our return to them with a full load of tortoise and firkt[49] pork.

As we were upon entering into the mouth of the harbor in a moonlight evening, we saw a great flash of light and heard the report of a gun—which we thought was much louder than a musket—out of a large peragua[50] which we saw near our Castle of Comfort.[51] This put us into a great consternation and we knew not what to make of it. Within a minute or two we heard a volley of eighteen or twenty small arms discharged upon the shore and heard some guns also fired off from the shore. Upon which we were satisfied that some enemy, pirates or Spaniards, were attacking our people; and being cut off from our companions by the peraguas which lay between us and them, we thought it our wisest way to save ourselves as well as we could. So we took down our little mast and sail that it might not betray us and rowed out of the harbor as fast as we could, thinking to make our escape from them undiscovered to an island about a mile and half off, but they either saw us before we had taken our sail down or heard the noise of our oars as we made out of the harbor and came after us with all speed in a peragua of eight or ten oars. We saw them coming and that they gained ground upon us apace and therefore [we] pulled up for life, resolving to reach the nearest shore if possible. The peragua overhaled us so fast that they discharged a swivel gun[52] at us which over-shot us, but we made a shift to gain the shore before they were come fairly within the reach of their small arms; which yet they fired upon us, as we were getting ashore.

Then they called to us and told us they were pirates and not Spaniards, and we need not fear, they would give us good quarter, supposing this would easily move us to surrender ourselves to them. But they could not have mentioned anything worse to discourage me from having anything to do with them, for I had the utmost dread of a pirate, and my first aversion to them was now strengthened with the just fears that if I should fall into their hands again, they would soon make a sacrifice of me for my deserting them. I therefore concluded to keep as clear of them as I could and the bay-men with me had no great inclination to be meddling with them, and so we made the best of our way into the woods. They took away our canoe from us and all that was in it, resolving if we would not come to them, they would strip us as far as they were able of all means of subsistence where we were. I, who had known what it was to be destitute of all things and alone, was not much concerned about that now that I had company, and they their arms with them so that we could have a supply of provision by hunting and fire to dress it with.

This company it seems were some of Sprigg's men, who was commander of the schooner when I ran away from them. This same Spriggs, I know not upon what occasion, had cast off the service of Low and set up for himself as the head of a party of rovers and had now a good ship of twenty-four guns and a Bermuda sloop of twelve guns under his command,[53] which were now lying in Roatán Harbor, where he put in to water and clean at the place where I first made my escape. He had discovered our people upon the small island where they resided and sent a peragua full of men to take them. Accordingly, they took all the men ashore and with them an Indian woman and child. Those of them that were ashore abused the woman shamefully. They killed one man after they were come ashore and threw him into one of the bay-men's canoes, where their tar was, and set fire to it and burnt him in it. Then they carried our people on board their vessels, where they were barbarously treated.

One of the bay-men, Thomas Grande, turned pirate, and he being acquainted that Old Father Hope (as we called him) had hid many things in the woods, told the pirates of it, who beat poor Hope unmercifully and made him go and show them where he had hid his treasure, which they took away from him.

After they had kept the bay-men on board their vessels for five days, then they gave them a flat of about five or six tons to carry them to the bay in, but they gave them no provision for their voyage, and before they sent them away, they made them swear to them not to come near us, who had made our escape upon another island. All the while the vessels rode in the harbor, we kept a good look out, but were put to some difficulties because we did not dare to make a fire to dress our victuals by, lest it should discover [i.e. reveal] whereabouts we were, so that we were forced to live upon raw provision for five days. But as soon as they were gone, Father Hope with his company of bay-men (little regarding an oath that was forced from them; and thinking it a wicked oath better broken than to leave four of us in such a helpless condition) came to us and acquainted us who they were and what they had done.

Thus the watchful providence of God, which had so often heretofore appeared on my behalf, again took special care of me and sent me out of the way of danger. It is very apparent that if I had been with my companions at the usual residence, I had been taken with them [sic]; and if I had, it is beyond question (humanely speaking) that I should not have escaped with life, if I should [sic] the most painful and cruel death that the madness and rage of Spriggs could have invented for me, who would now have called to mind the design I was engaged in while we were parted from Low, as well as my final deserting of them. But blessed be God, who had designs of favor for me and so ordered that I must at this time be absent from my company.

Philip Ashton was found by a Salem brigantine two years after his first escape from the pirates and was returned home on May 1, 1725—almost three years after his capture by pirates. He said, "I went the same evening to my father's house, where I was received as one coming to them from the dead, with all imaginable surprise and joy."

As to what happened to Captain Low: A month and a half after Ashton's first escape, Low's ships—the sloops Fortune *and* Ranger—*appeared off the coast of South Carolina and chased after a ship that suddenly whipped around and started firing at them. This ship turned out to be the man-of-war H.M.S.* Greyhound. *Low and the* Fortune *deserted the* Ranger, *then commanded by Capt. Charles Harris.*[54] *On seeing this, the men of the* Ranger *quickly surrendered. They were brought into Newport, Rhode Island, and of the forty-eight men on board, Capt. Harris and twenty-five of them were executed on July 19, 1723.*

Joseph Libbie, one of Ashton's three friends who were captured with him, was on the Ranger *when it was taken. Though he served the pirates unwillingly at first, it was determined that he had eventually joined them and he was hung with the rest.*

Low continued to terrorize the coast, but with increasing cruelty. After hacking off the head of the master of a New England fishing boat, he gave the boat to two Native Americans and sent them ashore with the body and a message that he intended to murder the master of every New England vessel he could find. On taking two whaling sloops later that day, he cut the heart out of one captain and the ears off the other. These were cooked and some of the crewmen were forced to eat them. The ears he served with salt and pepper. Though Low intended to kill more of these crews, his men talked him out of it.

After taking the ship Merry Christmas *and making a new Jolly Roger—a black flag with a red skeleton on it—Low and company set off for the Azores, Canaries, and Cape Verde Islands where he was joined by Capt. Lowther and then back to the Caribbean. What happened next is uncertain. There are a number of conflicting reports. One said his ship was wrecked in a storm with no survivors, while another said he retired in Brazil. But the most likely accounts reported that in the spring of 1724, Low got into an argument with his quartermaster and murdered him while he was sleeping. On discovering this the crew mutinied, setting Low and two others adrift in a small boat, where they were picked up by a French warship and hung in Martinique.*

After Spriggs separated from Low in the fall of 1723, Spriggs headed a pirate fleet that numbered up to five vessels. He was last reported capturing a ship in May 1725. Then a rumor went around that he and his cohort Capt. Shipton were marooned by their crews and "were got among the Mosquito Indians." This is probably accurate since Spriggs's quartermaster, Philip Lyne—now the captain of his own pirate sloop— took a prize off the coast of South Carolina on June 30th.

Whatever happened to Captains Spriggs and Low, they were never heard from again.

Notes

1. This is the same Capt. Low who captured Capt. George Roberts (see page 149).

2. Capt. Francis Farrington Spriggs was one of those who stayed with Low when Low and Lowther went their separate ways. It's thought that Spriggs originally became a pirate at the same time as Lowther, when, on a voyage that sailed from London in March 1721, Lowther led a mutiny and took over the ship.

3. Marblehead is a fishing port just north of Boston.

4. Shallop: a large boat with one or two masts, propelled by oars or sails, and rigged like a schooner.

5. Swivel guns: guns mounted on the ship's railing and could be swung from side to side.

6. Philip Ashton (age 19) was then the master of the schooner *Milton*. Nicholas Merritt (20) was master of the shallop *Jane*. Joseph Libbie (20) was one of Ashton's crew. Lawrence Fabens (about 20) was one of the crew on the schooner *Rebeckah*.

7. Steerage: the forward part of the stern cabin, under the quarter-deck.

8. The *Mary*, which Capt. Low later renamed the *Fancy*.

9. Quarter: to refrain from slaying someone and often to accept them as a prisoner.

10. St. John's Harbor, Newfoundland, Canada.

11. The *Solebay*.

12. Carbonear, Newfoundland.

13. League: a measurement usually of about three miles.

14. Banker: a vessel engaged in cod fishing on the coast of Newfoundland.

15. St. Michaels (São Miguel) is the largest island of the Azores, a group of islands which lie about 800 miles west of Portugal. Before heading for St. Michaels, they were caught in a hurricane and all hands were forced to work around the clock to save the ship. Trying to stay afloat amongst tremendous waves, they hoisted much of their goods, provisions, and six guns overboard. They cut their anchors and even considered chopping down their masts and pitching them over the side. After refitting their ship on a small island in the western Caribbean, Low and his crew decided to head for St. Michaels since there were several warships patrolling the Caribbean searching for pirates. They arrived at St. Michaels on August 3, 1722.

16. Pink: a general name given to a sailing ship with a very narrow, rounded stern.

17. This ship was also called the *Rose Pink*. Frigate: a light three-masted, fully-rigged ship with from 20 to 38 guns on a single gun deck. The deck is split-level with a rise of four or five steps from the waist up to the quarter-deck and the forecastle. It is a fast sailing man-of-war.

18. Actually, they let all of the Portuguese go, except one. This was the cook, who the pirates thought was "a greasy fellow who would fry well in the fire," so he was tied to the mast of the banker before they burned it. Also while at St. Michaels, on August 20th, they took the galley *Wright* after a short resistance. The crew, especially the Portuguese passengers (which included two friars), were tortured and mangled.

19. The Canary Islands are a group of seven major islands and six smaller ones that are scattered in a 300 mile arc and lie about 70 miles off the coast of Africa. Tenerife is one of these islands.

20. The Cape Verde Islands are a group of ten larger islands and several smaller ones that lie about 320 miles off the coast of Africa. The Isle of May (Maio) and Bonavista (Boa Vista) are two of the Cape Verde Islands.

21. Bristol man: a ship from Bristol, England.

22. Captain James Pease.

23. Tender: a boat that is carried or towed by a ship.

24. Careen: to lean a vessel over on its side so the bottom can be cleaned and repaired. Because of worms eating into the wood and the buildup of barnacles, cleaning the bottom of the ship was particular important to pirates because they wanted their vessels to sail as fast as possible so they could catch prizes or escape from a man-of-war sent to bring them to justice.

25. Nicholas Merritt, in his account of his escape wrote:

> I, who was on board the schooner, had been greatly abused by an old pirate, whom they called Jacob, but what his surname was I know not. I desired some that

were upon occasion going on board Low, to acquaint him how much I was beat and abused by old Jacob. They did so and Low ordered me to be put on board the sloop. Thus the foundation of my escape was laid, and my sufferings proved the means of my deliverance.

On board the sloop there were nine hands (one of them a Portugue) whom Low had no suspicion of, but thought he could trust them as much as any men he had; and when I came on board I made the tenth man. We perceived that the sloop greatly wronged both the pink and schooner, and there were six of us (as we found by sounding one another at a distance) that wanted to get away. When we understood one another's minds pretty fully, we resolved upon an escape. Accordingly the 5th of September, 1722, a little after break of day, all hands being upon deck, three of us six went forward, and three aft, and one John Rhodes, who was a stout hand, stepped into the cabin and took a couple of pistols in his hands and stood in the cabin door and said if there were any that would go along with him, they should be welcome, for he designed to carry the sloop home and surrender himself; but if any man attempted to make resistance, he swore he would shoot down the first man that stirred. There being five of us that wanted to gain our liberty, he was sure of us; and as for the other four they saw plainly it was in vain for them to attempt to oppose us. So we haled close upon a wind, and stood away.

When we parted with Low, we had but a very little water aboard, and but two or three pieces of meat among us all; but we had bread enough. We designed for England, but our want of water was so great, being put to half a pint a man, and that very muddy and foul . . . so we steered for St. Michaels, where we arrived on September 26.

Though they explained their situation to Portugese authorities, they were thrown in prison as pirates. Though he escaped hanging, he was held until June 1723. A severe illness and a sympathetic official facilitated his release, though his companions apparently remained in prison until they died. Merritt then caught a ship to Lisbon and another to Boston, finally arriving home on September 28th. He had been a prisoner of the pirates for three months and held as a prisoner at St. Michaels for nine months.

26. St. Nicholas (São Nicolau) is one of the Cape Verde Islands.

27. It was at this point that Capt. George Roberts was captured. See page 185.

28. Leeward: the side of the ship away from the wind.

29. This incident appears to be misplaced in the narrative and seems to be a description of the hurricane that occurred in July while they were in the Caribbean.

30. Hectors: bullies.

31. Nantes: probably a type of alcohol made in Nantes, France.

32. The Spanish Main was the mainland of the Americas adjacent to the Caribbean, primarily from the Isthmus of Panama to the mouth of the Orinoco River in Venezuela. Surinam is a country on the northern coast of South Amer-

ica, between Guyana and French Guiana with Brazil to the south.

33. Fathom: a measurement equal to six feet.

34. Tobago is an island off the coast of Venezuela between Trinadad and Granada.

35. Low took over the sloop and gave Capt. Spriggs the schooner *Fancy*.

36. It was at about this time that Low also captured the Portuguese ship *Nostra Signiora de Victoria* where he cut off the captain's lips and cooked them, as was mentioned earlier.

37. Santa Cruz is a small island near Puerto Rico.

38. St. Thomas is one of the Virgin Islands.

39. Curacao is an island off the coast of Venezuela.

40. Cartagena is a city on Columbia's Caribbean coast.

41. Portobello is a town on the Caribbean side of what is now Panama.

42. Guineaman: a ship engaged in trade with Guinea, probably a slave ship.

43. At this time they also had the snow *Unity* with them, which they had recently taken from a Captain Leonard on January 25, 1723.

44. Both Utila and Roatán are islands in the Gulf of Honduras.

45. A valuable purple dye was extracted from logwood. The English and colonials usually cut it illegally from Spanish territory.

46. Roatán Island is about 30 miles long and about 4 miles across.

47. Ashton didn't know it, but two months earlier, on April 4, 1724, Captain Spriggs marooned some men on another part of the island. Six of these men were from ships captured by Spriggs and a seventh was James Nelley, one of Sprigg's pirate crew that he wanted to get rid of. Spriggs left them with an old musket and some powder and ball. Ten days later they were discovered by two men in a canoe and transported to another island, where twelve days after that they were picked up by a sloop and carried to Jamaica.

48. Bonacca (or Guanaja) is an island to the east of Roatán. On December 23, 1724, Capt. Spriggs (who had parted with Low and was now sailing with his own pirate fleet) took a group of sixteen ships that were carrying logwood in the Bay of Honduras. One of these vessels, which was by Capt. Kelsey, was burned and the captain, along with his crew, were set adrift in a long boat. They reached the island of Bonacca, from which they were rescued by a passing sloop.

49. Firkt: (? Firked: beaten or pounded.)

50. Peragua: a native dugout canoe, or sometimes a plank-built, flat-bottomed boat with one sail.

51. Castle of Comfort was the name they gave to their group of shelters.

52. Swivel gun: a small cannon-like gun mounted on the ship's railing and could be swung from side to side.

53. In the Fall of 1723, Low and Spriggs captured the ship *Delight*. Spriggs was given command of this ship along with sixty men. Two days later, Spriggs

slipped away in the night after a quarrel with Low. It seems one member of the crew had murdered a man in cold blood and Spriggs felt he should be executed, but was overruled by Low. After departing from Low, Spriggs and his crew made a black flag like Low's, with a white skeleton holding an arrow piercing a bleeding heart in one hand and an hourglass in the other. Hoisting their new flag to the masthead, they fired all their guns in salute and set off in search of prizes. In twelve months, Spriggs and his men captured forty vessels.

54. Capt. Charles Harris joined Capt. Lowther after the ship he was on was taken on January 10, 1722. Originally from London, he was 25 years old when he went to the gallows. Spriggs was apparently on the *Fortune* for he appeared with Low at a later date and after that was commodore of two vessels that attacked the camp of Ashton and the bay-men, as related earlier.

Twenty Dollars for Every
Head They Cut Off

≈≈≈≈≈

Richard Glasspoole

At the age of 20, Richard Glasspoole was working for the British East India Company as the fourth mate on their ship Marquis of Ely. *In 1809 his ship reached the coast of China. He and several other men were sent off in a small boat to get someone familiar with these waters who could pilot the ship to the harbor. As they were returning, a storm forced the ship put out to sea. Unfortunately, this left them to hazard the storm in a ill-equipped, leaky, open boat. They were soon captured by the ladrones, which is what the Chinese pirates were called. "Ladrone" being Portuguese for "thief."*

Glasspoole's narrative of his adventure is probably the original report he wrote for the Select Committee of Supercargoes[1] at Macao following his release. This committee was responsible for buying and selling merchandise for the East India Company's factory (i.e. trading post). They also handled diplomatic duties, as there were no official British diplomats in China at this time. It was this committee that paid the ransom to secure Glasspoole's release.

After his return to England, Richard Glasspoole wrote an additional report on the ladrones which provide a background to his narrative. He titled it "A Few Remarks on the Origin, Progress, Manners and Customs of the Ladrones." Before moving on to his report on his capture, here is an excerpt from that second report.

The ladrones are a disaffected race of Chinese that revolted against the oppressions of the mandarins.[2] They first commenced their depredations on the Western coast (Cochin China [now the southern part of Vietnam]) by attacking small trading vessels in rowboats carrying from thirty to forty men each. They continued this system of piracy several years. At length their successes and the oppressive state of the Chinese had the effect of rapidly increasing their numbers. Hundreds of fishermen and others flocked to their standard, and as their number increased, they consequently became more desperate. They blockaded all the principal rivers and attacked several large junks[3] mounting from ten to fifteen guns each.

With these junks they formed a very formidable fleet, and no small vessels could trade on the coast with safety. They plundered several small villages and exercised such wanton barbarity as struck horror into the breasts of the Chinese.[4] To check these enormities, the government equipped a fleet of forty Imperial war-junks, mounting from eighteen to twenty guns each. On the very first *rencontre*,[5] twenty-eight of the Imperial junks struck[6] [i.e. surrendered] to the pirates. The rest saved themselves by a precipitate retreat.

These junks, fully equipped for war, were a great acquisition to them. Their numbers augmented so rapidly that at the period of my captivity, they were supposed to amount to near seventy thousand men, eight hundred large vessels, and nearly a thousand small ones, including rowboats. They were divided into five squadrons, distinguished by different colored flags,[7] each squadron commanded by an admiral (or chief), but all under the orders of A-juo-chay,[8] their Premier Chief—a most daring and enterprising man, who went so far as to declare his intention of displacing the present Tartar family from the throne of China, and to restore the ancient Chinese dynasty.[9] This extraordinary character would have certainly shaken the foundation of the government had he not been thwarted by the jealousy of the second in command who declared his independence and soon after surrendered to the mandarins with five hundred vessels on promise of a pardon.[10] Most of the inferior chiefs followed his example. A-juo-chay held out a few months longer, and at length surrendered with sixteen thousand men on condition of a general pardon and himself to be made a mandarin of distinction.

The ladrones have no settled residence on shore, but live constantly in their vessels. The after-part is appropriated to the captain and his wives; he generally has five or six. With respect to conjugal rights they are religiously strict; no person is allowed to have a woman on board unless married to her according to their laws. Every man is allowed a small berth about four feet square, where he stows with his wife and family.

From the number of souls crowded in so small a space, it must naturally be supposed they are horridly dirty, which is evidently the case, and their vessels swarm with all kinds of vermin—rats in particular, which they encourage to breed and eat them as great delicacies; in fact, there are very few creatures they will not eat. During our captivity, we lived three weeks on caterpillars boiled with rice. They are much addicted to gambling and spend all their leisure hours at cards and smoking opium.[. . .]

Now for Glasspoole's report of what happened to him during more than eleven weeks in captivity. He wrote this the day after his release.

On the 17th of September 1809,[11] the honorable company's ship *Marquis of Ely* anchored under the Island of Sam Chow in China, about twelve English miles from Macao,[12] where I was ordered to proceed in one of our cutters[13] to procure a pilot and also to land the purser with the packet [they had received at the Malaysian island of Pinang]. I left the ship at 5 P.M. with seven men under my command, [who were] well armed. It blew a fresh gale from the NE. We arrived at Macao at 9 P.M., where I delivered the packet to Mr. Roberts and sent the men with the boat's sails to sleep under the company's factory and left the boat in charge of one of the compradore's[14] men. During the night the gale increased.

At half-past three in the morning, I went to the beach and found the boat on shore half-filled with water, in consequence of the man having left her. I called the people and baled her out; found she was considerably damaged and very leaky. At half-past 5 A.M., the ebb-tide making, we left Macao with vegetables for the ship. One of the compradore's men who spoke English went with us for the purpose of piloting the ship to Lintin,[15] as the mandarins—in consequence of a late disturbance at Macao—would not grant chops [i.e. official permits or licenses] for the regular pilots. I had every reason to expect the ship in the roads,[16] as she was preparing to get under weigh when we left her. But on our rounding Cabaretta Point, we saw her five or six miles to leeward[17] under weigh, standing on the starboard tack.[18] It was then blowing fresh at NE. [We] bore up[19] and stood towards her. When about a cable's-length to windward of her, she tacked.[20] We hauled our wind and stood after her. A hard squall then coming on with a strong tide and heavy swell against us, we drifted fast to leeward, and the weather being hazy, we soon lost sight of the ship.[21] [We] struck [i.e. lowered] our masts and endeavored to pull [i.e. row]. Finding our efforts useless, [we] set a reefed[22] foresail and mizzen[23] and stood towards a country-ship[24] at anchor under the land to leeward of Cabaretta Point. When within a quarter of a mile of her she weighed and made sail, leaving us in a very critical situation, having no anchor and drifting bodily on the rocks to leeward. [We] struck the masts. After four or five hours hard pulling [we] succeeded in clearing them.

At this time [there was] not a ship in sight. The weather clearing up, we saw a ship to leeward, hull down.[25] [We] shipped [i.e. reinstalled] our masts and made sail towards her. She proved to be the honorable company's ship *Glatton*. We made signals to her with our handkerchiefs at the mast-head, she unfortunately took no notice of them, but tacked and stood from us. Our situation was now truly distressing, night closing fast with a threatening appearance, blows fresh with hard rain and a heavy sea. Our boat very leaky, without a compass, anchor or provisions, and drifting fast on a lee-shore, surrounded with dangerous rocks, and inhabited by the most barbarous pirates. I close-reefed my sails and kept tack and tack till daylight, when we were happy to find we had drifted very little to leeward of our situation in the evening. The night was very dark, with constant hard squalls and heavy rain.

Tuesday the 19th, no ships in sight. About ten o'clock in the morning it fell calm with very hard rain and a heavy swell. Struck our masts and pulled, not being able to see the land, [we] steered by the swell. When the weather broke up, [we] found we had drifted several miles to leeward. During the calm a fresh breeze springing up, [we] made sail and endeavored to reach the weather-shore, and [we made an] anchor with six muskets we had lashed together for that purpose. Finding the boat made no way against the swell and tide, bore up for a bay to leeward, and anchored about one A.M. close under the land in five or six fathoms[26] water, blowing fresh with hard rain.

Wednesday the 20th at daylight, supposing the flood tide making, [we] weighed and stood over to the weatherland, but found we were drifting fast to leeward. About ten o'clock perceived two Chinese boats steering for us. [We] bore up and stood towards them and made signals to induce them to come within hail. On nearing them, they bore up and passed to leeward of the islands. The Chinese [man] we had in the boat advised me to follow them and he would take us to Macao by the leeward passage. I expressed my fears of being taken by the ladrones. Our ammunition being wet and the muskets rendered useless, we had nothing to defend ourselves with but cutlasses and [were] in too distressed a situation to make much resistance with them, having been constantly wet and [having] eat[en] nothing but a few green oranges for three days.

As our present situation was a hopeless one and the man assured me there was no fear of encountering any ladrones, I complied with his request and stood in to leeward of the islands, where we found the water much smoother and apparently a direct passage to Macao. We continued pulling and sailing all day. At six o'clock in the evening I discovered three large boats at anchor in a bay to leeward. On seeing us they weighed and made sail towards us. The Chinese [man] said they were ladrones and that if they captured us they would most certainly put us all to death! Finding they gained fast on us, [we] struck the masts and pulled head to wind for five or six hours. The tide turning against us, [we] anchored close under the land to avoid being seen. Soon after we saw the boats pass us to leeward.

Thursday the 21st, at daylight, the flood making, [we] weighed and pulled along shore in great spirits, expecting to be at Macao in two or three hours, as by the Chinese [man's] account it was not above six or seven miles distant. After pulling a mile or two [we] perceived several people on shore, standing close to the beach. They were armed with pikes and lances. I ordered the interpreter to hail them and ask the most direct passage to Macao. They said if we came on shore they would inform us. Not liking their hostile appearance I did not think proper to comply with the request. [We] saw a large fleet of boats at anchor close under the opposite shore. Our interpreter said they were fishing-boats, and that by going there I should not only get provisions, but a pilot also to take to Macao.

I bore up and on nearing them perceived there were some large vessels very full of men and mounted with several guns. I hesitated to approach nearer, but the Chinese [man] assuring me they were mandarin junks and salt boats,[27] we stood close to one of them and asked the way to Macao. They gave no answer, but made some signs to us to go in shore. We passed on and a large rowboat pulled after us. She soon came alongside, when about twenty savage-looking villains, who were stowed at the bottom of the boat, leaped on board us. They were armed with a shortsword in each hand, one of which they laid on our necks and the other pointed to our breasts—keeping their eyes fixed on their officer, waiting his signal to cut or desist. Seeing we were incapable of making any resistance, he sheathed his sword and the others immediately followed his example. They then dragged us into their boat and carried us on board one of their junks with the most savage demonstrations of joy, and (as we supposed) to torture and put us to a cruel death. When on board the junk, they searched all our pockets, took the handkerchiefs from our necks, and brought heavy chains to chain us to the guns.

At this time a boat came and took me, with one of my men and an interpreter, on board the chief's vessel. I was then taken before the chief. He was seated on deck in a large chair dressed in purple silk with a black turban on. He appeared to be about thirty years of age, a stout commanding-looking man. He took me by the coat and drew me close to him, then questioned the interpreter very strictly, asking who we were and what was our business in that part of the country. I told him to say we were Englishmen in distress, having been four days at sea without provisions. This he would not credit, but said we were bad men and that he would put us all to death; and then ordered some men to put the interpreter to the torture until he confessed the truth.

Upon this occasion, a ladrone who had been once to England and spoke a few words of English, came to the chief and told him we were really Englishmen and that we had plenty of money, adding that the buttons on my coat were gold. The chief then ordered us some coarse brown rice, of which we made a tolerable meal, having eaten nothing for nearly four days except a few green oranges. During our repast, a number of ladrones crowded round us examining our clothes and hair and giving us every possible annoyance. Several of them brought swords, and laid them on our necks, making signs that they would soon take us on shore, and cut us in pieces, which I am sorry to say was the fate of some hundreds during my captivity.

I was now summoned before the chief, who had been conversing with the interpreter. He said I must write to my captain and tell him if he did not send a hundred thousand [Spanish] dollars[28] for our ransom in ten days he would put us all to death. In vain did I assure him it was useless writing unless he would agree to take a much smaller sum, saying we were all poor men and the most we could possibly raise would not exceed two thousand [Spanish] dollars. Finding that he was much exasperated at my expostulations, I embraced the offer of writing to inform my commander of our unfortunate situation, though there appeared not the least probability of relieving us. They said the letter should be conveyed to Macao in a fishing-boat, which would bring an answer in the morning. A small boat accordingly came alongside, and took the letter.

About six o'clock in the evening they gave us some rice and a little salt fish, which we ate, and they made signs for us to lay down on the deck to sleep; but such numbers of ladrones were constantly coming from different vessels to see us and examine our clothes and hair, they would not allow us a moment's quiet. They were particularly anxious for the buttons of my coat, which were new and as they supposed gold. I took it off and laid it on the deck to avoid being disturbed by them. It was taken away in the night and I saw it on the next day stripped of its buttons.

About nine o'clock a boat came and hailed the chief's vessel. He immediately hoisted his mainsail and the fleet weighed apparently in great confusion. They worked to windward all night and part of the next day, and anchored about one o'clock in a bay under the island of Lantau,[29] where the head admiral of ladrones was lying about at anchor with about two hundred vessels and a Portuguese brig they had captured a few days before, and [on which had] murdered the captain and part of the crew.

Saturday the 23rd, early in the morning, a fishing-boat came to the fleet to inquire if they had captured a European boat. Being answered in the affirmative, they came to the vessel I was in. One of them spoke a few words of English and told me he had a ladrone-pass and was sent by Captain Kay [of the *Marquis of Ely*] in search of us. I was rather surprised to find he had no letter. He appeared to be well acquainted with the chief and remained in his cabin smoking opium and playing cards all the day. In the evening I was summoned with the interpreter before the chief. He questioned us in a much milder tone, saying, he now believe we were Englishmen—a people he wished to be friendly with— and that if our captain would lend him seventy thousand [Spanish] dollars till he returned from his cruise up the river, he would repay him and send us all to Macao. I assured him it was useless writing on those terms, and unless our ransom was speedily settled, the English fleet would sail and render our enlargement [i.e. release] altogether ineffectual. He remained determined and said if it were not sent, he would keep us and make us fight or put us to death. I accordingly wrote and gave my letter to the man belonging to the boat before-mentioned. He said he could not return with an answer in less than five days.

The chief now gave me the letter I wrote when first taken. I have never been able to ascertain his reasons for detaining it, but suppose he dare not negotiate for our ransom without orders from the head admiral, who I understood was sorry at our being captured. [30] He said the English ships would join the mandarins and attack them. He told the chief that captured us to dispose of us as he pleased.

Monday the 24th, it blew a strong gale with constant hard rain. We suffered much from the cold and wet, being obliged to remain on deck with no covering but an old mat, which was frequently taken from us in the night by the ladrones who were on watch. During the night, the Portuguese who were left in the brig murdered the ladrones that were on board of her, cut the cables, and fortunately escaped through the darkness of the night. I have since been informed they ran her on shore near Macao.

Tuesday the 25th at daylight in the morning, the fleet—amounting to about five hundred sail of different sizes—weighed to proceed on their intended cruise up the rivers to levy contributions on the towns and villages. [31] It is impossible to describe what were my feelings at this critical time, having received no answers to my letters and the fleet underway to sail hundreds of miles up a country never visited by Europeans; there to remain probably for many months, which would render all opportunities of negotiating for our enlargement totally ineffectual, as the only method of communication is by boats that have a pass from the ladrones, and they dare not venture above twenty miles from Macao, being obliged to come and go in the night to avoid the mandarins; and if these boats should be detected in having any intercourse with the ladrones, they are immediately put to death, and all their relations—though they had not joined the crime—share in the punishment in order that not a single person of their families should be left to imitate their crimes or revenge their death. This severity renders communication both dangerous and expensive. No boat would venture out for less than a hundred Spanish dollars.

Wednesday the 26th of September at daylight, we passed in sight of our own ships at anchor under the island of Chun Po. The chief then called me, pointed to the ships and told the interpreter to tell us to look at them, for we should never see them again! About noon we entered a river to the westward of the Bogue.[32] Three or four miles from the entrance we passed a large town situated on the side of a beautiful hill, which is tributary to the ladrones. The inhabitants saluted them with songs as they passed.

The fleet now divided into two squadrons (the Red and the Black) and sailed up different branches of the river. At midnight the division we were in anchored close to an immense hill on the top of which a number of fires were burning, which at daylight I perceived proceeded from a Chinese camp. At the back of the hill was a most beautiful town[33] surrounded by water and embellished with groves of orange trees. The chophouse (customhouse) and a few cottages were immediately plundered and burnt down. Most of the inhabitants, however, escaped the camp.

The ladrones now prepared to attack a town[34] with a formidable force collected in rowboats from the different vessels. They sent a messenger to the town demanding a tribute of ten thousand [Spanish] dollars annually, saying if these terms were not complied with, they would land, destroy the town, and murder all the inhabitants—which they would certainly have done had the town laid in a more advantageous situation for their purpose, but being placed out of the reach of their shot, they allowed them to come to terms. The inhabitants agreed to pay six thousand [Spanish] dollars, which they were to collect by the time of our return down the river. This finesse had the desired effect, for during our absence they mounted a few guns on a hill which commanded the passage and gave us in lieu of the dollars, a warm salute on our return.

October the 1st, the fleet weighed in the night, dropped by the tide up the river, and anchored very quietly before a town[35] surrounded by a thick wood. Early in the morning, the ladrones assembled in rowboats and landed, then gave a shout and rushed into the town, sword in hand. The inhabitants fled to the adjacent hills in numbers apparently superior to the ladrones.[36] We may easily imagine to ourselves the horror with which these miserable people must be seized on being obliged to leave their homes and everything dear to them. It was a most melancholy sight to see women in tears, clasping their infants in their arms, and imploring mercy for them from those brutal robbers! The old and the sick, who were unable to fly or make resistance, were either made prisoners or most inhumanly butchered! The boats continued passing and repassing from the junks to the shore in quick succession, laden with booty and the men besmeared with blood!

Two hundred and fifty women and several children were made prisoners and sent on board different vessels. They were unable to escape with the men, owing to that abominable practice of cramping their feet. Several of them were not able to move without assistance. In fact, they might all be said to totter, rather than walk. Twenty of these poor women were sent on board the vessel I was in. They were hauled on board by the hair and treated in a most savage manner.

When the chief came on board, he questioned them respecting the circumstances of their friends and demanded ransoms accordingly from six thousand to six hundred [Spanish] dollars each. He ordered them a berth on deck at the after part of the vessel, where they had nothing to shelter them from the weather, which at this time was very variable— the days excessively hot and the nights cold with heavy rains. The town being plundered of everything valuable, it was set on fire and reduced to ashes by the morning. The fleet remained here three days, negotiating for the ransom of the prisoners and plundering the fish-tanks and gardens. During all this time, the Chinese never ventured from the hills, though there were frequently not more than a hundred ladrones on shore at a time and I am sure the people on the hills exceeded ten times that number.

October the 5th, the fleet proceeded up another branch of the river, stopping at several small villages to receive tribute, which was generally paid in dollars, sugar and rice, with a few large pigs roasted whole as presents for their Joss[37] (the idol they worship). Every person on being ransomed is obliged to present him with a pig or some fowls, which the priest offers him with prayers. It remains before him a few hours and is then divided amongst the crew. Nothing particular occurred till the 10th, except frequent skirmishes on shore between small parties of ladrones and Chinese soldiers. They frequently obliged my men to go on shore and fight with the muskets we had when taken, which did great execution, [since] the Chinese [were] principally using bows and arrows. They have matchlocks, but use them very unskillfully.[38]

On the 10th, we formed a junction with the Black Squadron and proceeded many miles up a wide and beautiful river, passing several ruins of villages that had been destroyed by the Black Squadron.

On the 17th, the fleet anchored abreast four mud batteries which defended a town so entirely surrounded with wood that it was impossible to form any idea of its size. The weather was very hazy with hard squalls of rain. The ladrones remained perfectly quiet for two days. On the third day, the forts commenced a brisk fire for several hours. The ladrones did not return a single shot, but weighed in the night and dropped down the river.

The reasons they gave for not attacking the town or returning the fire were that [their] Joss had not promised them success. They are very superstitious and consult their idol on all occasions. If his omens are good, they will undertake the most daring enterprises.

The fleet now anchored opposite the ruins of the town where the women had been made prisoners. Here we remained five or six days, during which time about an hundred of the women were ransomed. The remainder were offered for sale amongst the ladrones for forty dollars each. The woman is considered the lawful wife of the purchaser, who would be put to death if he discarded her. Several of them [i.e. the women] leaped overboard and drowned themselves rather than submit to such infamous degradation.[39]

The fleet then weighed and made sail down the river to receive the ransom from the town before-mentioned. As we passed the hill, they fired several shot at us, but without effect. The ladrones were much exasperated and determined to revenge themselves. They dropped out of reach of their shot and anchored. Every junk sent about a hundred men each on shore to cut paddy[40] and destroy their orange-groves, which was most effectually performed for several miles down the river. During our stay here, they received information of nine boats lying up a creek laden with paddy. Boats were immediately dispatched after them.

[The] next morning these boats were brought to the fleet. Ten or twelve men were taken in them. As these had made no resistance, the chief said he would allow them to become ladrones if they agreed to take the usual oaths before [their] Joss. Three or four of them refused to comply, for which they were punished in the following cruel manner: their hands were tied behind their backs, a rope from the mast-head rove through their arms. And [they were] hoisted three or four feet from the deck and five or six men flogged them with three rattans twisted together till they were apparently dead. Then [they were] hoisted them up to the mast-head and left them hanging nearly an hour. Then [they were] lowered them down and repeated the punishment till they died or complied with the oath.

October the 20th in the night, an express-boat came with the information that a large mandarin fleet was proceeding up the river to attack us. The chief immediately weighed with fifty of the largest vessels and let down the river to meet them.[41] About one in the morning they commenced a heavy fire till daylight, when an express was sent for the remainder of the fleet join them. About an hour after, a counter-order to anchor came; the mandarin fleet having run. Two or three hours afterwards the chief returned with three captured vessels in tow; having sunk two; and eighty-three sail made their escape. The admiral[42] of the mandarins blew his vessel up by throwing a lighted match into the magazine as the ladrones were boarding her. She ran on shore and they succeeded in getting twenty of her guns.

In this action, very few prisoners were taken. The men belonging to the captured vessels drowned themselves, as they were sure of suffering a lingering and cruel death if taken after making resistance. The admiral left the fleet in [the] charge of his brother, the second in command, and proceeded with his own vessel towards Lantau. The fleet remained in this river cutting paddy, the necessary supplies.

On the 28th of October, I received a letter from Captain Kay brought by a fisherman, who had told him he would get us all back for three thousand [Spanish] dollars. He advised me to offer three thousand, and if not accepted extend it to four, but not farther, as it was bad policy to offer much at first; at the same time [he was] assuring me we should be liberated, let the ransom be what it would. I offered the chief the three thousand, which he disdainfully refused, saying he was not to be played with and unless they sent ten thousand dollars and two large guns with several casks of gunpowder, he would soon put us to death. I wrote to Captain Kay and informed him of the chief's determination, requesting, if an opportunity offered, to send us a shift of clothes; for which it may be easily imagined we were much distressed, having been seven weeks without a shift although constantly exposed to the weather and of course frequently wet.

On the first of November, the fleet sailed up a narrow river and anchored at night within two miles of a town called Little Whampoa.[43] In front of it was a small fort and several mandarin vessels[44] lying in the harbor. The chief sent the interpreter to me, saying I must order my men to make cartridges and clean their muskets, ready to go on shore in the morning. I assured the interpreter I should give the men no such orders, that they must please themselves. Soon after the chief came on board, threatening to put us all to a cruel death if we refused to obey his orders. For my own part I remained determined and advised the men not to comply, as I thought by making ourselves useful we should be accounted too valuable.

A few hours afterwards he sent to me again, saying that if myself and the quartermaster would assist them at the great guns, that if also the rest of the men went on shore and succeeded in taking the place, he would then take the money offered for our ransom and give them twenty dollars for every Chinaman's head they cut off. To these proposals we cheerfully acceded, in hopes of facilitating our deliverance.

Early in the morning, the forces intended for landing were assembled in rowboats, amounting in the whole to three or four thousand men. The largest vessels weighed and hauled in shore to cover the landing of the forces and attack the fort and mandarin vessels. About nine o'clock the action commenced and continued with great spirit for nearly an hour, when the walls of the fort gave way and the men retreated in the greatest confusion.

The mandarin vessels continued firing, having blocked up the entrance of the harbor to prevent the ladrone boats entering. At this the ladrones were much exasperated and about three hundred of them swam on shore with a short sword lashed close under each arm. They then ran along the banks of the river till they came abreast of the vessels, and then swam off again and boarded them. The Chinese thus attacked, leaped overboard and endeavored to reach the opposite shore. The ladrones followed and cut the greater number of them to pieces in the water. They next towed the vessels out of the harbor and attacked the town with increased fury. The inhabitants fought about a quarter of an hour and then retreated to an adjacent hill, from which they were soon driven with great slaughter.

After this the ladrones returned and plundered the town, every boat leaving it with lading. The Chinese on the hills perceiving most of the boats were off, rallied and retook the town after killing near two hundred ladrones. One of my men was unfortunately lost in this dreadful massacre! The ladrones landed a second time, drove the Chinese out of the town, then reduced it to ashes and put all their prisoners to death, without regarding either age or sex!

I must not omit to mention a most horrid (though ludicrous) circumstance which happened at this place. The ladrones were paid by their
chief ten dollars for every Chinaman's head they produced. One of my
men, turning the corner of a street, was met by a ladrone running furiously after a Chinese. He had a drawn sword in his hand and two Chinaman's heads which he had cut off, tied by their tails and slung round his
neck. I was witness myself to some of them producing five or six to
obtain payment!!!

On the 4th of November, an order arrived from the admiral [Ching
Yih Saou] for the [Red Flag] fleet to proceed immediately to Lantau,
where [s]he[45] was lying with only two vessels and [with] three Portuguese ships[46] and a brig constantly annoying him [her], [plus] several
sail of mandarin vessels were daily expected. The fleet weighed and proceeded towards Lantau. On passing the island of Lintin, three ships and
a brig gave chase to us. The ladrones prepared to board, but night closing we lost sight of them.[47] I am convinced they altered their course and
stood from us. These vessels were in the pay of the Chinese government
and styled themselves "the Invincible Squadron," cruising in the river
Tigris[48] to annihilate the ladrones!

On the fifth in the morning, the Red Squadron anchored in a bay
under Lantau. The Black Squadron stood to the eastward. In the afternoon of the 8th of November, four ships, a brig, and a schooner came off
the mouth of the bay. At first the pirates were much alarmed, supposing
them to be English vessels come to rescue us. Some of them threatened
to hang us to the mast-head for them to fire at and with much difficulty
we persuaded them that they were Portuguese. The ladrones had only
seven junks in a fit state for action. These they hauled outside and
moored them head and stern across the bay, and manned all the boats
belonging to the repairing vessels ready for boarding.

The Portuguese observing these maneuvers hove to and communicated by boats. Soon afterwards they made sail, each ship firing her
broadside as she passed, but without effect, the shot falling far short. The
ladrones did not return a single shot, but waved their colors and threw up
rockets to induce them to come further in—which they might easily have
done, the outside junks lying in four fathoms water (which I sounded
myself), though the Portuguese in their letters to Macao lamented there
was not sufficient water for them to engage closer, but that they would
certainly prevent their escaping before the mandarin fleet arrived!

On the 20th of November early in the morning, [we] discovered an immense fleet of mandarin vessels standing for the bay.[49] On nearing us, they formed a line and stood close in. Each vessel, as she discharged her guns, tacked to join the rear and reload. They kept up a constant fire for about two hours, when one of their largest vessels was blown up by a firebrand thrown from a ladrone junk, after which they kept at a more respectful distance, but continued firing without intermission till the 21st at night, when it fell calm.

The ladrones towed out seven large vessels with about two hundred rowboats to board them, but a breeze springing up, they made sail and escaped. The ladrones returned into the bay and anchored. The Portuguese and mandarins followed and continued a heavy cannonading during that night and the next day. The vessel I was in had her foremast shot away, which they supplied very expeditiously by taking a mainmast from a smaller vessel.

On the 23rd in the evening, it again fell calm. The ladrones towed out fifteen junks in two divisions with the intention of surrounding them,[50] which was nearly effected, having come up with and boarded one when a breeze suddenly sprang up. The captured vessel mounted twenty-two guns. Most of her crew leaped overboard. Sixty or seventy were taken, immediately cut to pieces, and thrown into the river. Early in the morning the ladrones returned into the bay and anchored in the same situation as before. The Portuguese and mandarins followed, keeping up a constant fire. The ladrones never returned a single shot, but always kept in readiness to board, and the Portuguese were careful never to allow them an opportunity.

On the 28th at night, they [i.e. the Portuguese and mandarins] sent eight fire vessels,[51] which if properly constructed must have done great execution, having every advantage they could wish for to effect their purpose. A strong breeze and tide directed into the bay, and the vessels lying so close together that it was impossible to miss them. On their first appearance, the ladrones gave a general shout, supposing them to be mandarin vessels on fire, but were very soon convinced of their mistake. They came very regularly into the center of the fleet, two and two, burning furiously. One of them came alongside of the vessel I was in, but they succeeded in booming her off. She appeared to be a vessel of about thirty tons. Her hold was filled with straw and wood and there were a few small boxes of combustibles on her deck, which exploded alongside of us without doing any damage. The ladrones however towed them all on shore, extinguished the fire, and broke them up for firewood. The Portuguese claim the credit of constructing these destructive machines and actually sent a dispatch to the Governor of Macao, saying they had destroyed at least one-third of the ladrone's fleet, and hoped soon to effect their purpose by totally annihilating them.[52]

On the 29th of November, the ladrones being all ready for sea, they weighed and stood boldly out, bidding defiance to "the Invincible Squadron" and Imperial Fleet, consisting of ninety-three war-junks, six Portuguese ships, a brig, and a schooner. Immediately after the ladrones weighed, they made all sail. The ladrones chased them two or three hours, keeping up a constant fire. Finding they did not come up with them, they hauled their wind[53] and stood to the eastward.

Thus terminated the boasted blockade which lasted nine days, during which time the ladrones completed all their repairs.[54] In this action, not a single ladrone vessel was destroyed and their loss was about thirty or forty men. An American was also killed, one of three that remained out of eight taken in a schooner. I had two very narrow escapes: the first, a twelve pounder shot fell within three or four feet of me; another took a piece out of a small brass-swivel[55] on which I was standing. The chief's wife[56] frequently sprinkled me with garlic water, which they considered an effectual charm against shot. The fleet continued under sail all night, steering towards the eastward. In the morning they anchored in a large bay surrounded by lofty and barren mountains.

On the 2nd of December I received a letter from Lieutenant Maughn, commander of the honorable company's cruiser[57] *Antelope*, saying that he had the ransom board and had been three days cruising after us and wished me to settle with the chief on the securest method delivering it. The chief agreed to send us in a small gun-boat till we came within sight of the *Antelope*, then the compradore's boat was to bring the ransom and receive us.

I was so agitated at receiving this joyful news, that it was with difficulty I could scrawl about two or three lines to inform Lieutenant Maughn of the arrangements I had made. We were all so deeply affected by the gratifying tidings that we seldom closed our eyes, but continued watching day and night for the boat.

On the 6th she returned with Lieutenant Maughn's answer, saying he would respect any single boat, but would not allow the fleet to approach him. The chief then, according to his first proposal, ordered a gun-boat to take us, and with no small degree of pleasure we left the ladrone fleet about four o'clock in the morning.

At one P.M. [we] saw the *Antelope* under all sail, standing towards us. The ladrone boat immediately anchored and dispatched the com-pradore's boat for the ransom, saying that if she approached nearer they would return to the fleet. And they were just weighing, when she short-ened sail and anchored about two miles from us. The boat did not reach her till late in the afternoon, owing to the tide's being strong against her. She received the ransom and left the *Antelope* just before dark. A man-darin boat that had been lying concealed under the land and watching their maneuvers, gave chase to her and was within a few fathoms of tak-ing her when she saw a light, which the ladrones answered and the mandarin hauled off.

Our situation was now a most critical one. The ransom in the hands of the ladrones and the compradore dare not return with us for fear of a second attack from mandarin boat. The ladrones would not remain till morning, so we were obliged to return with them to the fleet.

In the morning the chief inspected the ransom, which consisted of the following articles: two bales of super-fine scarlet cloth, two chests of opium, two casks of gunpowder, and a telescope. The rest [was] in [Spanish] dollars.[58] He objected to the telescope not being new and said he should detain one of us till another was sent, or a hundred dollars in lieu of it. The compradore however agreed with him for the hundred dollars.

Everything being at length settled, the chief ordered two gunboats to convey us near the *Antelope*. We saw her just before dusk, when the ladrone boats left us. We had the inexpressible pleasure of arriving on board the *Antelope* at 7 P.M., where we were most cordially received and heartily congratulated on our safe and happy deliverance from a mis-erable captivity, which we endured for eleven weeks and three days.

Richard Glasspoole.

China, December 8th, 1809.

Notes

1. A supercargo is an official in charge of a cargo. The committee he's refer-ring to consisted of a president and three senior supercargoes.

2. Mandarins: officials of the Chinese government.

3. Junks: flat-bottomed ships with sails stiffened by rods to keep them from cupping, used in the orient. The larger junks carried twelve guns and also carried smaller boats that could hold twenty men and were armed with swivel guns. These boats were used for boarding other ships or making suprise attacks on coastal villages.

4. In another firsthand account, John Turner, who was a prisoner of the ladrones for five and a half months, described some of the horrors that he saw.

Among the captures made daily, there was taken on the 18th [of January, 1807], a small mandarin boat with four men in her—one of whom was brought on board the junk I was on board of. Their cruelty to him, as also to another, which I shall mention hereafter, has made an indellible impression on my mind. He was nailed to the deck through his feet with large nails, then beat with four rattans till he vomited blood. And after remaining some time in this horrid state, he was taken on shore and cut to pieces. The others, I believe, were treated in a similar manner.

The other incident he refers to in his narrative occurred on March 1, 1807.

At this place [where the pirates had stopped to career their vessels] a man was put to death with circumstances of particular horrors. Being fixed upright, his bowels were taken out and his heart likewise, which they after soaked in spirits and ate. The dead body I saw myself. I am well assured that this shocking threatment is frequently practiced to those, who having annoyed them in any particular manner, fall into their hands.

5. *Rencontre*: French for "rencounter," a hostile encounter or battle.

6. Struck: "struck their colors," meaning they lowered their flag to indicate their surrender.

7. Chinese sources say there were six squadrons distinguished by the color of their flags; these being red, black, blue, white, yellow and green, but captives Richard Glasspoole and John Turner both say there were only five. Turner says that three squadrons had red flags; one triangular with no border, one triangular with a scalloped border, and one square with no border. He said the fourth had a square flag of horizontal areas of blue, white and red and the last had a triangular black flag. It's possible the three types of red flags represented divisions of the Red Squadron.

8. The leader of the ladrones was actually a woman named Ching Yih Saou (which means "wife of Ching Yih"). Although her full name is not known, her family name was Shih, which means "stone." A former prostitute, she married the pirate leader Ching Yih and had two of his sons. After Ching Yih died in a typhoon in 1807, she took over. Chang Paou—who joined the pirates at age 15 and became Ching Yih's protégé, adopted son, and homosexual lover—was also

Ching Yih Saou's lover and later they were wed. Ching Yih Saou turned over control of most of the Red Squadron to Chang Paou and focused on overseeing the six squadrons and keeping them together. At the height of her career, she commanded a fleet of 800 large junks (some weighing almost 600 tons) and about 1,000 smaller boats. Her pirates numbered between seventy and eighty thousand men and women. It is Chang Paou that Glasspoole is referring to here. A-juo-chay is probably a title. Many of the ladrone leaders used titles or nicknames, such as "Scourge of the Eastern Sea," "Both Odor and Mountain" and "Frog's Meal." At this time, Chang Paou was 23 years old and Ching Yih Saou was 34.

9. The Sung Dynasty was the last Chinese dynasty. It ended in 1271 with the Mongol invasion which established the Yüan Dynasty, which in turn was followed by the Ming Dynasty. In 1644, a second period of foreign rule began with the Manchu emperors of the Ch'ing Dynasty, which continued until 1911.

10. This occurred after Glasspoole's release. After winning a major battle against the mandarins, the leader of the Black Squadron, Kwo Po Tai, became jealous of Chang Paou's power. Kwo Po Tai was also in love with Ching Yih Saou and resented her relationship with Chang Paou. Kwo Po Tai secretly began to seek a pardon from the government. After a battle between the Red and Black Squadrons, which the Black Squadron won, Kwo Po Tai was in a much better position to negotiate the pardon for his squadron and it was soon granted. He was made a naval mandarin in the Imperial Navy with the rank of sublieutenant and sent out to fight pirates. A short while later, Ching Yih Saou and Chang Paou also accepted pardons. Chang Paou was also made a naval mandarin. With several thousand of his men, he too set about subduing the remaining squadrons. This he quickly did. Despite being an opium addict and suffering the resentment of other military officers, Chang Paou eventually rose to the rank of brigade-general. He died at the age of 36, it is thought from natural causes. After her second-husband's death, Ching Yih Saou opened a gambling house in Canton and died at the age of 69.

11. The ship's log for the *Marquis of Ely* says this was the 18th.

12. Macao is the city in southern China across the bay from Hong Kong.

13. Cutters: a usually single-masted vessel with a sail suspended from a spar projecting diagonally upwards from the aft side of the mast, carried aboard large ships as a communications tender.

14. Compradore: a Chinese agent that works for a foreign business and is in charge of Chinese workers.

15. Lintin is an island to the northwest of the Pearl River estuary.

16. Roads: a protected area near shore where a ship can anchor that is not as enclosed as a harbor.

17. Leeward: the side of the ship away from the wind.

18. Starboard tack: changing direction towards the right side of the ship (when facing the bow) by changing the position of the sails.

19. Bore up: pushed forward or advanced.

20. Tacked: changing direction by changing the position of the sails.

21. The *Marquis of Ely*'s log says that a search party was sent out on the 19th and on the 21st three boats searched around the islands for them.

22. Reef: to take in a sail by folding or rolling it up and tying to its yard.

23. Foresail: the primary sail on the foremast. Mizzen: the sail on the mizzen mast, which is nearest the stern.

24. Country-ship: a native ship, here meaning a Chinese ship.

25. Hull down: far enough away that the hull was not visible over the horizon.

26. Fathom: a measurement equal to six feet.

27. Salt boats: junks transporting salt from the twenty-two salterns on Kwangtung to Canton. These boats had to pay protection money to the pirates in order to pass safely.

28. Probably pieces-of-eight.

29. Lantau is an island that lies just off what is now Hong Kong's mainland and to the west of what is now Hong Kong Island.

30. Glasspoole's letter was received on September 28, 1809, and was preserved in the East India Company's records. It read:

> Sir,
>
> I am sorry to inform you that this morning myself with the cutter's crew were made prisoners by a large ladrone boat mounting 20 guns they say if you will send 100,000 dollars ransom they will send us to Macao or they say they will behead us, be so good as to write me, and say what you can give, I think they will take much less; offer 20 or 30 thousand, send immediately an answer for God's sake an answer by this boat that brings this what can be given, the man that brings this knows w[h]ere to find us, I will send you the head man's answer, though if you send the dollars he will give us a chop to pass to Macao. I trust this will be legible we anxiously expect an answer.
>
> R. Glasspoole, 4th Mate and 6 Men
> Address to Captain Kay or any of the
> Supercargoes at Macao to be delivered immediately.
> Thursday, 21st September.

On receipt of this letter, the Select Committee of Supergargoes made the following resolution:

> As the ladrones by the foregoing letter seem disposed to accept ransom for these unfortunate men, we hope it may be practicable ultimately to effect their release. The sum now demanded it is considered impossible to grant as so great an encouragement would render it impracticable for a boat to move in security, but it is supposed for 8

or 10,000 dollars the object may be effected. This sum (should it not on more mature deliberation be considered that the honorable company and owners would willingly discharge it) in such an occasion we feel little doubt may be raised among the factory and shipping and though on every account the payment of ransom is extremely objectionable, we see no other mode at present of extricating our countrymen from their distressing situation.

The letter from Mr. Glasspoole therefore will be forwarded to Captain Kay together with some others addressed to him informing him of our sentiments on the subject and if on consultation with Captain Austen no better means of obtaining the release of his officer and men occurs to them, recommended his writing to Mr. Glasspoole urging him to place confidence in every possible measure being adopted for his release, and not to exceed 5,000 dollars in his first offer of a ransom. It was thought better to leave the negotiation entirely to Captain Kay, as it would through him be effected with greater economy than by the interference of anyone in the factory.

Capt. Kay began ransom negotiations by offering $4,000.

31. Because of a government attempt to cut off the pirates from their sources of food and supplies, the pirates began moving inland by sailing up the rivers and harvesting their own food. They forced the towns to buy protection documents from them to keep from being attacked. These documents could be bought from the ship's leaders or from their agents on shore. Flagships often carried between 50,000 and 100,000 Spanish dollars. The pirates set up finanical offices along the entire coast and even had a tax office in Canton where their fees could be paid. It appears their financial center was at Macao, where they bought much of their weapons and ammunition.

32. The Bogue—also known as Hu-men or Bocca Tigris (Tiger's Mouth), is a small strait formed by four tiny islands, each of which had a fort. It is one of the passages that access the Pearl River, which runs past Canton.

33. Sha-ting, about 70 miles south of Canton.

34. Kan-chiao.

35. Ch'en.

36. Their 3,000 men were not able to fight off the 500 pirates.

37. Joss: a Chinese idol or image used to represent a god or gods.

38. The Chinese firearms were of very poor quality and the pirates were not very skilled at using them, relying more on edged weapons such as swords, knives and spears. Chinese muskets were crudely made and of small calibers. Their touchholes were so large that if the charge didn't blow out of the back, it often escaped down the barrel since they inserted the ball without wad or ramming. Their flintlocks were modeled on sixteenth century European bird guns. The matchlocks, which fired by applying a slow-burning cord to the touchhole, were even worse. They also had a seven-foot long rifle called a gingall that was similar to an elephant gun and took two or three men to fire. The balls were nonstandard in size and sometimes didn't even fit into the gun. The gunpowder was

course, high in sulfur content, of uneven quality, and decomposed rapidly. Since the Europeans were much more skilled at using firearms, the pirates often forced them to provide assistance.

39. Yung Lun Yuen, writing in Canton twenty-one years after this event, gives some further information on this, saying, "In the paddy fields about a hundred women were hidden, but the pirates on hearing a child crying, went to the place and carried them away. Mei Ying, the wife of Ke Choo Yang, was very beautiful, and a pirate being about to seize her by the head, she abused him exceedingly. The pirate bound her to the yardarm, but on abusing him yet more, the pirate dragged her down and broke two of her teeth, which filled her mouth and jaws with blood. The pirates sprang up again to bind her. Ying allowed him to approach, but as soon as he came near her, she laid hold of his garments with her bleeding mouth and threw both him and herself into the river, where they were drowned. The remaining captives of both sexes were after some months liberated on having paid a ransom of 15,000 leang [or ounces] of silver."

40. Cut paddy: either to destroy them or harvest them for themselves.

41. Chang Paou meet the fleet near the town of Sha-wan—about 65 miles south of Canton and twenty miles east of Sha-ting.

42. Actually this was one of the captains. Admiral Sun Ch'üan-mou escaped, leaving his brother in charge (as Glasspoole mentions in the next paragraph).

43. Little Whampoa (Ta Huang-pu), a city about 120 miles south of Canton.

44. Actually twenty war-junks.

45. Apparently Glasspoole never knew the chief ladrone leader was a woman.

46. The Chinese government sought out the help of the British. In order to prevent this alliance, the Portuguese made a deal to assist them.

47. The Portuguese were stalling for time so that the Chinese could assemble their new provincial fleet.

48. The Pearl River which runs past Canton into the Bocca Tigris and then to the South China Sea.

49. This fleet consisted of 95 junks with 1,200 cannon and 18,000 men.

50. They weren't trying to surround the fleet, which would have been impossible. The fifteen ships with 2,000 men were actually planning to attack the garrison on Lantau Island.

51. Fire vessels (more commonly called fire ships): vessels loaded with flamable and explosive materials that are used as bombs by setting them on fire and directing them to drift among enemy warships.

52. Two of the fire ships were blown back into the Portuguese and mandarin fleet, setting two of their own junks on fire. The entire encounter was a disaster, which they tried to downplay to the Emperor by falsely reporting huge losses amoung the pirates. Following this success, Chang Paou wrote to the Por-

tuguese saying, "At the present time I have many ships and provisions and all that is necessary for ordinary use. Nothing is lacking to me. All that I have is enough for a long time.[. . .]At this time I beg of you to give me four of the armed vessels that are under your command to make use of as I wish, for with their help I'll be able to restore the lands of the empire. Be assured that when I have restored them and possess all the lands of the empire under my power, I will[. . .]give to you, my brothers[. . .]two or three provinces [of your choice]."

[53] Hauled their wind: directed their course as near as possible to the direction from which the wind was coming.

[54] In a letter to the President of the Select Committee of Supercargoes written after his release, Richard Glasspoole adds that the ladrone fleet consisted of five hundred ships and a landing force two thousand men; that the ladrones who swam out to board the Chinese ships had "two short swords lashed under the left arm" (not one sword under each arm as the narrative later states); and that they were able to cut to pieces Chinese who leapt into the water because of their superiority at swimming. He also says that while the government vessels were superior at sailing, preventing the ladrones coming to close quarters in the open sea, their shooting was not as good, with their broadsides falling "short of us by half a mile."

55. Swivel gun: a small cannon-like gun mounted on the ship's railing and could be swung from side to side.

56. Possibly Ching Yih Saou.

57. Cruiser: an armed patrol ship. The *Antelope* had been conducting survey work in the area, when it was assigned the task of delivering the ransom.

58. All together, a total of 4,220 Spanish dollars was paid in cash. The total ransom amounted to 7,654 dollars.

Like Mad Dogs They Killed
Six or Seven Boys

〰〰〰

Fernão Mendez Pinto

*Going back almost three centuries to the Age of Exploration,
we come to the account of the Portuguese explorer, Fernão[1]
Mendez Pinto, which is particularly interesting because he was
himself a pirate. Actually, he was many things during his life-
time, including a soldier, merchant, missionary, doctor, ambassador, and slave. During his twenty-one years of travel, he was
taken captive thirteen times (not always by pirates) and sold
seventeen times. He eventually recorded his adventures in a
book,* The Voyages and Adventures of Fernand Mendez
Pinto, *which was first published in 1614 after his death. In it
he describes several run ins he had with other pirates.*

*Pinto grew up hearing about the amazing discoveries of the
many explorers of that time. There was the tall, red-haired Ital-
ian named Columbus who got lost and landed in the Bahamas,
first thinking he was in Japan, then China, and finally deciding
he was on some unknown islands off Cathay. This was in 1492.
Six years later, the Portuguese Vasco da Gama found the sea
route to India. Then Cabral landed in Brazil in 1500, Balboa
crossed Panama to the Pacific Ocean in 1513, and Magellan cir-
cumnavigated the globe in 1522—the year after Cortéz wiped
out the Aztecs in what is now Mexico City.*

*It was about this time that Pinto had his first experience of
the seaman's life. At around the age of 13, he ran away and
was quickly captured by French pirates.*

I take for the beginning of my voyage the time which I spent in this
kingdom of Portugal, and say, that after I had lived there till I was about
eleven or twelve years old in the misery and poverty of my father's
house within the town of Montemor-o-Velho.[2] An uncle of mine—

desirous to advance me to a better fortune than that whereunto I was reduced at that time and to take me from the caresses and cockering [i.e. indulgence] of my mother—brought me to this city of Lisbon, where he put me into the service of a very honorable lady; to which he carried out of the hope he had, that by the favor of herself and her friends he might attain his desire for my advancement. And this was in the same year that the funeral pomp of the deceased King Manuel [1469–1521] of happy memory was celebrated at Lisbon, namely Saint Lucy's day, the thirteenth of December, 1521, which is the earliest thing I can remember.

In the meantime, my uncle's design had a success clean contrary to that which he had promised to himself in favor of me, for having been in the service of this lady about a year and an half, an accident befell me that cast me into manifest peril of my life, so that to save myself I was constrained to abandon her house with all the speed that possibly I could. Flying away then in very great fear, I arrived before I was aware at the Ford of Pedra,[3] which is a small port so called. There I found a caravel[4] of Alfama that was laden with the horses and stuff of a lord who was going to Setúbal,[5] where at that instant King John the Third [1502–1557][6] kept his court by reason of a great plague that reigned in diverse parts of the kingdom.

Perceiving then that this caravel was ready to put to sea, I embarked myself in her and departed the next day. But alas! a little after we had set sail, having gotten to a place named Sesimbra,[7] we were set upon by a French pirate, who having boarded us, caused fifteen or sixteen of his men to leap into our vessel, and finding no resistance, made themselves masters of her.

Now, after they had pillaged every one of us, they emptied all the merchandise with which ours was laden—which amounted to above 6,000 cruzados[8]—into their ship and then sank her so that of the seventeen of us that remained alive, not so much as one could escape slavery, for they clapped us up all bound hand and foot under hatches with an intent to go and sell us at Larache in Barbary,[9] whither also, as we found by being amongst them, they carried arms to the Muslims in way of trade. For this purpose they kept us thirteen days together, continually whipping us. But at the end thereof it fortuned that about sunset, they discovered a ship unto which they gave chase all the night, following her close, like old pirates long used to such thieveries.

Having fetched her up by break of day, they gave her a volley of three pieces of ordnance and presently invested her with a great deal of courage. Now, though at first they found some resistance, yet they quickly rendered themselves masters of her, killing six Portuguese and ten or eleven slaves. This was a goodly vessel, that belonged to a Portugal merchant in Vila do Condé[10] named Silvestré Godinho, which diverse other merchants of Lisbon had laden at São Tomé[11] with great store of sugar and slaves, in such sort that those poor merchants seeing themselves thus taken and robbed fell to lament their loss, which they estimated to be 40,000 cruzados. Whereupon these pirates, having gotten so rich a booty, changed their design for going to Larache and bent their course for the coast of France, carrying with them such of ourselves for slaves as they judged fit for the service of their navigation. The remainder of us they left at night in the road at a place called Melides,[12] where we were landed miserably naked, our bodies covered with nothing but with the stripes of the lashes which so cruelly we had received the days before. In this pitiful case we arrived the next morning at Santiago de Cacém,[13] where we were relieved by the inhabitants of the place.

> This didn't deter Pinto from taking up a life at sea, for in 1537 he left Portugal on his 21-year journey to the Far East, from which he wouldn't return until 1558. Initially he set off for India. After his arrival there, he was lured by the treasures to be gained by raiding Muslim shipping and headed off to the Red Sea. They attacked three ships off Ethiopia and were taken prisoner. He is sold twice before he escaped aboard a Portuguese cargo ship. Eventually he made his way to the Malay Peninsula, where he joined a business venture taking a shipload of merchandise to Siam.[14] After selling it for well over 50,000 cruzados, they were robbed by thieves. To avenge themselves, they turned pirate and quickly captured three junks. Then they had to figure out a way to convert their plundered merchandise into cash.

We arrived at Lugor roads[15] and anchored at the mouth of the river. There it was thought fit to pass the rest of the day to the end we might inform ourselves of what was best for us to do, for the sale of our commodities, as well as for the safety of our persons. And to tell the truth, we learned such good news that we were confident of making over 600 percent, and to be sure of freedom and liberty during all the month of September, according to the ordinance of the King of Siam, because it was the month of the king's *sumbayas*.[16] Now, to make this clear you must know that all along this coast of the Malay Peninsula and within the land, a great king commands, who for a more famous and recommendable title above all other kings, caused himself to be called *Prechau Saleu*, Emperor of all Sornau,[17] which is a country wherein there are thirteen kingdoms (by us commonly called Siam), to the which fourteen petty kings are subjected and yield homage. Anciently, they were obliged to personally go to Odiaa,[18] the capital city of this empire, and to bring their tribute there, so as to do the *sumbaya* to their emperor, which was indeed to kiss the sword that he wore by his side.

Now, because this city was seated fifty leagues[19] within the land and the currents of the rivers so strong, these kings were oftentimes forced to abide the whole winter there to their great expense, so they petitioned the *Prechau*, King of Siam, that the place of doing this their homage might be altered, whereupon he was pleased to ordain that in the future there should be a viceroy (which in their language is called Poyho) resident in the town of Lugor, to whom every three years those fourteen kings should render that duty and obedience they were accustomed to do to the emperor, and that during that time they spent there in performing the same—being the whole month of September—both their own merchandise and that of all others, natives as well as strangers, that either came in or went out of the country, should be free from all manner of imports whatsoever.

Since we arrived during this time of freedom, there was such a multitude of merchants that flocked here from all parts. We were assured there was no less then fifteen hundred vessels in the port, all laden with an infinity of commodities of very great value. This was the good news we learned as we arrived at the mouth of the river, with which we were so well pleased that we presently resolved to put in as soon as the wind would permit us. But alas! we were so unfortunate that we were never able to see what we so much desired. For at about ten of the clock, just as we had dined and were preparing to set sail, we saw a great junk coming upon us. Perceiving us to be Portuguese, few in number, and our vessel small, they fell close with our bow on the larboard[20] side and then those that were in her threw into us great grappling hooks fastened into two long chains, which they used to grapple us fast to them, dragging our ship with theirs. They had no sooner done this, when some seventy or eighty Muslims came flying out from under their hatches, where they had lain lurking, and with a mighty cry they cast so many stones, darts, and lances, that they fell as thick as hail upon us. Of us sixteen Portuguese, twelve rested dead in the place, together with thirty-six others, boys as well as mariners.

Now for us four remaining Portuguese, after we had escaped so dreadful an encounter, we all leapt into the sea, where one was drowned. And we three that were left getting to land as well as we could, being dangerously hurt and wading up to the waist in mud, went and hid ourselves in the next adjoining wood. In the meantime, the Muslims entered into our ship, and not contented with the slaughter they had made of our men, like mad dogs they killed six or seven boys outright whom they found wounded on the deck, not sparing so much as one of them. That done, they embarked all the goods of our vessel into their junk, then made a great hole in our ship and sank her. Immediately they set sail and made away as fast as ever they could for fear of being discovered, leaving their anchor in the sea and the grappling hooks which they used to grapple us to them.

After our escape, feeling ourselves all badly hurt and without any hope of help, we did nothing but weep and complain, for in this disaster we knew not what to resolve on, we were so amazed with that which had befallen us within the space of half an hour. In this desolation we spent the rest of that sad day, but considering with ourselves that the place was swampy and full of adders and lizards, we thought it our safest course to continue there all the night too, which we did, standing up to the chest in the ooze.

> *After six days in the swamp, they were rescued by a woman in a barge and eventually make their way back to their home on the Malay Peninsula, penniless. Swearing vengeance, they set out on May 9, 1540 in search of the pirates who stole their stolen loot. Sailing eastward, they came to a river in what is now southern Vietnam.*

The next morning we came to a river named Tobasoy, where [Captain] Antonio de Faria cast anchor because the pilot would not venture to enter into it since he had never been there before and did not know its depth. As we were arguing about whether to enter and not, we discerned a great sail making towards this port from the main sea. Without stirring from the place where we were, we prepared to receive them in a peaceable manner, so that as soon as they came near us we saluted them and hung up the flag of they call *charachina*, which is a sign of friendship used among them in such like occasions. Instead of answering us in the same manner as in reason it seemed they should have done, and knowing that we were Portuguese to whom they wished not well, they gave us very vile and base words, and from the top of their poop[21] made a kaffir[22] slave hold up his bare ass to us with a mighty noise and din of trumpets, drums and bells by way of scorn and derision of us.

Antonio de Faria was so offended, that he gave them a whole broadside to see if that would make them more courteous. To this shot of ours they returned an answer of five pieces of ordnance, namely three falcons and two little field pieces.[23] Whereupon consulting together what we should do, we resolved to abide where we were, for we held it not fit to undertake so doubtful an enterprise until such time as the next day's light might discover the forces of this vessel, so that we might either set upon her with the more security or let her pass by. This counsel was approved both by Antonio de Faria and us all, so that keeping good watch and giving order for all that was necessary, we continued in that place expecting day.

Now, about two of the clock in the morning we perceived three black things on the water close to the horizon coming towards us, which we could not well discern. Whereupon we wakened Antonio de Faria, who was then asleep on the hatches, and showed him what we had discovered, being by that time not far from us. He fearing, as we did, lest they were enemies, cried out presently, "Arm! Arm! Arm!" Wherein he was straightway obeyed, for now plainly perceiving that they were vessels rowing towards us, we betook us to our arms and were bestowed by our captain in places most necessary to defend ourselves.

We conceived by their silent approaching to us, that they were the enemies we had seen over night. Antonio de Faria said to us, "My masters, this is some pirate coming to set upon us who thinks we are not above six or seven at the most, as the manner is in such kind of vessels; therefore let every man stoop down so that they may not see any of us, and then we shall soon know their design. In the mean time, let the pots of powder[24] be made ready. With them and our swords, I hope we shall give a good end to this adventure. Let everyone also hide his match[25] so that they will not be spotted, whereby the pirates may be persuaded that we are asleep."

All of which, as he had prudently ordained, was immediately executed. These three vessels, having come within a crossbow shot of ours, went round about her, and after they had viewed her well, they joined all close together, as if they had entered into some new consultation, continuing so about a quarter of an hour. That done, they separated themselves into two parts, namely the two smaller went together to our poop and the third, that was greater and better armed, made to the starboard[26] of us. Hereupon they entered our lorcha[27] where most conveniently they could, so that in less than a quarter of an hour above forty men were gotten in, which seen by Antonio de Faria, he issued out from under the hatches with some forty soldiers, and invoking Saint James, our patron, he fell so courageously upon them that in a short time he killed almost all of them. Then with aid of the pots of powder that he caused to be cast in amongst those that were remaining in the three vessels, which he presently took, he made an end of defeating them—most of them being constrained to leap into the sea, where they were all drowned but five, whom we took up alive, whereof one was the kaffir slave that showed us his tail, and the other four were one Turk, two Atjehnese,[28] and the captain of the junk, named Similau, a notorious pirate and our mortal enemy. Antonio de Faria commanded them instantly to be put to torture in order to draw out of them who they were, from whence they came, and what they would have had of us; to which the two Atjehnese answered most brutishly. As we were getting ready to torment the slave in similar manner, he began with tears to beseech us to spare him because he was a Christian like we were and that without torture he would answer truly to all our demands. Whereupon Antonio de Faria caused him to be unbound, and setting him by him, gave him a piece of biscuit and a glass of wine. Then with fair words he persuaded him to declare the truth of everything to him, since he was a Christian, as he affirmed. To which he replied in this sort, "If I do not speak the truth unto you, then take me not for such as I am. My name is Sebastian and I was slave to Gaspar de Mello, whom this dog Similau, here present, slew about two years ago in Liampao[29] with twenty-five other Portuguese that were in his ship."

Antonio de Faria hearing this, cried out like a man amazed and said, "Nay, now I care not for knowing any more. Is this then that dog, Similau, that slew your master?" "Yes," answered he, "It was he, and he meant likewise to have done as much to you, thinking that you were not above six or seven, for which effect he came away in haste with a purpose, as he said, to take you alive so he could make your brains fly out of your heads with a frontal of cord,[30] as he did to my master. But I hope God will pay him for all the mischief he has committed."

Antonio de Faria being also advised by this slave, that this dog, Similau, had brought all his men of war along with him and left none in his junk but some Chinese mariners, he resolved to make use of this good fortune. After he had put Similau and his companions to death by making their brains fly out of their heads with a cord, as Similau had done to Gaspar de Mello and the other Portuguese in Liampao.

Wherefore he presently embarked himself with thirty soldiers in his boat and the three *manchuas*[31] wherein the enemies came, and by means of the flood[32] and a favorable wind, he arrived in less then an hour to where the junk rode at anchor within the river about a league from us. Whereupon he presently boarded her and made himself master of the poop, from whence he cast only four pots of powder among the rascals that were asleep upon the hatches, which made them all leap into the sea where nine or ten of them were drowned. The rest crying out for help were taken up and saved because we needed them for the navigation of the junk, which was a great tall vessel.

Thus you see how it pleased God out of his divine justice to make the arrogant confidence of this cursed dog a means to chastise him for his cruelties and to give him by the hands of Portuguese a just punishment for what he had done to them.

The next morning, taking an inventory of this prize, we found six and thirty thousand taels[33] in silver of Japan, which amounts in our money to fifty-four thousand cruzados, besides a variety of other commodities that were not then appraised for want of time because the country was all in an uproar and fires everywhere kindled, which they use to give warning one to another on any alarm or doubt of enemies, and this constrained us to make away with all speed.

Antonio de Faria parted from this river of Tobasoy on a Wednesday morning, being Corpus Christi Eve [May 26], in the year 1540.

Fernão Mendez Pinto continued his piratical adventures and even raided the tombs of the Chinese emperor. This expedition ended in a shipwreck and after being arrested for vagrancy, they were sentenced to work for a year repairing the Great Wall of China. Before they could complete this sentence, they were captured by the invading Tartars. They then showed the Tartars how to storm a fortress and in this way won their freedom. Eventually Pinto and two of his companions joined a Chinese pirate. Driven by a storm to Japan in 1542 or 1543, they apparently became the first Europeans to set foot in this country and they presented to a feudal lord Japan's first firearm.

Notes

1. His first name is also sometimes given as Ferdinand, Fernand, and Fernám.

2. Monte-mor Ovelho is about 160 miles north of Lisbon, near Coimbra.

3. The Ford of Pedra (Stone Wharf) used to be in the Alfama district of Lisbon.

4. Caravel: a ship with broad bows, a high poop (a raised deck at the stern) and triangular sails suspended from long diagonal yards.

5. Setúbal is a seaport 19 miles southeast of Lisbon.

6. It was during his reign that the Portuguese empire reached its height, but he also introduced the inquisition to Portugal.

7. Sesimbra (Ceznubra) is on the coast about 12 miles west of Setúbal.

8. Cruzado: a Portuguese silver or gold coin, roughly equal to a piece-of-eight.

9. Larache is on Morocco's Atlantic coast, about 40 miles south of Tangier and the Strait of Gibraltar. The Barbary States were the former countries of Morocco, Algiers, Tunis, and Tripoli. The Barbary Coast was thoroughly infested with corsairs.

10. Vila do Condé is a coastal city in northern Portugal, about 185 miles north of Lisbon.

11. São Tomé is an island off the central western coast of Africa, about 190 miles west of Gambon.

12. Melides is now part of Grândola, about 50 miles southeast of Lisbon.

13. Santiago de Cacén is about 20 miles southwest from Grândola.

14. Siam was the former name of Thailand.

15. Lugor is now Nakhon Si Thammarat, Thailand, on the Malay Peninsula about 400 miles south of Bangkok. Roads: a protected area near shore where a ship can anchor that is not as enclosed as a harbor.

16. *Sumbayas* (or *zumbaia*): an act of courtesy or reverence paid to some exaulted person.

17. Sornau: an area covering a large part of the Indochinese peninsula.

18. Odiaa (Phra Nakhon Si Ayutthaya) is about 40 miles north of Bangkok.

19. League: a measurement usually of about three miles.

20. Larboard: to the left (or port) side of a ship when facing the bow.

21. Poop deck.

22. Kaffir: literally means "infidel" or a non-believer in Islam. Arabs used it as a derogatory reference to Christians and blacks, and the Europeans adopted it to refer to blacks.

23. Falcon: a small cannon that fires a three-pound ball. Field pieces: mobile cannons.

24. Pots of powder: incendiary devices consisting of clay pots filled with gunpowder which were lit and thrown, similar to a Molotov cocktail.

25. Match: a slow-burning wick or cord used to light cannons, pots of powder, etc.

26. Starboard: to the right side (when facing the bow) of the ship.

27. Lorcha: a light Chinese vessel with a European-style hull but rigged as a junk.

28. Turk: a citizen of the Ottoman Empire that had Constantinople (now Istanbul, Turkey) as its capital. These Turks were usually Muslim Arabs. The Atjehnese are an ethnic group of Sumatra.

29. Liampao (Ningbo) is a seaport on the eastern coast of China, about 100 miles south of Shanghai.

30. Placing a cord with a bar through it around the person's head and turning the bar to tightly twist the cord like a tourniquet until the pressure splits the skull open. Esquemeling accused Capt. Morgan's men of doing this in Panama, saying "they twisted a cord around his forehead, which they wrung so hard that his eyes appeared as big as eggs and were ready to fall out of his skull."

31. *Manchuas*: a single-masted cargo boat used on the Malabar coast of India.

32. Flood tide: an rising or incoming tide; as opposed to an ebb tide.

33. Tael: a weight and also the amount of that weight in silver, used in the Far East. The weight was non-standard and tended to vary from place to place.

I Was Sold to an Alchemist

≋≋≋≋

Saint Vincent de Paul

Piracy dates back almost to the beginning of sailing. Over the centuries there have been several illustrious captives. The most famous being Julius Caesar, who was about 22 years old when he was captured in 78 B.C. by Aegean pirates. While the pirates discussed what ransom they should charge for his release, the second-in-command suggested to his leader that he thought they could get ten talents.[1] The leader decided to ask for twice that, but then Caesar remarked, "Twenty? If you knew your business, you'd realize I'm worth at least fifty!" He also told them he would have them crucified if he was released. They just laughed it off.

It took about a month for Caesar's friends to raise this ransom, but he set free. Caesar quickly borrowed four war galleys and five hundred soldiers and captured some 350 of the pirates in the middle of a drunken orgy. Only a few escaped. Having recovered the fifty talents, he then had them all executed—forty of them by crucifixion, though because they had treated him kindly, he allowed them to have their throats cut before they were crucified.

Another famous pirate captive was Miguel de Cervantes. He was taken on September 26, 1575 by an Albanian corsair. He was sold at Algiers to a Greek and was treated very cruelly. After several failed escape attempts and five years in captivity, he was finally ransomed. Of course, he later went on to write Don Quixote.

Then there was Saint Patrick, who, in about 405 A.D., fell into the clutches of Irish pirates at the age of 16 and was dragged off to Ireland, where he was sold into slavery. He escaped after six years and returned to England, but later he returned, bringing Christianity to the Emerald Isle.

Saint Vincent de Paul (1579–1660) was not yet consid-
ered a saint when the fell into the clutches of the Barbary cor-
sairs. In 1605, he was a young professor at the University of
Toulouse in southern France and everything was going well
for him. It's said he was even offered a bishopric by the Duc
(or Duke) d'Epernon. At the same time, an old woman died
leaving to him some property in Marseille, a city on France's
Mediterranean coast. In order to pay off his debts, he decided
to go there and sell off this land. Instead of returning by land,
he decided to sail across the Gulfe du Lion to Narbonne, about
120 miles to the west, and then travel by land back to
Toulouse. This was in late July of 1605. He would spent the
next two years as a slave. He wrote to his friend, Monsieur de
Comet, about his adventures in a letter dated July 24, 1607.

The wind would have been sufficiently favorable to bring us to Narbonne (fifty leagues) the same day, if God had not permitted three Turkish sloops coasting the Gulf of Lyons—lying in wait for ships coming from Beaucaire, where a fair was being held that is regarded as one of the finest in Christendom—who gave chase to us and made so sharp an attack upon us that two or three of us were killed and the rest all wounded, even myself receiving an arrow wound which has left its reminder for all my life. We were thus constrained to yield to these pickpockets, who were fiercer than tigers and, as a first expression of their rage, hewed our pilot in a thousand pieces to avenge the loss of one of theirs. After seven or eight days they set sail for Barbary, the robbers' den of the Grand Turk,[2] where, when we had arrived, we were put up for sale with a certificate of our capture on a Spanish vessel, because otherwise we should have been freed by the consul who is kept there by the king to safeguard French trading.

We were paraded through the streets of Tunis[3] where we were brought for sale and having gone round the town five or six times with chains on our necks, we were brought back to the ship that we might eat and in this way show the merchants that we had received no mortal injury [when they were captured]. When this was over, they brought us back to the market-place, where the merchants came to see us, for all the world just like people come to the sale of a horse or an ox, making us open our mouths to see our teeth, feeling our sides, examining our wounds, making us walk, trot and run, making us carry weights and fight so as to gauge the strength of each of us, as well as a thousand other forms of brutality.

I was sold to a fisherman, and by him to an aged alchemist—a man of great gentleness and humility. This last told me he had devoted fifty years to a search for the philosopher's stone,[4] but all in vain, as far as the stone was concerned, but most successfully in another manner of transmuting metals. For instance, I myself often saw him melt down equal quantities of gold and silver, arrange the metals in small plates, place over them a layer of certain powders, then another layer of the metals and then another of the powders in a crucible or goldsmiths' melting pot, place this in a furnace for twenty-four hours, then open it and find that the silver had become gold; and still more often did I see him freeze or fix quicksilver into fine silver,[5] which he sold and gave the proceeds to the poor. My duty was to keep up the heat of ten or twelve furnaces, in which office, thank God, I found more pleasure than pain. My master had great love for me and liked to discourse of alchemy and still more of his creed, towards which he did his best to draw me with the promise of wealth and all the secrets of his learning. God maintained my faith in the deliverance which was to be an answer to my continual prayers to Him and the Virgin Mary (to whose intercession I am confident my deliverance is due).

I was with this old man from September 1605 to the following August, when he was summoned to work for the Sultan [Ahmed I]—in vain for he died of regret on the way. He left me to his nephew, who sold me very soon after his uncle's death, on a rumor that M. de Brèves, the King's ambassador,[6] was coming armed with powers from the Grand Turk to emancipate Christian slaves. I was bought by a renegade from Nice in Savoie[7] and taken by him to his dwelling-place among the mountains in a part of the country that is very hot and arid. One of his three wives, a Greek who was a Christian, although a schismatic,[8] was highly gifted and displayed a great liking for me, as eventually and to a greater degree did another of them, who was herself Turkish, but who by the mercy of God became the instrument for reclaiming her husband from his apostasy, for bringing him back within the pale of the Church, and delivering me from slavery.

Her curiosity as to our manner of life brought her daily to the fields where I worked, and in the end she required me to sing the praises of my God. The thought of the "*Quomodo cantabimus in terra aliena*" of the children of Israel captive in Babylon, made me with tears in my eyes begin the psalm "*Super flumina Babilonis*," and afterwards the "*Salve Regina*" and other things, in which she took so much delight that it was amazing. In the evening she did not fail to say to her husband that he had made a mistake in deserting his religion, which she believed to be a very good one by reason of the account of our God, which I had given her and the praises of Him which I had sung in her hearing. In hearing these she said she had felt such pure delight that she could not believe that the paradise of her fathers and that to which she one day aspired would be so glorious or afford her anything to equal this sensation. This new representation of Balaam's ass[9] so won over her husband that the following day he said he was only waiting for an opportunity to fly to France and that in a short time he would go to such lengths as would be to the glory of God. This short time was ten months, during which he offered me only vain hopes, but at the end we took flight in a little skiff and arrived on the 28th of June [1607] at Aigues-Mortes,[10] and soon afterwards went to Avignon,[11] where Monseigneur the Vice-Legate[12] gave public readmission to the renegade with a tear in his eye and a sob in his throat in the Church of Saint Pierre to the glory of God and the edification of all beholders.

Monseigneur kept us both with him till he could take us to Rome, whither he went as soon as the successor to his three-year office arrived. He had promised to gain entrance for the penitent into the convent of the "*Fate ben fratelli*," where he made his vows, and he promised to find a good living for me. His reason for liking and making much of me was chiefly because of certain secrets of alchemy which I had taught him, and for which he had been vainly seeking all his life.

> *Both the monseigneur and St. Vincent seem to be quite open-minded regarding alchemy. Half a century later it would be considered one of the black arts.*
>
> *St. Vincent de Paul started numerous charities—one of which was the Daughters of Charity—to help the poor, convicts, and galley slaves. He also founded a missionary organization known as the Lazarists. His influence was felt as far away as Madagascar and the Scotland's Hebrides. He was canonized in 1737 and in 1885 he was made the Universal Patron of Works of Charity. His feast day is July 19th.*

Notes

1. Talent: a nonstandard weight (roughly sixty pounds) in gold or silver.

2. The Grand Turk referred to here was Ahmed I, one of the sultans of Turkey and a ruler of the Ottoman Empire.

3. Tunis in Tunisia is on Africa's Mediterranean coast about 150 miles southwest of Sicily.

4. Philosopher's stone: an imaginary substance that alchemist's believed would transform base metals into gold or silver.

5. This alchemist was probably using deception since in other letters St. Vincent tells of an "artificial spring" the old man put in a skull that made it sound like it was talking "to deceive the people[. . .]saying that his god Mohammed taught him what the god's will was by means of this voice."

6. Francis Savary de Brèves, the French Ambassador at Constantinople. Because of a treaty of May 21, 1604 between the French King Henry IV and Sultan Ahmed I, the ambassador was on his way to Tunis to demand the liberation of all Christian slaves and the restitution of all that had been captured by pirates. In the end, only seventy-two slaves were set free. St. Vincent wasn't one of them.

7. This was William Gauntier, a priest and Friar Minor who had denied his faith to gain his liberty. He was from Nice in the Savoie region of the French Alps, just south of Geneva.

8. Schismatic: someone separated from an established church. In this case, she may have been a member of the Eastern Orthodox Church.

9. Numbers 22:21-33, where Balaam was riding his ass down a road and is suddenly confronted by an angel of the Lord, who the ass sees but not Balaam. The ass refuses to move, so Balaam beats her. The ass starts talking and asks why he's beating her. The angel then reveals himself to Balaam, explaining that if the ass hadn't stopped, he (the angel) would have slaughtered Balaam. Balaam promptly pleaded for forgiveness.

10. Aigues-Mortes is on the Mediterranean coast of southern France, about 60 miles west of Marseille.

11. Avignon is about fifty miles northwest of Marseille.

12. Monseigneur Peter Montorio, Vice-Ligate of Avignon.

Oh My God, I am Killed!

≈≈≈≈≈

Captain John Stairs

Pirates did not always work in gangs. Sometimes they were just a couple of criminals committing robbery and murder on water. One of these was Edward Jordan, who, along with his wife, was tried for the crimes of murder and piracy in a special Court of Admiralty on November 16, 1809 in Halifax, a town in the Canadian province of Nova Scotia.

Years before, Edward Jordan had been one of the leaders of Ireland's "rebellion of 1789." Prior to the rebellion he was caught one night drilling a company of pikemen and was sentenced to death for treason, but he escaped before the sentence was carried out. After the rebellion failed, the British government offered amnesty to all who turned in their arms. Jordan took advantage of this. He soon married and had a son, followed by three daughters.

Moving to New York and then to Canada, he worked as a fisherman and after five years had saved enough money to start building his own schooner. Using the ship as collateral, he secured a loan from the Halifax firm of J. and J. Tremain in June 1808 to complete the ship and outfit her. He named her the Three Sisters *after his three daughters.*

In July 1809 he was arrested for debt, but was bailed by J. and J. Tremain on the promise he would turn over to them a cargo of 100,000 pounds of dried fish. They sent him off to get it and sent Capt. John Stairs along to make sure he delivered the goods. On arriving at his home in Gaspé, Quebec, he could only come up with a tenth of what he owed, so acting for the firm, Capt. Stairs foreclosed on the ship. They were returning to Halifax with the Jordans as passengers when Edward Jordan decided to turn pirate.

What follows is the testimony of Capt. Stairs, taken from the transcripts of the Jordans's trial.

[The Solicitor-General:] Q. What is your profession and occupation in life?

[Capt. John Stairs:] A. A mariner and ship master.

Q. What ship or vessel did you last command?

A. The schooner *Three Sisters*.

Q. Who gave you the command of the *Three Sisters*?

A. Jonathan and John Tremain.

Q. Where and when did you take command?

A. The 15th of July last at Halifax.

Q. On what voyage did you sail with her?

A. To Perce,[1] for the purpose of procuring a cargo of fish Jordan had promised to deliver. We sailed on or about the 17th of July.

Q. Who sailed with you in the schooner?

A. John Kelly, mate; Thomas Heath seaman and pilot; Benjamin Matthews, seaman; and Edward Jordan and Patrick Cinnet, passengers—the latter was sickly.

Q. When did you arrive at Perce?

A. The latter end of July or first of August.

Q. Did you take in a cargo at Perce?

A. Part of a cargo—on freight 200 quintals[2] from Theophilus Fox; 300 from Wm. Driscoll; and about 90 or 100 from the prisoner Jordan, on account of my owners Jonathan and John Tremain.

Q. When did you sail from Perce?

A. On the 10th of September, for Halifax.

Q. Name the crew and passengers then on board.

A. Myself, John Kelly, Thomas Heath, Benjamin Matthews, Edward and Margaret Jordan (the prisoners), and their four children—three girls and one boy.

Q. Relate, fully and distinctly, all the circumstances that occurred on your voyage from Perce to Halifax?

A. Nothing material happened until the 13th of September, when between Cape Canso and White Head, myself and crew—except Kelly, who was at the helm—went forward to trim the sails, the wind coming off the land. Between 11 and 12 o'clock, I went below for the purpose of getting my quadrant to take the sun, and was soon followed by Heath. I was standing near the table directly below the skylight turning over the leaves of a book—Heath [was] near, but rather behind me—when looking up, I saw Jordan presenting a pistol down the skylight, I thought at me. I was startled. And then pistol was discharged, the ball from which grazed my nose and side of my face and entered the breast of Heath, who fell on his knees and cried, "Oh my God, I am killed!" Heath soon after crawled on deck. When I recovered from my fright and the first effects of the powder which lodged in my face, I went to my trunk for my pistols, but I found the trunk had been forced open and the pistols taken. I then searched for my cutlass, but could not find it. I then determined to go on deck. On going up the ladder, I met the prisoner, Edward Jordan, in the act of descending. One of his feet was on the ladder, he held an ax in his right hand and a pistol in his left. I seized his arms, and begged him for God's sake to spare my life, shoved him backwards. When he snapped the pistol, I instantly grasped it by the muzzle, wrested it from him, and threw it overboard, and called Kelly the mate to my assistance, but he made no answer. Benjamin Matthews came hastily aft, he appeared to be wounded and fell down. By this time I had taken the ax from Jordan and endeavored to strike him, but he held me so forcibly as to prevent me. I however threw the ax overboard. I again called Kelly, but his back was towards me and he in the attitude of loading a pistol,[3] when Margaret Jordan struck me several times with a boat hook[4] handle, observing, "Is it Kelly you want? I'll give you Kelly."

Before I went on deck I distinctly heard four or five pistol reports. On coming on deck, I saw Heath lying dead on the starboard side of the vessel, bleeding very much. After disentangling myself from Jordan, I went forward [and] Jordan aft for another ax, with which returning he struck Matthews three or four times on the back of the head. Finding no chance of my life if I remained on board and that I might as well be drowned as shot, I threw the hatch overboard, jumped after it, and got on; where I remained about three hours and a half, when I was picked up by an American fishing schooner[5] in a weak and almost senseless state. On recovering a little, I told the captain what had happened, then went on deck and borrowed a spy glass, with which I saw one or two sail of vessels at a great distance to leeward. I asked the captain to bear away and see what they were, thinking one might be the *Three Sisters*, but they [*sic*] refused, saying that if he went out of his voyage and any accident happened to him, the underwriters would not pay the insurance. I then asked him to keep the shore aboard [i.e. along side] and land me at Halifax. He said he would, was he not afraid of having his men impressed,[6] as on his outward bound passage he had his pilot taken by the Bream or Mullet schooner. I then told him he might perhaps be enabled to put me ashore before he passed Cape Sable,[7] but as the wind was not favorable, we went directly to Hingham, (Massachusetts,) from thence I traveled to Boston, where I published the circumstances in the newspapers and had circular letters describing the vessel and persons of Kelly, Jordan, his wife and family sent to the collectors in the American ports by W. S. Skinner, Esq., acting British Consul.

The other passenger on the Three Sisters, *Patrick Cinnet, was probably also murdered, joining Heath and Matthews in the deep. The pirates then went off in search of a new crew, especially since they now had no navigator. Edward Jordan masqueraded as one of the ship's owners, John Tremain, while John Kelly pretended to be Capt. Stairs. They tried to get to Ireland, but never made it off the coast of Canada. Eventually, when Jordan and Kelly were drunk, they got into a fight. Kelly stole the ship's boat and went ashore somewhere in Newfoundland. Then sometime in late October or early November 1809, the Jordans were captured by the H.M.S.* Cuttle *and brought back to Halifax to stand trial.*

Margaret Jordan testified that for the first half of their ten year marriage, they lived happily in Ireland. Then on moving to the United States, her husband became extremely jealous of her and abused her very badly. Several members of the new crew testified that Edward Jordan often threatened to kill his wife, especially when in drunken rages, and they often had to stop him. She admitted she might have struck Capt. Stairs during the struggle, but was out of her mind at the time. The court found her innocent and released her to care for her children. A fund was established for them in Halifax and they were eventually able to return to Ireland.

Edward Jordan was found guilty and executed on November 20, 1809. His body was left hanging as a warning until a storm blew his skeleton out to sea. Years later his skull washed ashore and was turned over to the Halifax Museum.

John Kelly was caught in Newfoundland and sentenced to death, but was later pardoned.

Notes

1. Perce is in the New Brunswick province on the Gulf of St. Lawrence.

2. Quintal: a weight equal to one hundred pounds.

3. Kelly, who was also Irish, had joined the Jordans in taking over the ship and may have been the one who shot Matthews.

4. Boat hook: a long pole with an iron hook on the end, used for pulling or pushing boats.

5. This was the *Eliza*, which was commanded by Capt. Levi Stoddard.

6. Canada was still part of the British Empire at this time and because the British Navy often found itself short of recruits, they would often press sailors into service. Sometimes they would even stop a ship and take its crew. This is what happened to Capt. Kidd. As he set out on his fateful voyage, he failed to fire the appropriate salute to the navy. Even though Kidd had a commission from the King, the offended naval ships pressed his crew into service and replaced it with some criminals and trouble-makers they wanted to get rid of. At the time of Capt. Stair's account, Britain was at war with Napoleon, and as the British tended to look down on the colonials, they probably felt the fishing ports of Canada were excellent places to press sailors into service.

7. Cape Sable is the southern tip of Nova Scotia.

I Made Signs for Assistance

≈≈≈≈≈

Captain Rufus Frink

Capt. Rufus Frink was captured by pirates off the coast of Cuba. After surviving the attack, he wrote a letter to the owner of his schooner, Shepherdess, *who lived in Warren, Rhode Island. It was dated Havana, February 2, 1822, and was reprinted on March 6th in the Salem* Register.

I arrived at Matanzas on the 29th ult.[1] [i.e. January 29, 1822], but finding the markets extremely unfavorable, I thought it would be most for the interest of the voyage to proceed to Havana for which place I accordingly sailed on the 31st ult., at four o'clock P.M., with a fine breeze. At about two o'clock A.M. I discovered a boat in shore of me standing to the eastward, and was apprehensive that it was a pirate. Thinking to avail myself of the assistance and protection of the steamboat, then in sight, I continued my course. The steamboat more rapidly approached, and the pirates being nearly abreast of me, it being now eight o'clock in the morning, I made signs to the steamboat for assistance. The pirates, thinking probably that they would not have time to effect their object before she came up, hauled their wind in shore; not so far, however, but that the steamboat passed them within half pistol shot without taking the least notice of them. She also passed by us totally regardless of our signal of distress and the maneuvering of the pirates, whose object she could not possibly have mistaken. A calm now succeeding, the steamboat was soon out of sight. Being thus abandoned and in a defenseless situation, the only alternative that remained was to secrete my most valuable property and resign myself to their barbarity. The pirates now returned and boarded us. After having secured the mate and crew, beating them at the same time most inhumanly with swords and cutlasses, they ordered me into the cabin and demanded my money or my life, attempting at the same time to cut my throat. I then surrendered up to them about sixty dollars; but this only increased their savage ferocity to obtain more, and threatened to murder me and burn my vessel instantly unless I gave up all I had. But as I persisted in saying that it was all I had by me, they ceased beating me for a moment and commenced a general pillage of the cabin, and after rifling it on everything to the amount of a real,[2] they ordered me on deck and commenced beating me again with increased barbarity. Being nearly exhausted in consequence of their inhuman cruelty, they ordered me to rig a rope to hang me with and threatened to put it into execution instantly unless I gave them more money. At this moment I cast my eyes towards the stern of my vessel and saw that she was on fire. They immediately charged me with having kindled it, and began to beat me again most unmercifully. They, however, extinguished the fire before it had arrived to a dangerous extent.

Seeing there was no chance for my life unless I made a total surrender of all my property, I entreated them to spare my life and I would give them more money. After having surrendered up all I had, they insisted on more and again commenced the savage work of beating me, and finally forced me overboard. They then cast loose the stern boat and let her go adrift. I was not so far exhausted but that I was able to recover [i.e. get back into] the vessel.

They then called up the mate and began to beat him most barbarously, when luckily a vessel hove in sight, having the appearance of a man-of-war. After having hastily stripped me of my clothes, their captain offered me his hand and wished me a good passage to Havana, and they all repaired to the boat. They robbed me in money and articles to the amount of about $1,200. Their boat was about thirty feet long, carrying fifteen men armed with cutlasses, muskets and blunderbusses,[3] with a swivel[4] mounted on the bow. I then proceeded for Havana, where I arrived yesterday, the 1st inst.[5]

Notes

1. Ult. is the abbreviation for "ultimo," meaning the previous month.

2. Real: a Spanish silver coin. Pronounced "ree'-al" or "ree'-al-lay," it is sometimes spelled reale, rial, riyal or ryal. A piece-of-eight was eight reals.

3. Blunderbuss: a short rifle with a flared muzzle.

4. Swivel: a small cannon-like gun mounted on the ship's railing and could be swung from side to side.

5. Inst. is the abbreviation for "instant," meaning this month.

Americans were Very Good Beef for Their Knives

≋≋≋≋≋

Daniel Collins

Oddly enough, the following excerpt from his pamphlet was used to introduce Lucretia Parker's account in her pamphlet, Piratical Barbarity or The Female Captive *(1825).*[1] *Given the religious emphasis of Parker's narrative, it is interesting that they should choose such a violently explicit report to precede hers.*

Like Lucretia Parker, Daniel Collins was the lone survivor of a piratical attack. It was on the night of December 20, 1824 that the brigantine Betsey of Wiscasset, Maine, was shipwrecked on the Double Headed Shot Keys in the lower Florida strait near Cuba. After striking a rock, it only took ten minutes for the ship to break apart. Abandoning their stricken ship for their long boat, they were only able to save the ship's money and themselves. By using a blanket as their sail, they were able to make it to Cruz del Padre Key, which is about fifteen miles from mainland Cuba. Here they found two or three fishermen's shacks, where they were given food and water.

Unfortunately, the crew escaped one disaster only to be confronted by something even worse. One of their hosts, "the Master Fisherman," had secretly sent word of their arrival to a nearby gang of pirates.

The pirates quickly came and, with knives and cutlasses drawn, seized the stricken Americans. Binding the captives' arms behind their backs, the pirate captain exclaimed, "We will now cut your throats, Yankees."

Four fishermen and seven pirates loaded their captives into two canoes—Capt. Hilton, Mr. Merry (the first mate), Bridge (the cook) and another crewman into one, and Daniel Collins *(the second mate), Seth Russel and Charles Manuel into the other. The captives were taken to a nearby lagoon, all the while knowing they were about to be slaughtered.*

The seven pirates and four fishermen, mentioned, now proceeded with us towards the beach until the water was about three feet deep, when they all got out; the two fishermen to each canoe, hauling us along, and the pirates walking by the side of us, one to each of our crew, torturing us all the way by drawing their knives across our throats, grasping the same, and pushing us back under the water which had been taken in by rocking the canoes. While some of us were in the most humiliating manner beseeching of them to spare our lives and others with uplifted eyes were again supplicating that Divine mercy which had preserved them from the fury of the elements, they (the pirates) were laughing, and occasionally telling us in broken English that "Americans were very good beef for their knives." Thus they proceeded with us nearly a mile from the vessel, which we were now losing sight of by doubling [i.e. rounding] a point at the entrance of the cove before described and when within a few rods[2] of its head—where we had before seen human bones—the canoes were hauled abreast of each other preparatory to our execution.

The stillness of death was now around us, for the very flood gates of feeling had been burst asunder and exhausted grief at its fountain. It was a beautiful morning—not a cloud to obscure the rays of the sun— and the clear blue sky presented a scene too pure for deeds of darkness. But the lonely sheet of water, on which, side by side, we lay, presented that hopeless prospect which is more ably described by another:

———————— "No friend, no refuge near
All, all is false and treacherous around;
All that they touch, or taste, or breathe, is Death."

We had scarcely passed the last passing look at each other, when the work of death commenced.

They seized Capt. Hilton by the hair, bent his head and shoulders over the gunwale,[3] and I could distinctly hear them chopping the bone of the neck. They then wrung his neck, separated the head from the body by a slight draw of the sword, and let it drop into the water. There was a dying shriek, a convulsive struggle, and all I could discern was the arms dangling over the side of the canoe and the ragged stump pouring out the blood like a torrent.

There was an imploring look in the innocent and youthful face of Mr. Merry, that would have appealed to the heart of anyone but a pirate. As he rose on his knees, in the posture of a penitent, supplicating for mercy even on the verge of eternity, he was prostrated with a blow of the cutlass, his bowels gushing out of the wound. They then pierced him through the breast in several places with a long pointed knife and cut his throat from ear to ear.

The captain's dog—repulsed in his repeated attempts to rescue his master—sat whining beside his lifeless body, looking up to these blood hounds in human shape, as if to tell them that even brutal cruelty would be glutted with the blood of two innocent, unoffending victims.

Bridge, the cook, they pierced through the breast, as they had Merry, in several places with their knives, and then split their [sic] heads open with their cutlasses. Their dying groans had scarcely ceased, and I was improving the moment of life that yet remained, when I heard the blow behind me. The blood and brains that fled all over my head and shoulders warned me that poor Russel had shared the fate of the others. And as I turned my head to catch the eye of my executioner, I saw the head of Russel severed in two nearly its whole length with a single blow of the cutlass, and even without the decency of removing his cap. At the sound of the blow, Manuel, who sat before me, leaped overboard and four of the pirates were in full chase after him. In what manner he loosed his hands, I am unable to say. His escape, I shall hereafter explain. My eyes were fixed on my supposed executioner, watching the signal of my death. He was on my right hand and partly behind me. My head, which was covered with a firm tarpaulin hat, was turned in a direction that brought my shoulders fore and aft the canoe. The blow came. It divided the top of my hat, struck my head so severely as to stun me, and glanced off my left shoulder, taking the skin and some flesh in its way, and divided my pinion cord on the arm. I was so severely stunned that I did not leap from the canoe but pitched over the left side, and was just arising from the water, not my length from her, as a pirate threw his knife which struck me but did not retard my flight an instant; and I leaped forward through the water, expecting a blow from behind at every step.

The shrieks of the dying had ceased. The scene of horrid butchery in the canoes was now over. Manuel and I were in the water about knee deep. Two of the pirates after me, and all the rest, except one, after Manuel. We ran in different directions. By the interposition of Divine Providence, I escaped and succeeded in reaching the island of Cuba. Poor Manuel was less fortunate. He was overtaken by his unmerciful pursuers and instantly destroyed.[4]

Notes

1. Unfortunately I have yet to locate a copy of his pamphlet, so I can only include what was quoted in hers.

2. Rod: a measurement equal to 16½ feet or 5½ yards.

3. Gunwale: the upper edge of the ship's side, or the piece of timber that extends on either side from the quarter-deck to the forecastle.

4. It's reported that while on the streets of Matanzas, Collins suddenly found himself face to face with Charles Manuel, who had survived in much the same way that Collins had. If this true, it must have happened after Collins wrote his account of the ordeal.

A Bloody, Merciless Ruffian

≋

John Fillmore

*John Phillips, a carpenter from England, was aboard a ship cap-
tured by the pirate captain Thomas Anstis. He joined them and
continued with them until the company broke up. Some of the
pirates wanted to give up piracy and return England, so they
decided to sent a petition to the King requesting a pardon. Each
of them signed it and they sent to London aboard a merchant
ship. Phillips and several of the other pirates went along, confident the pardon would be granted. Most of those who remained
behind were taken by a man-of-war and hanged.*

*Shortly after their arrival, Phillips learned that some of
his companions had been arrested and thrown in jail. Thinking
he would be next, he immediately shipped out for St. Peters,
Newfoundland. Once there he deserted ship and got a job as a
fish splitter. He soon convinced four others to join him and on
the night of August 29, 1723, they seized a schooner while it
lay at anchor in the harbor[1] and set off in search of prizes and
to enlarge their crew. Phillips was made captain, John Nutt
navigator, James Sparks gunner, Thomas Fern carpenter, and
William White was the crew.[2] They renamed their vessel the*
Revenge *and began capturing fishing vessels off the coast of
Newfoundland, Canada. On one of their prizes they found
John Rose Archer who had previously been a pirate under
Blackbeard. He immediately joined with them and Phillips
appointed him quartermaster. Then on September 5th they fell
upon a ship from Massachusetts which contained John Fill-
more, the great-grandfather of President Millard Fillmore.
His account was later printed in the pamphlet* A Narrative
of the Captivity of John Fillmore and His Escape from the
Pirates *(1802). It seems this is the first time this account has
been reprinted since then.*

The depravity of the [————————————]³ so universally acknowledged in the present enlightened age, and a belief of the universal pres-
idency of providence over the affairs of men so evidently established, as
to need no argument to enforce the reception of a narrative in which
both are peculiarly manifest.

Convinced of the truth of the above sentiment I shall proceed in my
narrative, endeavoring on the one hand to avoid tedious repetitions, and
on the other to omit no incident that may afford entertainment to my
cherished reader.

My father dying when I was young, my mother put me apprentice to
learn the [——]⁴ occupation of a carpenter. On the [——]⁵ side of the
road, opposite to the house where I lived [in Wenham, Massachusetts],
there dwelt a tailor who had an apprentice named William White with
whom I was very intimate during the time of his apprenticeship, but he
was out of his time and went to sea some time before I was free, being
about three years older than myself.

White, as I before observed, went to sea sometime before I was free,
but he did not return, nor do I remember that I ever saw or heard of him
afterwards till I found him among the pirates.

From my youth I had an almost irresistible desire for undertaking a
voyage to sea, which I referred to all events to gratify as soon as I
obtained the right to dispose of myself. In establishing this resolution,
a love of novelty joined to a secret delight I enjoyed in hearing sailors
relate the curiosities they met with in their voyages doubtless had a
great effect, and the older I grew the impression became stronger.

But however strong my desire was to follow the sea, a sense of the duty
I owed my surviving parent so far overbalanced my inclination as to
occasion me to form a determination not to gratify it until I should be of
age, unless I could gain her consent. The propensity however was so
strong as to induce me at the age of 17 to apply to my mother and request
liberty to go [on] a voyage to sea. My mother was very uneasy at the
request and used every art of persuasion that maternal tenderness could
dictate to induce me to relinquish the design. Expressing some surprise
that I should entertain any idea of following the sea, as it was a life most
evidently attended with innumerable fatigues and dangers: urging, in
particular reason for her disapprobation of the measure, the melancholy
fate of my father, who being a seafaring man was taken by a French
frigate [while] on a voyage homeward and carried into Martinico⁶ a

number of years before, where he underwent all the hardships of a close and cruel confinement, and although ultimately redeemed with many others, was supposed to be most inhumanly poisoned by the French on board the cartel,[7] as they principally died on their passage home.

However strong an argument this might have appeared to my mother, it failed in its desired effect on me. It only lulled my desire for a while, but by no means eradicated it. I waited, however, with a great degree of impatience about two years longer, when I again asked leave to go [on] a voyage to the West Indies, and my mother—finding my res-olution unabated—concluded she could as well part with me then as when I became of age, after which she imagined she should not be able to detain me. Upon the whole she told me she was unwilling I should go to the West Indies, but that the sloop *Dolphin*, Capt. Haskell, was then in the harbor fitting out for a fishing voyage and if I would go with him she would give her consent. To this proposal I readily assented.

I accordingly shipped on board the sloop and had a tolerable passage to the fishing ground [off Newfoundland], but soon after our arrival there we were surprised by the appearance of a ship, which from exter-nal signs we suspected to be a pirate. We were not by any means pre-pared to oppose so formidable an enemy, and she was so close upon us before we suspected her as to render it impossible for us to escape by run-ning away, we were therefore obliged to abide our fate peaceably, let the consequence be what it would.

The pirate soon came up and sent a boat on board our sloop, demanding who we were and where we were bound; to which our cap-tain gave a direct answer. By this boat's crew we learned that the noted pirate captain Phillips commanded their ship. This intelligence it will readily be conceived gave us great uneasiness, most of the crew being quite young, and having often heard of the cruelties committed by that execrable pirate, which made us dread to fall into his hands.

The pirate's boat soon boarded us again, demanding the name of every hand on board. In this boat came White the tailor, as before men-tioned. I was greatly surprised to find him employed in so criminal a course of life, though I said nothing to him. On the return of the pirate's boat with a list of our names, White, as I was afterwards informed, acquainted Phillips of his knowledge of me, informing him that if he could engage me in his service, he would gain a stout, resolute fellow, [and in] every way he supposed such a hand as he wanted.

On receiving this information—as he stood in need of a hand and found we had no property he wanted on board—he sent his boat once more with orders to Capt. Haskell to send me on board his ship and the rest of the crew with the sloop may go free. My worthy commander, with much visible concern in his countenance, took me aside and informed me of Phillips's orders, adding that although it would be exceedingly disagreeable and painful to him to let me go. Yet as we were entirely in the power of a bloody, merciless ruffian and [had] no hopes of escape but by giving me up, "I believe," says he, "you must go and try your fortune with them."[8]

The thought of being sacrificed, as it were, to procure liberty for the rest of the crew operated greatly on my spirits and the first conclusion I drew up was that I would not on any conditions agree to go on board the pirate. I therefore told my captain that I had ever been faithful to his interest and commands, that I had always wished to do my duty punctually and well, but that I was determined not to go on board the pirate, let the consequence be what it would. Our conversation ended here for that time and the boat returned without me.

Phillips was greatly incensed when the boat returned without me and sent again with orders to bring me either dead or alive. My captain took me aside again and told me the pirate's resolution and message, adding that he believed I should do well to go with them, for if I refused to go and made resistance, it would be inevitable death to me and probably to our whole crew, and there would at least be a probability of making an escape from them sometime or other. But if I could not find a way to escape, it was not impossible but Phillips might discharge me for he had sent word that if I would agree to serve him faithfully for two months, he would set me at liberty.

Those only who have been in familiar circumstances can form an adequate idea of the distress I experienced at this time. If I obstinately refused to join the pirates, instant death stared me and my comrades in the face. If I consented to go with them, I expected to be massacred for refusing to sign their piratical articles,[9] which I had fully determined never to do, though I should be put to the extremity of torture for refusal. Into so critical a situation had my bad fortune plunged me that inevitable destruction seemed to stare me in the face from every quarter. I took the matter however into serious consideration and after the most mature deliberation, determined to venture myself among them rather than bring the vengeance of the pirates on my comrades. I therefore went with them seemingly contentedly and the captain renewing his promise to set me at liberty in two months, I engaged to serve him to the best of my abilities during that term. I was likewise agreeably disappointed in their not urging so strenuously as I expected the thing I most of all dreaded, viz. the signing of their articles. To induce me to join them they used more arguments of a persuasive than a compulsory nature, judging I suppose that youth would be more easily enticed than compelled to join in sharing their ill-gotten gain.

When I first went aboard of the pirate, their crew consisted of ten men including their captain, and on the whole of them I think as stout, daring, hardy-looking fellows as ever I saw together. As I was then the only hand on board who had not subscribed their articles, the captain assigned me to the helm, where I kept my station during the greatest part of the time I stayed with them.

No captures of any consequence were made during the first two months. Some small vessels were taken, but their lading was too inconsiderable to satisfy the insatiable dispositions of the pirates.

The period being now arrived when I had a right according to agreement to demand my liberty, I thought it a proper season at least to remind the captain of the manumission[10] he had engaged me. For this purpose I went to him and in language the least offensive I could frame, remind him of his promise and request him to fulfill it. Phillips, in tolerable good humor, replied that we had done but little business since I came on board, that he could not well spare me yet, but if I would stay with him three months longer he would then set me at liberty upon his honor and I was obliged quietly to submit, comply with his demands, and trust to his honor, though it turned out in the end that it did but mock me.

Nothing of any importance occurred during this three months. Some few small vessels were taken and plundered, their cargoes were of no great value and their hands were dismissed with their vessels, except two or three robust, stout-looking men whom Phillips picked from among them and compelled to sign articles.

When the three months were expired, I went to the captain and once more reminded him of the expiration of my servitude and handsomely requested him to set me ashore according to his promise, that I might go to my mother, who had not heard from me since my first captain returned from his fishing voyage.

"Set you at liberty, damn you. You shall be set at liberty when I'm damned and not before," replied Phillips in a rage more compatible with his diabolical disposition of an infernal fiend than a being endowed with a reaion [sic] soul susceptible of human sensations.

It is evident, and experience daily evinces, that persons by habituating themselves to any particular vice become so familiarized thereto as to be unable to distinguish it from a real virtue, and in such case conscience ceases to alarm the understanding and suffers the culprit to pursue it to its extremity. This was undoubtedly the case with Captain Phillips, who was not addicted to one particular vice, but to every vice.

Having now lost all hope and probability of being liberated, there was no alternative more eligible for me than to sustain my servitude with as much patience, resolution and fortitude as possible. Although the captain had assured that I should not be set at liberty till he was damned, I was still in hopes that we might be taken by some vessel or that we might take more prisoners, who in concert with myself might be able to contrive some plan whereby we might take the ship and thereby incapacitate Phillips to determine whether I should obtain my freedom before he received his final doom, or not.

As we were sailing one day we came within view of a fine merchant vessel, the appearance of pleased the captain much, who swore by heaven he would have her, accordingly I was ordered to beat[11] off for her as [——][12] as possible. Phillips, being extremely anxious for to take this vessel, walked the deck with his glass in his hands viewing of her the greatest part of the day, [——————][13] me, because, as I said, I did not steer so well as I might.

Eleven holes he cut through my hat and the skin of my head without the least provocation with his broad sword. But the merchantman, being lightly built and completely rigged, left sight of us before night. Phillips exclaiming in a horrid rage that the loss of that fine ship was all my damned doings, adding that he wanted the damned thing just long enough to sail to Hell in.[14]

We had sundry prisoners on board, Frenchmen and Negroes[15]; we had also an American with whom I had been acquainted when young and whom the pirates could neither persuade nor compel to sign their articles. Thus, fortune had sent me one friend with whom I could sympathize under my almost insupportable calamities, though our sympathy was chiefly confined to looks and private gestures, for we dared not complain in the hearing of the crew.

About the end of the seventh month from my entering on board, we took a merchantman belonging to Boston, Capt. Harridon,[16] commander—a young man only 22 years of age. The father of this young man was a merchant in Boston and had given this son the education requisite for a mariner and sent him to the West Indies [as] captain of this vessel, in which he was returning home when we took him.

All except Harridon, James Cheeseman (a ship carpenter),[17] and a Spanish Indian[18] who was with Harridon, my friend whom I mentioned above, and myself had been compelled to sign the pirates' articles. We had been enjoined to sign them but had utterly refused, choosing rather to be killed by the villains than to be taken, condemned and executed for being their associates. But I suppose they deemed [—————]19 to dispatch us yet.

One day we took a large vessel after considerable trouble in chasing, but found nothing on board worthy the attention of the pirates except their provision and water—which being in some want of, Phillips striped them of it entirely, took out one or two of their hands, and then let them go.[20]

Some of the pirates having been sent on board Harridon's vessel, there remained only six of the old pirates on board besides those who had been forced to sign their articles, and as there were five of us who wished to escape from them, we began to think and even to suggest something about trying some scheme to effect that purpose. There was no time that we could confer together without being discovered, except in the dead of night, and even then we dared not be all together, and consequently could not without great difficulty succeed in forming any regular plan to effect our escape.

One day we came in sight of a merchantman which Phillips imagining would prove a valuable prize gave orders for chasing. His orders were put in execution immediately, but the merchantman being lightly built and a prime sailer, we chased her three days before we were able to capture them. Having made what disposition he pleased of their hands, etc. he found on board the new prize, Phillips ordered one Fern,[21] a daring resolute fellow of the old pirate crew, to go on board of her and take command, taking some of the old crew along with him.

Phillips had now become so exceedingly arbitrary as to be hated by his own crew, but they stood in such dread of him that they dared no more contradict his orders than they dared to die. Soon after night came on, Fern proposed to the pirates with him that as they were now in possession of a fine vessel, every way [——][22] for a cruiser, and as good a sailer as Phillips's, if they would join him he would put out his lights, and steering by the light of the old pirate, make their escape from the tyranny of Phillips and set up for themselves. The crew accordingly joined and they began to execute their plan, but Phillips suspecting their design on finding they darkened their ship, put out his own light and endeavored to follow them in which he succeeded so well as to be in a fight with them the next morning. We continued to chase the new pirate till the third day before we came up with her, when a fierce engagement ensued, but Fern soon finding himself overpowered and no hope of escape, sent word to Phillips that if he would grant him a pardon he would strike to him and once more serve him faithfully, but if not they would all fight till they died. Phillips immediately complied with their demand and sent orders for Fern to come on board his ship, which he did, and Phillips, not regarding his engagement to pardon, immediately ran his sword through his body and then blew his brains out with his pistol, and thus glutted his own vengeance and ridded us of a desperate enemy.[23]

I mentioned before that there were five of us who had not signed the pirates' articles, and as Phillips by killing Fern had left but five of the old pirate crew alive, we began to conceive it a proper opportunity to make our escape. We were however exceedingly cautious, and had not yet had an opportunity to communicate our plans to my New England friend before mentioned, yet conscience made the pirates suspicious of something of the kind being in agitation, and from the consequent murderous procedure of Phillips we had reason to apprehend they had in reality discovered our intentions.

My friend—the American before mentioned—being on board the vessel lately taken from Capt. Harridon, Phillips ordered out a boat and went on board where he accused him with joining in a plot—assisted by me—to kill him and all his crew and take the vessel.[24] My friend solemnly denied the accusation and declared he knew nothing of such a plan, which was in fact the case, for I afterwards learned that there had nothing been said to him about it. This reply, however true, did not mitigate the captain's passion in the least, for he damned him, swore he would send him to Hell and instantly ran him through the body with his sword in such a manner that he twisted the point of it off, leaving it in the backbone.

My friend, I suppose, not being conscious of having received his death wound still denied the charge and with great earnestness begged that his life might be spared, but the captain, whose insatiable thirst for slaughter was not sufficiently gorged, damned him, presented his pistol and shot him through the head, exclaiming, "I have sent one of the devil's to Hell and where is Fillmore, he shall go next." I was ordered to go aboard Harridon's vessel.

My long familiarity with and constant apprehension of my death rendered its near approaches less terrifying than formerly, but I did not receive this message without heart-rending sensations and thrilling emotions of trepidation and fear. But Phillips was completely despotic, and there was no such thing as evading his commands. I therefore drew up a resolution that if I found he was bent on my death, I would sell my life as dear as possible and endeavor to kill him first. With this resolution and as much fortitude as I could muster, I went on board Phillips and stood by a handspeak[25] that lay upon the deck, Phillips charged me as he had done my friend with contriving to betray him and take the ship. The accusation was true enough, but I concluded a lie was warrantable in that case and consequently replied that I knew nothing of any conspiracy either against him or his crew. I had prepared myself to make resistance in case he offered any abuse, but he had a pistol concealed under his coat which he presented to my breast and snapped it before I had time to make any evasion, but happily for me it missed fire. He drew it back, cocked and presented it again but I struck it aside with my hand, so that it went off by my side without doing any injury.

I thought of knocking out his brains with the handspeak that lay near me, but I knew it would be instant death for me and therefore concluded if he would leave me, I would not meddle with him at that juncture. He then swung his sword over my head, damned me, and bid me go about my business, adding that he only did that to try me. These last words raised my spirits one degree higher than they had been before, for I confess I thought that snapping a loaded pistol at a man's breast was a harsh mode of trial and such an one as I had by no means been accustomed to before. I stooped to take up the handspeak, thinking to try him with the butt end of that, but on mature consideration concluded to let the matter rest a little longer and watch for a more convenient opportunity to resent the injury. The pistol missing fire when snapped at my breast and then going off by my side was a strong indication to me that providence had interposed graciously in my preservation, that our final deliverance from the barbarity of the savage Phillips and his abandoned banditti might be the more speedily effected.

A few weeks now ensued which were spent in tolerable good humor and peace among all hands on board, and myself and friends put on the semblance of content as much as possible, though we were incessantly seeking opportunities to confer with each other upon some mode of escape, but no proper opportunity occurred nor indeed were our measures properly concerted as yet.

Again we were called upon to sign their flagitious[26] articles and become willing members of the piratical band with menaces of immediate death in case we still refused, but we had heard their threats too often to be frightened into a compliance by them now.

A short time after this, being about nine months after I was taken and about two from the time we fell in with and made a prize of the vessel on board of which Harridon was taken,[27] the crew in commemoration of some signal [i.e. memorable] advantage which they had obtained, had a grand carouse, eating, drinking, and spending the day in such diversions as their gross inclinations required. A favorable opportunity now seemed to offer to extricate us from our suffering and we determined to improve it if possible. Cheeseman was ordered by Phillips to bring some tools on deck and do something towards repairing the ship early next morning and the master [i.e. navigator][28] was ordered to take an observation next day at noon to find out where we were. Thus far providence seemed to favor our design and we felt firm in the determination of executing of it the next day.

It was late in the evening before the pirates retired to rest and White and one more of the old pirates got into the caboose[29] as drunk as beasts and lay down before the fire. A favorable opportunity now seemed to offer for us to improve in conferring upon some means for our [meeting ?].[30] We got together, held a consultation and concluded to risk ourselves in trying to win our deliverance, considering [that it would be ?][31] better to die in so just a cause than to share in the fate of our late New England friend, which we had no doubt would soon overtake us if we persisted in our determination never to sign their articles or share in their unlawful gain.

When I mentioned that we had determined on an immediate execution of our design, I would inform the reader that there were but three of us, viz. Cheeseman, myself, and the Spanish Indian[32] before mentioned, for poor Harridon declared that his heart was broken, his resolution and courage gone by a series of ill-usage and that he dared not engage to assist but would not discover [i.e. reveal] our plot. Thus there remained only three of us to engage the whole crew, and the Indian we felt rather dubious about though we gained confidence in him from his having firmly refused several times though threatened with immediate death to subscribe to pirating articles. However I must do him the honor to say he was true to his trust and it not have been for him our plot would most probably have failed in the execution.

Cheeseman, the Indian and myself got together[. We agreed that ?][33] Cheeseman should leave broadax on the main deck when he had done using it and when I saw Cheeseman make ready to grasp the master, I was to catch it up and make the best use of it I could cutting and slashing all that offered to oppose me, while the Indian was to stand ready to help as occasion may require. And each of us in the meantime was to do everything he could think of to forward the design.

Our plan being thus concerted, I went down into the caboose where White and John Rose Archer, a desperate fellow who had been taken in one of the prizes and immediately joined the pirates, laid on the floor as before mentioned drunk as beasts. I took fire and burnt these two villains in the feet while they lay senseless so badly as to render them unable to be upon the deck the next day. There were only four left now of the old pirate gang and five who had joined them since, besides the two who I rendered incapable of injuring us.

We were up early in the morning and Cheeseman used the broadax and left it as agreed. It was very late in the morning and the pirates were none of them up and we were afraid they would arise out too late to take an observation and our plan of consequence must fall through. To prevent this, about 10 o'clock I went to the cabin door and told the captain the sun was almost up to the meridian. "Damn you," said he, "it is none of your business." This was all the thanks I got, and indeed all I expected for my service. However, it answered the [call ?][34] designed, for the captain, boatswain, quartermaster[35] and master came upon deck a little after 11 o'clock. Inquiry was [made] for [how] White and Archer [——————————————]36 to accident. Harridon was [——————————]37 and the Indian became near as white as any of us. Phillips took notice of Harridon's paleness and I cloaked the matter by informing him that Harridon had been sick all night and I believed a dram would help him. Phillips told me to go to his case and get a bottle of brandy, which I did, and we all drank heartily except the Indian who refused to take a dram, though something apt to drink at other times.

The important crisis now drew near when three of us were to attack the whole crew. The master prepared to take his observations and Cheeseman was walking the deck with a hammer in his hand. The quartermaster was in the cabin drawing out some leaden slugs for a musket and the Spanish Indian stood by the cabin door. The captain and boatswain stood by the mainsail talking upon some matters and I stood partly behind them whirring the ax round with my foot till my knees fairly smote together.

The master being busied, I saw Cheeseman make the motion to heave him over[38] and I at that instant split the boatswain's head in twain with the ax, and dropped him from upon the deck to [————][39] in his [————].[40] [Before the captain ?][41] had time to put himself into a position of defense, I gave him a stroke with the head of my ax, which partly stunned him. At the same time, Cheeseman dispatched the master overboard, and then made to my assistance and gave the captain a blow with his hammer on the back of the head, which put an immediate end to his mortal existence.[42]

The quartermaster hearing the bustle, came running out of the cabin with his hand up to strike Cheeseman with his hammer and would probably have killed him had not the Indian [———— him by ?][43] the elbow, [———— well-bringing the hammer ?][44] down, and there held him until I came up and gave him a blow upon the back side of the head, cutting his wig and neck almost off so that his head hung down before him.[45]

We had now dispatched all the old pirates except White and demanded surrender of the vessel, which was granted and those poor Frenchmen and Negroes came to us, fell down and embraced our legs and feet, begging for their lives.

White, Archer, and one more of the pirates were tried, condemned and executed in Boston.[46] The three other pirates were sent to England with the vessel, with whom my friend Cheeseman and the Indian went likewise, whom [the] government liberally rewarded for their services, and gave Cheeseman an honorable [——]⁴⁷ in one of the king's ship-yards. The three pirates who went home with the vessel were hung at the Execution Dock⁴⁸ and the vessel made [——————]⁴⁹ by [——————].⁵⁰

Apparently, when they arrived at Annisquam on April 24, 1724, Capt. Phillips's head was hanging from the mast-head and was later pickled. During the period from August 29, 1723 (when Phillips and four of his men stole their ship) to April 14, 1724 (when all but one of these men had suffered violent deaths), they plundered thirty-four vessels.

After his escape from the pirates, John Fillmore got married and his great-grandson, Millard Fillmore, became president of the United States.

Notes

1. Later, Phillips and his pirates captured another vessel owned by the same man who owned this one. When he found this out, Phillips ordered his men to repair the ship and allow the captured crew to take back to the owner, saying, "We have done him enough injury already."

2. Fillmore happened to be in the harbor of St. Peters when the pirates stole their ship. William White later told him that he was drunk at the time and later regretted his actions.

3. The only copy of this pamphlet I've been able to locate has suffered some damage and a few words are indecipherable. About three words are missing here.

4. One word indecipherable ending in "-or."

5. One word indecipherable.

6. Martinico: (? Martinique: one of the islands of the Lesser Antilles at the eastern end of the Caribbean Sea.)

7. Cartel ship: a ship employed in the exchange of prisoners.

8. Forced men usually had some special skill or knowledge that the pirates needed. They included surgeons, navigators, carpenters, blacksmiths and musicians.

9. The following are Capt. Phillips's articles from this voyage in 1723 as printed in Capt. Charles Johnson's *A General History of the Robberies and Murders of the Most Notorious Pyrates* (vol. 1, 1726 edition):

1. Every man shall obey civil command. The captain shall have one full share and a half in all prizes. The master, carpenter, boatswain and gunner shall have one share and quarter.

2. If any man shall offer to run away or keep any secret from the company, he shall be marooned with one bottle of powder, one bottle of water, one small arm and shot.

3. If any man shall steal anything in the company or game to the value of a piece-of-eight, he shall be marooned or shot.

4. If at anytime we should meet another marooner [pirate], that man that shall sign his articles without the consent of our company shall suffer such punishment as the captain and company shall think fit.

5. That man that shall strike another whilst these articles are in force shall receive Moses's Law (that is, forty stripes lacking one) on the bare back.

6. That man that shall snap his arms or smoke tobacco in the hold without a cap to his pipe, or carry a candle lighted without a lantern, shall suffer the same punishment as in the former article.

7. That man that shall not keep his arms clean, fit for an engagement, or neglect his business, shall be cut off from his share and suffer such other punishment as the captain and the company shall think fit.

8. If any man shall lose a joint in time of an engagement, he shall have 400 pieces-of-eight. If a limb, 800.

9. If at anytime we meet with a prudent woman, that man that offers to meddle with her without her consent, shall suffer present death.

10. Manumission: a freeing from slavery.

11. Beat: to sail against the wind, especially on alternate tacks.

12. One word indecipherable.

13. Two words indecipherable.

14. On one occasion after capturing a ship they had to chase, Phillips punished the master of the vessel by making him dance the deck until he keeled over from exhaustion.

15. There were two Frenchmen (John Baptis and Peter Taffery) and three Negro slaves (Pedro, Francisco, and Pierro). All were later found to be forced men and therefore innocent of piracy.

16. Capt. Andrew Harridon was taking his sloop *Squirrel* on her maiden voyage on April 14, 1724, when he was captured by Capt. Phillips. Fillmore confused the taking of this ship with that another, since the taking of Harridon and the *Squirrel* occurred much later in the narrative following many of the events he has yet to describe. Fillmore wrote his account in his old age from memory, which resulted in a few inaccuracies. It was actually on a snow (which is the largest of the two-masted ships and similar to a brig) taken from Capt. Laws on February 4, 1724, that some of the following events took place.

17. Other records give his name as Edward Cheeseman. Phillips took him unwillingly on board to replace carpenter Thomas Fern. Cheeseman was captured on March 27, 1724—after the incidents with Fern that Fillmore relates a little later.

18. This was Isaac Larsen, who was taken the same day as Fillmore.

19. Two words indecipherable.

20. At one point they were so short of provisions that the ten men were forced to split one pound of meat as their daily ration. They became so desperate that they decided to attack a French ship with thirty-five hands and twelve guns, but after they ran up their black flag, the Frenchmen surrendered without firing a single shot.

21. Thomas Fern, the carpenter.

22. One word indecipherable ending in "-ed" and about five letters long.

23. Fillmore seems to be combining two occasions where Fern tried to escape. Apparently, Fern was a bit put out over John Rose Archer's being made quartermaster, since Archer was not one of the original crew (though he had served under Blackbeard). The first time was shortly after the snow of Capt. Laws was captured on February 4, 1724. In this ship, Fern, James Wood, William Taylor and William Phillips ran away from Phillips. In an ensuing battle, James Wood was killed and William Phillips was wounded in the leg, which they then had to amputate. Fern and Taylor surrendered. The second time apparently was several weeks later. This was when Phillips killed him.

24. This incident occurred just a few days after Fern was killed, but a month or so before Harridon's ship was taken.

25. Handspeak: (Handspike?: a sort of crowbar or lever, usually made of wood).

26. Flagitious: atrocious or heinous.

27. Fillmore appears to be a bit confused here. Other records show that the following events happened on the 16th and 17th of April—just two days after Harridon's ship was taken—but it would have been about two months since Thomas Fern was murdered and seven months after Fillmore was kidnapped.

28. John Nutt.

29. Caboose: the galley, or ship's kitchen.

30. One word indecipherable.

31. Several words indecipherable.

32. Isaac Larsen.

33. Several words indecipherable.

34. One word indecipherable.

35. Fillmore already states that he had incapacitated the quartermaster, John Rose Archer, by burning his feet. He is actually referring to the gunner, James Sparks.

36. Several words indecipherable.

37. Several words indecipherable.

38. Cheeseman took hold of John Nutt's collar with one hand and grabbed him between the legs with the other and pitched him over the side. Nutt caught Cheeseman's arm and while dangling against the side of the ship exclaimed, "Lord, have mercy upon me! What are you trying to do, carpenter?" Cheeseman

answered that that was an unnecessary question "for, master, you are a dead man" and struck Nutt on the arm. Losing his grip, Nutt fell into the sea and drowned.

39. One word indecipherable.

40. One word indecipherable.

41. Several words indecipherable.

42. Actually, when Cheeseman struck Capt. Phillips, it broke his jaw but did not knock him down. It was Capt. Harridon who killed him with a blow from an adz.

43. Several words indecipherable.

44. Several words indecipherable.

45. Fillmore is confusing elements from the death of Capt. Phillips with that of the gunner, James Sparks. On hearing Nutt's cry, Sparks ran on deck and started toward Harridon who was about to dispatch Capt. Phillips, but he was tripped up by Cheeseman and fell into the hands of Charles Ivemay who was another of the conspirators. With the help of the two Frenchmen, Ivemay pitched Sparks overboard. Cheeseman then leapt below deck and had given Archer several blows to the head with his mallet when he was stopped by Harry Giles who insisted Archer should be spared as evidence of their innocence.

46. William White (age 22) and John Rose Archer (about 27) were hung on June 2, 1724. The *Boston News-Letter* reported, "At one end of the gallows was their own dark flag, in the middle of which an anatomy, and at one side of it a dart in the heart, with drops of blood proceeding from it; and on the other side an hour-glass." William Taylor was condemned with White and Archer, but given a reprieve. The one-legged William Phillips, who was tried with those who were found to be forced men, was also condemned and reprieved. Both were later pardoned. The reason for their pardons is uncertain. In his dying declaration (which was written with the help of two Boston ministers) John Rose Archer said, "I greatly bewail my profanations of the Lord's Day and my disobedience to my parents. And my cursing and swearing, and my blaspheming the name of the glorious God. Unto which I have added the sins of unchastity. And I have provoked the Holy One, at length, to leave me unto the crimes of piracy and robbery; wherein, at last, I have brought myself under the guilt of murder also. But one wickedness that has led me as much as any to all the rest, has been my brutish drunkenness. By strong drink I have been heated and hardened into the crimes that are now more bitter than death unto me. I could wish that masters of vessels would not use their men with so much severity, as many of them do, which exposes us to great temptations." William White's dying declaration says, "I am now, with sorrow, reaping the fruits of my disobedience to my parents, who used their endeavors to have me instructed in my Bible, and my catechism. And the fruits of my neglecting the public worship of God and profan-

ing the Holy Sabbath. And of my blaspheming the name of God, my maker. But my drunkenness has had a great hand in bringing my ruin upon me. I was drunk when I was enticed aboard the pirate. And now, for all the vile things I did aboard, I own the justice of God and man, in what is done unto me."

47. One word indecipherable.

48. Execution Dock: the usual place for pirate hangings in London. It is at Wapping Old Stairs on the Thames.

49. One, two or three words indecipherable.

50. One word indecipherable. If there was another page, it's missing.

To Save Ourselves
We Must Join These Pirates

≋≋≋

Captain Samuel Samuels

Now we move to the coast of a country that's not usually associated with piracy, though it is famous for crimes of a different nature. This is Italy. While the Mediterranean was full of pirates in the early nineteenth century, these were primarily the corsairs of the Barbary Coast, which stretched along the northern coast of Africa. By the middle of that century—when the following incident took place—the U.S. and British fleets had disbanded the corsairs. Even the heyday of the pirates in the Caribbean was over, having been essentially destroyed by the U.S. and British navies by around 1835.

Though shipping was made much safer, there were still a few pirates around—as there still are today. Captain Samuel Samuels happened to have an encounter with some from Italy.

In about 1844, shortly before this incident, Samuels was made a captain at the age of 21. This was his second voyage as captain and he decided to take his wife and two children along. As he recorded in his book From the Forecastle to the Cabin (1887), he had some trouble at the town of Livorno, which is on the northwestern coast of Italy. As he neared the harbor, two boats offered to guide him in, which he accepted only to find there were actually just fishermen when the proper pilots showed up. He refused to pay them and they brought him before the magistrate, who found in his favor.

The situation became increasingly dangerous when, while on a sightseeing trip with his wife to Pisa—which was only about 15 miles away—they were confronted by a group of these fishermen and their friends armed with knives. They were rescued when an armed group of U.S. Naval officers

showed up searching for them. The officers had expected trou-
ble. They decided the bandits probably intended to kidnap his
wife and hold her for ransom. At any rate, a few days later the
money for his cargo—80,000 Spanish dollars[1]—was safely
loaded aboard his ship and they set sail.

About three o'clock the breeze began to freshen, and at five o'clock we were twelve miles from shore when I felt somewhat uneasy at seeing two small vessels steering directly for us, and gaining rapidly. My uneasiness grew when they got close enough for me to see that they were the two [Italian] fishing-craft that had offered to be my pilots and that they were crowded with men. I had no doubt they meant to board us. Piracy was a well-known crime in the Mediterranean. They could pillage and sink our ship and she would merely be reported as "missing." In a moment I decided upon my line of action. I had two twelve-pound carronades[2] on board. These were brought aft and loaded to the muzzle with grape and canister.[3] I did not intend to let these rascals come within pistol range of us.

We had changed our course four points on two occasions to be certain that they were following us, and in each case they changed theirs, pointing directly for us. The gap between us lessened rapidly. I no longer needed the telescope to distinguish their piratical visages. Below me was the ship and treasure for which I was responsible, as well as for the lives on board. To hesitate longer would have been criminal. I must say that my Christian spirit forsook me for the time and that I felt a grim satisfaction in anticipating revenge for the Pisa episode and in having an opportunity to blow these dogs out of water. The sun was setting and the land just visible astern. I had taken in the port studding sails[4] to let everything draw well on the starboard[5] quarter to increase, if possible, our speed. Further, I could do nothing to avoid being boarded, except to sink our pursuers before they came too close. My crew were too few to meet their number at close quarters. I took good aim at the nearest craft, which was now about a quarter of a mile off.

The pirates saw my movement and dropped flat on their decks, firing at me as they saw me apply the red-hot salamander[6] to the gun. The next instant their yells rent the air. There was no occasion for a second shot, as the first took the mast out of the boat it was aimed at and swept her decks. The second craft luffed to[7] to get out of our reach. She was not so close to us as the one fired into, but I was determined to cripple her if possible, to prevent her from crawling up to us during the night. As she was broadside to, she presented a good mark. I fired my second gun, and the grape and canister did their work. Her sails were riddled and her gaff[8] dropped. The water around her was plowed up as though struck by a tornado. How many were killed or hurt I never knew.

We kept our course with the wind over our starboard quarter till nightfall, then edged off on the regular course to pass about four miles north of Corsica.

> *This was not the first time Samuels had a run in with pirates. His first experience occurred when he was 14 years old. He had shipped out on a voyage from Liverpool, England, to Galveston, Texas, in the British brig* Emily. *The year was 1837 and they were had reached the Gulf of Mexico. The "Peter" he mentions was a middle-aged sailor, who had befriended the young Samuels.*

The vessel came down on us like a meteor. Before we got on deck she was close aboard on our starboard beam. Peter told me to look at her carefully. She was a two topsail schooner; that is, she had a square fore and main-topsail,[9] with topgallant sails[10] over. When these square sails were furled, the yards on deck and the masts housed, the fore and aft sails would equal single reefs.[11] This rig is now obsolete; though if I were going to build a large sailing yacht, I would rig her in this way. She would be the most rakish and saucy-looking craft afloat. The stranger had a long swivel[12] amidships and a smaller one mounted forward of the foremast. She was painted black, had a flush deck and four quarter boats. No flag was flying. We were hailed in good English, though he who hailed us looked like a Spaniard.

"What ship is that?" he asked. "Where are you from and where are you bound?"

We replied to all these interrogations. Our captain was too much astonished at her extraordinary speed and appearance to ask any questions. There was no name on her stern and only three men were to be seen on deck. Captain Gillette asked the mate what he made her out. He replied that she was a mystery and that he did not like her looks, as she appeared like neither a warship nor a merchantman.

At ten o'clock the wind moderated enough to let us set all light sails, including the starboard studding sails. At noon we sighted the mysterious stranger again right ahead. At 1 P.M. a heavy squall was coming down on us. Then we took in the studding sails and royal.[13] The main top-gallant studding sail fouled over the brace block[14] and I went aloft to clear it. While I was on the yard the squall struck us with terrific force. Everything had to be let go by the run to save the masts. The studding sail blew to ribbons in my hands. The top-sail halyards[15] had been let go and down I went with the yard. I had secured myself on the foot-rope near the brace block. This I did to save myself from being knocked off by the slapping of the top-gallant sheet. It was marvelous that I was not thrown from the yard when it came down on the cap.[16] The squall was soon over, but it took the rest of the day to repair the split sails.

About four o'clock the stranger hove to till we passed her, when she trimmed her canvas and was alongside again like magic.

"What does your cargo consist of?" he asked.

"Coal, salt, crates, and iron," we replied.

She starboarded her helm and hauled to the southward, but before dark was ahead of us again. By this time all hands showed uneasiness, but said nothing. Supper was announced, but no one had any appetite. We all sat on the forecastle, straining our eyes into the darkness to see if we could discern the schooner. The captain came forward at eleven o'clock to join the mate, who had been sitting forward among us all the evening.

"Mr. Crawford," he said, "let us trim the yards and haul up four points to the southward. I don't like that craft. She was right ahead when last seen. We had better give her the slip during the night."

Peter now joined in and said, "If you don't want them to board us, we had better keep our course. They have their eye on us and if we attempt to avoid them they may suppose we are not bound for Galveston and that our cargo is not of such small value as we told them. Once on board of us they will show their true character and before daylight we shall all have walked the plank and the *Emily* will be sunk five thousand fathoms[17] deep. None of us will be left to tell the tale. I have been on these waters before, Captain Gillette, and know these crafts and what I am talking about."

Peter's words were ominous. They sent a thrill of horror through us all. They sounded like the death sentence pronounced by a judge in deep, solemn tones to a prisoner whose hours are numbered.

The course was not changed. Silence pervaded the whole crew. The night was very dark. Suddenly Peter nudged me and motioned me to follow him aft. When abreast of the gangway he whispered in my ear, "Boy, be a man. Don't tremble so. Your teeth chatter as if you had the ague.[18] Slip down below and bring up a pannikin[19] of rum; you know where it is stowed. You need courage to carry out what you will have to undertake before sunrise. By that time there will be no more of the *Emily* or her crew, except you and me. Get the rum and then hear the rest."

I groped my way down the after hatch and into the storeroom and got the rum. I begged him not to take too much, as I knew his desperate character when in liquor.

"Don't fear," he said, "I never take too much in serious times. Now drink a little yourself; it will brace you up. Put the cup where we can get it again and let us walk the deck where we can be seen but not heard. Much of my life you have heard me relate, from boyhood to manhood. The rest you shall hear now. My first criminal act, when I was a mere child led on by others, landed me and them in the galleys, whence we escaped after murdering the guard. All except me were taken and guillotined. I was too small to have a hand in the murder. At the trial my plea of ignorance of an evil intent saved me from the extreme penalty of the law, but I was sent on board a French man-of-war, from which I escaped after many years of service. Then I found myself in the Spanish navy, and after the battle of Trafalgar I shipped in a slaver.

"We were on our way from the Congo, bound to San Domingo with four hundred slaves stored in the hold. The prospects were good for a profitable voyage. When we were off Puerto Rico, a schooner—just like the one you have seen this morning—came up and hailed us. It was just getting dark and she passed ahead. When the next day was breaking, she hailed us to heave to and brought her guns to bear. In a moment we were grappled and boarded. Part of our crew at once attacked our officers and, with the pirates who had boarded us, made short work of those who showed any resistance. We who had done this were allowed to join the pirate crew, as we had proved ourselves worthy of them. If we had acted otherwise, we would have been slain also.

"An officer with a prize crew took charge of our schooner—after we had been sent aboard the pirate—and took the slaver into Havana, where she and her cargo were sold. I stayed with the pirates three years, but their life did not suit me and I made my escape during a battle with two English ships-of-war which had discovered our stronghold in the bay of San Lorenzo.

"Now, boy," Peter cautioned, "to save ourselves we must join these pirates, who will board us about daybreak. You take your position behind Mr. Crawford and as soon as they board, strike him with the knife between the shoulders."

At these instructions, my knees began to give way. Peter seized me or I should have fallen. The story he told me was all very well until it became my turn to be an actor. But a nip of rum, administered by him, set me all right. He said it would be better to kill the mate than to be killed myself, and our crew would all be slaughtered anyway. He called it justifiable self-defense and said that after we had joined the pirates, he would find a way for us to escape. He so worked on my imagination that I really felt I was going to do an excusable deed. The knife he gave me was his favorite one. It had a very long blade encased in a wooden sheath, instead of the leather usually used for sheath-knives. I agreed to do as he bade me and took my place behind the mate. Peter took his place near the captain. It had just struck seven bells. There had been scarcely a word spoken forward during the night. The sound of the bells fell upon me like a funeral knell. Tears began to run down my cheeks. Mr. Crawford had always been good to me, why should I kill him? Everybody had treated me well on board. I thought of home and the plans I had laid for the future. Now my aspirations and hopes would all be ruined in the next half hour. A horror of the situation seized me. I slipped off the bitts[20] upon which I had been sitting and walked aft. Peter followed me.

He said, "You had better take a little more rum. I don't think the cook will serve us with coffee this morning. It is chilly for you after the long night's watch. I see that you have a slight attack of ague."

"No, Peter, I don't want to drink. I am not cold. But I would rather be killed than commit murder in such cold blood."

But his pleadings, his love for me, and the review of his friendship had their effect. The demon that seduced our great mother was whispering in my ear. I again did as he told me and stationed myself behind the mate.

The silence was broken by the captain saying he wished it was daylight.

"It will be here soon enough," I heard Peter say. "I see it breaking in the east, and before the sun is up all will be over."

The day was indeed breaking, and night was furling her black flag. The light mounted slowly towards the zenith, and as our eyes were strained to catch a glimpse of the mysterious craft, we saw her shoot out of the darkness, heading across our bow to the northward. We looked in that direction and saw a large West India merchantman about four miles on our starboard beam. She was running before the wind with studding-sails set on both sides and was evidently Dutch from her build.

"She is doomed," Peter said, "and we are safe. Those poor fellows will never muster round the grog-pail again. Presently you will see the schooner make her heave to."

The words were scarcely spoken when we saw the smoke from her Long Tom.[21] The signal was unheeded and a shot brought down her foremast, which took the main topmast with it. This crippled her so that in less than an hour she was out of sight astern.

While in Amsterdam years after, my curiosity led me to ascertain what ships were lost during the year in which the above incident occurred and I learned that the ship *Crown Prince William* from Rotterdam, bound for Curacao,[22] was never heard from.

We felt ourselves safe for the time being, but changed our course, fearing that after she had pillaged and sunk the ship, she might overtake and destroy us to avoid being reported. We did not consider ourselves out of danger until we entered the harbor of Galveston.

Notes

1. Probably pieces-of-eight.

2. Carronades: light cannons of large caliber used for short range. The twelve and six-pounds referring to the weight of the cannonballs they fire.

3. Grapeshot: a cluster of connected iron balls shot from a cannon. Canister shot: a metal can filled with small shot and scrap metal that scatter when fired.

4. Studding sails: the sail extending beyond the side edge of a square sail, used to make the most of light winds.

5. Starboard: towards the right side of the ship when facing the bow.

6. Salamander: a slow-burning wick or cord used to light cannons.

7. Luffed to: turned to put the ship's head windward.

8. Gaff: a spar extending diagonally upward behind a mast and which supports a primary sail.

9. Fore-topsail: the sail above the foresail on the foremast, or the second sail in ascending order from the deck on the ship's forward mast. Main-topsail: the

topsail on the mainmast, or the second sail in ascending order from the deck on the ship's primary mast.

10. Topgallant sail: the sail above the topsail, or the third sail in ascending order from the deck.

11. Reefs: sails that have been folded or rolled up and tied to their yards.

12. Swivel: a small cannon-like gun mounted on the ship's railing and could be swung from side to side.

13. Royal: the sail above the topgallant, or the fourth sail in ascending order from the deck.

14. Brace block: a block at the end of a yard that a rope passes through, enabling the yard to be swung by someone on the deck.

15. Halyards: vertical ropes for hoisting sails.

16. Cap: a large block of wood by which the base of an upper mast is fitted to the top of the next lower one.

17. Fathom: a measurement equal to six feet.

18. Ague: chills caused by a severe fever.

19. Pannikin: a metal cup.

20. Bitts: deck posts around which ropes and cables are wound to hold them fast.

21. Long Tom: a heavy swivel gun.

22. Curacao Island is off the coast of Venezuela.

Index

A Little Bit About John Richard Stephens

John has had many different occupations ranging from driving an armored truck and working as a professional photographer to being a psychiatric counselor at a couple hospitals and a security officer for the U.S. Navy. He was an intelligence officer and squadron commander in the U.S. Air Force before he moved on to writing full time in 1990. Since then, he's written over three dozen articles, poems, and short stories for newspapers and magazines that range widely from a short story for the literary journal *Nexus* to an article about anti-American propaganda on postage stamps for *Penthouse*. He's also the author/editor of the following books:

> *Weird History 101*
> *Wyatt Earp Speaks!*
> *Wyatt Earp Tells of the Gunfight Near the O.K. Corral*
> *Into the Mummy's Tomb*
> *Vampires, Wine and Roses*
> *The King of the Cats and Other Feline Fairy Tales*
> *Mysterious Cat Stories* (co-edited with Kim Smith)
> *The Dog Lover's Literary Companion*
> *The Enchanted Cat*

John's books have been selections of the Preferred Choice Book Club, the Quality Paperback Book Club and the Book of the Month Club. His work has been published as far away as India and Singapore and has been translated into Japanese and Finnish.